Effective Software Maintenance and Evolution

A Reuse-Based Approach

Other Auerbach Publications in Software Development, Software Engineering, and Project Management

Effective Software Maintenance and Evolution

A Reuse-Based Approach

Stanislaw Jarzabek

CRC Press
Taylor & Francis Group
Boca Raton London New York

CRC Press is an imprint of the
Taylor & Francis Group, an **informa** business

AN AUERBACH BOOK

CRC Press
Taylor & Francis Group
6000 Broken Sound Parkway NW, Suite 300
Boca Raton, FL 33487-2742

First issued in hardback 2019

© 2007 by Taylor & Francis Group, LLC
CRC Press is an imprint of Taylor & Francis Group, an Informa business

No claim to original U.S. Government works

ISBN-13: 978-0-8493-3592-1 (hbk)

Library of Congress Cataloging-in-Publication Data

Jarzabek, Stan.
   Effective software maintenance and evolution : a reuse-based approach / Stanislaw Jarzabek.
      p. cm.
   Includes bibliographical references and index.
   ISBN-13: 978-0-8493-3592-1 (alk. paper)
   ISBN-10: 0-8493-3592-2 (alk. paper)
   1. Computer software--Reusability. 2. Software maintenance. 3. Software reengineering. I. Title.

QA76.76.R47.J375 2007
005.1'6--dc22   2006025796

Visit the Taylor & Francis Web site at
http://www.taylorandfrancis.com

and the CRC Press Web site at
http://www.crcpress.com

For my Wife Malgosia,
who's been my love and inspiration
in all possible ways.

Contents

Foreword

Almost three decades ago, while teaching at Toronto's York University, serendipity struck me in the form of frame technology. Frustrated at having to reedit my customizations over and over each time I reused my code generators, I became determined to automate the splicing process. I soon discovered I had a tiger by the tail. Tigers are powerful and hard to tame. Regarding power, frames turn out to greatly alleviate many persistent software engineering concerns, including development productivity, system quality, and maintainability. As to taming this tiger, I'm still learning what gives the technology its power.

In 1981 I cofounded Netron, Inc., to bring frame technology to the world. Ironically, its best users received such an immensely competitive edge that they did not want outsiders to know their secret. One such Fortune 500 company's entire software staff numbered no more than 50 people — that's worldwide, with no outside contractors. Their proudest statistic, revealed to me only after much wheedling: in a typical year they would satisfy approximately 18,000 user requests. In the 90s a group of Netron customers (not its best) commissioned a study by software project auditors QSM Associates. The study reported that, compared to industry norms, these companies were, on average, completing their software projects (ranging up to 10 million noncomment source lines) in 70 percent less time with 84 percent less effort (staff months), and typical reuse levels were 90 percent. Such statistics, even gathered at arm's length, are hard to believe. There's got to be a catch, right? Read on.

My 1997 book, *Framing Software Reuse: Lessons from the Real World*, distilled my then-best understanding of frame technology, explaining how frames raise quality while greatly reducing the time and effort to design, construct, and test complex software systems. Prof. Stan Jarzabek has greatly extended my efforts, lucidly presenting his insights and hard evidence in the following pages. He tackles that most expensive part of software's life cycle, maintenance and evolution, first presenting a comprehensive analysis of the topic, then showing how to improve the practice through the use of frame technology.

In particular, he affords a new perspective on software development via his mixed-strategy approach to adding frame technology to a host of object-oriented programming environments. He provides a detailed analysis of the many modern techniques that deal with generics, aspects, domain-specific languages, and feature combinatorics. His analysis confirms what one might expect: each technique offers advantages for its particular engineering goal. However, he also shows how to use frames to do much the same things. Moreover, his mixed-strategy is a single, unified approach for designing, constructing, and evolving adaptable software for any domain and using any programming language.

No longer should we tolerate developing large systems from scratch. An inventory of generic frames and architectures allows so-called new development to itself be an evolutionary process. Hence, this book is relevant to software's entire life cycle. In my book I remarked that although the basic frame rules are simple, like chess, master play is not. With this book you learn from a master.

The surpassing software engineering issue of our era, and the main focus of this book, is complexity reduction. A problem's intrinsic complexity is the size of its smallest solution (executable on a canonical computer). Sadly, almost all programs ever written possess complexities far above their minima. Excessive complexity saps productivity, creates enormous costs, compromises safety, and causes failures and errors. Most troubling, it limits the sophistication of the systems we can build.

Why are systems so full of crippling complexity? A cynic might say job protection. But at the most basic level, we rarely can even know what the least complex solution is. So although we cannot achieve absolute minimization, why do we almost seem driven to implement system designs in unnecessarily complex ways? A common habit in softwaredom is to copy code that works and then modify it to be compatible with a new context. Copy-and-modify may be expedient but we pay an unacceptable price in redundancy, hence gratuitous complexity. I say "gratuitous" because Stan Jarzabek's deconstruction of complexity shows us all the ways it creeps into our systems and how to prevent or minimize most of them. By following the prescriptions in this book you will be able to shift complexity from being proportional to program size, from being proportional to novelty — a far smaller measure.

If this is your first acquaintance with frame technology, I would like you to approach it with an open mind. In my experience, the technology has been confused with macro processors and text editors. True, there are elements of both in the frame processor, but the combination yields novel properties, akin to hydrogen and oxygen combining to form water. This technology's power derives from subtle properties, such as an inversion of the block scoping rule that governs variables in programming languages.

So, is there a catch? Our software engineering ethos has heretofore been focused on modeling and design. This was entirely appropriate when the field was new. But now, over a half-century later, it's high time that adaptability gained equal prominence. When it comes to engineering software for change, our industry has a large blind spot, even though software's infinite malleability cries out for formalization. This book attempts to redress this oversight. But it can be difficult to accept that so many of the things programmers consider to be their exclusive prerogative can, in fact, be done much more reliably by machines, not to mention much faster. Programmers used to automating other people's jobs may balk when automation knocks on their own doors. Aha! There *is* a catch!

Dr. Jarzabek fully explains how to use the open-source frame processor XVCL (XML-based Variant Configuration Language). Thus, all of the valuable insights to be found in the following pages can be immediately applied. And that is none too soon!

Paul G. Bassett

The Author

Stan Jarzabek is an associate professor at the Department of Computer Science, School of Computing, National University of Singapore (NUS). He spent 12 years of his professional career in industry and 20 years in academia. He is interested in all aspects of software design, in particular techniques for design of adaptable, easy to change (high-variability) software. He has published over 90 papers in international journals and conference proceedings (his recent paper received the ACM Distinguished Paper Award, and two other papers were selected as "best papers" at leading conferences). Stan was a principal investigator in a multinational collaborative project involving universities (NUS and the University of Waterloo) and companies in Singapore and Toronto. He has given tutorials and public courses on software maintenance, reengineering, and reuse.

Acknowledgments

I am grateful to all the students in the Software Engineering Lab at the National University of Singapore (NUS) and collaborators with whom I have had the privilege to work over the last eight years. I extend my appreciation to the Department of Computer Science, School of Computing, National University of Singapore for generous support for the research program that led to formulation of XVCL and the mixed-strategy approach.

Collaboration with Paul Bassett, a cofounder of Netron, Inc., and Ulf Pettersson, a technical director of ST Electronics (Info-Software Systems) Pte. Ltd., contributed much to the results and interpretations described in this book. In particular, these collaborations were very important in formulating and validating the mixed-strategy approach. XVCL is based on concepts of Frame Technology™ by Netron, Inc. Paul was instrumental in extracting the essence of frame principles, which led to formulating XVCL as a source language-independent and application domain-independent method and tool that can enhance modern programming methods in areas of maintainability and reusability. Paul gave insightful feedback to our XVCL team on all the experiments and papers describing their analytical interpretations.

Ulf Pettersson gave us invaluable industry feedback on XVCL and was the author of the first commercial applications of XVCL, which evidenced the benefits of the approach on a larger scale in the industrial context. Mixed-strategy approach would not be possible without Ulf's continue involvement in our projects.

I am thankful to Paul Bassett, Ulrich Eisenecker, Nicholas Zvegintzov and anonymous reviewers for many insightful comments and suggestions, regarding earlier drafts of this book.

The following NUS students contributed to studies described in this book:

Part I

Chapter 2: Wang Guo Sheng implemented a PQL-based SPA for COBOL as a part of his master's degree thesis. PQL for model language SIMPLE was implemented by students in the Software Engineering Project Course CS3215 at NUS.

Chapter 3: Honors student Tan Poh Keam implemented a first prototype of a reverse engineering assistant. Wang Guo Sheng and Ding Xin (master's degree student) followed up with design of a PQL-based reverse engineering assistant.

Chapter 4: Teh Hsin Yee implemented a first prototype of a model-based project support environment (PSE) in Java and JavaScript™ as a part of her master's thesis. Her work was later followed by Damith Rajapakse (Ph.D. student) and numerous honors students who experimented with project support environments in their research using various emerging Web technologies (PHP, .NET, J2EE, and others).

Chapter 5: Seow Junling conducted step-by-step experiments comparing evolution with CVS, and also with the mixed-strategy approach. Ulf Pettersson provided invaluable feedback about using CVS to support evolution in industrial projects.

Many students contributed to the XVCL Processor, Workbench, and Web site. Students conducted numerous studies applying XVCL in a variety of application domains and technological contexts. The mixed-strategy approach described in Part II was formulated based on their experimental and analytical work.

Part II

Creating XVCL has been a team effort. It included the definition of the XVCL formalism, implementation of the XVCL processor, design of the tool support called XVCL Workbench, and numerous experiments in which we applied XVCL in a variety of application domains, together with a wide range of software technologies. Experimental and analytical work with XVCL conducted with talent and dedication by Ph.D., master's degree, and honors students at the National University of Singapore was instrumental in formulating mixed-strategy methods described in Part II of this book.

Wong Tak Wai did a prototype implementation of an XVCL subset using XML as a part of his master's thesis. His work was followed by Soe Myat Swe (master's student) who, together with Paul Bassett, contributed to defining XVCL. Soe also implemented full XVCL using XML open parser. Soe's work enabled us to experiment with XVCL on a larger scale. Li Shubiao, a visitor from Xi'an Jiaotong University, reimplemented the XVCL processor using newer technology, considerably improving its performance. Vu Tung Lam (honors student, research assistant, and Ph.D. student) redesigned large parts of the XVCL processor for maintainability and interoperability with other XVCL tools, further improving its performance. Valentin Weckerle (an exchange student from Germany) proposed and implemented improvements of XVCL features.

A number of students developed XVCL tool prototypes supporting the mixed-strategy approach. Shen Ru (master's student), Vu Tung Lam, and Sun Zhenxin (honors student) developed a static analyzer to help developers understand x-frameworks. Chen Liang (master's student) developed an XVCL debugger. Cao Yang (research assistant) developed a first prototype of the XVCL Workbench. Vu Tung

Lam redesigned the XVCL Workbench on the Eclipse, and advanced its development to reach a near-production-quality level. Pradeepika Irangani (research assistant) contributed much to the XVCL processor and Workbench development.

Soe Myat Swe designed the first XVCL Web site on SourceForge, which was then replaced by a Web site designed by Vu Tung Lam. All the members of the XVCL team contributed contents to the Web site over many years. Zhang Hongyu (Ph.D. student) and Soe Myat Swe contributed educational examples and tutorials.

Numerous students applied XVCL in the experimental part of their research work. Zhang Hongyu (Ph.D. student) was a chief designer of the first large project in which we applied XVCL to support a computer-aided dispatch system product line. This project was done with the involvement of Ulf Pettersson of ST Electronics, Paul Bassett, and Rudolph Seviora (University of Waterloo), under the joint Singapore–Ontario research project "Software Reuse Framework For Reliable Mission-Critical Systems." The project was funded by the Singapore Agency for Science, Technology, and Research (A*STAR) and the Canadian Ministry of Energy, Science, and Technology. Damith Rajapakse conducted extensive studies on the application of XVCL in Web application development. More than ten honors students applied XVCL with other Web technologies such as .NET, J2EE, and Ruby on Rails.

Hamid Basit (Ph.D. student) came up with a method and tool called Clone Miner for automated detection of similarity patterns in legacy code, for possible reuse with XVCL. Honors students Melvin Low, Chan Jun Liang, and Goh Kwan Kee conducted experimental studies applying Clone Miner to class libraries and application software.

Prologue

Change is inherent in software. Whether we develop a new program or reengineer an old one, software is in a constant flux. Change is the essence of bread-and-butter, day-to-day maintenance and long-term evolution.

Software maintenance takes up a large share of computing costs — 50 percent on average, but in some companies over 80 percent. Any solutions that can improve maintenance productivity are bound to have dramatic impact on software costs and the overall profitability of companies. Advancements in software technology of the last two decades have changed the computing landscape. Interestingly, with all those investments, the cost of maintenance, rather than dropping, is on the rise.

This book sheds light on this situation. It explains fundamental reasons why software change is technically hard, and why conventional techniques fail to bring visible improvements in software maintenance productivity. With particular focus on complexities of long-term software evolution, the book describes a novel mixed-strategy approach that makes software change a first-class citizen and promises to tackle challenges of software maintenance and evolution in a more effective way.

This book treats only technical aspects of effective change management during maintenance and evolution. Managerial aspects of maintenance and evolution are not discussed. Of course, an overall solution to effective maintenance and evolution must necessarily address both technical and managerial issues.

We make the following distinction between software maintenance and evolution: The term *software maintenance* means day-to-day changes implemented into a software system. The term *software evolution* refers to what happens to software long-term, during its entire life span.

This book starts with the Introduction in which we set the stage for the rest of the book. The Introduction provides the background, discusses the challenges of software evolution that we address, and introduces techniques described in both parts of the book.

Part I discusses some of the state-of-the-art conventional techniques, such as static program analysis, reverse engineering, and model-based design for change. The first three chapters of Part I primarily focus on maintenance techniques. Part I ends with two chapters that bridge software maintenance and evolution, namely a chapter on evolution with software configuration management tools, and a chapter on analysis of software maintenance and evolution problems that are difficult to solve with conventional techniques. The two main problems are the poor visibility of changes that have been applied to software over time, and the lack of generic, adaptable software representations that can evolve gracefully, avoiding an explosion of look-alike components, without degrading the software structure. These two limitations, among other technical and managerial problems, contribute much to the growing complexity of software over years of evolution, which in turn triggers the growing cost of any further changes.

Part II is about both software maintenance and evolution, with the main focus on evolution. It presents a mixed-strategy approach that lifts the above-mentioned limitations, radically improving software productivity during maintenance and evolution. Mixed-strategy relies on synergistic application of modern architecture-centric, component-based, and object-oriented methods, and a generative frame-based technique of XVCL (xvcl.comp.nus.edu.sg). XVCL provides for both simplifying and making explicit the variants that a software system creates as it undergoes evolution. The essence of the mixed-strategy approach is identifying and unifying similarity patterns in evolving software, as well as in evolutionary changes applied to software over time. XVCL provides technical means for doing that in a systematic and cost-effective way. Non-redundant mixed-strategy program representation reduces the conceptual complexity of software and emphasizes software relationships that matter during maintenance and evolution. It facilitates reuse-based evolution, bridging the gap between reuse and evolution. The approach leads to easier maintenance and helps to keep software complexity under control during long-term evolution.

Mixed-strategy is a practical and common sense approach. It has been applied in industrial projects demonstrating the increase in maintenance productivity much beyond levels possible with conventional approaches alone.

Although this book primarily focuses on practical aspects of maintenance and evolution, it also highlights techniques from the wider, research perspective.

Advanced problems and solutions are presented in an easy to grasp way via case studies. Generalization of findings follows an intuitive, example-based presentation.

The book is meant for a wide audience of researchers, practitioners, and students interested in software design in general and technical aspects of maintenance and evolution in particular. For researchers, the book points to challenging problems in software maintenance that call for more research and more advanced solutions. Practitioners will find in the book ideas on where to look for improvements in current maintenance practices and see in which areas advanced methods and tools can help. The book provides a perspective and a reference point for evaluating technological innovations in the area of software maintenance. It can be adopted for graduate level courses on advanced software engineering and specialized courses in software maintenance. Most of the materials have been used by the author in graduate courses on software reengineering and software reuse.

How to read this book

The Introduction should be read first.
Part I and Part II can be read independently of each other.
Chapters of Part I can be read in any order.

Readers interested in mixed-strategy only should read the Introduction, Chapter 5 and Chapter 6 of Part I, and Part II. Chapter 12 can be skipped at the first reading.

Chapter 1

Introduction

Chapter Summary

In this chapter, we set the stage for the book. We discuss the problem of software change, motivating the mixed-strategy approach. We characterize the evolution situations that we focus on in this book, and discuss their main challenges. We illustrate evolution with an example of a facility reservation system (FRS), which will be our running example in Part II. The last section guides the reader through themes addressed in various chapters of the two parts of the book.

1.1 Background

Companies spend more time on maintenance of existing software than on development of new software. According to various studies, software maintenance accounts for the following percentages of total software costs: 90 [11,17], 75 [9], 60–70 [13,18], and 66 [12,21]. Earlier studies reported the following percentages: 50 [15], 70 [9], and 65–75 [16].

Maintenance is undoubtedly the most expensive software activity. Any solutions that can improve maintenance productivity are bound to have a dramatic impact on software costs and the overall profitability of companies. It is interesting to note that advancements in software technology over the last two decades, as well as much research on maintenance methods, have not improved the situation. The cost of maintenance, rather than dropping, is on the increase. Understanding the reasons why this is so and exploring an alternative technical approach to managing

1

changes during maintenance and evolution that is more effective than conventional techniques used today is the theme of this book.

High maintenance cost has serious practical implications, as it limits the capabilities of IT divisions to deliver new systems that might be of strategic importance to their companies. Outsourcing has emerged as a main strategy to address these problems and cut software costs. Outsourcing may be an economically justifiable option today, but it also has well-known negative consequences, such as the possibility of losing control over the company's critical software assets, or not being able to respond to change requests in a timely manner. In any case, as the global economic situation changes, outsourcing can hardly be considered a viable solution to software problems in the long term. Should today's software technology allow companies to develop and maintain software themselves, in a cost-effective way, there is no doubt that fewer companies would outsource their software operations. Therefore, one could also argue that the growing importance of outsourcing is a symptom of the failure of software technology to deliver solutions to satisfy today's software needs in a cost-effective way.

Many years ago, the role of maintenance was understood as fixing errors in released programs. Today, we know that what happens to software after the first release is much more complicated than that. Functional enhancements are inevitable in the evolution of any successful software: As the business environment changes, users come up with new requirements. Only our imagination is the limit for the ever-increasing expectations regarding how software can better support our work and make us more productive. At times, we must reengineer existing software to take advantage of technological advances such as new platforms and architectures, improve software structure, reach new clients, or win new market share. A new term, *software evolution*, has been coined to better reflect this wide range of postrelease processes affecting software systems.

In this book, we use the term *software maintenance* to mean day-to-day changes implemented into a software system, and the term *software evolution* when referring to what happens to software in the long term, during the whole of its life span.

With maintenance consuming an increasing share of computing costs, much attention has been drawn to methods and tools that can improve maintenance productivity. This is clear from work published in reputed international forums devoted to software maintenance, such as *Journal of Software Maintenance and Evolution: Research and Practice*, International Conference on Software Maintenance (22nd event in 2006), Working Conference on Software Reverse Engineering (13th event in 2006), European Conference on Software Maintenance and Reengineering (10th event in 2006), International Workshop on Program Comprehension (14th event in 2006), and the International Workshop on Principles of Software Evolution (9th event in 2006). It is common to find papers on software maintenance at prime general software engineering forums such as *IEEE Transactions on Software Engineering*, International Conference on Software Engineering, Symposium on Foundation of Software Engineering, or the European Software Engineering Conference.

1.2 The Problem of Software Change

Software maintenance is about change. It may be a small change to fix a bug or enhance software requirements to better satisfy users. Sometimes, the situation calls for a massive change to reengineer programs and port them to a new platform, solve the Y2K problem, or facilitate a switch to the Euro system. Software evolution comprises the long-term process of changing software and managing the cumulative consequences of the changes made. ISO 9126 quality standards mention changeability among the four most important characteristics of maintainable software (the other three are analyzability, testability, and stability). Still, change is known to be conceptually challenging, technically difficult, and risky [6].

To understand change means to know how to apply a sequence of program modifications to satisfy a given source of change (e.g., to enhance a program with a new user requirement, fix a bug, or support a new platform). Each modification may cause unexpected ripple effects that trigger the need for yet more modifications. To understand change also means to understand those impacts. We need to manage changes at the design level to avoid code decay [10]. Finally, we need to understand changes in the context of long-term software evolution, which often leads to multiple releases of similar programs. Although mechanisms for effective management of software changes must necessarily relate to software component architecture and code, they should also reach beyond them to reflect this historical perspective of changes that happen to software over time.

The sheer size and complexity of programs make change hard. The complexity of understanding and maintaining a program is proportional to its size and complexity. In his famous paper, "No Silver Bullet" [2], Frederick Brooks argues that programming is inherently complex. Whether we use a machine language or a high-level programming language, on general grounds, we cannot simplify a program below a certain threshold that he calls an *essential program complexity*. Two main factors that determine this complexity threshold are: (1) the complexity of a problem and its solution at the conceptual level, and (2) the fact that not only do programs express problem solution, but also must address a range of issues related to solving a problem by a computer. These two factors cannot be cleanly separated one from one another in program components, which constrains our efforts in using conventional decomposition ("divide and conquer") in combating software complexity. Very often, we cannot make software conform to the rules of a LEGO model, which works so well for hardware construction [1,19]. This difficulty of achieving clean decomposability is an important difference between hardware and software. Another important difference is that we never try to change hardware as often and in such drastic ways as we do software. The difficulty of cleanly separating concerns by means of decomposition necessarily hinders changeability. Generative techniques [7], such as aspect-oriented programming [14] and XVCL [22], which is described in detail in Part II of this book, propose unconventional approaches to software decomposition to address these problems.

What makes change hard is ripple effects of modifications, coupled with invisible and obscure mappings between reasons why we want to change a program and code that must be modified: One source of change (say, change in user requirements) may affect multiple software components. Sometimes, it may affect the design — the component architecture. Any change that affects component interfaces or global system properties may unpredictably impact many components.

Then, there is the problem of redundancies. Similar code structures, often copied and duplicated with suitable modifications in many places in a program, may make change hard and contribute significantly to high maintenance costs. Yet, programs are often polluted by redundant code. Some of the unwanted redundancies can be refactored, but refactoring may not necessarily be in tune with other important design goals and software qualities. Any changes expose programs to risks of malfunctioning, so at times refactoring to eliminate redundancies may not be a viable option for business reasons. Some of the redundancies are created intentionally and for a good reason, for example, to improve software performance or reliability. Some are induced by a programming technology used. Apparently, such redundancies cannot be refactored at all within constraints of a given technology.

A single change may itself be quite a challenge. Once a program has been changed, the change gets buried in the existing code; it becomes invisible. If not immediately, then after some time, it becomes unclear which parts of the code relate to which source of change and why they are there. Maintenance problems aggravate during software evolution, when many changes get implemented over time. The impact of various sources of change on code is mostly undocumented and attempts to delegate the problem to external tools have not been successful so far. Poor visibility of changes that have affected software over time makes any future changes even harder. This vicious cycle of program evolution adds to program complexity, increasing the complexity of change. Software configuration management (SCM) tools [5] are used to ease the problem, but understanding changes from the evolution history managed by SCM tools is often insufficient for effective maintenance (Chapter 5). SCM tools are mainly concerned with the end result of changes; they do not explicate the whole process that leads to implementing a change in an operational and replicable form. To achieve higher levels of automation for managing changes during evolution, we need to understand this process at architecture and code levels, and repeat or undo changes at will.

Programming languages include rich abstractions to model runtime program structures. Historically, the main role of programming languages has been to provide abstractions for code structures to be executed on a computer, such as assignment statements, loops, selection, procedures, procedure invocations, classes, objects, methods, message passing, or components. Problems of program evolution did not receive much recognition in the early days of computing when the fundamentals of programming paradigms were formed. Mechanisms for change have become second-class citizens in today's programming languages and environments, as well as in modeling notations such as Unified Modeling Language (UML) [20].

There seems to be no easy way out of it; change is bound to be difficult. Rising maintenance costs and problems with software reuse underline the gravity of this situation.

1.3 Software Evolution and Its Challenges

Evolution problems and the suitability of various techniques to address them depend on many factors, such as the size of a software system, the nature of similarities and differences among system releases, or quality requirements (e.g., reliability, time performance, or memory consumption) [3]. Below, we clarify the assumptions about the evolution situations that we address in this book.

We may have a single evolving system or many system versions released to different customers. From the technical perspective, the first situation is a special case of the second one. The second situation is also by far more challenging than the first one, so in this book we primarily concentrate on the second situation.

Suppose a successful software system S evolves into a family of similar software systems released to various customers over time. We consider software evolution situations that require fine levels of feature management in software system releases. This includes: (1) the ability to inject combinations of variant features arising during evolution into system releases, in a flexible way, with minimum effort; (2) propagating new features in variant forms to selected releases; and (3) reuse of already implemented features in future system releases.

In particular:

1. Each system release may implement:
   a. Common features shared by all releases of S.
   b. Variant features shared with some other releases.
   c. Some unique features.
2. Feature implementation may vary across system releases.
3. Each release should contain only features that its customers wish to have. This may be important for:
   a. Reliability reasons.
   b. Strict time performance or memory consumption requirements, for example, in real-time process control software, embedded system software, applications running on mobile devices, etc.
   c. Large packages such as SAP that need to be tailored for different operating environments. Because of the huge number of features implemented in such packages, it is important to selectively include in each custom release only those features that a customer needs.

Evolution in the preceding sense poses a number of practical problems that must be addressed no matter what technique we use to support evolution. We discuss them here, as possible criteria to evaluate capabilities of various techniques to support evolution.

The first challenge is to cope with a large number of variant features and feature dependencies, and the complexity arising from them. Explosion of variant features triggers many other related problems. Various combinations of these features have been implemented into released systems, and may be needed in future releases. The explosion of look-alike component versions is a common symptom of failing to address this challenge during evolution. It is not uncommon in industrial projects for the number of variant features to reach several thousand [8]. The problem of variant feature explosion is inherent in both single-system evolution and a multi-system product line [4]. The weakness of existing variability realization mechanisms has been identified as one of the obstacles that impedes implementation of reuse strategies via the product line architecture approach [8]. The number of features and the nature of their dependencies are conditioned by real-world business needs, and cannot be reduced without compromising them. Therefore, we can only try to alleviate the problem by considering other issues related to it. Some form of generic components capable of unifying groups of similar concrete components is needed to avoid such explosion.

The preceding problem is aggravated by feature dependencies, which is the second challenge. Functional dependencies among features imply that only certain combinations of variant features may coexist in any given system release. Feature f_2 is functionally dependent on feature f_1 (in short notation $f_1 \overset{f}{\rightarrow} f_2$) if feature f_2 cannot exist without f_1. Feature f_2 is implementation-dependent on feature f_1 (in short $f_1 \overset{i}{\rightarrow} f_2$) if the presence or absence of f_1 affects the way f_2 is implemented. We use symbols $f_1 \overset{f}{\leftrightarrow} f_2$ and $f_1 \overset{i}{\leftrightarrow} f_2$ to indicate mutual dependencies among features, and $f_1 \overset{-f}{\leftrightarrow} f_2$ and $f_1 \overset{-i}{\leftrightarrow} f_2$ to indicate mutual independence of features. Insufficient information about such dependency rules may result in an incomplete or impractical system. It is not our goal in this book to study formal properties of feature dependency relationships in a systematic way, but we use the above notions and notation for convenience.

The third challenge is reuse of features implemented in past releases when building new system releases. When a new system release is requested, we make use of previous releases to save the time and effort of implementing a new system. Implementation of the same variant feature across system releases may vary, because of the impact of other features. Therefore, features implemented in past releases may need to be adapted to the context of a new release. The ease with which we can reuse functionality already implemented in past releases determines the *evolution productivity*, and makes the whole difference between ad hoc and systematic evolution.

The fourth challenge is selective propagation of new features (and any changes) to past releases. Often, new features implemented into a certain system release can be beneficial in other existing systems releases. Then, it is useful to include new features into systems released in the past. However, not all such systems may need the feature and some of them may need the feature with slight modifications. In addition, each released system may evolve independently of others.

The fifth challenge is to preserve the visibility of feature implementation during evolution. For any variant feature, we must know the whole chain of changes associated with that feature.

The sixth challenge is to enhance the overall understanding, as well as maintain a detailed description of, similarities and differences among system releases.

The seventh challenge is to minimize the effort of selecting or customizing components from past releases during development of new systems. This effort directly translates into productivity gains; therefore, it is a final test of effectiveness of an adopted approach to evolution.

We believe the preceding considerations are a representative, though not exhaustive, list of technical problems arising in evolution.

1.3.1 The Concept of Reuse-Based Evolution

The idea behind reuse-based evolution is to reuse the knowledge of past changes to effectively implement future changes. The essence of reuse-based evolution is clear visibility of changes, clear understanding of software similarities and differences at all granularity levels, and nonredundancy achieved by unifying similarity patterns of evolutionary changes with generic structures. Reuse-based evolution attempts to explicitly address evolution challenges.

Reuse-based software evolution is a concept, or a principle, of how to address changes so that evolution is easier, faster, and cheaper. Different techniques can be used to realize reuse-based evolution.

1.3.2 An Example

We illustrate evolution with an example of a Facility Reservation System (FRS). This FRS will serve as a working example in later chapters of the book.

An FRS helps users reserve facilities such as meeting rooms. Figure 1.1 shows a sample FRS evolution history. Circled numbers attached to FRS releases indicate the order in which the releases were implemented. Solid arrows between releases X and Y indicate that X was chosen as a baseline for Y. Dashed arrows between releases X and Y indicate that some features implemented in X were adapted for Y.

The initial FRS includes the functions to reserve the facilities and supports a method for viewing reservations by facility (FAC, for short). In the diagram of Figure 1.1, it is numbered "0."

> Stage 1: Suppose one of our customers requests a new feature, to view reservations by date (DATE, for short). Having implemented the required enhancement, we have two versions of the FRS in use, namely, the original FRS and the enhanced system FRS^{DATE}.

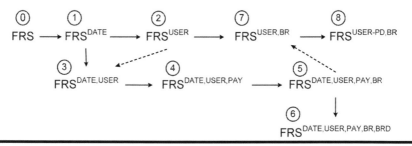

Figure 1.1   Stages in facility reservation system (FRS) evolution.

Stage 2: After some time, yet another customer would like to view reservations by user (USER). Having implemented this new enhancement, we have three versions of the FRS in use: the original FRS, FRS^{DATE}, and FRS^{USER}.

Stage 3: We also realize that the new features may be generally useful for other customers and yet another version, FRS^{DATE,USER}, may make perfect sense to some of them.

Stage 4: Sometime later, a new customer wants an FRS that supports the concept of payment for reservations (PAY). This includes computing and displaying reservation charges (RC), cancellation charges (CC), bill construction (BC), and frequent customer discount (FCD). The name PAY refers to all such payment features. FRS^{DATE,USER,PAY} results from that enhancement.

Stage 5: Another customer would like to make block reservations (BR), as well as have support for payment (FRS$^{DATE,USER,\ PAY,BR}$).

Stage 6: We include block reservation discount (FRS^{DATE,USER,PAY,BR,BRD}).

Stage 7: We need an FRS with existing features USER and BR (FRS^{USER,BR}).

Stage 8: A customer asks us to customize the USER feature to view reservations made for only a preferred range of dates (FRS$^{USER-PD,BR}$).

1.4   About This Book

This book focuses on technical aspects of change management in the context of long-term software evolution. We present technologies that help us address some of the maintenance and evolution problems discussed earlier. Part I of the book discusses conventional maintenance techniques, and problems that are difficult to solve using conventional methods. Part II presents a constructive and practical way of solving those problems, with a mixed-strategy approach.

In Part I we discuss static program analysis and reverse engineering, model-based design (a technique that can ease the handling of unanticipated changes), as well as SCM tools. Although these techniques help, certain problems related to change remain inherently difficult to address with conventional approaches. Part I ends with a chapter on analysis of software maintenance and evolution problems that are difficult to solve with conventional techniques. The last two chapters of Part I bridge software maintenance and evolution.

In Part II, we focus on software evolution and describe a novel approach called *mixed-strategy*. Mixed-strategy is a synergistic merger of conventional and generative programming techniques to enhance software maintainability and impart engineering qualities to software solutions that cannot be achieved otherwise. Mixed-strategy relies on modern architecture-centric techniques, component platforms, and any conventional programming language (e.g., Java or C++) to design a core program solution in terms of its user interfaces, business logic, and database. A generative frame-based technique of XVCL [22] is then applied on top of a conventional program solution to enhance the program's maintainability, and to facilitate long-term evolution. A programming language expresses the syntax and semantics of a program. XVCL expresses the syntax and semantics of change. XVCL provides for both simplifying and making explicit the variants that a software system creates as it undergoes evolution.

In the mixed-strategy approach, we identify and unify similarity patterns in evolving software, as well as in evolutionary changes applied to software over time. XVCL provides technical means for doing that in a systematic and cost-effective way. The nonredundant and adaptable mixed-strategy program representation emphasizes software relationships that matter during maintenance and evolution. Mixed-strategy representation has a unique capability to retain simplicity and robust software structure under the pressure of multiple changes occurring over years of program evolution. These engineering qualities make the mixed-strategy approach well-suited to supporting reuse-based evolution, bridging the gap between reuse and evolution.

The principles behind XVCL are not new. They have been the basis of the Frame Technology™, developed by Netron, Inc. [1]. Frames have been extensively applied to maintain multi-million-line COBOL-based information systems and to build reuse frameworks in companies [1]. An independent analysis showed that frames could achieve up to 90 percent reuse, reduce project costs by over 84 percent, and their time to market by 70 percent when compared to industry norms [1]. Project experiences with the mixed-strategy approach described in this book show that frame principles have their role to play in the world of modern software technologies. Most importantly, they enhance modern technologies in the area of unifying software similarity patterns of any kind and granularity, with generic software representations that can be easily adapted to form concrete software components in required variant forms.

This book is based on the author's papers published in journals and conference proceedings, as well as new material. The previously published material has been rewritten for this book.

The intended audience of the book comprises researchers, practitioners, and students interested in software design in general, and in technical aspects of evolution and maintenance in particular. For researchers, the book points to challenging problems in software maintenance that call for more research and more advanced solutions. Researchers will use the book as a background and a reference for further research on topics covered in the book. Practitioners will find in the book ideas regarding where to look for improvements in current maintenance practices, and in which areas advanced methods and tools can help. Techniques and tools discussed in the book provide a perspective and a reference point for evaluating technological innovations in the area of software maintenance. The book can be adopted for graduate-level courses on advanced software engineering. Most of the materials have been used by the author in graduate courses on software reengineering and software reuse.

References

1. Bassett, P., *Framing Software Reuse — Lessons from Real World*, Yourdon Press, Prentice Hall, Englewood Cliffs, NJ, 1997.
2. Brooks, F.P., No Silver Bullet, *Computer Magazine*, April 1986.
3. Chapin, N., Hale, J.E., Khan, K.M., Ramil, J.F., and Tan, W.G., Types of software evolution and software maintenance, *Journal of Software Maintenance and Evolution: Research and Practice*, 13(1), 3–30, January–February 2001.
4. Clements, P. and Northrop, L., *Software Product Lines: Practices and Patterns*, Addison-Wesley, Boston, 2002.
5. Conradi, R. and Westfechtel, B., Version models for software configuration management, *ACM Computing Surveys*, 30(2), 232–282, 1998.
6. Cordy, J.R., Comprehending reality: practical challenges to software maintenance automation, *Proceedings of the 11th International Workshop on Program Comprehension, IWPC'03*, Portland, OR, May 2003, pp. 196–206 (keynote paper).
7. Czarnecki, K. and Eisenecker, U., *Generative Programming: Methods, Tools, and Applications*, Addison-Wesley, Boston, 2000.
8. Deelstra, S., Sinnema, M., and Bosch, J., Experiences in software product families: problems and issues during product derivation, *Proceedings of the Software Product Lines Conference, SPLC3*, Boston, MA, August 2004, LNCS 3154, Springer-Verlag, pp. 165–182.
9. Eastwood, A., Firm Fires Shots at Legacy Systems, *Computing Canada,* 19(2), 1993, p. 17.
10. Eick, S.G., Graves, T.L., Karr, A.F., Marron, J.S., and Mockus, A., Does code decay? Assessing the evidence from change management data, *IEEE Transactions on Software Engineering*, 27(1), 1–12, January 2001.
11. Erlikh, L., Leveraging Legacy System Dollars for E-Business, *(IEEE) IT Pro*, May–June 2000, pp. 17–23.
12. Harrison, R., Maintenance Giant Sleeps Undisturbed in Federal Data Centers, *Computerworld*, March 9, 1987, pp. 81–86.
13. Huff, S., Information systems maintenance, *The Business Quarterly,* 55, 30–32, 1990.

14. Kiczales, G., Lamping, J., Mendhekar, A., Maeda, C., Lopes, C., Loingtier, J-M., and Irwin, J., Aspect-oriented programming, *European Conference on Object-Oriented Programming*, Finland, Springer-Verlag LNCS 1241, 1997, pp. 220–242.
15. Lientz, B.P. and Swanson, E., Problems in Application Software Maintenance, *Communications of the ACM,* 24(11), 1981, pp. 763–769.
16. McKee, J., Maintenance as a function of design, *Proceedings of the AFIPS National Computer Conference*, Las Vegas, NV, 1984, pp. 187–193.
17. Moad, J., Maintaining the Competitive Edge, *Datamation,* 1990, pp. 61, 62, 64, 66.
18. Port, O., The Software Trap — Automate or Else, *Business Week,* 3051(9), 1998, pp.142–154.
19. Ran, A., Software Isn't Built From Lego Blocks, *ACM Symposium on Software Reusability*, 1999, pp. 164–169.
20. Rumbaugh, J., Jacobson, I., and Booch, G., *The Unified Modeling Languages Reference Manual*, Addison-Wesley, Boston, 1999.
21. Tan, W.G. and Jarzabek, S., Current practices and future needs of software maintenance in Singapore, *Proceedings of the SCS Silver Jubilee Conference on Software Engineering: New Technologies and Business Payoffs*, Singapore, October 1992, pp. 121–135.
22. XVCL (XML-based variant configuration language) method and tool for managing software changes during evolution and reuse, xvcl.comp.nus.edu.sg.

Part I

CONVENTIONAL METHODS OF SOFTWARE MAINTENANCE AND EVOLUTION

As maintenance programmers spend more than 50 percent of their time just trying to understand programs [1], methods and tools that can ease program understanding are of great importance and have attracted much attention in the software engineering community.

Static program analysis methods, discussed in Chapter 2, address the problem of understanding large and complex programs. A static program analyzer (SPA) is a tool that automatically answers queries about program properties related to specific maintenance tasks at hand.

Reverse engineering methods (Chapter 3) recover abstract program views from code, addressing problems of missing documentation. Some of the low-level program abstractions can be extracted automatically. Missing links between code structures and application domain concepts can be recovered in a semiautomatic way by human analysts assisted by reverse engineering tools. In particular, we describe a specification formalism for reverse engineering heuristics that facilitates design of a generic reverse engineering tool. Examples focus on reverse engineering heuristics for object recovery.

The above two chapters also provide a comprehensive review of static program analysis and reverse engineering methods. Technical solutions presented in detail are intended to give the reader a feel for what can be realistically achieved with advanced static program analysis and reverse engineering tools.

Model-based design is discussed in Chapter 4. Programs designed with the model-based technique are highly customizable.

Software configuration management tools are commonly used to support software evolution. Chapter 5 is a case study in evolution supported by Concurrent Versions System (CVS).

Chapter 6 extends and summarizes our discussion of the strengths and limitations of conventional techniques in supporting software evolution.

References

1. Parikh, G. and Zvegintzov, N., Eds., *Tutorial on Software Maintenance*, IEEE Computer Society Press, Silver Spring, MD, 1983.

Chapter 2

Static Program Analysis Methods

Chapter Summary

The reader is introduced to a general-purpose facility to define and perform a range of static program analysis methods. Such a facility can be implemented in any IDE (integrated development environment). This chapter gives the reader an idea of what we can realistically expect from static program analysis methods and tools in terms of their benefits, and also the limitations in software development, maintenance, and evolution.

2.1 Introduction to Static Program Analysis

To implement change, we must know a great deal about global and detail relationships among program elements such as classes, procedures (methods or functions), and variables. Program modifications often have ripple effects: Modifications of code at one program point may affect other parts of code in unexpected and undesirable ways, introducing errors. We fix one problem, but unwittingly introduce another one. Tracing the impact of change in a large, undocumented program is a challenge, and may take up a significant portion of the overall maintenance effort.

To better understand a maintenance task at hand, programmers often examine relationships among program elements and study detailed properties of programs.

Sometimes, what programmers need to know about a program can be stated in the form of queries, such as:

Q1. Which procedures are called from procedure p?
Q2. Which variables have their values modified in procedure p?
Q3. Find assignment statements where variable x appears on the left-hand side.
Q4. Find statements that contain the subexpression x*y+z.
Q5. Is there a control path from statement #20 to statement #620?
Q6. Which program statements affect the value of x at statement #120?
Q7. If I change the value of x in statement #20, which other statements will be affected?

Manually digging out all the information needed to answer such queries for large programs is time consuming and error-prone. Most advanced IDEs incorporate some analysis features to help programmers with the information they need to understand a program. For example, Oracle JDeveloper 10g™ shows variable definition for a selected variable reference, finds all points where a given variable is used, and displays graphical views of a class inheritance hierarchy. IntelliJ™IDEA detects unused classes, redundant declarations, unreachable code, and code duplications. Microsoft Visual Studio .Net™ shows variable definition for a selected variable reference, displays graphical views of class inheritance hierarchy, shows classes in namespaces, methods and properties of each class, base classes and interfaces of a class, and base class content.

It is difficult to predict all types of program views that programmers may want to see and queries about program properties that they may require. In this chapter, we address the problem of static program analysis in a systematic and general way. Rather than trying to guess what kind of program analysis method (or program query) a programmer may need, we describe a general-purpose facility that enables programmers to ask queries and get answers. A static program analyzer (SPA) is a tool that implements a general-purpose facility to support programmer-defined analysis methods, helping a programmer understand a program under maintenance. SPA concepts discussed in this chapter can be implemented in any IDE.

Of course, an SPA cannot answer all possible program queries. But the class of program queries it can answer is wide enough to make an SPA a useful tool.

With an SPA concept, a programmer is not restricted to a fixed set of program analysis methods supported by a development tool. Instead, an SPA provides programmers with the flexibility to define types of program analysis methods, which a tool will implement for them. This is user-level flexibility, which means that a programmer can formulate a possibly wide class of program queries that a tool can answer.

However, an SPA also needs design-level flexibility, so that it can be easily extended and adapted to work with different programming languages, on different platforms, using different media for storing program design information. The same tool can then be customized to serve in many different projects. In this chapter, we focus on user-level flexibility. We talk about design-level flexibility in Chapter 4, where we describe model-based design methods.

2.2 Approaches to Static Program Analysis

Many SPAs and program query languages have been described in the literature. PQL [8–11] is a conceptual level, source-language-independent notation to specify static program analysis methods in the form of program queries. PQL queries are answered automatically by a query evaluation mechanism built into an SPA.

RIGI [24] concentrates on architectural aspects of programs. Views produced by RIGI mirror mental models used by software maintainers. RIGI does not provide a general-purpose query facility, but views can be customized by means of a scripting language. GENOA [5] provides specification methods and algorithms that allow the extraction of program design information from the source code. In GENOA, new types of queries can be formulated without actually modifying the SPA front end at the cost of a more complex query specification language. Incremental attribute evaluation methods have been extended from single to multiple interrelated syntax trees [12]. Using these extensions, we can store and query families of interrelated programs and incrementally update program information after modifications.

REFINE [16] and SCA [19] provide powerful query languages that were designed with objectives similar to PQL. The main difference between REFINE, SCA, and PQL is in the underlying models of program design information and in the way queries are formulated. REFINE uses an object-oriented database to store program designs. SCA models programs as many-sorted algebras and offers a set of algebraic operations to form program queries. In PQL, we write program queries in terms of program models expressed as Unified Modeling Language (UML) class diagrams. PQL uses a uniform and intuitive notation to specify all aspects of program design, such as global program properties, detailed program structures, and control/data flow information. This results in a uniform and simple notation for program queries. Similar to REFINE and SCA, PQL is capable of querying global program design, statement-level structural program patterns, and control/data flow information derived by static program analysis. All three formalisms handle atomic data types, composite object types (such as structured loop constructs or expressions), and list objects; they also allow us to organize program objects into subtyping hierarchies with inheritance.

PQL emphasizes the uniformity of program modeling conventions, simplicity of the query language, and clear separation of conceptual SPA models from implementation decisions. In databases, separation of the conceptual data design from the physical database schema has become a standard practice as it facilitates design of flexible applications. We use a similar approach to aid the design of flexible SPAs. In particular, we can implement the same specifications of SPA capabilities on a variety of program representations to obtain desirable SPA characteristics such as performance and simplicity of the design.

CIA [3] stores program information in a relational database. The advantage of using a relational database is that we can write program queries in SQL [4]. As CIA shows, we can obtain an interesting class of program views based on a relatively simple program model stored in the database. However, CIA stores only the global descriptions of programs. Unlike CIA, PQL allows a programmer to query both global program design and detailed program structures (such as abstract syntax trees), using a uniform SQL-like program query notation. If we store too much detailed information about programs in a relational database, the performance of an SPA might be poor. In particular, displaying complex, structured program views (such as recreating program text) can be especially slow. Also, SQL is not power-ful enough to support types of queries that involve traversals of graph structures (such as syntax trees and control/data flow graphs). To evaluate such queries, we must embed SQL into procedural code. The reader can find a detailed discussion of problems with storing and querying low-granularity structured objects (such as syntax trees and dependency graphs) in a relational database in Chapter 19 of the REDO Compendium [23].

A number of alternative approaches for storing program information for effi-cient static program analysis have been proposed. Dependency graphs [18] rely on explicit representation of program control and data flow relations in one unified form. Very efficient for performing certain types of program analysis, this represen-tation is difficult to modify and has limited value in design of tools that combine analysis and editing features. Logic-based representation were well-suited to on-demand interprocedural analysis [20].

There seems to be no ideal storage for program design information (and, gen-erally, for software project information). Systems based on relational databases are strong in global queries, but weak in dealing with statement-level structural information. Systems based on attribute grammars effectively deal with detailed program structures, but are weak in supporting global queries. Therefore, in the design of PQL we make no assumptions about how program design information is stored. PQL can be implemented on any storage medium, such as relational database, abstract syntax trees, or any hybrid of these program storage media [12]. PQL queries are written in terms of conceptual program design models that are independent of the way the design models are actually computed and stored. The choice of the program storage medium affects PQL characteristics such as ease of PQL implementation or the performance of a query evaluator. We feel we still have to experiment with alternative implementations to better understand their impact on SPAs. PQL is a good vehicle to conduct such experiments.

To avoid problems of storing and updating program information after modifi-cations, some authors have proposed methods for specifying program model extrac-tion algorithms at the level of source code. In [17], nested lexical rules with actions are used to search for code patterns to extract a required program model. Pattern matching and program model analysis modules are generated from program model specifications. Although not all program models can be easily extracted based on source-code-level specifications, the method described in [17] has the advantages of being simple, efficient, and tolerant, as program model extraction can be done on an incomplete or incorrect program.

2.3   How Does an SPA Work?

To answer program queries, an SPA must first extract relevant program design abstractions from source programs. Program design abstractions that are useful in answering queries include an abstract program syntax tree, program control flow graph, and cross-reference lists indicating usage of program variables, procedure invocations, etc. An SPA front end parses a source program, extracts program design abstractions, and stores them in a program knowledge base (PKB).

A programmer formulates questions about programs in a semiformal program query language, PQL for short [8–11]. A query processor subsystem validates a query and builds a query internal representation suitable for evaluation (a so-called query tree). Then, the query processor answers queries and the query result projector displays query results for the programmer to view. Major SPA components are depicted in Figure 2.1.

We use a simple model language to present essential concepts of Program Query Language (PQL). Later, we show how our approach to *static program analysis* (SPA)

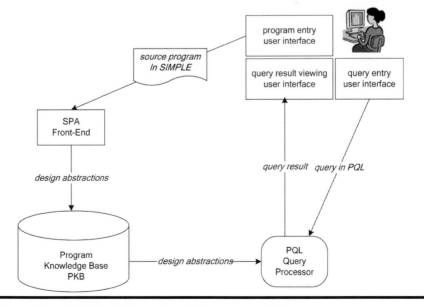

Figure 2.1   A high-level view of a static program analyzer.

scales up to any real-world programming language (for example, we described SPA for COBOL in [8]).

PQL is similar to SQL, but it is a higher-level language. For example, the query, "Which procedures are called from procedure "Push"?" can be written in PQL as follows:

procedure p;
Select p **such that** Calls ("Push", p)

To answer queries, the query evaluator maps program design entities referenced in a query (such as "procedure") and their relationships (such as "Calls") into the program design abstractions stored in the PKB. Then, the query evaluator interprets query conditions in **such that** to extract from the PKB program design entities that match the conditions.

The following scenario describes how an SPA is used by programmers:

1. John, a programmer, is given a task to fix an error in a program.
2. John feeds the program into an SPA for automated analysis. The SPA parses a program into the internal representation stored in a program knowledge base (PKB).
3. Now John can start using an SPA to help him find program statements that cause the crash. John repeatedly enters queries to the SPA. The SPA evaluates queries and displays results. John analyzes query results and examines related sections of the program, trying to locate the source of the error.
4. John finds program statements responsible for an error. Now he is ready to modify the program to fix the error. Before that, John can query the SPA further to examine a possible unwanted ripple effect of changes he intends to make.

2.4 Source Language: SIMPLE

We describe PQL using a model language called *SIMPLE*. SIMPLE is meant for explaining PQL and SPA concepts, and contains the minimum number of constructs necessary for this purpose. SIMPLE is not a language for solving real programming problems. PQL relies on abstract models of programming concepts, rather than on the syntax of any specific programming language. In that sense, we say that PQL is model-based. This model-based character of PQL makes it possible for concepts associated with SIMPLE to scale up to any real-world programming language. Furthermore, the model-based design of PQL makes the SPA tool itself easily adaptable to different programming languages. For example, we implemented an SPA for COBOL by plugging COBOL models into an SPA that was initially developed for SIMPLE [8]. We look into model-based design in Chapter 4, as it is an important technique in designing maintainable programs.

```
procedure First {
  x = 2;
  z = 3;
  call Second; }
procedure Second {
1.  x = 0;
2.  i = 5;
3.  while i {
4.    x = x + 2 * y;
5.      call Third;
6.    i = i - 1; }
7.  if x then {
8.    x = x + 1; }
    else {
9.    z = 1; }
10. z = z + x + i;
11. y = z + 2;
12. x = x * y + z;}
procedure Third {
  z = 5;
  v = z;  }
```

Figure 2.2   Sample program in *SIMPLE.*

The following example depicts (Figure 2.2) language constructs of *SIMPLE*. Program lines in procedure Second are numbered for ease of reference in examples.

Here is a summary of the language rules for *SIMPLE*: A program consists of one or more procedures. Program execution starts by calling the first procedure in a program. By convention, the name of the first procedure is also the name of the whole program. Procedures have no parameters and cannot be nested in each other or called recursively. A procedure contains a body of statements. Variables have unique names and global scope. Variables can be introduced in a program at any time. All the variables are of integer type, require no declarations, and are initialized to 0. There are four types of statements, namely, procedure call, assignment, while loop, and if-then-else. Decisions in while and if statements are made based on the value of a control variable: TRUE for values different than 0, and FALSE for 0.

Below is the grammar for *SIMPLE*. Lexical tokens are written in capital letters, e.g., NAME, VAR, INTEGER. Keywords are between apostrophes, e.g., 'procedure'. Nonterminals are in lowercase letters.

Meta symbols:

a* — repetition 0 or more times of "a"
a+ — repetition 1 or more times of "a"
a | b — a or b
brackets (and) — used for grouping

Lexical elements:

LETTER : A–Z | a–z —- capital or small letter
DIGIT : 0–9
NAME, VAR : LETTER (LETTER | DIGIT)* —- procedure names and variables are strings of letters and digits, starting with a letter.
INTEGER : DIGIT+ — Constants are sequences of digits.

Grammar rules:

program : procedure +
procedure : 'procedure' NAME '{' stmtLst '}'
stmtLst : (stmt)+
stmt : call | while | if | assign
call : 'call' NAME ';'
while : 'while' VAR '{' stmtLst '}'
if : 'if' VAR 'then' '{' stmtLst '}' 'else' '{' stmtLst '}'
assign : VAR '=' expr ';'
expr : expr '+' term | expr '-' term | term
term : term '*' factor | factor
factor : VAR | constant | '(' expr ')'
constant : INTEGER

2.5 Program Design Abstractions for SIMPLE

An SPA front-end parses source programs, derives program design abstractions from sources, and stores them in the PKB (Figure 2.1). The PQL query subsystem consults the PKB to validate and evaluate program queries. In this section, we address two important issues:

1. How do we specify program design abstractions to be stored in the PKB?
2. How do we refer to program design abstractions in PQL queries?

Conceptual models of program design information described in this section provide the answer to the preceding questions. Why is it better to use models rather than the actual data structures in the PKB? Data structures in the PKB may be complex. Writing queries directly in terms of data structures would be unnecessarily complicated, and PQL should be easy to use for programmers. Program design abstractions described in this section are "conceptual" in the sense that they make no assumptions about their physical data representation in the PKB. At the same time, models are sufficient to formulate program queries in a precise but simple and natural way. This is the most important reason for modeling program design abstractions. There are more reasons that make conceptual modeling worthwhile, but as these reasons have to do with the model-based design of a language-independent SPA, we defer their discussion to Chapter 4.

For convenience, we divide program design abstraction models into three parts, namely, a global program design model, a syntax structure model, and a control/data flow model. The three models are defined in terms of program design entities (such as procedure, variable, or assignment), entity relationships (such as Calls or Follows), and entity attributes (such as procedure.procName or variable.varName). For each model, we provide a graphical definition (as a UML class diagram) and an equivalent textual definition.

2.5.1 A Model of Global Program Design Abstractions

In Figure 2.3, we see global program design abstractions modeled as a UML class diagram [22].

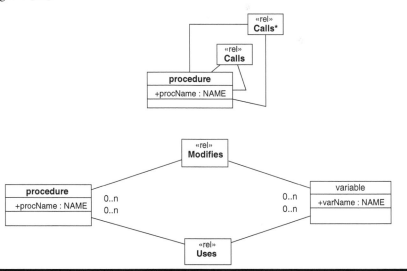

Figure 2.3   A model of global program design abstractions for *SIMPLE* **programs.**

Program design entities are represented as classes. Relationships among program design entities are represented by class stereotypes <<rel>>. The meaning of relationships is explained as follows. For any program P, procedures p and q, and variable v:

Modifies (p, v) holds if procedure p modifies the value of variable v. That is, if variable v appears on the left-hand side in some assignment statement in procedure p, or v is modified in some other procedure called (directly or indirectly) from p.

Uses (p, v) holds if procedure p uses the value of variable v. That is, if variable v appears on the right-hand side of an assignment statement in procedure p, or in the condition in p, or v is used in other procedure called (directly or indirectly) from p.

Calls (p, q) holds if procedure p directly calls q.
Calls* (p, q) holds if procedure p directly or indirectly calls q, that is:

Calls* (p, q) if:
    Calls (p, q) or
    Calls (p, p1) and Calls* (p1, q) for some procedure p1.

Program design entities have the following attributes:

program.progName (type NAME),
procedure.procName (type NAME),
variable.varName (type NAME).

For example, the following relationships hold in procedure First of Figure 2.2 (we refer to procedures and variables via their names given as strings):

Modifies ("First", "x"), Modifies ("First", "z") — as there are assignments to variables x and z in procedure First,
Modifies ("Second"," i") — as there is an assignment to variable i in procedure Second,
Modifies ("First", "i") — as procedure First calls Second and procedure Second modifies variable i,
Modifies ("Third", "v"), Modifies ("Second", "v"), Modifies ("First", "v"),
Uses ("Second", "i"), Uses ("Second", "x"), Uses ("Second", "y"), Uses ("Second", "z"),
Uses ("First", "i"), Uses ("First", "x"), Uses ("First", "y") , Uses ("First", "z"),
Calls ("First", "Second"), Calls ("Second", "Third"),
Calls* ("First", "Second"), Calls* ("Second"," Third"), Calls* ("First", "Third").

The SPA front end will be designed to derive program design abstractions specified by this model from source programs and to store them in the PKB.

2.5.2 A Model of Abstract Syntax of SIMPLE

An abstract syntax tree (AST) for a source program is another important model. The rules shown in Figure 2.4 model the abstract syntax structure of programs in *SIMPLE*.

A graphical model of an abstract syntax of *SIMPLE* in UML class diagram notation is given in Figure 2.5. The textual definition of abstract syntax in Figure 2.4 and the graphical definition of Figure 2.5 are equivalent.

Figure 2.6 shows a partial AST for program First (Figure 2.2), built according to the rules defined in the abstract syntax models of Figure 2.4 and Figure 2.5. We use a UML object diagram to depict an AST. Nodes in the AST are instances of design entities in Figure 2.5. An instance name is reflected at the node using UML convention (e.g., Second:call represents a call to the procedure named Second).

Relationships Parent and Follows (Figure 2.7) describe the nesting structures of program statements within a procedure. Relationships Parent and Follows are implicitly defined in the AST. For any two statements s1 and s2, the relationship Parent (s1, s2) holds if s2 is directly nested in s1. Therefore, s1 must be a "container" statement. In *SIMPLE* there are two containers, namely while and if. For example, in procedure Second (Figure 2.2) we have: Parent (3,4), Parent (3,5), Parent (3,6), Parent (7,8), Parent (7,9), etc. For convenience, we refer to statements via their

Meta-symbols: a+ means a list of 1 or more a's; '|' means or
1. program : procedure+
2. procedure : stmtLst
3. stmtLst : stmt+
4. stmt : assign | call | while | if
5. assign : variable expr
6. expr : plus | minus | times | ref
7. plus : expr expr
8. minus : expr expr
9. times : expr expr
10. ref : variable | const
11. while: variable stmtLst
12. if : variable stmtLst stmtLst

Attributes and attribute value types:
program.progName, procedure.procName, variable.varName : NAME
const.value : INTEGER
stmt.stmt# : INTEGER (program line number of a given statement, see Figure 2.2)

Figure 2.4   A model of abstract syntax structure for *SIMPLE*.

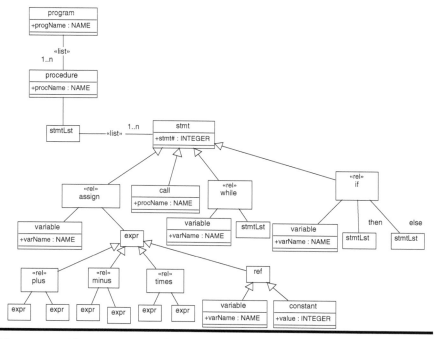

Figure 2.5   Abstract syntax rules for *SIMPLE* as UML class diagrams.

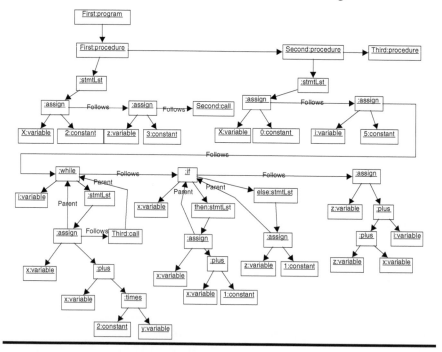

Figure 2.6   A partial abstract syntax tree (AST) for program First.

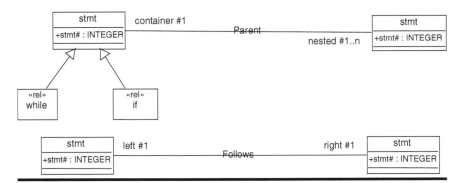

Figure 2.7   Relationships Parent and Follows.

respective program line numbers. As Parent relationship is defined for program statements, number 3 refers to the whole while statement, including lines 3–6, rather than to the program line "while i (" alone. Similarly, number 7 refers to the whole if statement, including lines 7–9.

Relationship Parent* is the transitive closure of relationship Parent, i.e.,

Parent* (s1, s2) if:
    Parent (s1, s2) or
    Parent (s1, s) and Parent* (s, s2) for some statement s.

For any two statements relationship Follows (s1, s2) holds if s2 follows s1 in the statement sequence. Follows* is the transitive closure of Follows, i.e.,

Follows* (s1, s2) if:
    Follows (s1, s2) or
    Follows (s1, s) and Follows* (s, s2) for some statement s.

Here are some examples from procedure Second: Follows(1, 2), Follows(2, 3), Follows(3, 7), Follows(4, 5), Follows(7, 10), Follows*(1, 2), Follows*(1, 3), Follows*(1, 7), Follows* (1, 12), Follows*(3, 12). Statement 6 is not followed by any statement. Note that statement 9 does not follow statement 8. As in the case of the Parent relationship, number 3 refers to the whole while statement and number 7 refers to the whole if statement.

2.5.3 A Model of Program Control and Data Flow

For a given statement s, the relationships Modifies and Uses define which variables are modified and used in statement s, respectively. For example, in procedure Second we have (Figure 2.8):

Modifies(1, "x"), Modifies(2, "i"), Modifies(6, "i")
Uses (4, "x"), Uses (4, "y")

Note that if a number refers to statement s that is a procedure call, then Modifies(s, v) holds for any variable v modified in the called procedure (or in any procedure called directly or indirectly from that procedure), and likewise for relationship Uses. Also, if a number refers to a container statement s (i.e., while or if statement), then Modifies (s, v) holds for any variable modified by any statement in the container s. Likewise for relationship Uses. For example:

Modifies (3,"x"), Modifies (3,"z"), Modifies (3,"i")

The relationship Next is defined among program lines within the same procedure. Program lines belonging to two different procedures are not related by means of relationship Next.

Let n1 and n2 be program lines. Relationship Next (n1, n2) holds if n2 can be executed immediately after n1 in some program execution sequence.

In the case of assignments or procedure calls, a line number also corresponds to a statement. But for container statements, line numbers refer to the "header" of the container rather than the whole statement as was the case earlier. For example, line number 3 refers to "while i {" and line number 7 refers to "if x then {".

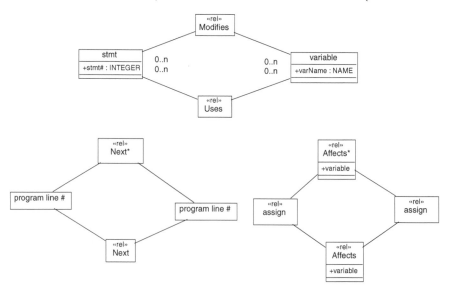

Figure 2.8   A model of program control and data flow.

For example, in procedure Second we have:

Next (1, 2), Next (2, 3), Next (3, 4), Next (4, 5), Next (5, 6), Next (6, 3), Next
(3, 7),
Next (7, 8), Next (7, 9), Next (8, 10), Next (9, 10), Next(10, 11) and Next(11, 12)

Based on the relationship Next, we can define the control flow graph (CFG) in
a program. A CFG is a compact and intuitive model of control flows in a program.
Nodes in the CFG are so-called basic blocks. A basic block contains statements that
are known to be executed in sequence; that is, a decision point in while or if always
marks the end of a basic block. As statements within a node are known to execute
sequentially, we only need to explicitly show control flows among basic blocks.
Figure 2.9 shows a CFG for procedure Second.

```
procedure Second {
  1. x = 0;
  2. i = 5;
  3. while i {
  4. x = x + 2 * y;
  5. call Third;
  6. i = i - 1; }
  7.if x then {
  8. x = x + 1; }
else {
  9. z = 1; }
  10. z = z + x + i;
  11. y = z + 2;
  12. x = x * y + z;}
```

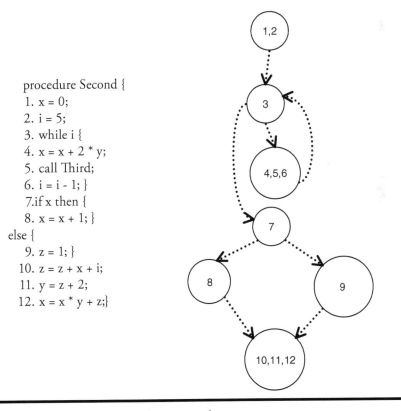

Figure 2.9   A CFG for procedure Second.

Relationship Next* is the transitive closure of relationship Next:

Next*(n1, n2) if
  Next (n1, n2) or
  Next(n1, n) and Next*(n, n2) for some program line n.

In procedure Second we have:

Next*(1, 2), Next*(1, 3), Next*(4, 7), Next*(3, 4), Next*(4, 3), Next*(6, 5), etc.

Relationship Next* describes possible computational paths in a program. It complements relationship Calls in the global design model that describes possible sequences of procedure activation.

The relationship Affects models data flows in a program. As indicated in the model of Figure 2.8, relationship Affects is defined only among assignment statements and involves a variable (shown as an attribute of relationship Affects).

Suppose we have two assignment statements a1 and a2 such that a1 modifies the value of variable v, and a2 uses the value of variable v. The relationship Affects (a1, a2) holds if the value of v as computed at a1 may be used at a2; that is, there must exist at least one computational path from a1 to a2 on which v is not modified.

Note that relationship Affects can only hold between assignments related by means of relationship Next*. So as in the case of Next, Affects may only hold among statements within the same procedure.

In procedure Second we have:

Affects (1, 4), Affects (1, 8), Affects (1, 10), Affects (1, 12)
Affects (2, 6), Affects (2, 10),
Affects (4, 8), Affects (4, 10), Affects (4, 12)
Affects (9, 10)

But Affects (9, 12) does not hold as the value of z is modified by assignment 10, that is, on any computational path between assignments 9 and 12.

In the following program, Affects (1, 5) and Affects (2, 5) do not hold, as both x and y are modified in procedure q. Even though modification of variable y in procedure q is only conditional, we take it that variable y is always modified when procedure q is called. Affects (3, 5) holds as variable z is not modified in procedure q.

```
procedure p {
1. x = 1;
2. y = 2;
3. z = y;
4. call q;
5. z = x + y + z;}
```

```
procedure q {
6. x = 5;
7.    if z then {
8. t = x + 1;}
else {
9. y = z + x;} }
```

At the same time, we see that the value assigned to z in statement 9 indirectly affects the use of z in statement 12. Transitive closure Affects* caters to this: the relationship Affects* (a1, a2) holds if assignment statement a1 has either direct or indirect impact on the use of v in assignment a2:

Affects* (a1, a2) if
    Affects (a1, a2) or
    Affects (a1, a) and Affects* (a, a2) for some assignment statement a.

Consider the following program fragment as an illustration of the basic principle:

```
1. x = a;
2. v = x;
3. z = v;
```

Modification of x in statement 1 affects variable v in statement 2, and modification of v in statement 2 affects use of variable v in statement 3. So we have: Affects (1, 2), Affects (2, 3), and Affects*(1, 3).

In procedure Second, we have: Affects* (1, 4,), Affects*(1, 10), Affects*(1, 11), Affects*(1, 12), etc.

Suppose we have the following code:

```
1. x = a;
2. call p;
3. v = x;
```

If procedure p modifies variable x, that is Modifies (p, "x") holds, then assignment Affects (1, 3) does not hold, as procedure call "kills" the value of x as assigned in statement 1. If procedure p does not modify variable x; then Affects (1, 3) holds.

To compute relationships Affects and Affects*, you will need to have a CFG and also relationship Modifies for all the procedures.

2.5.4 Summary of Program Design Models

Here is a summary of program design entities, attributes, and relationships for SIMPLE defined in program design models. When writing program queries, we can refer only to listed entities, attributes, and relationships:

Program design entities:
    program, procedure,
    stmtLst, stmt, assign, call, while, if
    plus, minus, times
    variable, constant
    program line

Attributes and attribute value types:
    program.progName, procedure.procName, variable.varName : NAME
    constant.value : INTEGER
    stmt.stmt# : INTEGER (numbers assigned to statements for the purpose
       of reference)

Program design entity relationships:
    Modifies (procedure, variable)
    Modifies (stmt, variable)
    Uses (procedure, variable)
    Uses (stmt, variable)
    Calls (procedure 1, procedure 2)
    Calls* (procedure 1, procedure 2)
    Parent (stmt 1, stmt 2)
    Parent* (stmt 1, stmt 2)
    Follows (stmt 1, stmt 2)
    Follows* (stmt 1, stmt 2)
    Next (program line 1, program line 2)
    Next* (program line 1, program line 2)
    Affects (assign 1, assign2)
    Affects* (assign 1, assign2)

2.5.5 Types of Relationship Arguments in Program Queries

In addition to argument types indicated in program design models, we adopt the following conventions:

> 1. A placeholder "_" (that is, an unconstrained argument) may appear in place of any argument, with the exception that Modifies (_, "x") and Uses (_, "x") are not allowed.
>
> 2. If it does not lead to ambiguity in Next and Next*, instead of program line, we can put a statement (that is a design entity stmt, assign, call, if, or while) that is interpreted as a program line of that statement (Remark: We shall use this in examples but you do not have to implement this feature. When you implement PQL, you can assume that arguments in Next and Next* must be program lines).

3. We can use program lines to denote respective statements whenever it makes sense. For example, we can put a program line in place of an argument representing a statement (that is a design entity stmt, assign, call, if, or while) in relationships Modifies, Uses, Parent, Parent*, Follows, and Follows*. Similarly, we can put a program line in place of an argument representing an assignment statement in relationships Affects and Affects*.

2.6 Querying Programs with PQL

Here, we describe a simplified form of PQL. Appendix A summarizes PQL rules as they are discussed in the scope of this book. An interested reader can refer to [8] for a full definition of PQL.

PQL queries are expressed in terms of program design models described in the previous section and summarized in Section 2.5.4. We express queries in terms of design entities (such as procedure, variable, assign, etc.), attributes (such as procedure.procName or variable.varName), entity relationships (such as Calls (procedure, procedure)) and syntactic patterns (such as assign (variable, expr)). Evaluation of a query yields a list of program elements that match a query. Program elements are specific instances of design entities, for example, procedure named "Second", statement number 35, or variable x.

In a query, after keyword **Select**, we list query results; that is, program design entities we are interested in finding and **Select** from the program or the keyword BOOLEAN. We can further constrain the results by writing (optional) conditions that the results should satisfy. These conditions will include **with**, **such that**, and **pattern** clauses. In PQL, all the keywords are in bold font.

Here are examples of queries without conditions:

procedure p;
Select p
Meaning: This query returns as a result all the procedures in a program. You could then display the result, for example, as a list of procedure names along with statement numbers. You could also display procedures along with source code (i.e., the whole program) if you wanted to. The issue of displaying query results is handled separately from the PQL by the SPA components query result projector and user interface (Figure 2.1).

procedure p;
Select p.procName
Meaning: Returns as a result names of all procedures in a program.

procedure p; assign a; variable v;

Select <a.stmt#, p.procName, v.varName>

Meaning: Query result may be a tuple of program items. Here, the result will contain all possible combinations of all assignment statement numbers, procedure names, and variable names in a program.

The preceding query examples did not include any conditions. However, in most situations, we wish to select only specific program elements; for example, we may want to select only those statements that modify a certain variable.

We specify properties of program elements to be selected in conditions that follow **Select**. Conditions are expressed in terms of:

a. Entity attribute values and constants (**with** clause)
b. Participation of entities in relationships (**such that** clause)
c. Syntactic patterns (**pattern** clause)

All the clauses are optional. Clauses **such that, with,** and **pattern** may occur many times in the same query. There is an implicit **and** operator between clauses — that means a query result must satisfy the conditions specified in all the clauses.

Declarations introduce synonyms that refer to design entities. Synonyms can be used in the remaining part of the query to mean a corresponding entity. So we can write:

stmt s;

Select s **such that** Modifies (s, "x") — Here we introduce a synonym for statement s and constrain the result with the condition. As you can guess, in this query, you **Select** all the statements that modify variable x.

A typical query has the following format:

Select ... such that ... with ... pattern ...

In the following sections, we shall introduce queries by examples, referring to program design models explained earlier.

2.6.1 Querying Global Program Design Information

These queries refer to the global program design model described in Section 2.5.1.

Q1. Which procedures call at least one procedure?
    procedure p, q;
    Select p **such that** Calls (p, q)
    Explanation: Declaration introduces two variables p and q that can be used in a query to mean "procedure". Keywords are in bold. This query means

exactly: "**Select** all the procedures p **such that there exists** a procedure q that satisfies Calls (p, q)".

Important: Note that the existential qualifier is always implicit in PQL queries. That means, you select any result for which there exists a combination of synonym instances satisfying the conditions specified in **such that**, **with**, and **pattern** clauses.

Example: In program First, the answer is: First, Second

A better way to write this query is:

procedure p;

Select p **such that** Calls (p, _)

Explanation: This query is the same as the preceding one. The underscore symbol is a placeholder for an unconstrained variable (procedure in this case). Symbol "_" can only be used when the context uniquely implies the type of the argument denoted by the underscore symbol. Here, we infer from the program design model that "_" stands for the design entity "procedure."

Q2. Which procedures are called by at least one other procedure?

procedure q;

Select q **such that** Calls (_, q)

Q3. Find all pairs of procedures p and q such that p calls q.

Select <p, q > **such that** Calls (p, q)

Example: In program First, the answer is: <First, Second>, <Second, Third>.

Q4. Find the procedure named Second.

procedure p;

Select p **with** p.procName = "Second"

Explanation: Dot "." notation means a reference to the attribute value of an entity (procedure name in this case).

Q5. Which procedures are called from Second?

procedure p, q;

Select q **such that** Calls (p, q) **with** p.procName="Second"

We can also write the preceding query in short form, referring to procedure p in Calls via its name:

Select q **such that** Calls ("Second", q)

Here, we infer from the program design model that the first argument of relationship Calls is the design entity "procedure." By convention, Second refers to a procedure name. We shall use the short form whenever it does not lead to misunderstanding.

Q6. Find procedures that call procedure Second and modify variable x.

procedure p;

Select p **such that** Calls (p, "Second") **and** Modifies (p, "x")

Explanation: The **and** operator can be used in relationship conditions with the **such that** clause and in equations under **with** clause. We infer from the program design model that the second argument of relationship Calls is design entity "procedure" and the second argument of relationship

Modifies is design entity "variable." By convention, Second refers to procedure name and x refers to the variable name.

2.6.2 Querying Control and Data Flow Information

Using the same rules, we can write queries about control and data flow relations.

Q7. Is there a control path from program line 20 to program line 620?
Select BOOLEAN **such that** Next* (20, 620)
Explanation: BOOLEAN after **Select** means that the result is TRUE (if there exist values for which the conditions are satisfied) or FALSE otherwise.

Q8. Find all the program lines that can be executed between program line 20 and program line 620.
program line n;
Select n **such that** Next* (20, n) **and** Next* (n, 620)
The following query selects only assignment statements (rather than all the program lines) that can be executed between program line 20 and program line 620:
assign a;
Select a **such that** Next* (20, a) **and** Next* (a, 620)

Q9. Is there a control path in the CFG from program line 20 to program line 620 that passes through program line 40?
Select BOOLEAN **such that** Next* (20, 40) **and** Next* (40, 620)

Q10. Which assignment statements are directly affected by variable x assigned value at program line 20?
assign a;
Select a **such that** Affects (20, a)
Explanation: We can refer to program statements via their respective program line numbers.

Q11.   Which assignments directly affect a value assigned to a variable in the assignment statement at program line 120?
assign a;
Select s **such that** Affects (a, 120)

2.6.3 Finding Syntactic Code Patterns

We can specify code patterns that we wish to find. Code patterns are based on abstract syntax model and, in *SIMPLE*, may involve the following design entities: stmtLst, stmt, assign, call, while, if, ref, constant, variable, expr, plus, minus, and times.

Q12.   Find all while statements.
while w;
Select w

Q13.   Find all while statements directly nested in some if statement.
while w;
if if;
Select w **such that** Parent (if, w)

Q14.   Find three while loops nested one in another.
while w1, w2, w3;
Select <w1, w2, w3> **such that** Parent* (w1, w2) **and** Parent* (w2, w3)
Explanation: Note that the query returns all the instances of three nested while loops in a program, not just the first one that is found.

Q15.   Find all assignments with variable x at the left-hand side located in some while loop, and that can be reached (in terms of control flow) from program line 60.
assign a; while w;
Select a **such that** Parent* (w, a) **and** Next* (60, a) **pattern** a("x", _)
Explanation: In a("x", _), we refer to a variable in the left-hand side of the assignment via its name and in Next*(60, a) we refer to the statement whose number is 60. Patterns are specified using relational notation so they look the same as conditions in a **such that** clause. Think about a node in the AST as a relationship among its children. So the assignment is written as assign (variable, expr), and the while loop is written as while(variable, _). Patterns are specified in **pattern** clause. Conditions that follow pattern specification can further constrain patterns to be matched.
Remark: The two queries below yield the same result for *SIMPLE* programs. Note also that this might not be the case in other languages. Why?
assign a;
Select a **pattern** a ("x", _)
Select a **such that** Modifies (a, "x")

Q16. Find all while statements with x as a control variable.
while w;
Select w **pattern** w ("x", _)
Explanation: We use a placeholder underscore "_", as statements in the while loop body (stmtLst) are not constrained in the query (they are irrelevant to the query).

Q17. Find assignment statements where variable x appears on the left-hand side.
assign a;
Select a **pattern** a ("x", _)

Q18.   Find assignments that contain expression x*y+z on the right-hand side.
assign a;
Select a **pattern** a (_, "x*y+z")

Q19.   Find assignments that contain the subexpression x*y+z on the right-hand side.
assign a;
Select a **pattern** a (_, _"x*y+z"_)

Explanation: Underscores on both sides of x*y+z indicate that it may be part of a larger expression. An underscore in front of "x*y+z" would mean that it must appear at the end of the expression and one after "x*y+z"_ would mean that it must appear at the beginning of the expression. Note that "x*y+z"_ means that the subexpression may or may not be followed by other symbols (that is, "_" may mean an empty subexpression). Matching of subexpressions takes into account priorities of operators (operator * has higher priority than + and -; operators + and – have equal priority). Therefore, _"x*y+z"_ is a subexpression of expression "x*y+z-v" but it is not a subexpression of "x*y+z*v". Matching of subexpressions is done on the AST that reflects priorities of operators rather than on the program text.

Q20. Find all assignments to variable x such that its value is subsequently reassigned recursively in an assignment statement that is nested inside two loops.

assign a1, a2; while w1, w2;

Select a2 **pattern** a1 ("x", _) **and** a2 ("x",_"x"_) **such that** Affects (a1, a2) **and** Parent* (w2, a2) **and** Parent* (w1, w2)

2.6.4 A Summary of PQL Rules

The following is a general format of a program query:

select-cl : declaration* **Select** result (with-cl | suchthat-cl | pattern-cl)*

Asterisks denote repetition zero or more times. Declarations introduce variables representing program design entities. Synonyms can be used in the remaining part of the query to mean a corresponding entity. The *result* clause specifies a program view to be produced (i.e., tuples or a BOOLEAN value). In the *with*-cl clause, we constrain attribute values (e.g., procedure.procName="Parse"). The *suchthat*-cl clause specifies conditions in terms of relationship participation. The *pattern*-cl describes code patterns to be searched for. The PQL grammar is described in Appendix A.

2.6.5 Comments on Query Semantics

Examples in this section are meant to further clarify interpretation of program queries in PQL.

The existential qualifier is always implicit in PQL queries, which means you select any result for which there exists a combination of synonym instances satisfying the conditions specified in **such that**, **with**, and **pattern** clauses.

procedure p, q;

Select p **such that** Calls (p, q)

Answer: This query means exactly: **Select** all the procedures p **such that there exists** a procedure q that satisfies Calls (p,q). In program First of Figure 2.2, the result is procedures First and Second.

procedure p, q; assign a;
Select <p, a> **such that** Calls (p, q) **with** p.procName="Second" **pattern** a("x", _)

To qualify for the result, a procedure and assignment statement must satisfy all the conditions specified in the query. Note that a query may have any number of **such that**, **with**, and **pattern** clauses that can be mixed in any order. There is an implicit **and** operator among all those clauses.

2.6.6 Use of Free Variables

A free variable is not constrained by any condition in the query. Underscore denotes a free variable. You can always replace underscore with a synonym. The following two queries are equivalent:

procedure p, q;
Select p **such that** Calls (p, _)
Select p **such that** Calls (p, q)

Use of an underscore must not lead to ambiguities. For example, the following query should be rejected as incorrect as it is not clear if underscore refers to the statement or to the procedure:

Select BOOLEAN **such that** Modifies (_, "x")

2.7 Design of PQL and SPA

In this section, we give the reader a glimpse of SPA design and internal workings. The two desirable qualities and objectives of SPA design are efficiency of query processing and independence of SPA components on the source language being analyzed. The first quality is important for usability reasons: As an SPA is an interactive tool, it must process queries and show query results to a programmer in a reasonable amount of time. The second design quality ensures that, rather than implementing an SPA for each source language from scratch, we can customize SPA components to work with different source languages.

An SPA consists of four subsystems that we have shown in Figure 2.1, namely, SPA front end, program knowledge base (PKB), query processor, and user interface subsystems. Figure 2.10 is a refined view of the SPA design initially sketched in Figure 2.1: We decomposed an SPA front end into a parser and design extractor,

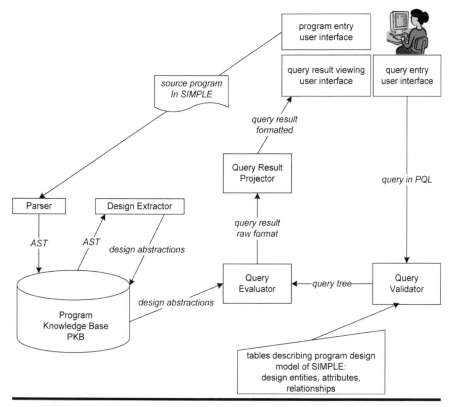

Figure 2.10 Static program analyzer (SPA) design — a refined view.

and a PQL processor into a query validator and query evaluator. Arrows indicate information flows among components.

An SPA front end builds a PKB. A parser checks the syntactic correctness of a source program and builds an AST (abstract syntax tree) representation and a symbol table. Then, the design extractor traverses an AST and derives other program design abstractions such as CFG, relationships Calls, Modifies, Uses, and other information according to program design models. Once an AST is created, there is no need to analyze program text anymore. Other program design abstractions can be more conveniently derived from the AST rather than by repeatedly parsing the program text.

The PKB is the heart of an SPA architecture. It provides a storage (data structures) for program design abstractions. Design abstractions such as AST, CFG, Modifies, and Uses are stored in the data structures of the PKB. Design abstractions such as Follows*, Parent*, Next*, Affects, and Affects* are computed on demand by calling suitable PKB interface operations.

A PKB API (abstract program interface) is the key to managing the complexity of SPA design. All the major SPA components communicate one each other via PKB API. The PKB only exposes the API to its clients, which are other SPA components, such as the design extractor or query evaluator. The actual storage media — data structures that store program design abstractions — remain hidden from the clients, as are many PKB internal mechanisms that provide fast access to the stored information and help in efficient manipulation of program information during query evaluation (such as hash tables and mappings across program design abstractions used for efficient implementation).

SPA components communicate with the PKB by calling API operations to build and then access program information. For example:

ASTNode createASTNode (NodeType) — to create a new AST node during parsing
ASTNode getParent (ASTNode) — to access a parent node
assertCalls (Proc p, q) — records the fact that procedure p calls q
ProcSet getCalled (Proc p) — returns all the procedures called from procedure p

The PKB API is a key concept in design of a flexible SPA and plays a central role in the SPA architecture:

1. PKB API allows SPA developers to experiment with various strategies for storing program information without affecting other SPA components.
2. PKB API is based on program design models. As other SPA components (except the parser) rely only on PKB API rather than a source program itself, they become independent of a source language.
3. Once PKB API has been stabilized, other SPA components can be developed in a fairly independent way one from one other.

The query processing subsystem consists of a query validator and query evaluator. The *query validator* checks a program query for correctness and builds a query tree (Figure 2.11), a data structure that is convenient for query optimization and evaluation. Query validation includes checking if references to design entities, attributes, and relationships are used according with their definition in the program design model.

The *query evaluator* traverses the query tree and consults the PKB to produce a query result. A simple strategy is to evaluate queries incrementally as follows: Query fragments contained in the **such that**, **with**, and **pattern** clauses are evaluated one by one. Evaluation of each query fragment produces an intermediate result that approximates the final query result. The incremental evaluation is relatively straightforward to implement, but without optimizations the query evaluation will be slow and will take up much memory. We discuss query optimizations in a separate subsection in the following text.

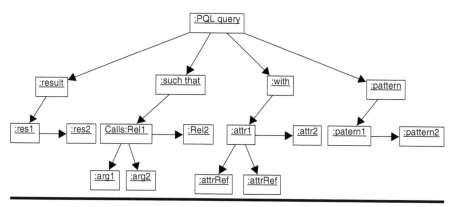

Figure 2.11   A query tree

The query result projector is the final SPA component. It formats the query results in a format suitable for display. It is useful to separate the query result projector from the query evaluator, as we may want to show query results in many different ways, such as a simple table of program elements that satisfy the query (e.g., which procedure calls which other procedures), or in a graphical form. A separate query result projector component can work with the query result produced by the query evaluator in some standard form that is easy to read and manipulate, displaying views of the result in multiple formats.

2.8   Optimizing the Performance of Query Evaluation

The design of a general and efficient query evaluation mechanism that can answer any PQL query is a nontrivial task. Performance is a major problem in implementing descriptive notation for program queries such as PQL. Query evaluation must be optimized with respect to time and memory usage. Of course, query evaluation time depends on the size of the source program. However, design decisions considering the PKB and query evaluator also have a great impact on the efficiency of query evaluation.

The choice of data representation in the PKB affects performance of query evaluation. To answer some queries, we may need to do multiple traversals of the AST and CFG, sometimes switching among PKB data structures that store different program representations. The proper choice of data structures and mappings among data structures can significantly improve the efficiency of query evaluation. When computing relationship Affects among program statements, we traverse a CFG and repeatedly access and manipulate information about variables Modified/Used. The way we store Modify/Use relationships has a significant impact on the evaluation time of queries.

Designing a program representation in the PKB that can be easily manipulated during query evaluation is a prerequisite for efficient query evaluation. Still, there is much room for further optimization in the query evaluator. A query evaluator may produce large sets of tuples at intermediate steps of the query evaluation process. If we subsequently perform join operations on large sets of tuples, then query evaluation will use a large amount of computer memory and time. There are some possible remedies to these problems.

First, we observe that the query results do not depend on the order in which we evaluate search conditions specified in query clauses. However, the actual evaluation time and memory requirements may drastically change as we vary the order of conditions. Therefore, by rearranging the order of search conditions in a query, we may reduce the time and memory needed for query evaluation. For example, it will take much longer to evaluate query:

assign a1; a2; while w;
Select a1 **such that** Follows (a1, a2) **and** Follows (a2, w)
than an equivalent query:
Select a1 **such that** Follows (a2, w) **and** Follows (a1, a2)

Generally, we should try to rearrange conditions so that we compute the most restrictive conditions first. By following this rule, intermediate sets of tuples are smaller and the query evaluation time is minimized.

Further improvements can be achieved by precomputing sizes of design entity sets (e.g., the number of procedures, variables, assignments, etc., in a source program) and sizes of relationships (e.g., the number of pairs related by relationship Calls). This information can help us fine-tune performance of query evaluation by evaluating conditions that are likely to produce a smaller number of intermediate results first. For example, in the following query, if a program contains more assignments than while loops (most programs do), we should evaluate condition Follows (a2, w) first:

assign a1; a2; while w;
Select a1 **such that** Follows (a1, a2) **and** Follows (a2, w)

Furthermore, when evaluating Follows (a2, w), the query evaluator should find while loops first and then compute assignments that satisfy condition Follow (a2, w) rather than the other way round.

These are some of the optimization strategies for efficient evaluation of PQL queries.

2.9   PQL for COBOL

Due to model-based, table-driven design of SPA, SPA for *SIMPLE* described in the earlier sections can be adapted to real-world languages. We described PQL for COBOL in [8]. For the reader's reference, we have summarized program design models for COBOL in Appendix B. All the PQL concepts and SPA design solutions that work for *SIMPLE* also work for COBOL.

2.10   Conclusions

Static analysis can help programmers understand a program under maintenance. An SPA can automatically compute some of the program properties and software relations that programmers typically need to know to implement changes. On the downside, only a small subset of the overall information pertinent to maintenance can be obtained in the course of static analysis. The use of pointers and dynamic binding impose severe practical limits on the depth and breadth of program information that static analysis can effectively compute.

Static program analysis techniques can help in implementing change requests during day-to-day maintenance. Current static analysis methods deal with a single program rather than with families of programs arising during evolution. Helping developers to see what is common and what is different among software releases seems to be outside the scope of current static analysis methods. In conclusion, static program analysis can only be indirectly helpful in addressing long-term software evolution challenges discussed in Chapter 1.

It is important to note a difference between static and dynamic program analysis methods. Static analysis means analysis of a program text, without executing a program, such as is typically done by a complier front end. In dynamic analysis, on the other hand, we execute a program, keep record of program states during execution, and allow programmers to examine the information collected at program runtime. Debuggers exemplify tools based on dynamic analysis concepts. Static and dynamic program analysis methods have different strengths and weaknesses. The strength of static analysis is that it gives an understanding of program properties in general, properties that hold for all possible program executions. The weakness of static analysis methods is that much of the interesting program information that matters in program understanding is only evident at runtime and cannot be computed in the course of static program analysis. The strengths and weaknesses of dynamic program analysis methods are exactly opposite. Program execution reveals much more useful information about interesting software relations, but this information is specific to a given program execution and may not apply to other program executions. Therefore, static and dynamic program analysis methods complement each other [6].

Concepts of PQL have been applied in the project management domain. Here, PQL queries have bridged the gap between high-level questions project managers typically ask about the progress of a project and its possible problem areas, and low-level metrics collected during project development [1,2]. These high-level project views were expressed as PQL queries, which were then answered by interpreting the project metrics.

An SPA for the model language *SIMPLE* has been used in a software engineering project course developed by the author that has been offered at National University of Singapore since 2000. The goal of the course is to let students apply software design principles and "best practices" in team projects. We refer the reader to the publication describing the philosophy and organization of the course, and lessons learned from teaching it over five years [13].

References

1. Chee, C.L., Jarzabek, S., and Paul, R., F-metric: a WWW-based framework for intelligent formulation and analysis of metric queries, *Journal of Systems and Software*, No. 43, 119–132, 1998.
2. Chee, C.L., Jarzabek, S., and Ramamoorthy, C.V., An intelligent process for formulating and answering project queries, *Proceedings of the 6th International Conference on Software Engineering and Knowledge Engineering, SEKE'96*, Nevada, June 1996, pp. 309–316.
3. Chen, Y., Nishimito, M., and Ramamoorthy, C., C Information abstraction system, *IEEE Transactions on Software Engineering*, 16(3), 325–333, March 1990.
4. Date, C. and Darwen, H.A., *Guide to the SQL Standard*, Addison-Wesley, Boston, 1993.
5. Devanhu, P., GENOA — a customizable, language — and front-end independent code analyzer, *Proceedings of the 14th International Conference on Software Engineering*, 1992, pp. 307–319.
6. Eisenbarth, T., Koschke, R., and Simon, D., Aiding program comprehension by static and dynamic feature analysis, *International Conference on Software Maintenance, ICSM'01*, Florence, Italy, November 2001, pp. 602–611.
7. Eisenbarth, T., Koschke, R., and Simon, D., Locating features in source code, *IEEE Transactions on Software Engineering*, 29(3), 210–224, March 2003.
8. Jarzabek, S., Design of flexible static program analyzers with PQL, *IEEE Transactions on Software Engineering*, 197–215, March 1998.
9. Jarzabek, S., PQL: a language for specifying abstract program views, *Proceedings of the 5th European Software Engineering Conference, ESEC'95*, Barcelona, September 1995, Lecture Notes in Computer Science, No. 989, Springer Verlag, pp. 324–342.
10. Jarzabek, S., Systematic design of static program analyzers, *Proceedings of the 18th Annual International Computer Software and Applications Conference COMPSAC'94*, Taipei, November 9–11, 1994, IEEE Computer Society Press, Los Alamitos, CA, pp. 281–286.

11. Jarzabek, S., Shen, H. and Chan, H.C., A hybrid program knowledge base system for static program analyzers, *Proceedings of the First Asia Pacific Software Engineering Conference, APSEC'94*, Tokyo, December 1994, IEEE Computer Society Press, Los Alamitos, CA, pp. 400–409.

12. Jarzabek, S., Specifying and generating multilanguage software development environments, *Software Engineering Journal*, 5(2), 125–137, March 1990.

13. Jarzabek, S. and Eng, P.K., Teaching an advanced design, team-oriented software project course, *18th International Conference on Software Engineering Education and Training (CSEE&T)*, IEEE CS, April 2005, Ottawa, pp. 223–230.

14. Kirkegaard, C., Moller, A., and Schwartzbach, M.I., Static analysis of XML transformations in java, *IEEE Transactions on Software Engineering*, 30(3), 181–192, March 2004.

15. Kozaczynski, W., Ning, J., and Engberts, A., Program concept recognition and transformation, *IEEE Transactions on Software Engineering*, 18(12), 1065–1075, December 1992.

16. Maletic, J. and Marcus, A., Supporting program comprehension using semantic and structural information, *23rd International Conference on Software Engineering ICSE'01*, Toronto, Canada, May 2001, pp. 103–112.

17. Murphy, C. and Notkin, D., Lightweight lexical source model extraction, *ACM Transactions on Software Engineering and Methodology*, 5(3), 262–292, July 1996.

18. Ottenstein, K. and Ottenstein, L., The program dependence graph in a software development environment, *Proceedings of the Software Engineering Symposium on Practical Software Development Environments*, ACM Press, pp. 177–184.

19. Paul, S. and Prakash, A., A query algebra for program data bases, *IEEE Transactions on Software Engineering*, 22(3), 202–217, March 1996.

20. Reps, T., Demand interprocedural program analysis using logic databases, in *Applications of Logic Databases*, Ramakrishnan, R., Ed., Kluwer Academic Publishers, Boston, MA, pp. 163–196.

21. Robillard, M.P. and Murphy, G.C., Static analysis to support the evolution of exception structure in object-oriented systems, *ACM Transactions on Software Engineering and Methodology*, 12(2), 191–221, April 2003.

22. Rumbaugh, J., Jacobson, I., and Booch, G., *The Unified Modeling Languages Reference Manual*, Addison-Wesley, 1999.

23. van Zuylen, H.J., Ed., *The REDO Compendium: Reverse Engineering. for Software Maintenance*, John Wiley and Sons, New York, 1992.

24. Wong, K., Tilley, S., Muller, H., and Storye, M., Structural Redocumentation: A Case Study, *IEEE Software*, January 1995, pp. 46–54.

Chapter 3

Reverse Engineering Methods

Chapter Summary

The objective of reverse engineering is to extract design information from code automatically or in the interaction with a programmer. During program maintenance, programmers often extract abstract program views such as cross-reference lists, control flow relations, or procedure call trees to better understand a maintenance task at hand. Techniques for object and component recovery have received much attention because of the market need. Reverse engineering techniques can be helpful in any project that involves poorly documented legacy software, such as maintenance, reengineering of legacy software into new architectures, or reengineering for reuse.

In this chapter, the reader learns about the capabilities of reverse engineering techniques, and about the incremental, interactive reverse engineering process, with examples from object recovery.

3.1 Review of Approaches to Reverse Engineering

The objective of reverse engineering is to extract design information, functional specifications and, eventually, requirements from the program code, documents, and any other available sources [4,11,16,25,53]. Reverse engineering techniques can help in maintenance of poorly documented programs and in software reengineering projects.

When analyzing a program for understanding, programmers create multiple mental models of a program. They identify concepts in each model and try to establish relationships among those concepts within and across models [7,25]. If mental program models that programmers need are not readily available in documentation, programmers repeatedly recover them (usually in an incomplete and approximate form) from code and from other sources. Automated reverse engineering can ease a tedious and error-prone manual process of recovering models from code. As a research discipline, reverse engineering is not new, but the debate about its objectives, potentials, and levels of possible automation still continues [8,17].

Reverse engineering of data was of great practical importance when companies were migrating their data from old databases (or data stored in flat files) to relational databases (sometimes object-oriented databases). Typically, the first step in such migration was recovering of the entity-relationship data model [15] from the existing program code [3,18,19,23,61].

Recovering objects (or classes) and object-oriented models from programs received much attention when companies migrated from the procedural to the object-oriented software paradigm [11,12,14,26,27,31,32,37,42,53,56,57]. Practical situations in which these techniques can be useful include reengineering programs into object-oriented architectures and reengineering code for reuse [11]. Most often, reengineering cannot be conducted in one big-bang project because of the variety of business constraints. Incremental approaches to gradually reengineer legacy software into an object-oriented architecture have been proposed [30].

Methods for object recovery have been complemented with detecting relationships among objects. In [21], authors analyze persistent data stores as well as procedural code, applying specialized heuristics to recover associations among objects.

Methods for recovering software decompositions [44,51] are generally useful. Independent of a programming paradigm, knowing how software is partitioned into fairly independent components or subsystems is critical to understanding fundamental software structure.

When component-based technologies started dominating the software development arena, methods for object recovery were extended to methods for component recovery [43] and architecture recovery [29,46,50]. The RIGI system [60] concentrated on recovering the architectural structure of large legacy software and provided a user with a flexible interface to customize multiple views of software architecture produced by the system.

Research on reverse engineering using AI techniques, mainly pattern matching, concentrated on identifying higher-level design abstractions and domain concepts in programs. In DESIRE [4], the domain model was built first and then code patterns were used to find instances of domain concepts in code. In Recogniser [47], so-called plans represented commonly used program structures. *"Programming plans* are units of programming knowledge connecting abstract concepts and their implementations" [28]. In the process of program recognition, a program was searched for instances of plans. Although these early approaches to applying pattern matching for design recovery purposes did not scale up, the idea of looking for patterns in code as a means of identifying architectural concepts was further explored in new, more practical ways [45,46,50].

External documentation often becomes inconsistent with an evolving program. Reverse engineering can help recover traceability links between code and documentation [1,2] or Unified Modeling Language (UML) models [6]. RIGI [60] recovers a rich set of program views that constitute valuable program documentation. The possibility of reverse engineering formal specifications from programs has also been explored [8,40,58]. In the RECAST method [23], COBOL applications were reverse-engineered into logical descriptions in the format of Structured System Analysis and Design Method (SSADM).

Despite the relatively short history of the World Wide Web, recently, a number of researchers reported on methods for reverse engineering web applications [5,20,54].

New software technologies often promise improved maintainability and better grasp of software design. Ironically, not long after new technologies become popular, we invariably see a growing need for reverse engineering, or even reengineering, software written using those technologies.

Success stories with reverse engineering have been reported [10,53]; many tools have been implemented both in industry [9,48,39] and academia [4,11,13,23,34, 40,47,58,60], but more experimentation is needed to fully explore the potential and limits of automated reverse engineering. Cordy [17] makes interesting observations about the limited practical value of program abstractions that become disconnected from the code being maintained. Cordy's paper sheds light on technology transfer problems, and on the reasons why programmers are not willing to adopt tools in their maintenance work. In [13], we read about yet other problems that hinder wide adoption of reverse engineering tools. Authors claim that that reverse engineering tools fail to identify the right level of details in recovered design and lack proper design presentation strategies, recover only a small portion of the design information software maintainers need, are not flexible enough, and cannot be easily tailored and enriched in the operating environment. The authors further point out that reverse engineering tools recover design views that are commonly used during forward engineering, such as structure charts. However, the design information that is essential during software maintenance (and, therefore, should be produced by reverse engineering tools) is different from that used during forward engineering.

3.2 Incremental and Interactive Reverse Engineering Process

Suppose we are reengineering C programs into C++ and wish to identify candidate classes in C code. We would typically start by building an object model for a program. Analysis and reverse engineering of existing data structures, file definitions, and program code can help in building such a model. The process that leads to identifying classes is semiautomatic and involves applying heuristics (such as data coupling between C functions) and manual analysis of programs by a human expert. A human expert is aware of application domain concepts that are candidates for classes, and the software engineering expert can judge which design and implementation concepts are candidates for sound and useful classes. Automatically identified classes must be presented to human experts for acceptance and refinement.

Effective reverse engineering must be goal oriented. There is plenty of design information and abstract program views that we can possibly extract from code, but we want to extract only the information that is helpful for the maintenance or reengineering task at hand. Therefore, we need to identify proper heuristic rules to map program code to low-level program designs, and from there move further to recovering higher-level design views.

Reverse engineering is a knowledge-intensive process. Some of the well-understood and clear-cut heuristics can be encoded into a reverse engineering tool. However, many reverse engineering tasks cannot be done automatically, as the relevant information (design decisions and application domain knowledge, for example) are not explicit in code. Heuristics that cannot be automatically recovered must be solicited from a human expert. We believe that involvement of a human expert is critical in any but trivial reverse engineering tasks.

Such a semiautomated, human-guided reverse engineering process assumes that intermediate abstract program views, extracted possibly by a reverse engineering assistant (REA) tool, are examined by a human expert, filtered, and further analyzed. The approach to reverse engineering described in this chapter assumes close cooperation between a human expert and an REA.

We summarize these observations in an incremental and semiautomatic reverse engineering process model shown in Figure 3.1.

The horizontal dimension shows the progress of a reverse engineering task. The vertical dimension reflects the level of abstraction of recovered program views.

Reverse engineering progresses in stages, shown in rectangular boxes in Figure 3.1. At each process stage, REA applies heuristic rules to extract design abstractions, and a human expert accepts or rejects decisions made by the tool. In our discussion of SPAs in Chapter 2, we introduced a PKB (program knowledge base) as a repository of program information to answer program queries. To make this concept work in the context of interactive reverse engineering, we extend the concept of PKB so that program design views recovered at each stage are stored in intermediate repositories. We call such repositories DKB (design knowledge base). DKBs store program design views recovered so far and make that information available for the follow-up analysis, with the objective of recovering yet higher-level program views.

"Refronte" parses source programs and builds a PKB. Refronte is analogical to the SPA front-end described in Chapter 2. The PKB contains program design views

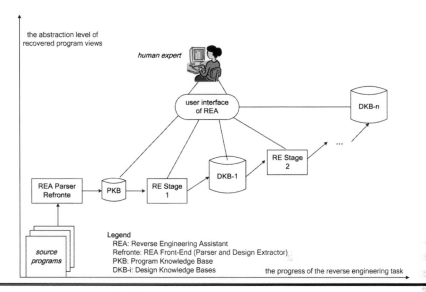

Figure 3.1   An incremental reverse engineering process with the involvement of a human expert.

that can be automatically computed from code using conventional compilation techniques, such as ASTs annotated with static semantic information (attributes), control flow graphs (CFG), and data flow relations. The actual types of design abstractions that we compute depend on the specific objectives of a reverse engineering project.

DKB-1, DKB2, ... , DKB-n in Figure 3.1 are DKBs that store design views recovered at various reverse engineering stages, with the possible involvement of a human expert.

A human expert (data analyst, programmer, or application domain expert) inspects intermediate design views and provides inputs that can influence the reverse engineering process.

3.3   Recovering Object Models from Code

We illustrate reverse engineering with examples from object recovery. One application of object recovery methods is in reengineering of legacy programs written in a procedural language into object-oriented programs. Another application is in reengineering for reuse [11].

An object model comprises data structures and operations that act on those data structures. In well-designed procedural programs, some of the object's operations might be already implemented as separate procedural modules. In poorly designed programs, code implementing operations may be intermixed with implementation of other program functionalities. Sometimes, such intermixing of code may occur even in well-designed programs, as the result of crosscutting concerns [38]. If object's operations are not cleanly isolated from the rest of a program code, finding an operation pertaining to objects may be a nontrivial task. Program slicing [59] is one of the techniques that can help programmers identify code that manipulates object's data, even if such code has not been locally defined.

A number of methods have been proposed to identify objects in code [11,12,13,27,42,53]. In [53], we start by identifying global data structures that are likely to represent the state of some object. Procedures that refer to global data are considered candidates for an object's operations. To filter out "false-positive" operations, relationships between candidate operations are analyzed. In yet another method described in the same source, dependencies between data types in a program are analyzed, and then procedures whose arguments refer to common data types are grouped together. Such procedures, along with data types, form candidate objects.

In [11], the authors propose to classify objectlike abstractions into four groups: abstract objects (data structures + operations), abstract data types (data types + operations + instantiation), generic data structures (abstract objects parameterized by types for generality), and generic abstract data types. Then, the authors identify heuristic rules that are used as candidature criteria to test which code might pertain to which objects. A logic-based notation can be used for specifying such candidature criteria, and other program information relevant to finding object candidates [13]. We could also approach the problem of finding candidate objects from yet another angle, namely by reverse engineering structure charts and data flow diagrams [27]. We then attempt to build objects around data store entities, and around other nonpersistent, but important application domain concepts. In [53], we find useful hints as to what kind of objects we should be looking for so that the eventual result is useful in reengineering of business applications. These useful object types include user interface objects, data objects, file objects, view objects, and many others. There may be no set of universal heuristics for identifying objects. Given the application domain, project objectives, and even a design technique and a programming language used, we may need to identify suitable heuristics to find useful objects.

Research on locating features in code [24] is also related to recovery of operations on objects. A feature realizes some functional requirement. Most often, feature implementation spreads across system components, and finding all code that contributes to implementation of a certain feature may be a difficult task requiring intimate knowledge of system design and a tedious examination of system component implementation details. In [24] a combination of static and dynamic program analysis is applied to recover such delocalized features.

3.4 Object Recovery Heuristics

We illustrate general capabilities of reverse engineering methods and principles of systematic design of reverse engineering tools with an example of object recovery. Our object recovery heuristics are based on object identification rules proposed by others [11,12,27,42]:

H-1 A globally declared data structure, say DS-X, directly referred to (used or modified) by two or more procedural modules (e.g., functions in C language) is considered a possible element of data representation for some program object X.

H-2 Any procedural module that uses or modifies DS-X should be considered a candidate method for object X.

H-3 Any two candidate data structures, say, DS-X and DS-Y, identified by applying rule H-1, considered as possible representations for objects X and Y, respectively, and such that there is a procedural module that refers to both DS-X and DS-Y, are likely to together form a data representation of the same object. Candidate methods for this object are procedural modules that refer to any of the data that forms the object's data representation.

H-4 Any user-defined data type, say, DT-X, that appears as an argument in signatures of two or more procedural modules such that the signatures of those procedural modules do not include any parent class of DT-X should be considered as a possible element of data representation for some class X.

H-5 Any procedural module whose signature includes argument of type DT-X should be considered a candidate method for class X.

H-6 Any two candidate data representations, say, DT-X and DT-Y, identified by applying rule H4, and such that there is a procedural module whose signature includes arguments of both types DT-X and DT-Y, are likely to form together a data representation for the same class. Candidate methods for this class are procedural modules whose signatures include an argument of any of the data types that forms the data representation of the class.

Note that we consider both abstract objects (global data structures + operations) and ADTs (user-defined data types + operations + instantiation) as candidates for classes.

3.5 Semiautomatic Recovery of Abstract Objects as Candidates for Classes

To see how the heuristics just described are used, we outline a plan for semiautomatic recovery of candidate classes. First, we focus on abstract objects:

O-1. Apply rule H-1 to find candidate data representations for objects.

O-2. A domain expert examines candidates, selects one of the data representations, say DS-X, and decides whether or not it forms a basis for a sound object. To help in making the decision, the domain expert views procedural modules that refer to DS-X (rule H-2).

O-3. If the domain expert decides that DS-X is not a suitable data representation for some object, he or she repeats step O-2 trying other data; otherwise, the domain expert proceeds to step O-4.

O-4. Repeatedly rule H-3 to find other data that, together with DS-X, are likely to form a data representation for object X. To help in making the decision, the domain expert views procedural modules that refer to candidate data representations (rule H-3).

O-5. At this point, the domain expert has already identified a set of data structures that, together with DS-X, form a data representation for object X.

O-6. Find candidate methods for object X (rules H-2 and H-3). Again, the domain expert views and verifies the candidate methods. This ends recovery of object X.

O-7. Repeat steps 2–6 until all the candidate data representations have been considered.

O-8. Map recovered objects to classes.

3.6 A Plan for Semiautomatic Recovery of Abstract Data Types as Candidates for Classes

A-1. Apply rule H-4 to find user-defined types that may be candidates for ADTs.

A-2. A domain expert examines candidates, selects one of the candidate types, say DT-X, and decides whether or not it forms a sound ADT. To help in making the decision, the domain expert views procedural modules whose signatures include DT-X (rule H-4).

A-3. If the domain expert decides that DT-X is not a suitable data representation for some ADT, he or she repeats step A-2 for another data type; otherwise, the domain expert proceeds to step A-4.

A-4. Apply rule H-6 repeatedly to find other data types that, together with DT-X, are likely to form an ADT-X. To help in making the decision, the domain expert views procedural modules whose signatures include arguments of data types under consideration (rule H-6).

A-5. At this point, the domain expert already has identified a set of data types that, together with DT-X, form a sound ADT-X.

A-6. Find candidate methods for ADT-X (rules H-5 and H-6). The domain expert views and verifies the candidate methods. This ends recovery of ADT-X.

A-7. Repeat steps 2–6 until all the candidate-type representations have been considered.

A-8. Map recovered ADTs to classes.

3.7 Specifying Reverse Engineering Heuristics in PQL

We now show how the concepts of PQL, described in Chapter 2, can be extended to formalize reverse engineering heuristics. The value of doing so is that we can use the same formalism and, to some extent, the same tool for both static program analysis and reverse engineering. The idea is to let program queries express reverse engineering heuristics. These and other PQLs are described in [36].

Before reading further, the reader should briefly review PQL concepts described in Chapter 2.

As discussed in Section 3.2, reverse engineering is an incremental, semiautomatic process that greatly relies on the involvement of human experts. Object recovery heuristics described in previous sections also suggest a highly interactive reverse engineering process. In particular, abstract program views already recovered at certain reverse engineering stages (shown as DKB-i in Figure 3.1) should be amenable to analysis in subsequent stages.

We explain the required extensions of PQL using a partial design model for C language shown in Figure 3.2. We follow UML modeling conventions used in Chapter 2 for PQL: Rectangular boxes represent C program design entities such as source files (Cfile), functions (Cfunction), types (Ctype), or globally declared data (globData). Attributes are shown below a design entity name. Association links show relationships among design entities.

Our first extension is to allow a query result to be named and stored, so that we can progress from low-level code views to higher-level program views. Naming query results allows us to build higher-level program views out of previously constructed, simpler ones.

A query result is called a **view**. Views are named and typed. For example:

view FunRefersToAccount
globData Account;
Cfunction f;
Select f **such that** RefersTo (f, X) **with** X.dataName="Account"

The result of this query includes functions that refer to global data Account. The query result is named FunRefersToAccount and its type is Cfunction.

Having evaluated this query, we can use its result in subsequent queries, as long as there is no type conflict.

We further extend PQL with operation IS-IN, which allows us to check membership of an element in a given set. For example:

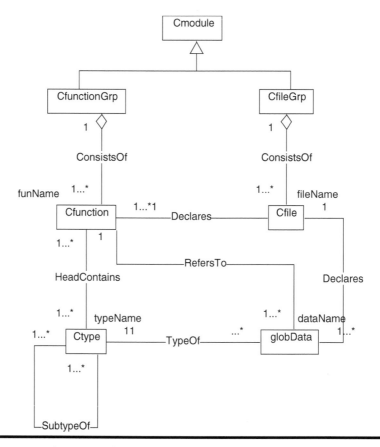

Figure 3.2 A fragment of a design model for C.

view HeadContainsInt

Ctype arg;

Cfunction f;

Select f **such that** IS-IN(f, FunRefersToAccount) **and** HeadContains (f, arg)
  with arg.typeName="int"

This query further restricts the result of the previous query to only those functions whose header (signature) contains an argument of type integer. A new query result is named HeadContainsInt.

Similarly, operation NOT-IN allows us to check nonmembership of an element in a given set.

Another useful extension allows one to constrain cardinality of arguments in query conditions. For example:

view MoreThanTwoArgs
Ctype arg;
Cfunction f;
Select f **such that** HeadContains (f, arg > 2)

This view contains functions that contain more than two arguments. We can also use logical **or** in formulating queries:

view AnyAccount
globData ac;
Select ac **with** ac.dataName="CurrentAccount"
  or ac.dataName= "SavingAccount"

This query returns global data named CurrentAccount or SavingAccount.

3.8 Specifying Object Recovery Heuristics for C Programs

We now focus discussion on reverse-engineering C programs to find candidate objects for a C++ program. We start by modeling those aspects of C and C++ program designs that are relevant to object recovery. As notions of a class, method, and data representation for objects are not present in C programs, we need to model objects independently of C programs.

With reference to the C program design models of Figure 3.2, we now formulate object recovery heuristics in PQL.

The following PQL declarations introduce synonyms used in the following PQL queries:

globData data, d, DS-X
Cfunction fun

The definition of first-cut candidate objects (heuristics H-1):

view objects
Select < data, fun > **such that** RefersTo (_, data > 1) **and** RefersTo (fun, data)
Explanation: Underscore means an unbounded variable. This view contains all pairs of globData "data" and Cfunction "fun" such that "data" is referred to by more than one function, one of which is "fun."

The definition of first-cut candidate methods (heuristics H-2):

view methods
Select < fun > **such that IS-IN** (<_, fun >, objects)
Explanation: Type of the **view** objects is a pair < globData, Cfunction >. This
view returns all the functions that appear as the second argument in some
pair of the **view** objects.

The definition of first-cut candidate data representations for objects (heuristics H-3):

view data-rep
Select < data > **such that IS-IN** (<data, _>, objects)
Explanation: This view is presented to the human expert in steps O-1 and O-2.

For a selected DS-X from the set data-rep, we now produce first-cut methods for
a candidate object X with data representation DS-X (rule H2):

view method-X-1
Select < fun > **from** methods **such that** RefersTo (fun, DS-X)
Explanation: This view is presented to the human expert in steps O-2 and O-3.

view data-rep-X
Select < data > **such that** data = DS-X
Explanation: DS-X is judged to be a data representation for a sound object.

For a selected globData d from **view** data-rep-X, we find other data that,
together with DS-X, form a data representation for the same object:

view data-rep-X-more
Select < data > **from** data-rep **such that NOT-IN** (data, data-rep-X) **and**
IS-IN (fun, methods) **and** RefersTo (fun, d) **and** RefersTo (fun, data)
Explanation: Each data from **view** data-rep-X-more is presented to the expert,
who can decide whether the data should be included into the set data-rep-X
or not. This view is computed repeatedly as long as new data is contributed to
the set data-rep-X (step O-4 and rule H3).

The alternative solution to computing the data representation for object X might
be to compute all the candidate data representations of object X and then ask the
expert to review the candidates and decide which ones should collectively form a

data representation for object X. Computing of candidate data representations is formalized in the following recursive view:

recursive view data-rep-X
Select < data > **such that IS-IN** (data, data-rep) **and IS-IN** (fun, methods) **and IS-IN** (d, data-rep-X) **and** RefersTo (fun, d) **and** RefersTo (fun, data)
Explanation: Here, we find other data that, together with DS-X, possibly form a data representation for object X, based on rule H-3. A recursive view is executed repeatedly as long as new data is inserted to the set data-rep-X.

The definition of methods for object X (heuristics H-3):

view methods-X
Select < fun > **such that IS-IN** (fun, methods) **and** IS-IN (data, data-rep-X) **and** RefersTo (fun, data)
Explanation: The expert reviews and verifies candidate methods (step O-6).

This completes recovery of design views relevant to object X as a candidate class for a C++ program. We do not formalize heuristics for recovery of ADTs as they are similar to those described earlier.

3.9 Generation of Recovered Design Views in Extended PQL

In the preceding discussion, we have recovered design views that correspond to elements in the object model, but we did not create object models in an explicit way.

We now extend PQL [33] to allow for generating design fragments of the target design of the C++ object model shown on the right-hand side of Figure 3.3. Generation rules have the following format:

source-pattern   =>   (**CreateEnt** entitySpec |
                          CreateRel relSpec |
                          AssignAttr attrValueSpec |
                          CreateLink linkedEntitiesSpec)*

The "source-pattern" is a pattern definition in PQL. The right-hand side of the formula shows how to create fragments of the reverse-engineered target design when instances of "source-pattern" are found in the PKB. Operator **CreateEnt** creates a new instance of a design entity, **CreateRel** establishes a relationship between two design entities, **AssignAttr** assigns a value to the entity or relationship attribute, and **CreateLink** links design entities from different program design models

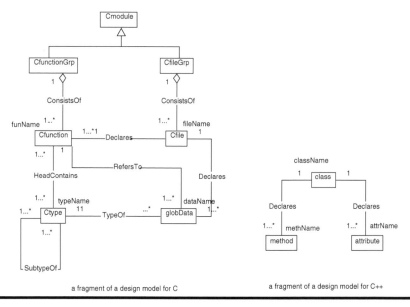

a fragment of a design model for C   a fragment of a design model for C++

Figure 3.3   Partial design models for C and C++ programs.

for the purpose of traceability. Operators may appear any number of times and in any order on the right-hand side of the formula.

In the object recovery example, the "source-pattern" refers to C models (on the left-hand side of Figure 3.3), whereas target design entities are classes, attributes, and methods of the object-oriented design model (on the right-hand side of Figure 3.3). In the extended PQL, we can map data from set data-rep-X to class attributes and procedural modules from set methods-X to class methods:

CreateEnt class **with** class.className = ?X
Explanation: ?X indicates that the class name must be provided by the human expert.
Select fun **from** methods-X
CreateEnt method **with** method.methName = fun.funName
CreateRel Declares (class, method) **with** class.className = ?X
CreateLink (fun, method)
Select data **from** data-rep-X
CreateEnt attribute **with** attribute.attrName = data.dataName
CreateRel Declares (class, attribute) **with** class.className = ?X
CreateLink (data, attribute)

3.10 Conclusions

We described general capabilities of reverse engineering techniques. We pointed to limitations of fully automated reverse engineering methods in recovering higher-level design views. We described an interactive and incremental reverse engineering process model that assumes close cooperation between an REA tool and a human expert. We extended PQL to provide a unified formalism for specifying program queries and reverse engineering heuristics.

Reverse engineering methods can be helpful in day-to-day maintenance, but they show similar limitations in addressing the challenges of long-term evolution as static program analysis methods. In particular, current reverse engineering methods cannot build a clear picture of similarities and differences among systems released during evolution.

References

1. Antoniol, G., Canfora, G., Casazza, G., De Lucia, A., and Merlo, E., Recovering traceability links between code and documentation, *IEEE Transactions on Software Engineering*, 28(10), 970–983, October 2002.
2. Antoniol, G., Canfora, G., De Lucia, A., and Merlo, E., Recovering code to documentation links in OO systems, *Working Conference on Reverse Engineering, WCRE'99*, Atlanta, GA, October 1999, pp.136–144.
3. Arora, A.K. and Davis, K.H., A methodology for translating a conventional file system into an entity-relationship model, in Chen, P.P., Ed., Entity relationship approach: the use of ER concepts in knowledge representation, North Holland, The Netherlands, pp. 148–159.
4. Biggerstaff, T., Design Recovery for Maintenance and Reuse, *IEEE Computer*, 7, 1989, pp. 36–49.
5. Boldyreff, C. and Kewish, R., Reverse engineering to achieve maintainable WWW sites, *Working Conference on Reverse Engineering, WCRE'01*, Stuttgart, Germany, May 2001, pp. 249–257.
6. Briand, L.C., Labiche, Y., and Miao, Y., Towards the reverse engineering of UML sequence diagrams, *Working Conference on Reverse Engineering, WCRE'02*, Victoria, B.C., Canada, November 2003, pp. 57–66.
7. Brooks, R., Towards a theory of the comprehension of computer programs, *International Journal of Man-Machine Studies*, 18, 543–554, 1983.
8. Brown, A., Specifications and reverse engineering, *Journal of Software Maintenance: Research and Practice*, 5, 147–153, 1993.
9. Burson, S., Kotik, G., and Markosian, L., A program transformation approach to automating software re-engineering, *Proceedings of COMPSAC'90*, IEEE Computer Society Press, Los Alamitos, CA, pp. 314–322.
10. Byrne, E.J., Software reverse engineering: a case study, *Software-Practice and Experience*, 21, 1349–1364, 1991.

11. Canfora, G., Cimitile, A., and Munro, M., RE2: reverse engineering and reuse re-engineering, *Journal of Software Maintenance: Research and Practice*, 6(2), 53–72, 1994.

12. Canfora, G., Cimitile, A., Munro, M., and Tortorella, M., A precise method for identifying reusable abstract data types in code, *Proceedings of the Conference on Software Maintenance*, IEEE Computer Society Press, Los Alamitos, CA, 1994, pp. 404–413.

13. Canfora, G., Cimitile, A., and de Carlini, U., A logic-based approach to reverse engineering tools production, *IEEE Transactions on Software Engineering*, 18(12), 1053–1064, 1992.

14. Carver, D.L. and Valasareddi, R., Object localization in procedural programs: a graph-based approach, *Journal of Software Maintenance: Research and Practice*, 12(5), 305–323, September–October 2000.

15. Chen, P.P., The entity-relationship model: towards a unified view of data, *ACM Transactions on Database Systems*, 1(1), 9–36, 1976.

16. Chikofsky, E.J. and Cross, J.H., Reverse Engineering and Design Recovery: a Taxonomy, *IEEE Software*, 7(1), January 1990, pp. 13–18.

17. Cordy, J.R., Comprehending reality: practical challenges to software maintenance automation, *Proceedings of the IWPC 2003, IEEE 11th International Workshop on Program Comprehension*, Portland, OR, May 2003, pp. 196–206 (keynote paper).

18. Darlison, A.G. and Sabanis, N., Data remodeling, *The REDO Compendium: Reverse Engineering for Software Maintenance*, van Zuylen, H.J., Ed., John Wiley and Sons, Chichester, U.K., chap. 20, pp. 311–325.

19. Davis, K.H. and Alken, P.H., Data reverse engineering: a historical survey, *Working Conference on Reverse Engineering, WCRE'01*, Brisbane, Australia, November 2000, pp. 70–78.

20. Di Lucca, G.A., Fasolino, A.R., Pace, F., Tramontana, P., and De Carlini, U., WARE: a tool for the reverse engineering of Web applications, *European Conference on Software Maintenance and Reengineering, CSMR'02*, Budapest, Hungary, March 2002, pp. 241–250.

21. Di Lucca, G.A., Fasolino, A.R., and De Carlini, U., Recovering class diagrams from data-intensive legacy systems, *International Conference on Software Maintenance, ICSM'00*, San Jose, CA, pp. 52–63.

22. Di Lucca, G.A., Fasolino, A.R., and Tramontana, P., Reverse engineering Web applications: the WARE approach, *Journal of Software Maintenance and Evolution: Research and Practice*, 16(1–2), January/April 2004, pp. 71–101.

23. Edwards, H.M. and Munro, M., Deriving a logical data model for a system using the RECAST method, *Proceedings of the 2nd Working Conference on Reverse Engineering, WCRE' 95*, IEEE Computer Society Press, Los Alamitos, CA, pp. 126–135.

24. Eisenbarth, T., Koschke, R., and Simon, D., Locating features in source code, *IEEE Transactions on Software Engineering*, 29(3), 210–224, March 2003.

25. Estadale, J. and Zuylen, H.J., Views, representations and development methods in *The REDO Compendium: Reverse Engineering for Software Maintenance*, van Zuylen, H.J., Ed., John Wiley and Sons, Chichester, U.K., 1993, pp. 93–109.

26. Ferenc, R., Beszedes, A., Tarkiainen, M., and Gyimothy, T., Columbus — reverse engineering tool and schema for C++, *International Conference on Software Maintenance, ICSM'02*, Montreal, Canada, October 2002, pp. 172–181.

27. Gall, H. and Klosch, R., Finding objects in procedural programs: an alternative approach, *Proceedings of the 2nd Working Conference on Reverse Engineering, WCRE'95*, Toronto, 1995, 208–216.

28. Hartman, J., Technical introduction to the first workshop on artificial intelligence and automated program understanding, *Workshop Notes AAAI-92 AI and Automated Program Understanding*, American Association of Artificial Intelligence, San Jose, CA, pp. 8–13.

29. Hassan, A. and Holt, R., Architecture recovery of web applications, *22nd International Conference on Software Engineering ICSE'02*, Orlando, FL, 2002, pp. 349–359 .

30. Jackobson, I. and Lindstrom, F., Re-engineering of old systems to an object-oriented architecture, *Proceedings of the OOPSLA'91*, Phoenix, ACM Press, pp. 340–350.

31. Jackson, D. and Waingold, A., Lightweight extraction of object models from bytecode, *IEEE Transactions on Software Engineering*, 27(2), February 2001, pp. 156–169.

32. Jarzabek, S., Tan, C.L., and Tham, K., An Object-oriented model for recovered designs in software reengineering, *Information Technology Journal*, 6(2), 80–94, December 1994; also in *Proceedings of the InfoScience'93*, Seoul, Korea, October 1993, pp. 217–224.

33. Jarzabek, S., Specifying program transformations with PQTL, *Proceedings of the ICSE-17 Workshop on Program Transformations for Software Evolution*, April 24, 1995, Seatle, U.S., William Griswold, Ed., TRCS95-418, University of California, San Diego, CA, pp. 35–46.

34. Jarzabek, S. and Tan, P.K., Design of a generic reverse engineering assistant tool, *Proceedings of the 2nd Working Conference on Reverse Engineering, WCRE*, Toronto, Canada, July 14–16, 1995, IEEE Computer Society Press, Los Alamitos, CA, pp. 61–70.

35. Jarzabek, S. and Woon, I., Towards precise description of reverse engineering heuristics, *Proceedings of the EUROMICRO Working Conference on Software Maintenance and Reengineering*, IEEE Computer Society Press, Berlin, March 1997, pp. 3–9.

36. Jarzabek, S., Design of flexible static program analysers with *PQL*, *IEEE Transactions on Software Engineering*, 24(3), 197–215, March 1998.

37. Jarzabek, S. and Wang, G., Model-based design of reverse engineering tools, *Journal of Software Maintenance: Research and Practice,* No. 10, 1998, pp. 353–380.

38. Kiczales, G., Lamping, J., Mendhekar, A., Maeda, C., Lopes, C., Loingtier, J-M., and Irwin, J., Aspect-oriented programming, *European Conference on Object-Oriented Programming*, Finland, Springer-Verlag LNCS 1241, 1997, pp. 220–242.

39. Kozaczynski, W., Ning, J., and Engberts, A., Program concept recognition and transformation, *IEEE Transactions on Software Engineering*, 18(12), 1065–1075, 1992.

40. Lano, K.C., Breuer, P.T., and Haughton, H., Reverse engineering COBOL via formal methods, *Journal of Software Maintenance: Research and Practice*, pp. 13–35.

41. Linton, M.A., Implementing relational views of programs, *Proceedings of the Software Engineering Symposium on Practical Software Development Environments*, ACM Press, pp. 65–72.

42. Liu, S. and Wilde, N., Identifying objects in a conventional procedural language: an example of data design recovery, *Proceedings on the Conference on Software Maintenance*, IEEE Computer Society Press, Los Alamitos, CA, pp. 266–271.

43. Mancoridis, S., Mitchell, B.S., Chen, Y., and Gansner, E.R., Bunch: a clustering tool for the recovery and maintenance of software system structures, *International Conference on Software Maintenance, ICSM'99*, Oxford, England, October 1999, pp. 50–59.

44. Mitchell, B.S. and Mancoridis, S., Comparing the decompositions produced by software clustering algorithms using similarity measurements, *International Conference on Software Maintenance, ICSM'01*, Florence, Italy, November 2001, pp. 744–753.

45. Niere, J., Schäfer, W., Wadsack, J.P., Wendehals, L., Welsh, J., Towards pattern-based design recovery, *22nd International Conference on Software Engineering ICSE'02*, Orlando, FL, 2002, pp. 338–348.

46. Pinzger, M., Fischer, M., Gall, H., and Jazayeri, M., Revealer: a lexical pattern matcher for architecture recovery, *Working Conference on Reverse Engineering, WCRE'02*, Richmond, VA, October 2002, pp. 170–178.

47. Rich, C. and Wills, L., Recognising Programs Design: A Graph-Parsing Approach, *IEEE Software*, 1, pp. 82–89, 1990.

48. Rock-Evans, R. and Hales, K., *Reverse Engineering: Markets, Methods and Tools*, 1, Ovum, London, 1990.

49. Rumbaugh, J., Jacobson, I., and Booch, G., *The Unified Modeling Language — Reference Manual*, 1999, Addison-Wesley.

50. Sartipi, K., Software architecture recovery based on pattern matching, *International Conference on Software Maintenance, ICSM'03*, Amsterdam, The Netherlands, September 2003, pp. 293–296.

51. Sartipi, K. and Kontogiannis, K., A user-assisted approach to component clustering, *Journal of Software Maintenance and Evolution: Research and Practice*, 15(4), July–August 2003, pp. 265–295.

52. Sneed, H., Recycling software components extracted from legacy programs, *International Workshop on Principles of Software Evolution, IWPSE'01*, Vienna, Austria, September 2001, pp. 43–51.

53. Sneed, H. and Nyary, E., Extracting object-oriented specification from procedurally oriented programs, *Proceedings of the 2nd Working Conference on Reverse Engineering, WCRE'95*, Toronto, 1995, 217–226.

54. Tilley, S. and Huang, S., Evaluating the reverse engineering capabilities of Web tools for understanding site content and structure: a case study, *23rd International Conference on Software Engineering ICSE'01*, Toronto, Canada, May 2001, pp. 514–523.

55. Tonella, P., Concept analysis for module restructuring, *IEEE Transactions on Software Engineering*, 27(4), 351–363, April 2001.

56. Tonella, P. and Potrich, A., Reverse engineering of the interaction diagrams from C++ code, *International Conference on Software Maintenance, ICSM'03*, Amsterdam, The Netherlands, September 2003, pp.159–168.

57. Tonella, P. and Potrich, A., Static and dynamic C++ code analysis for the recovery of the object diagram, *International Conference on Software Maintenance, ICSM'02*, Montreal, Canada, October 2002, pp. 54–63.

58. Ward, M., Calliss, F.W., and Munro, M., The maintainer's assistant, *Proceedings of the Conference on Software Maintenance*, IEEE Computer Society Press, Los Alamitos, CA, pp. 307–315.

59. Weiser, M., Program slicing, *IEEE Transactions on Software Engineering*, 10(4), 353–357.
60. Wong, K., Tilley, S., Muller, H., and Storye, M., Structural Redocumentation: A Case Study, *IEEE Software*, 1995, pp. 46–54.
61. Yang, H. and Bennett, K., Acquisition of ERA models from data intensive code, *Proceedings of the Conference on Software Maintenance*, IEEE Computer Society Press, Los Alamitos, CA, pp. 116–123.

Chapter 4

Model-Based Design for Ease of Maintenance

Chapter Summary

In this chapter, the reader learns about model-based design of extensible, adaptable programs. Models encode the problem domain semantics. At the conceptual level, models can be expressed in a variety of forms, for example, as Unified Modeling Language (UML) class diagrams. At the program level, models are stored in data structures (e.g., tables) and play the role of parameters driving operation of generic programs. Along with information hiding, model-based techniques are a powerful means of realizing design for change [20]. We illustrate model-based design with examples of static program analyzers (SPAs), reverse engineering, and project-support environment. Although our examples are from the domain of software tools, model-based techniques can be applied to improve maintainability of programs in any application domain.

4.1 The Role of Models in the Design of Software Tools

Tools built in an ad hoc way often display problems for both tool users and designers. First, without systematic analysis and a good understanding of the underlying software process, we have little chance to design a tool that will adequately address the user's needs [15]. Next, because one tool is often used in many different situations and by people who have different working habits, tools should be highly customizable. Tools built in an ad hoc manner are usually not flexible enough, as possible variations in tool functions are typically not incorporated into the tool architecture to make future customization possible. Ad hoc design practice does not lead to accumulating tool design know-how, makes it difficult to repeat successful solutions, and slows down the process of understanding and improving tool design methods.

There are many variations in software maintenance and reengineering projects that affect tool features. For example, tools such as SPA (discussed in Chapter 2) and reverse engineering assistant (REA; discussed in Chapter 3) should be as independent of source language and program design abstraction as possible, so that various tool components can be adapted to a specific source language and reused, rather than developed from scratch.

Project-support tools must be adaptable to realities of a given project.

Models have a vital role to play in building successful software tools. Designing tools involves analysis of a software process to be supported by a tool, habits of people who use a tool, and information processed and produced by a tool. By expressing a software process and tool external behavior in the form of precise, interrelated models, we can better understand tool features. Incorrect assumptions about the human-related issues in software development processes were in part responsible for CASE tool failure to deliver promised benefits [15].

If we carry on modeling from analysis to the tool design level, we can come up with model-based, adaptable tool architecture, based on which we can develop tools faster and cheaper [12,27]. We can start viewing tools in a given category as different variants of the same generic tool concept. In the past, we saw how this process of growing understanding, modeling, and formalization led to elegant, cost-effective, and generic solutions in the compiler domain. Business applications and tools supporting development of business programs (CASE and program generators [18]) benefited greatly from the design centered around a data model, initially an entity-relationship, and today as UML class diagrams [24].

In this chapter, we describe a model-based design technique that is helpful in designing flexible, adaptable, and extensible software tools. Model-based design can be also applied in development of any program, not only software tools, for benefits of extensibility and improved maintainability.

4.2 The Concept of Model-Based Design

Conceptual modeling is an integral part of many mature approaches to problem solving. The structure of a domain and the nature of a problem to be solved determines types of models we need [19]. Models have a long history of being useful in formalizing, analyzing and communicating software requirements and design.

Models pertaining to application domain and to design solutions can be equally useful. In our discussion in this chapter, we concentrate only on models that capture information a tool (or any program) has to understand and process.

The idea of model-based design is to carry on models into the software design and implementation stages. We store models in tables (or other suitable data structures). In that way, all the information contained in models is defined separately from the algorithms defining tool behavior, rather than being hard-coded into a tool. The tables with models drive the tool behavior. Precisely speaking, the algorithmic part of tool definition communicates with models via an abstract program interface (API). An API allows a tool to create, modify, and access the information contained in models.

What do we gain by using such a model-based, table-driven design? Any changes affecting a tool that can be achieved by modifying models become very easy to implement. Such changes require us to only modify information in tables (or other data structures), but do not affect the algorithmic part of the tool definition. Modifying data stored in tables is usually much simpler than modifying algorithmic code. We gain extensibility and adaptability: certain types of extensions and adaptations can be achieved by modifying models only.

Program design models described for SPA in Chapter 2 are an example of models that can be useful in designing a flexible model-based SPA. In particular, we can change program design models without affecting model-based PKB construction (design extractor) and PQL query processor subsystems. We can even make many of the SPA components work with different source languages just by plugging in different program design models. Of course, certain SPA components need some modifications as we move from one source language to another. An example is the parser of an SPA front-end. Although we can generate the parser from a BNF definition of source language syntax rules, we still need to write code for actions that require knowledge to source language semantics (e.g., AST and CFG generation actions).

A compiler-compiler is a classical example of a powerful model-based, table-driven design solution. Models comprise regular expressions (drive generic lexer), BNF grammar (drives generic parser), attribute grammars (drive generic static semantic analyzer), and target machine definition (drives generic optimizer and code generator). The same generic compilation algorithms can be used to compile programs written in different source languages, by plugging in source language models. The amount of code that must be written by hand is substantially reduced, as it is confined to actions that depend on language semantics not captured in models. A model-based solution improves productivity in compiler implementation by orders of magnitude over hand-crafted compiler development.

Today IDEs, developed based on experience with earlier CASE tools [18], also generate much custom functionality from models. The entity-relationship model [1], and its later incarnation as a UML class diagram [24], provides much useful information that facilitates generation of normalized database schema and user interface screens to manipulate data processed by a program.

Not every tool/program can benefit from model-based design to the same extent as compiler-compilers and CASE tools. However, quite often a model-based approach can help design certain parts of a tool, easing implementation of certain types of changes. Even then, clarity of design and productivity gains may give us enough good reasons to apply the model-based technique.

4.3 Model-Based PQL Query Validator in SPA and REA

Model-based design is one of the basic techniques of achieving language independence of an SPA and REA. By making an SPA design based on models of a source language and storing those models in tables, we can design most of the SPA components in a table-driven way.

We describe model-based design of a query validator, a component in a PQL query processing subsystem of an SPA (Chapter 2) or REA (Chapter 3).

We briefly describe what is involved in query validation. As a programmer enters a query, the query validator needs to check if the query is valid with respect to program design models for *SIMPLE*. This involves checking if all the references to entities, attributes, and relationships in a program query agree with the program design model definition. In particular:

1. All the program design entities in declaration of synonyms should be defined in the program design model. In the case of *SIMPLE*, valid program design entities are procedure, variable, assign, while, etc.
2. All the relationships in query conditions should be syntactically correct. In particular, they should have the required number of arguments and the type of arguments should be the same as in the program design model. For example, in relationship Calls (p, q), p and q should be synonyms of the design entity procedure. Cluster (p, s) is not valid as we do not have relationship Cluster () in the program design model. Reference to Calls (p, q, v) is not valid either as Calls expects only two arguments of type procedure.
3. All the references to entity attributes should be valid. First, attributes should be defined in the program design model. For example, procedure.value is not a reference to a valid attribute. Equation p.procName=2 in **with** clause is not valid, as the type of attribute procName is string, not integer.

A simple solution to a query validator is to hard-code program design models into the query validation algorithms. The code for query validation would contain switch statements such as:

```
switch ( relationship) {
case Calls: expect two arguments; each argument should be either procedure
    synonym or '_'
case Next: expect two arguments; each argument should be either statement
    number or synonym of statement, assign, if, while or '_'
etc.
}
```

In case of changes to the program design model, we have to find and modify affected parts of the code. A table-driven technique provides a better solution. Rather than hard-coding program design models into query validation algorithms, we put the program design model schema into tables (Table 4.1 and Table 4.2).

An entity attribute table can be defined in a similar way. All the information the query validator needs to validate queries is now stored in the tables. The query validator refers to the tables to check whether all the references to entities, attributes, and relationships in a query agree with the program design model definition. The query validator becomes more generic and much simpler. Instead of switch statements, we have the following code:

```
rel = getRelTabIndex (R)
if (#args ≠ RelTab [rel, 2] ) Error()
if (arg1 ∉ RelTab [rel, 3] then Error()
if (arg2 ∉ RelTab [rel, 4] then Error()
etc.
```

where R is a relationship referenced in a query, #args is the number of arguments of R as it appears in the query, arg1 is the first argument of R, etc. The preceding fragment of the query validator definition checks if the actual references in a query agree with their respective definitions in the tables.

The advantage of the table-driven solution is that any changes to the program design models will affect only tables but not the code of the query preprocessor. Changing data in tables is much easier than changing procedural code.

Table 4.1 Design Entity Table

1	program
2	procedure
3	stmtLst
4	stmt
5	assign
6	...

Table 4.2   Relationship Table

Relationship	# Arguments	Type of arg 1	Type of arg 2	Type of arg 3
Calls	2	Procedure	Procedure	Nil
Calls*	2	Procedure	Procedure	Nil
Modifies	2	Procedure	Variable	Nil
Modifies	2	stmt, assign, call, while, if	Variable	Nil
...				

4.4   Model-Based Design of the PQL Query Evaluator in SPA and REA

The PQL query evaluator is another SPA and REA tool component that greatly benefits from model-based design in terms of extensibility and adaptability to varying tool features. Query evaluation is difficult to implement, so its reusability across SPA and REA tools dealing with different source language program design abstractions is particularly attractive.

The query evaluator needs to know all the details of program design models, such as shown in Chapter 2 for *SIMPLE*, in Chapter 3 for C and C++, and in Appendix B for COBOL85. It also needs to access program information stored in the PKB to evaluate program queries.

To make query evaluation algorithms independent of program design models, we store the model schema in the tables, as shown in the previous section. Tables contain the definition of design entities, their attributes, and relationships.

To make query evaluation algorithms independent of how program information is represented in the PKB, we define mappings between the conceptual models and their physical representations in the PKB. The PKB API defines those mappings in an operational way. The operations are abstract in the sense that they refer to design entities, entity attribute values, and relationships in program design models rather than to their physical representations in the PKB. Reference to program design models always goes via tables containing model definition.

Complex operations, such as traversing abstract syntax trees to do pattern matching, or traversing a control flow graph to compute data flow relations are also included in the abstract PKB interface. The PKB API isolates and hides the knowledge of how to manipulate the physical program design in the PKB from the query evaluator, as well as other form components of an SPA tool. For example, when a query refers to an entity attribute, the query evaluator calls a suitable operation from the PKB API to fetch the value of the required attribute from the PKB. As the PKB API hides the physical program design in the PKB, we can reuse the query evaluator even if we decide to change the physical representation of data in the PKB. Such a change requires reimplementation of PKB API operations, but does not require any modifications to the query evaluator.

4.5 Model-Based Design of a Software Project-Support Environment

A software project-support environment (PSE) is a collaboration tool helping in planning, executing, and monitoring progress of software projects. Because of many variations across software projects, PSE must be flexible, extensible, and adaptable to realities of various projects.

The following is a brief, informal description of the software project domain: Project planning includes selecting a development methodology and tools, dividing a project into phases and activities, estimating the schedule and resources required for the project, setting up milestones, defining project deliverables, defining the project metrics to be collected for progress monitoring purposes, etc. As companies organize and run software projects in many different ways, there are many variations in the software project domain.

We conduct domain analysis [17] and large-granularity decomposition of a software project domain first. Domain analysis paves a foundation for setting up PSE architecture, identifying PSE models, and for follow up model-based design of an extensible and adaptable PSE. Further benefit of domain analysis could be reuse of common functions across tool components.

In the domain of software projects, we identified project management and project development subdomains (arrows in Figure 4.1 represent *PartOf* relationship). We further decomposed the project management subdomain into project planning and project monitoring subdomains. Finally, we distinguished a software process subdomain, as a *PartOf* all other project subdomains. *PartOf* relationship decomposes domains horizontally into domain parts that can be described separately from one another.

We call a subdomain that is *PartOf* more than one other domain problem domains. Problem domains are interesting as they often create reuse opportunities. A software process (box 4 in Figure 4.1) is a problem domain. Models of problem domains need to be specialized for different reuse contexts.

As demonstrated in other work [7–9,16,17], problem orientation is useful in domain analysis. First, it helps identify the right components: problems are good candidates for domain model and reference architecture components. Second, reuse of problem solutions often crosses the boundaries of a single application domain. Problem domains and their model-based software solutions blur the traditional difference between application-domain-specific and domain-independent reuse.

We chose a software process model to play an integrating role among many information models describing different views of a PSE. By a software process model

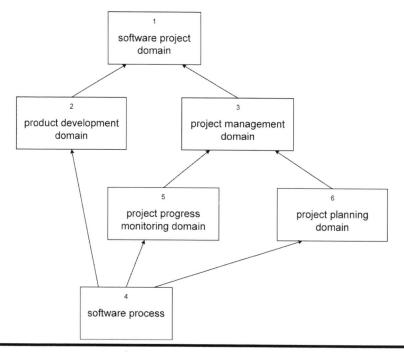

Figure 4.1   Decomposition of a software project domain.

(SPM) we mean the whole range of issues involved in planning and executing a project, including life-cycle style, activities, development methods and tools to be used to complete project activities, deliverables, project team structure, resources allocated to a project, project metrics, etc. Through the SPM, project managers communicate to software developers what they should do, when, and how: project managers define an SPM for a project, and software developers develop a software system by following the SPM. During project development, matters may not go exactly as the managers had initially planned. A development team may face unexpected technical problems, some phases may take longer than planned, iterations over phases may be needed to remove bugs or to incorporate new features, etc. All this may affect the SPM as the project work progresses. Project managers assess the actual status of the project and make the necessary adjustments to the SPM definition.

In real-life software projects, the SPM appears with varying degrees of rigor, ranging from explicit and formal process models to informal and fuzzy process models, existing only in the minds of people working on a project. The issues of software process modeling and process-centered software engineering environments have received much attention in recent years. The discussion of various approaches to process modeling is not within the scope of this chapter and we refer the reader to other sources, such as [5].

4.5.1 Stable and Customizable PSE Features

We classify PSE features as stable features or variant features. Variant features can be user-customizable features or designer-customizable features:

1. *Stable features*: These cannot be changed without much rework by the PSE designers. They are defined in the SPM shown in Figure 4.3 to Figure 4.7. This means project entity types, relationships, and attributes in the SPM characterize all software projects and the core of a PSE can be based on an SPM.

2. *User-customizable variant features*: These are the features that a PSE user, a manager or developer, should be able to customize either during runtime or in the customize–compile–run cycle.

   a. *Runtime variant features*: A project plan differs from one project to another and is often changed during the project lifetime. Therefore, the user must be able to change the details of a project plan on the fly. Note that the project plan is an instance of the SPM. The user changes the details of an instance of the SPM, not the SPM itself. Having changed the project plan, the user should be able to run the PSE without recompilation.

   b. *Variant features customizable in the "customize–compile–run" cycle*: Here, variant features include different development life-cycle styles, development phases and activities, activity flowcharts, team organizations, project schedules, development methods, physical resources, and many other elements. The user should be able to specialize the SPM before the project starts. This may involve adding new project entity types, attributes, and relationships to the SPM (an example is given in Figure 4.8). The PSE should provide user-level means for extending the SPM, so that no manual code modifications are required.

3. *Designer-customizable variant features*: These features require modifying PSE code. Designer-customizable features include porting a software process component to other platforms, changing the way the PSE stores an SPM instance, user interface, etc. Some of the variant user features that cannot be addressed by methods 2a or 2b may also belong to this category.

4.5.2 Use Cases in Modeling Multiple Domains

A use case [24] is a notation used in features analysis to describe processes that lead to achieving user-level tasks. Use cases help identify workflows that will be supported by applications and help us understand how applications will interact with one another and with the users. Following examples from [8], we extended use case notations to make use cases useful in domain analysis. Jacobson et al. [8] expresses use case variability using forms, macros and parameters, inheritance, and use case extensions. Our use cases include optional and alternative steps. In addition, various steps of a given use case may spread through a number of software project subdomains (Figure 4.1). Naming conventions allow us to cross-reference use cases contained in different subdomains. In that way, we can describe a complex use case as a collection of smaller, interlinked use cases from different subdomains. Finally, our use cases may involve decision points and control structures such as loops and conditional if-then-else control structures. An example of a global project use case in the software project domain (box 1 in Figure 4.1) follows:

Use case [1;1] *Global project use case*

1. Project Managers (PMs) kick off the project [1;2].
2. PMs create an initial project plan [6;1].
3. **while** (project **is not** completed **and** project **is not** scrapped) **do**

   3.1 Software Developers (SDs) build a software product according to the project plan [2;1].
   3.2 PMs monitor the progress of the project [5;1].
   3.3 PMs modify the SPM for the project [4;1-1].
   3.4 **if** (schedule is affected) **then**
   3.4.1 PMs adjust project estimates [6;6-1]
   3.4.2 <Estimate-DB OPT> PMs enter new project estimates into the project database [4;7]
   end if
   3.5 **if** (resources are affected) **then** PMs reallocate physical resources [6;8-1]
   end if
   end while

Explanation: [n;m] is a unique use case identifier: "n" is a domain identifier (digits in boxes of Figure 4.1) and "m" uniquely identifies a use case in that domain. [1;1] is an identifier of a root use case. Using use case identifiers, we can interlink use cases specified at different levels of details, as well as use cases described in different component domains. Step 2 in the preceding use case refers to a use case in the project planning domain and step 3 to use cases in the project development, project monitoring, and software process model domains. Notation [4;1-1] means that a given use case is a variant of some basic use case, [4;1] in this case PM and SD are formal project entities that we discuss later.

Step 3.4.2 in the preceding use case is optional and occurs only in situations when project estimates are recorded in the project database. (In our terminology, project estimates are part of the SPM definition.) By qualifying certain steps in a use case as optional or alternative, we can describe variations. Variant steps help us write concise and general use cases. When we try to write use cases for a family of applications, our use cases become either overly simplistic or imprecise. Optional and alternative steps are a means to deal with this problem: we can describe use cases for a family of applications at a nontrivial level of detail. A use case with optional and alternative steps is a generic use case, i.e., one from which we may derive many concrete use cases that fit specific reuse contexts.

In the following text, we show examples of use cases from other software project component domains.

Use case [6;1] *Create an initial project plan*

1. PMs analyze software product features [6;3].
2. <Reuse OPT> PMs analyze similarities with other projects done in the past [6;5].
3. PMs define the first-cut SPM for the project [4;1].
4. PMs estimate effort, schedule, and other resources for the project [6;6].
5. <Estimate-DB OPT> PMs enter project estimates into the project database [4;7].
6. PMs allocate physical resources to the project [6;8].

There are two optional steps in the preceding use case: step 2 occurs in reuse-based software development and step 5 occurs if project estimates are recorded in the project database.

Use case [4;1] *Define the SPM for the project*

1. PMs define the life-cycle model for the project [4;5]
2. PMs define the first-cut architecture for the product [6;15]
3. PMs define software development phases and milestones [4;6]
4. PMs decompose phases into tasks, draw task workflows [4;7], and write guidelines for completing tasks [4;8].

Use case [4;1-1] *Modify the SPM for the project*

1. PMs refine the life-cycle model for the project [4-5-1].
2. PMs refine the architecture for the product [6;15-1].
3. PMs update development phases and milestones [4;6-1].
4. PMs update phases, tasks workflows [4;7-1], and guidelines for completing tasks [4;8-1.]

Use case [2;1] (John : SD) *Build a software product according to the project plan*

1. John examines the SPM for the project [4;10] {SD} (John : SD).
2. John retrieves a list of tasks assigned to him.
3. John selects one of the tasks assigned to him.
4. John reviews task description.
5. John performs the task.
6. John records project metrics and <Metric-DB OPT> enters project metrics into the project database.

A parameter in the preceding use case indicates that each software developer (SD) may have a different instance of the use case assigned to him or her. Using parameters, we can also create formal links between use cases and other domain views. Use case [4;10] *Examine the SPM for the project* is parameterized by both the role (PM or SD) and an instance (John and Albert). All the steps in the use case [2;1] are performed in any order for an unspecified period of time.

Use case [5;1] (Albert : PM) *Monitor the progress of the project*

1. Albert examines the SPM for the project [4;10] {PM} (Albert : PM).
2. Albert analyzes the status of the project.

Use cases create a natural and intuitive link between real-world processes and supporting them in software applications. The problem is that when the use cases grow in size and number, it becomes difficult to make sense out of mostly informal and overly complex use cases. This may limit the role of use cases in deriving features for applications. As illustrated earlier, we introduced elements of formality to the use case notation to overcome this problem during domain analysis. We built use cases in a hierarchical way and broke potentially large use cases into small subuse cases that could be described within component domains. We further created links between subuse cases so that the interactions between the environment and applications can be understood at various levels of abstraction.

Still, use cases describe only one view of a domain. In particular, use cases do not capture information models, communication among operational steps, and external events. Therefore, we complemented use cases with other views to provide a more comprehensive domain description and a better foundation for designing software project support tools.

Use cases do not precisely define execution sequences. In many domains execution sequences must be precisely defined. For example, in modeling an ATM domain, we used state transition diagrams to specify execution sequences triggered by events. We introduced optional and alternative states and transitions to model variations in this domain. In the software project domain, most of the steps are not executed in any a priori defined order. Furthermore, steps intertwine with each other and are executed repeatedly, on demand. This is indicated by double lines along most of the steps in use cases. For this reason, we did not find state transition diagrams particularly useful in modeling the software project domain. On the other hand, information models and information flow models convey a great deal of knowledge that helps us understand the software project domain. We discuss these models in the following sections.

4.5.3 An Information Model for the Software Process Domain

A software process is the heart of our software project domain. Project management and project development domains are based on the software process model. The following is an informal description of the software process domain: We model software processes in terms of project entities such as phase, activity, decision, event, rule, agent, deliverable, etc. A *process* is a sequence of phases. A *phase* consists

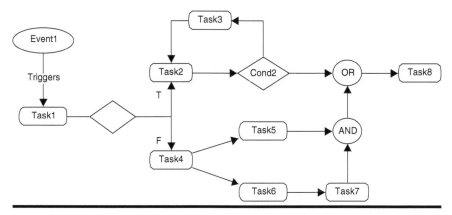

Figure 4.2   A task workflow.

of *activities* to be performed, *decisions* to be made, *agents* (humans and tools) who perform activities, etc. Task workflows (Figure 4.2), where task denotes either a phase or activity, depict sequences of task execution, iterations, tasks that can be executed in parallel (an AND circle) and decision points (a diamond and an OR circle). We use UML activity diagrams to model task workflows.

Each task can be decomposed into a lower-level task workflow. *Rules* govern task execution. Rules describe what happens at the decision points or indicate chains of tasks that can be performed in parallel. Timing constraints are also modeled as rules. *Agents* model people and tools responsible for activities. Deliverables are inputs to and outputs from tasks.

Task workflows are an essential component of the SPM. Similarity between a task workflow and use cases might suggest that we could describe the software process domain in terms of use cases. However, this is not the case. SPM is concerned with plans for all possible software projects that can be based on different development life cycles, development methods, and project development and management styles. The software process domain encompasses an infinite number of specific process models.

Therefore, enumeration of specific process models is not a good approach to describing the software process domain. Our SPM should allow us to describe any specific process model that we need. SPM must be based on generic concepts that apply to a wide class of software projects.

We use UML [24] to define the SPM. Figure 4.3 and Figure 4.4 and describe classifications of project entities as class diagrams. One project entity can participate in many classifications. Taxonomies are important as they provide insights into the domain semantics and often allow us to identify commonalties that lead to reuse.

The diagram of Figure 4.4 shows a set of rules for defining task workflows (such as the one in Figure 4.2). A task is either a phase or an activity. By applying rules

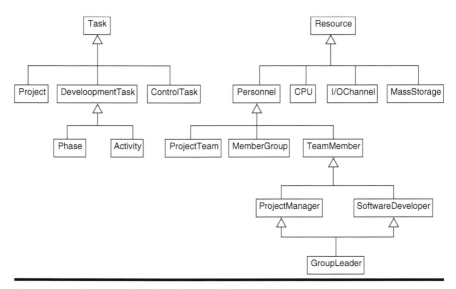

Figure 4.3   Taxonomies of project entities.

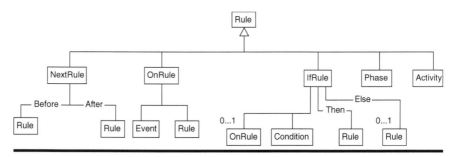

Figure 4.4   Taxonomies of project entities, continued.

recursively, we can obtain task workflows of any size and complexity. The following is the textual representation and meaning of the rules:

Task1 NEXT Task2
meaning: Task1 must be completed before TASK2 can be initiated.
ON Event1 Task1
meaning: Event1 triggers Task1
ON Event1 IF Cond1 THEN Task1 ELSE Task2
meaning: when event Event1 occurs and if condition Cond1 is TRUE, then start Task1; otherwise, start Task2. In the above rule, the ON and ELSE clauses are optional.

In our experience, these three rules are enough to conveniently model workflows with alternative and parallel paths and loops. Of course, we can think about more sophisticated modeling methods, but we decided to keep the SPM general and simple. For example, the following rules describe a task workflow of Figure 4.2:

```
ON Event1 Task1
Task1 NEXT Lab1
Lab1: IF Cond1 THEN Task2 ELSE Task4
    Task2 NEXT Lab2
Lab2: IF Cond2 THEN Task3 ELSE Task8
    Task4 NEXT Task5
    Task5 NEXT Task8
    Task4 NEXT Task6
    Task6 NEXT Task7
    Task7 NEXT Task8
```

In the preceding specifications, we used labels to provide references between rules.

The schema of Figure 4.5 provides a mechanism for defining the hierarchical structure of processes in terms of phases and activities. Phases are decomposed into activities. Each activity can be further divided into more detailed activities. Decomposition of activities may continue to any required level of details.

The schema of Figure 4.6 provides a mechanism for defining the structure of the development team. Using these schemas, we can model hierarchical, flat, and other project team organization styles.

Figure 4.7 depicts the remaining project entities from our generic software process SPM.

4.5.4 Specializations of SPM

An important and difficult part of modeling is finding the right level of abstraction. Being too abstract is as bad as being too specific. Models that are too abstract do not contain enough information to fuel model-based design of PSE; that is, it

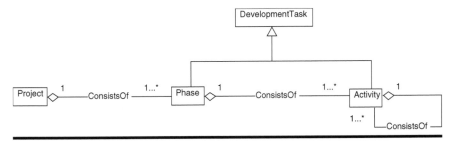

Figure 4.5   Project structure.

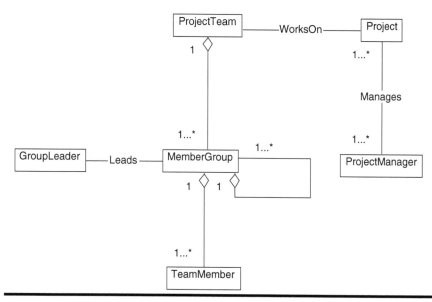

Figure 4.6 Project team structure.

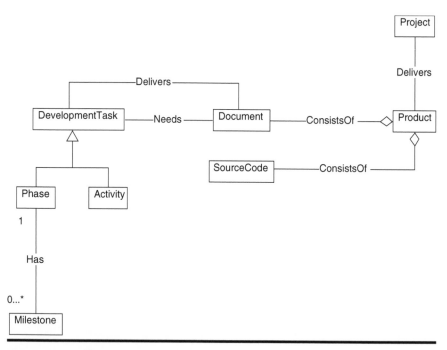

Figure 4.7 Milestones, products, and documents.

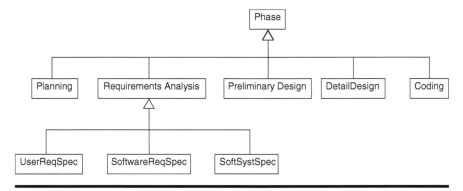

Figure 4.8   Refinement of phase taxonomy.

is difficult to define useful PSE components based on such models. On the other hand, too-specific models are likely to make assumptions that do not apply to some of the required PSEs. The SPM defined in the preceding section is based on analysis of software projects and project support tools in both academic and industrial settings. Design of process-driven PSE based on those models shows that models were rich enough to implement much of the PSE functionality in a generic, model-based manner.

However, the choice of the modeling concepts upon which to build an SPM is arbitrary. Therefore, a domain model will not be perfect, no matter how extensively the software project domain is analyzed. To solve this dilemma, we provide a specialization mechanism for creating multiple domain models, expressed at different levels of abstraction.

By specializing the SPM, we can address variations in software processes such as specific characteristics of various development life cycles, development methods, project management styles, etc. Also, we need software process models specialized to the needs of project management and the project development team. Specialization of an SPM is done before instantiation, that is, before defining an SPM for a given project.

There is no universal method to achieving specialization of domain models. A suitable specialization mechanism depends on the actual modeling methods that have been used. Our SPM can be specialized by adding new project entities, refining project entity taxonomies (Figure 4.8), and adding relationships and attributes.

Some attributes in the software process SPM specialized to the project development domain follow:

Task

> name : TEXT
> id : IDENT   // id is unique though names may not be unique
> objective : TEXT
> description : TEXT
> methods : TEXT
> tools : TEXT
> expertise-required : TEXT
> comments : TEXT

DevelopmentTask

> as in the Task plus:
> entry-criteria : TEXT
> reviews : TEXT
> approved-by : PM*   // PM* is a reference to the entity ProjectManager
> exit-criteria : TEXT

Project

> as in the Task plus:
> currentPhase: Phase*

Milestone

> name : TEXT
> id : IDENT
> reviews : TEXT
> approved-by : PM*
> comments : TEXT

Document

> name : TEXT
> id : IDENT
> description : TEXT
> contents : NOTATION // document may contain text, design specs, ER dia-
>   grams, DFD diagrams, etc.

An SPM specialized to the project management style based on rigorous collection and monitoring of project measurements includes the following attributes:

Task

> expected-start-date : DATE
> actual-start-date : DATE
> expected-end-date : DATE
> actual-end-date : DATE
> percentage-completed : INTEGER
> expected-cost : $$
> actual-cost-to-date : $$

SPM defines a conceptual schema for a project repository storing all the project information manipulated by the PSE. For a given software project, PSE allows the user to instantiate the SPM in the repository, and then modify it as the project progresses.

4.5.5 Model-Based Design of PSE

We extract experiences from a number of laboratory studies and industrial projects in which model-based PSEs were designed with various Web technologies. The initial PSE was implemented with JavaScript™ and Java. The software project domain model described in previous sections was built during this early experiment. Our industry partner shared with us lessons learned for a model-based collaboration Web portal in ASP [21] and J2EE™ [28]. We built yet other PCE variants with PHP™ in other laboratory studies [23].

Software project domain models are useful in clarifying functional features for PSE. Software project subdomains depicted in Figure 4.1 represent high-level functions that can be supported by tools. Use cases describe detailed functions within subdomains. Some of those functions can be supported by a PSE, and the domain model helps determine which functions should be packaged to which PSE modules. There are functional overlaps between subdomains depicted in Figure 4.1. For example, function "query project data" occurs in project planning, project progress monitoring, and project development component domains. Similarly, function "view the software process model definition" occurs in most of the component domains. Overlapping functions may indicate that we should introduce a new subdomain and refine our domain decomposition of Figure 4.1. This is precisely why it is good to distinguish software process as a separate subdomain. We package groups of tightly coupled functions into different PSE modules. Then, we make functions driven by SPM, and in such a way that different tools can reuse them, after possible customizations.

To give the reader a better idea of PSE capabilities and the fundamental role of models in its design, we comment on some of the PSE modules.

The project cost estimation (PCE) module maintains a database of past project experiences and supports estimation by analogy, function points, and COCOMO.

Many cost estimation tools are commercially available, and they can be reused in PSE. We chose to implement our own PCE, so that the cost estimation function was well integrated with all the PSE modules that needed that function. In particular, we wanted project estimations to be based on task workflows (and attached to various development stages), as well as other information defined in the SPM. Being based on a common domain model, PCE can then be fully integrated with the software process definition task, as well as with other PSE modules that need access to PCE functions or project estimates.

The project plan definition (PPD) module allows project managers to define a project plan for developers. The project plan is defined according to the SPM schema. Strictly speaking, a project plan is an instance of a specialized SPM. For example, scenario [4;1-1] in Section 4.5.2 refers to the PPD.

The project development support (PDS) module guides software developers in following the project plan. The project plan is defined, according to the SPM schema, by project managers. For example, scenario [2;1] in Section 4.5.2 refers to the PDS.

The project metrics query (PMQ) module answers queries about the status and progress of a software project under development. The PMQ bridges the gap between the project managers' and developers' mental models of a project and raw software metrics collected during development and stored in the project repository [2,3]. PMQ is a variant of PQL [10] described in the context of static program analysis (Chapter 2) and reverse engineering needs (Chapter 3). Although the project query function was primarily meant for the PM module, it was also useful in most other PSE modules.

We now outline the PSE architecture and illustrate model-based design of some of the PSE modules.

4.5.5.1 A PSE Architecture

A PSE architecture reflects the structure of the domain model. Main PSE modules correspond to software project subdomains. PSE modules are built out of smaller components that correspond to lower-level functions described in the software project domain model. In Section 4.5.3, we described software project management and development subdomains in terms of the SPM. In line with that, we placed the SPM in the center of a PCE architecture, building all the PCE modules in reference to the SPM module.

The SPM module supports features listed in Section 4.5.1 by providing the means to (1) specialize the SPM to the needs of a given project, (2) instantiate the SPM for a given project (i.e., to create a project repository), and (3) retrieve and modify information from a repository storing project information (i.e., an SPM instance). The SPM module provides an API supporting the aforementioned functions. Examples of interface operations from each of the three API groups are given in the following text.

(1)   *API operations to specialize SPM*

These SPM API operations allow the user to specialize SPM to the realities of a given software project by adding new project entities, attributes, and relationships. For example:

NewEntity (ent)	// adds new project entity "ent" to the SPM
NewAttr (ent, attr, type)	// adds new attribute "attr" of type "type" to entity "ent"
NewIsA (ent-p, ent-c)	// makes entity "nt-p" a parent of entity "ent-c"
NewRel (rel, ent1, ent2)	// establishes relationship "rel" between entities "ent1" and "ent2"
AttrList GetAttrs (ent)	// returns attributes of entity "emt"
Type GetAttrType (ent, attr)	// returns the type of an attribute "attr" of entity "ent"
DisplaySPM ()	// displays SPM in graphical form

(2)   *API operations to instantiate SPM*

These operations facilitate defining a specific project plan, which technically means creating an SPM instance in the project repository. This includes definition of team structure, development phases, activity flowcharts, schedule definition, allocation of resources, etc.

EntityId CreateEntityInstance (ent)	// creates a new instance of entity "ent"
CreateRel (rel, entId1, entId2)	// establishes relationship "rel" between link between two entity instances "entId1" and "entId2"
CreateNextRule (task1, task2)	// asserts that "task1" should be completed before "task2"

(3)   *API operations to retrieve project information from the project repository and modify project information as the project progresses*

TaskList GetNextTask (task)	// returns tasks to be initiated once "task" has been completed
TaskList GetNextTask (task, memb)	// returns tasks assigned to a team member "memb"
EnterMetric (entId, metric, value)	// enters a project metric to the project repository
QueryProjectData (query)	// evaluates a project query
DeleteEntityInst (entId)	// deletes an entity instance "entId"

DeleteRel (rel, entId1, entId2)   // deletes relationship "rel" between
                                        two entity instances
                                        "entId1" and "entId2"

Different groups of interface operations are selectively exposed to different PSE modules.

4.5.5.2 Model-Based Design of PSE Modules: An Example

Model-based design ensures the required level of adaptability of PSE modules to accommodate variant features (Section 4.5.1). As in model-based design of SPA and REA described in previous sections, we store the SPM schema definition — entities, relationships and attributes — in suitable tables and let tables drive SPM-independent PSE modules.

Based on the project domain model, we adopted PQL (described in detail in Chapter 2) for the purpose of answering queries about project metrics [2,3]. The PMQ module was an adaptation of the model-based PQL query processor (validator and evaluator). We plugged the SPM definition into the PQL query processor. Software project queries could be expressed in PQL driven by SPM. To answer queries, the query evaluator communicated with the project repository via its API.

We now comment on model-based design of a project development support (PDS) module. The role of the PDS is to guide software developers in project development according to a project plan. The project plan is defined, according to the SPM schema, by project managers. For example, see scenario [2;1] in Section 4.5.2, which refers to the project plan definition supported by the PM module.

The following dialogue, in which John is a member of a project development team, further clarifies the role of the PDS:

John: Asks, "What tasks are assigned to me?"
PDS: Displays a list of tasks that are assigned to John. Tasks already completed, tasks that John started but has not finished, and tasks that are yet to be done are marked accordingly.
John: Asks, "Which task should I do now?"
PDS: Displays a list of tasks John should do (based on satisfaction of task entry criteria, task priorities, etc.) For example, if other developers wait for deliverables from John's task X, John should do X first.
John: Wants to see an overview of the SPM for the project.
PDS: Displays a view of the SPM and allows John to navigate through it.
John: Selects a task, say, X, he wants to work on.
PDS: Displays a task form for X.
John: Wants to see a part of the SPM that is related to task X.
PDS: Displays the requested part of the SPM.

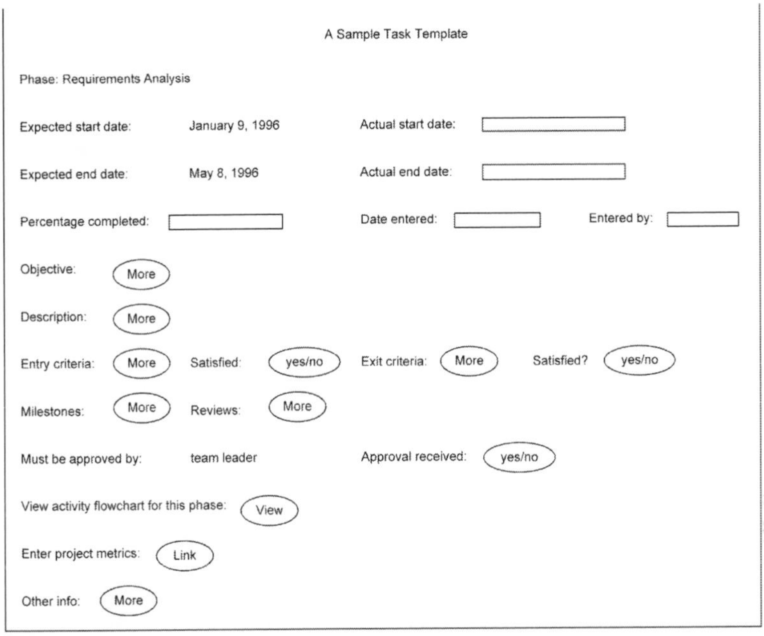

Figure 4.9   A task form.

John: Executes task X; enters project metrics — the task form provides slots for John to enter required data.

PDS: Stores project metrics in the SPM database.

John: Once all exit criteria for task X are completed, the task is completed; so John asks again, "what tasks are assigned to me?"

For each task (phase or activity) defined in the project plan, the PDS provides a task form. A task form tells developers when a task can begin, who should approve the task, what to do when the task has been completed, etc. A task form also allows developers to enter project metrics to convey information about the task progress to project managers.

Technically, a task form contains slots that correspond to attributes of project entities according to the SPM. For example, a task form is likely to have slots with task name, objective, description, methods, etc. (refer to the task attributes in Section 4.5.4), and slots to enter project metrics. Figure 4.9 depicts a sample task form for the requirements analysis phase.

Rectangular boxes denote input slots. "More" buttons allow one to display long text attached to a slot in the flying window. "View" buttons activate tools to view, for example, diagrams. "Link" buttons activate another form, for example, to enter project metrics. Slot values can be formally linked to entities or entity attributes. In the example, the value of the slot "Expected start date" is linked to the attribute

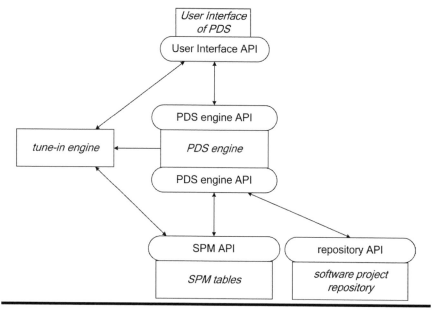

Figure 4.10   Components of the project development support (PDS) module.

"expected-start-date" of a task entity (refer to the task entity at the end of Section 4.5.4). In that way, the project plan can be viewed and modified via task forms.

Figure 4.10 depicts the components of the PDS module.

The component "PDS engine" is an algorithmic part of the PDS, driven by tables storing the SPM schema. In this case, *PartOf* relationship between project development and software process sub-domain models becomes *UsesResourcesOf* relationship between the corresponding components.

The component "tune-in engine" provides a means for defining task forms and SPM interpretation rules. The "PDS engine" displays task forms and provides other project development support functions required in the PDS.

One of the main functions of the PDS is to generate and display task forms based on the SPM schema definition. Much flexibility is required in creating task forms; ideally, we should have a user-level mechanism for creating task forms that would be available to project managers. A model-based task form generator (TFG) provides such a mechanism: all the information to create a custom form is placed in tables, and the TFG interprets the table entries to create task forms. Table entries specify how to display the form, which values can be entered/modified, where to store entered values, where to get read-only values from, etc. Each table entry speci-fies one slot in a task form. The TFG supports slot types such as text, value, more button, view button, and link button. The following descriptors specify slots:

Table 4.3   A Task Form Definition Table

Slot Type	Layout			Read/Enter	Attribute-Link		
	Position	*Mul*	*Font*		*Entity Type*	*Entity Key*	*Attribute-Ind*

C — Display this slot in the center.

L — Display this slot on the left side.

R — Display this slot on the right side.

k — Display this and the following k-1 slots in one line, if possible.

* — Display this and as many as possible following slots in one line.

b — Display slot name in bold.

i — Display slot name in italic.

n — Display slot name in font of size n.

c — Display slot name in capital letters.

We used Table 4.3 to define the structure and layout of task forms.

Columns describe different properties of a given slot: slot type, position (C, L, or R), multiplier (a digit or *), font (size, bold, italic, etc.), whether a slot is read-only or can be modified, and a link to an entity or attribute in the SPM.

Another function of the "tune-in engine" component is to customize the SPM interpretation rules that define the overall behavior of the PDS. We can predefine a pool of functionalities that may be useful in different versions of PDS. These functionalities include a synchronization mechanism for concurrent activities, event handling, sending notification about events to interested parties over e-mail, displaying task flowcharts in graphical form, and standard task navigation use cases. All these facilities are designed based on the SPM and can be customized to the realities of a given project.

4.6   Conclusions

Model-based design is effective in designing adaptable software. The idea is to create an explicit mode of an application domain (or any part of it), store the model in tables, and let tables drive the algorithmic part of tool implementation. By changing models (that is, data in tables) we can adapt tool behavior without the need to modify algorithms.

We illustrated model-based design of software tools; however, the approach can be applied to enhance maintainability of any program, not only software tools.

The model-based approach addresses a class of variations and changes that can be expressed in terms of model modifications. The limitation of model-based design is that variant features and changes whose impact goes beyond model capabilities must be implemented in an ad hoc way.

In cases when most of the evolutionary changes are confined to a priori developed models, model-based design is to some extent effective in long-term evolution, as all the system releases are produced by model instantiation. Still, we face problems in the area of selective feature injection into certain system releases, other releases remaining unaffected. By implementing selective features in the generic algorithmic core of software definition, we propagate features to all the releases, which is not desirable. Therefore, such features must be manually implemented into system releases that need them. Such a solution, however, disconnects modified system releases from the generic core. Consequently, each release modified in such an ad hoc way must be further maintained as a separate product. This problem is common to development approaches based on software generation from higher-level specifications.

References

1. Chen, P.P., The entity-relationship model: towards a unified view of data, *ACM Transactions on Database Systems*, 1(1), 9–36, 1976.
2. Chee, C.L., Jarzabek, S., and Paul, R., F-metric: a WWW-based framework for intelligent formulation and analysis of metric queries, *Journal of Systems and Software*, No. 43, 119–132, 1998.
3. Chee, C.L., Jarzabek, S., and Ramamoorthy, C.V., An intelligent process for formulating and answering project queries, *Proceedings of the 6th International Conference on Software Engineering and Knowledge Engineering, SEKE'96*, Nevada, June 1996, pp. 309–316.
4. Clements, P. and Northrop, L., *Software Product Lines: Practices and Patterns*, Addison-Wesley, Boston, 2002.
5. Finkelstein, A., Kramer, J., Nusebeh, B., Eds., *Software Process Modeling*, Research Studies Press, England.
6. Hayes, J., Griswold, W.G., and Moskovics, S., Component design of retargetable program analysis tools that reuse intermediate representations, *22nd International Conference on Software Engineering ICSE'00*, Limerick, Ireland, June 2000, pp. 356–365.
7. Jackson, D. and Jackson, M., Problem decomposition for reuse, *Software Engineering Journal*, 19–30, January 1996.
8. Jacobson, I., Griss, M., and Jonsson, P., *Software Reuse: Architecture, Process and Organization for Business Success*, ACM Press, New York, Addison Wesley Longman, 1997.

9. Jarzabek, S., Modeling multiple domains for software reuse, *Proceedings of the Symposium on Software Reusability, SSR'97*, Boston, May 1997, ACM Press, pp. 65–79.

10. Jarzabek, S., Design of flexible static program analysers with *PQL, IEEE Transactions on Software Engineering*, 24(3), 197–215, March 1998.

11. Jarzabek, S., Specifying and generating multilanguage software development environments, *Software Engineering Journal*, 5(2), 125–137, March 1990.

12. Jarzabek, S. and Wang, G., Model-based design of reverse engineering tools, *Journal of Software Maintenance: Research and Practice*, No. 10, 353–380, 1998.

13. Jarzabek, S. and Ling, T.W., A conceptual model for business re-engineering methods and tools, *Proceedings of the 14th International Conference on Object-Oriented and Entity-Relationship Modeling, OO-ER'95*, Queensland, Australia, December 12–15, 1995, in Lecture Notes in Computer Science, Springer-Verlag, Germany, December 1995, pp. 260–269.

14. Jarzabek, S. and Ling, T.W., Model-based design of tools for business understanding and re-engineering, *Appendum: Proceedings of the 2nd Working Conference on Reverse Engineering, WCRE*, Toronto, Canada, July 14–16, 1995, IEEE Computer Society Press, Los Alamitos, CA, pp. 324–333; also published in *Proceedings of the 7th International Workshop on Computer Aided Software Engineering, CASE'95*, Toronto, Canada, July 10–14, 1995, IEEE Computer Society Press, Los Alamitos, CA, pp. 328–337.

15. Jarzabek, S. and Huang, R., The Case for User-Centered CASE Tools, *Communications of ACM*, August 1998, pp. 93–99.

16. Lung, C. and Urban, J., Analogical approach for software reuse, *Proceedings of the Golden West International Conference On Intelligent Systems*, Reno, NV, June 1992, pp. 194–200.

17. Lung, C. and Urban, J., An approach to the classification of domain models in support of analogical reuse, *ACM SIGSOFT Symposium on Software Reusability, SSR'95*, Seatle, 1995, pp. 169–178.

18. McClure, C., *CASE is Software Automation*, Prentice Hall, 1989.

19. Ohsuga, S., Role of model in intelligent activity — a unified approach to automation of model building, in *Information Modelling and Knowledge Bases VI*, Kangassalo, H., Jaakkola, H, Ohsuga, S., and Wangler, B., Eds., IOS Press, Amsterdam, pp. 27–42.

20. Parnas, D., On the Criteria to Be Used in Decomposing Software into Modules, *Communications of the ACM*, 15(12), December 1972, pp.1053–1058.

21. Pettersson, U. and Jarzabek, S., Industrial experience with building a web portal product line using a lightweight, reactive approach, *ESEC-FSE'05, European Software Engineering Conference and ACM SIGSOFT Symposium on the Foundations of Software Engineering*, ACM Press, Lisbon, September 2005, pp. 326–335 .

22. Prieto-Diaz, R., Domain analysis for reusability, *Proceedings of the COMPSAC'87*, 1987, pp. 23–29.

23. Rajapakse, D.C., Exploiting Similarity Patterns in Web Applications for Enhanced Genericity and Maintainability, Ph.D. thesis, National University of Singapore, 2006.

24. Rumbaugh, J., Jacobson, I., and Booch, G., *The Unified Modeling Language — Reference Manual*, Addison-Wesley, 1999.

25. Stirewalt, R.E. and Dillon, L.K., A component-based approach to building formal analysis tools, *23rd International Conference on Software Engineering ICSE'01*, Toronto, Canada, May 2001, pp. 67–176.

26. Teh, H.Y., Jarzabek, S., and Tiako, P., WWW-based communication tool for distributed team-based software development, *Proceedings of the Conference Systemics, Cybernetics and Informatics and the International Conference on Information Systems Analysis and Synthesis*, SCI'99/ISAS'99, Florida, August 1999.

27. Viljamaa, J., Reverse engineering framework reuse interfaces, *Proceedings of the 9th European Software Engineering Conference* held jointly with *10th ACM SIGSOFT International Symposium on Foundations of Software Engineering*, Helsinki, Finland, September 2003, pp. 217–226.

28. Yang, J. and Jarzabek, S., Applying a generative technique for enhanced reuse on J2EE platform, *4th International Conference on Generative Programming and Component Engineering, GPCE'05*, September 29–October 1, 2005, pp. 237–255.

Chapter 5

Evolution of Versions and Configuration Management

Chapter Summary

We move on now from the maintenance of the function of the system's code (considered in Chapter 2 and Chapter 3), and of the functionality of the application (considered in Chapter 4), to the evolution of the system's code and a sequence of system releases. Software configuration management (SCM) is "the discipline of controlling the evolution of complex software systems" [18]. SCM tools [5,18] are commonly used in industry to manage software changes, especially to support evolution. SCMs store the history of component versions and their configurations, created in the response to evolutionary changes. Each system release is a configuration of component versions stored in an SCM repository.

In this chapter, we go through an example of software evolution with Concurrent Versions System (CVS) (http://www.nongnu.org/cvs/). CVS is probably the most widely used SCM tool in industry, especially in the development of open source projects [9]. CVS is based on concepts of the pioneering and highly influential versioning system called RCS [17].

We focus on some typical situations that arise during evolution, and try to address them with CVS. We observe that some of the evolution problems, notably

95

explosion of similar component versions, are difficult to avoid as long as evolution is managed in terms of specific component versions.

5.1 A Working Example: FRS Evolution

A facility reservation system (FRS) was introduced in Chapter 1. Its functions and multiple versions are now briefly summarized. The facility reservation system (FRS) helps users reserve facilities such as meeting rooms. FRS users manage (add, delete, and modify) their own reservations or reservations requested by others (middleman). We briefly discussed an FRS evolution example in Chapter 1. For ease of reference, we repeat the FRS description here, with some more details.

The following FRS features are discussed in the evolution example described in this chapter:

- VIEW-RES: reservation viewing methods:
  - FAC: view reservations by facility
  - RES-ID: view reservations by reservation ID
  - DATE: view reservations by date
  - USER: view reservations by user
  - USR-PD: view reservations made for only preferred range of dates
- BR: block reservation — making reservations in bulk
- PAY: charges for reserving facilities
- BRD: discount for block reservations

Figure 5.1 shows the FRS evolution scenario in our study. Circled numbers attached to FRS releases indicate the order in which the releases were implemented. Solid arrows between releases X and Y indicate that X was chosen as a baseline for Y. Dashed arrows between releases X and Y indicate that some features implemented in X were adapted for Y.

We illustrate evolution of FRS supported by the evolution history stored in the CVS repository.

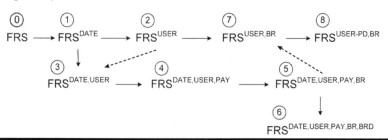

Figure 5.1   Stages in facility reservation system (FRS) evolution.

Stage 1: Suppose one of our customers requests a new feature, to view reservations by date (DATE, for short). Having implemented the required enhancement, we have two versions of the FRS in use, namely, the original FRS and the enhanced system FRS^{DATE}.

Stage 2: After some time, yet another customer would like to view reservations by user (USER). Having implemented this new enhancement, we have three versions of the FRS in use: the original FRS, FRS^{DATE}, and FRS^{USER}.

Stage 3: We also realize that the new features may be generally useful for other customers and yet another version $FRS^{DATE,USER}$ may make perfect sense to some of them.

Stage 4: Sometime later, a new customer wants an FRS that supports the concept of payment for reservations (PAY). This includes computing and displaying reservation charges (RC), cancellation charges (CC), bill construction (BC), and Frequent Customer Discount (FCD). Name PAY refers to all such payment features. $FRS^{DATE,USER,PAY}$ results from that enhancement.

Stage 5: Another customer would require block reservations (BR) as well as support for payment ($FRS^{DATE,USER,\ PAY,BR}$)

Stage 6: We include a block reservation discount ($FRS^{DATE,USER,PAY,BR,BRD}$).

Stage 7: We need an FRS with existing features USER and BR ($FRS^{USER,BR}$).

Stage 8: A customer asks us to customize the USER feature to view reservations made for only preferred range of dates (($FRS^{USER-PD,BR}$).

Analysis of FRS requirements and implementation revealed the following dependencies among features (revisit definitions in Section 1.3):

- DATE $\overset{-i}{\leftrightarrow}$ USER (mutually implementation-independent features)
- PAY $\overset{-f}{\leftrightarrow}$ BR (mutually functionally-independent features)
- PAY $\overset{i}{\leftrightarrow}$ BR
- PAY $\overset{i}{\rightarrow}$ {DATE, USER}
- PAY $\overset{i}{\rightarrow}$ FRS (meaning that most FRS components are implementation dependent on PAY)
- {BR, PAY} $\overset{f}{\rightarrow}$ BRD

5.2   FRS Component Architecture

A component architecture, design assumptions, and implementation technologies, as well as underlying platforms (such as J2EE™ or .NET™) define the context within which software is evolved. A software architecture is described by a set of components that interact with one another through well-defined interfaces (connectors) to deliver the required system behavior. In this chapter, we focus on components only, and will address connectors in Chapter 12.

FRS components are organized into three tiers, namely, the user interface, business logic, and database tiers, depicted in Figure 5.2. In the architecture terminology, a "tier" is just a large-granularity component that may contain many smaller components. Each tier provides services to the tier above it and serves requests from the tier below it. User interface (UI) components allow FRS administrators and reservation requestors to interact with the system to manage users, facilities, and reservations. The UI components handle the initialization, display, and event handling for the various Java panels used in reservation, user, and facility management. The server, business logic (BL) tier, defines the functionality of the FRS to accomplish various actions. Server components provide the actual event-handling code for the various user interface widgets (e.g., buttons). There are also components that set up and shut down connections with the DBMS component. The database tier is responsible for providing data access and storage services to the business logic tier. The database components include tables or databases to store data related to users, facilities, and reservations.

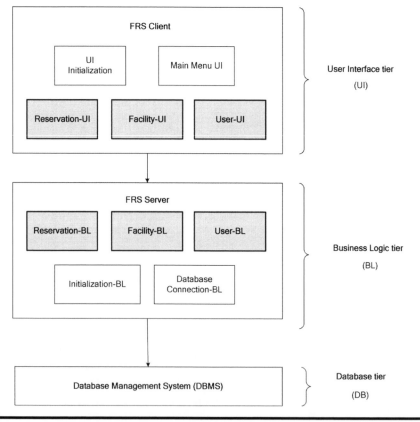

Figure 5.2 Tiers and component groups in facility reservation system (FRS) architecture.

FRS is implemented in EJB™ and Java, with MySQL as the database server.

FRS is structured as follows: FRS consists of subsystems, modules, and components to manage reservations (Reservation), facilities (Facility), and users (User). Each module (e.g., ViewRes to view reservations) is implemented by a user interface component (ViewRes-UI) and a business logic component (ViewRes-BL).

Shaded boxes in Figure 5.2 denote component groupings in FRS subsystems as follows:

Reservation-UI: all the user interface components for the Reservation subsystem
Reservation-BL: all the business logic components for the Reservation subsystem
Facility-UI: all the user interface components for the Facility subsystem
Facility-BL: all the business logic components for the Facility subsystem
User-UI: all the user interface components for the User subsystem
User-BL: all the business logic components for the User subsystem

Table 5.1 shows some of modules and components in user interface and business logic tiers.

5.3 Evolution of FRS with CVS

CVS keeps track of versions of source code files, documents, and other software artifacts resulting from changes applied to software during evolution. Versions of software artifacts are stored under unique identifiers. Each version of a software artifact may branch into subversions, as shown in Figure 5.3.

Each system release is defined as a configuration of specific versions of system components.

Besides usual SCM capabilities such as version control, CVS also performs conflict resolution and provides check-in and check-out facilities to assist parallel development. Here, we concentrate only on version control and management of system releases. We store component versions and their configurations that occurred in released systems in a CVS repository. Each such component (or component configuration) accommodates some combination of variant features. Typically, components are files. The following is a development life cycle for a new system release, S^{NEW}:

1. Analyze requirements for S^{NEW}.
2. Understand similarities and differences among S^{NEW} and earlier releases.
3. Select from the CVS repository configurations of component versions "best matching" S^{NEW}. We call this S^{NEW} component the *baseline*.
4. Customize the selected component baseline to fully meet the requirements of S^{NEW}.
5. Test and integrate customized components to obtain S^{NEW}.
6. Validate S^{NEW} to see if it meets its requirements.

Table 5.1   FRS Component Architecture: User Interface and Business Logic Tiers

Subsystem	Modules	User Interface Components	Business Logic Components
Reservation	ViewRes	ViewRes-UI	ViewRes-BL
	CreateRes	CreateRes-UI	CreateRes-BL
	DeleteRes	DeleteRes-UI	DeleteRes-BL
	UpdateRes	UpdateRes-UI	UpdateRes-BL
Facility	ViewFac	ViewFac-UI	ViewFac-BL
	CreateFac	CreateFac-UI	CreateFac-BL
	DeleteFac	DeleteFac-UI	DeleteFac-BL
	UpdateFac	UpdateFac-UI	UpdateFac-BL
User	ViewUser	ViewUser-UI	ViewUser-BL
	CreateUser	CreateUser-UI	CreateUser-BL
	DeleteUser	DeleteUser-UI	DeleteUser-BL
	UpdateUser	UpdateUser-UI	UpdateUser-BL

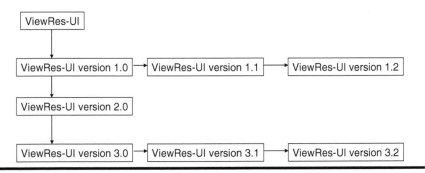

Figure 5.3   Version tree of ViewRes-UI facility reservation system (FRS) component.

We may need to iterate over the preceding life cycle, changing component selection or customization, even revising some of the requirements, until we obtain an acceptable S^{NEW}.

In this study, we focus on issues related to component selection (Step 3) and customization (Step 4). These two activities greatly impact productivity of programmers during evolution: The quality of selection determines the follow-up customization effort. In the following sections, typical problems developers must solve during these two steps are analyzed. Our analysis is based on the evolution scenario depicted in Figure 5.1.

5.4 Reuse of Features Implemented in Past Releases When Building New System Releases

Reuse of features already implemented in past releases is the main concern when selecting components. Based on CVS release history, selecting components "best matching" a newly built system release is a problem in itself. We must take into account functionality as well as the follow-up customization and integration effort.

We start with $FRS^{DATE,USER}$. We can build $FRS^{DATE,USER}$ by (1) selecting FRS^{DATE} and then customizing it according to FRS^{USER}, or, vice versa, (2) selecting FRS^{USER} and then customizing it according to FRS^{DATE}. If we choose scenario (1), the customization effort is a combined effort of:

- Finding components affected by feature USER in FRS^{USER}, and extracting relevant code
- Analyzing the impact of feature USER on FRS^{DATE}
- Implementing feature USER on FRS^{DATE}

As feature USER has been implemented in FRS^{USER}, we would like to reuse feature implementation in $FRS^{DATE,USER}$. For illustration, we show steps involved in scenario 1:

1. Select a previous version of FRS as a starting point. Here, we choose FRS^{DATE}.
2. Retrieve version FRS^{USER}. We make use of this version to update the FRS^{DATE}, rather than reimplement the USER feature from scratch.
3. Extract business logic action to "view reservation by user" from FRS^{USER} and modify ReservationManager component.
4. Extract user interface code to "view reservations by user" and code to call the business logic action to "view reservation by user" from FRS^{USER} and modify reservation user interface, Reservation-UI, accordingly.

For implementation-independent features, such as DATE and USER, the preceding steps are quite simple and are accomplished by branch and merge ("update" command) facilities of CVS. As all the implications of scenarios 1 and 2 on evolution are the same, we conclude that it makes no difference whether we choose 1 or 2.

Should scenarios 1 and 2 require different customizations to accommodate the new feature, the logical choice would be to pick components from FRS releases in which adding the new feature requires less customization effort. A number of issues may complicate the follow-up customization, and therefore may impact the right selection of components. In particular:

1. DATE and USER might impact FRS components differently; for example, DATE could affect more components and in more complicated ways than USER; or implementation of feature USER might be well documented, whereas the documentation for the implementation of DATE might be missing.

2. DATE might be implementation dependent on USER, but USER might also be implementation independent of DATE.

3. DATE might be implementation dependent on yet other features that are not relevant to USER.

4. DATE might have been modified in FRS^{DATE} in a way that is not required for FRS^{USER}.

All of these considerations could affect the customization effort of scenario 1 versus scenario 2, and should be taken into account when selecting the component baseline for $FRS^{DATE,USER}$.

We now illustrate point 3 in the previous list. Suppose we have already implemented features f_1 and f_2 in releases FRS^{f1} and $FRS^{f1,f2}$, and would like to have feature f_1 and a new feature, f_3, in release $FRS^{f1,f3}$. Intuitively, we would pick FRS^{f1} as the closest configuration, because for $FRS^{f1,f2}$, we would have to remove f_2 before adding in f_3. This would probably be the right selection if f_3 and f_2 were not similar to each other. However, if f_3 was similar to f_2, $FRS^{f1,f2}$ would be a better choice, as it would be easy to turn f_2 into f_3. We see an instance of this situation when implementing FRS^{USER}, with the initial FRS and FRS^{DATE} as starting points. As features DATE and USER are similar, we should pick FRS^{DATE} as an FRS^{USER} baseline.

The usual situation is that any new system release, say, S^{NEW}, may include many features implemented in variant forms in past releases. Variant forms of the same feature stem from implementation dependencies among features. Existing features may also be implementation dependent on new features required in S^{NEW}. The following example illustrates reuse of features in view of implementation dependencies among them. In developing $FRS^{USER,BR}$, we select FRS^{USER} as our baseline and add BR (block reservation) to it. As BR has been implemented only in $FRS^{DATE,USER,PAY,BR}$ previously, we make use of this implementation. The customization of FRS^{USER} includes:

1. Finding components affected by feature BR in $FRS^{DATE,USER,PAY,BR}$ and extracting relevant code

2. Analyzing the impact of feature BR on FRS^{USER}

3. Implementing feature BR on FRS^{USER}

In step 1 the code extracted for BR is inclusive of code to calculate payment for BR. In step 2 we realize that the code needed for BR here should be independent of the code for PAY (payment). This causes a conflict with code extracted in step 1, as implementation of BR was according to the implementation dependency PAY $\leftrightarrow$ BR (payment and block reservation are mutually implementation dependent) previously. Thus, in step 3 we are unable to reuse BR directly. The parts where PAY was involved in BR need to be removed. If information on modifications made for PAY in BR is not available, implementation becomes more difficult. Upon implementation, a new variant form of BR is produced.

Suppose we have picked a configuration of component versions that we believe makes a good baseline for a new release, and removed unwanted features (if any) from that configuration. To add in new features, we fetch the previous version that contains a given feature, and extract the relevant code from that version. Reuse of features is hindered by the fact that the same feature may be implemented differently in different system releases. The implementation of a feature may span many system components. The process of (possibly) retrieving many versions of feature implementation and extracting the correct portions of that feature implementation may be tedious and time consuming. Tools such as diff and Bonsai [3] are typically used to aid in feature extraction and reuse. However, diff shows all the differences between two files, not modifications relevant to a specific feature. If it is too difficult to reuse a feature from a previous version, a feature must be implemented from scratch, increasing redundancy and complexity.

The preceding discussion shows that, at times, the knowledge of already-implemented features and of feature similarities may not be readily available from the CVS repository. We can improve the situation by linking logical groupings of detailed changes done to system components to relevant sources of change (e.g., a request for a new feature or for a modification of a certain feature in some system release). The concept of a "change set" has been introduced in SCM research [5,13,14], and is available in some SCMs (e.g., Synergy/CM [16]). In CVS, we can do frequent check-in and check-out to avoid intermixing, in any single component version, multiple changes done for different purposes. This can help in extracting feature implementation. Enumerating "change sets" corresponding to interdependent features, especially in the presence of variant ways in which the same feature can be implemented in different system releases, may produce a complicated web of information that may pose nontrivial problems for effective feature reuse and modification. In Part II we describe an alternative way of addressing these problems, with mixed-strategy mechanisms capable of representing changes and affected components in a unified, generic form amenable to automation.

We also try to address the preceding problems with external documentation. For example, we have recorded code lines inserted/deleted/modified with respect to a baseline. Such documentation can help when we deal with simple situations such as reusing implementation of feature DATE to build FRS^{USER}, but in other cases different information may be required. For example, when modifying FRS^{DATE} to accommodate USER feature and build $FRS^{DATE,USER}$, we would only need to modify the lines that differ between the two, as both DATE and USER are implemented in a similar way. As there are possibly many other different cases to consider, the external documentation complementing the information we can get from the CVS repository would have to vary to cater to those nuances. In addition, there are well-known problems with keeping documentation up to date with evolving programs. A study of software development in two industries [6] showed that despite the fact that documentation comprised thousands of pages, selected components often implemented requirements insufficiently or turned out to be incompatible.

The process of selecting components to minimize the customization effort may be quite complicated. Much information has to be repeatedly extracted but is not explicitly represented in the evolution history stored in the CVS repository. As it is difficult to see all the implications of component selection, often the choice of components for customization is suboptimal, leading to a high cost of evolution.

Deelstra et al. [6] mention that, using such an approach, "development effort is spent on implementing functionality that highly resembles the functionality already implemented in reusable assets or in previous projects." In their case studies, it was observed that product derivation at a company consisted of selecting several hundreds of components, and this occasionally led to a situation where components were not found, though they were present. Many of the functionalities, though already implemented in earlier releases, could not be reused and had to be reimplemented all over again.

5.5   Adding New Features to a System Release

The new feature is either completely different from the existing features, or it is similar to an existing one. A completely different feature must be implemented from scratch, as no previous knowledge of it exists. This situation was observed when developing $FRS^{DATE,USER,PAY,BR}$. We selected $FRS^{DATE,USER,PAY}$ as a component baseline for implementing a new feature BR (block reservation). However, PAY (payment feature) and BR are mutually implementation dependent: PAY $\leftrightarrow$ BR. The customization of $FRS^{DATE,USER,PAY}$ includes:

1. Implementing the BR feature while adding code to calculate payment for BR
2. Modifying the PAY feature to accommodate specific needs of block reservation

We end up with two variant forms for PAY: PAY implemented without BR in $FRS^{DATE,USER,PAY}$, and PAY implemented with BR in $FRS^{DATE,USER,PAY,BR}$.

We can save effort (and also enhance the clarity of the design) if we implement similar features in a similar way. FRS^{DATE} illustrates a simple case. DATE (view-by-date) is similar to the FAC (view-reservation-by-facility) method implemented in the initial FRS. The customization effort includes:

1. Finding components affected by feature FAC in FRS and extracting relevant code
2. Customizing copied code to obtain DATE

Recognizing similar features based on the information stored in CVS, especially in relation to feature dependencies, is not easy.

5.6 Selective Propagation of New Features to Past Releases

To accommodate a new feature into past releases, we must upgrade each release separately, taking into account unique feature dependencies that may exist in different releases.

The propagation process is time consuming, error prone, and contributes to component version explosion.

Consider the case of $FRS^{USER-PD,BR}$. USER-PD (view-by-user for a preferred date) is a slight modification of the USER (view-by-user) reservation method. The feature USER-PD is implemented by simply customizing code for USER. The same modifications must be manually implemented in every other system release in which the PD feature has to be incorporated.

5.7 The Visibility of Changes during Evolution

The visibility of changes is hindered by feature dependencies and the fact that implementation of a feature may span many components. To illustrate how implementation dependencies affect the visibility of changes, we show steps involved in enhancing $FRS^{DATE,USER,PAY}$ with feature BR (features PAY and BR are mutually implementation dependent: PAY $\leftrightarrow$ BR):

1. Add an option for selecting block reservations to the reservation user interface menu in Reservation-UI components.
2. Add options for selecting different block reservation methods (reserving multiple facilities or multiple time slots) to the Reservation-UI. Upon selecting an option, the user is asked to provide input needed for that option.
3. Add code to call block reservation methods for each option. Add an option to delete block reservations in the menu of Reservation-UI and code for deleting block reservations in a relevant business logic component.
4. Calculate the payment for block reservation.
5. Modify Payment component to accommodate block reservation as follows: add methods to calculate the total cost of all the block reservations, store the reservation cost in a vector (rather than a single value as it was in the case of a single reservation), and store the total number of block reservations.

In step 4, we modify code for BR to deal with payment. In step 5, we modify code for PAY to accommodate BR. Changes are embedded into the code and we cannot discriminate among parts of the code in BR that have been modified to accommodate PAY and vice versa.

In FRS^{DATE,USER,PAY,BR,BRD}, block reservation discount is functionally dependent on both block reservation and payment: {BR, PAY} $\xrightarrow{f}$ BRD, in addition to the implementation dependency mentioned earlier. Steps to implement this FRS release are as follows:

1. Modify code in PAY (payment). For BR (block reservation), different calculations are needed due to BRD (block reservation discount).
2. Modify code in block reservation methods to inform the user that BRD is included when calculating payment.

As before, it is not clear which modifications relate to a feature in question (BRD, in this case). However, the difficulty is more severe now owing to the complicated dependencies. In step 2, to modify PAY, we must first find code for BR in PAY, and then embed the code for BRD in it. Similarly, in step 2, we embed code for BRD into the code for PAY in BR.

5.8 Explosion of Variant Features and Feature Dependencies

In studies described in [6] it was observed that even small changes to interfaces led to new component versions. This was also observed in our case study. For example, we created eight versions of component Reservation-UI, as each FRS release (Figure 5.1) required some modifications of that component. Feature dependencies also caused component versions to multiply. For example, component Payment had three different versions: PAY implemented alone, PAY implemented with BR, and PAY with BR and BRD.

As more variant features are added, the number of component versions explodes. Just adding six features (DATE, USER, PAY, BR, BRD, USER-PD) to the FRS produced 22 new component versions.

A technique sometimes used to limit version explosion is to add features in a permanent way, and to control their availability in a specific system installation using runtime parameters. As this technique addresses the problem at the program implementation rather than at the design level, it leads to complex programs. This approach also results in a larger resource footprint with "dead code," which may be undesirable. An example of a solution trying to address this problem is the one by Koala [15].

The problem of explosion of similar component versions seems to be inherent in object and component technologies [1,2,10–12]. Although supporting techniques can be used to extract change information from the component history [5,8,9], these techniques deal with symptoms and do not attack the root of the problem.

5.9 Lessons Learned

Reuse of existing features and propagation of new features in CVS is based on extraction of relevant code from past releases, using the CVS update operation. When a component is modified, only the differences between the original version and a modified one are stored to minimize storage. However, different versions of the same component are treated as different entities in the sense that a change done in version 1 of component A will not be reflected in version 2 of component A. Therefore, changes meant for many component versions must be manually propagated to the versions in question, taking into account possible subtle variations in change implementation across component versions, not to mention the likelihood of making errors. Reuse of existing and new features is therefore tedious, time consuming, and error prone.

Tools such as diff and Bonsai [3] are helpful, but the former shows all the differences between two files, not modifications relevant to a specific feature. When feature dependencies are involved, the modifications needed may be different in each release, and usefulness of diff becomes even more problematic. Propagation of new features to past releases also poses problems. Table 5.2 summarizes modifications of FRS components at various evolution stages.

Consecutive changes affecting code over time are absorbed into the code, and it becomes difficult to see relationships among features. The concept of "change set" is a significant step toward addressing these problems.

It is quite significant that we could observe some very basic difficulties despite the simplicity of our case study. These difficulties will necessarily become magnified when we move into the deeper waters of evolution.

5.10 Related Work

Advanced SCM features [5,13,14] and commercial tools such as Synergy/CM [16] improve the visibility of information that matters in evolution. So do techniques for extracting a release history stored in an SCM repository [7–9]. One such advanced SCM concept is a change set (or change package) [5,14,16]. A change set represents a logical grouping of modifications spanning multiple system components. As each source of change usually affects more than one component, the changes across all the affected components are classified under one change identifier. Change sets increase the visibility of changes, and propagating changes across component versions becomes easier. SCMs such as Molhado [19] allow developers to control changes at the level of system architecture and manage versions of architectural elements (e.g., subsystems). Change sets and the ability to manage evolution at the architecture level are powerful concepts. Still, we believe that even with application of advanced approaches, system evolution in terms of concrete component versions faces some inherent difficulties; in particular, the problem of component version

Table 5.2   Summary of Evolution Stages

Stage	#mod	Comments
FRS^{DATE}	3	Simple implementation
FRS^{USER}	3	Simple implementation
FRS^{DATE,USER}	3	Simple code extraction from the previous version
FRS^{DATE,USER,PAY}	35	Implementation is not difficult though it affects many components
FRS^{DATE,USER,PAY,BR}	9	Difficult to see where code was added for BR in PAY and vice versa
FRS^{DATE,USER,PAY,BR,BRD}	3	Difficult to see relationship between features
FRS^{USER,BR}	12	Difficulty in extracting the BR code without PAY
FRS$^{USER-PD,BR}$	4	Simple customization of USER method

explosion is difficult to solve within the SCM-based approach to evolution. Working with hundreds of similar components is bound to be a challenge, even if we provide extra means to help one understand changes that affected the components.

Techniques for visualization of release history stored in an SCM repository [9] and for mining useful information from it [7,8] attack the problem from yet another angle: by applying heuristics, these techniques can extract groups of modifications possibly related to the same source of change.

We believe advanced SCM tools and techniques for information mining from SCM repositories alleviates some of the problems observed when working with CVS. However, we have been unable to find a detailed-enough study demonstrating how the evolution challenges discussed in this chapter can be mitigated using advanced SCM approaches.

Work on product line approach to reuse [4] is relevant to evolution problems addressed in this chapter. Industrial practice shows that the evolution challenges discussed in Chapter 1 often remain unsolved in the context of product lines [6].

5.11   Conclusions

We described a study of problems arising in evolution supported by CVS. We identified the following difficulties: (1) the difficulty of controlling explosion of component versions in view of many new features and feature dependencies arising in evolution; (2) the difficulty of propagating new features in variant forms to selected releases; and (3) the difficulty of reusing functionality implemented in past system releases in building new releases. As we were progressing through evolutionary changes, the overall complexity of the knowledge of an evolving system was growing rapidly at a rate disproportionate to the complexity of each individual change.

We believe the preceding problems, in some form and to some extent emerge when trying to manage similarities and differences in evolving software at the level of specific component versions (files or architecture level components). The net effect of these problems is that one fails to see the impact of variant features implemented in various system releases clearly enough to make practical use of the accumulated evolution knowledge. As a result, one tends to view each system release as a separate product. Failing to fully exploit commonalities inherent across a family of releases leads to more evolution effort than necessary.

Newer SCM tools [5,13,14,19] implement change sets and other features that considerably advance support for evolution; however, we have been unable to find a detailed-enough study demonstrating how they mitigate evolution challenges discussed in this chapter, in particular, explosion of component versions. Furthermore, these advanced SCM tools have not been widely used in industry as of yet.

References

1. Batory, D., Sarvela, J.N., and Rauschmayer, A., Scaling step-wise refinement, *Proceedings of the International Conference on Software Engineering, ICSE'03*, May 2003, Portland, OR, pp. 187–197.
2. Biggerstaff, T., The library scaling problem and the limits of concrete component reuse, *3rd International Conference on Software Reuse, ICSR'94*, 1994, pp. 102–109.
3. Bonsai, a tool that performs queries on CVS repositories, http://www.mozilla.org/bonsai.html.
4. Clements, P. and Northrop, L., *Software Product Lines: Practices and Patterns*, Addison-Wesley, Boston, 2002.
5. Conradi, R. and Westfechtel, B., Version models for software configuration management, *ACM Computing Surveys*, 30(2), 232–282, 1998.
6. Deelstra, S., Sinnema, M., and Bosch, J., Experiences in software product families: problems and issues during product derivation, *Proceedings of the Software Product Lines Conference, SPLC3*, Boston, August 2004, LNCS 3154, Springer-Verlag, pp. 165–182.
7. Fischer, M., Pinzger, M., and Gall, H., Populating a release database from version control and bug tracking systems, *International Conference on Software Maintenance, ICSM'03*, September 2003, pp. 23–32.
8. Gall, H., Jazayeri, M., and Krajewski, J., CVS release history data for detecting logical couplings, *Proceedings of the International Workshop on Principles of Software Evolution, IWPSE'03*, September 2003, Helsinki, pp. 13–23.

9. German, D., Hindle, A., and Jordan, N., Visualizing the evolution of software using softChange, *Proceedings of the 16th International Conference on Software Engineering and Knowledge Engineering, SEKE'04,* Banff, Canada, June 2004, pp. 1–6.

10. Jarzabek, S. and Li, S., Eliminating redundancies with a composition with adaptation meta-programming technique, *Proceedings of the ESEC-FSE'03, European Software Engineering Conference and Symposium on the Foundations of Software Engineering,* ACM Press, September 2003, Helsinki, pp. 237–246.

11. Jarzabek, S. and Li, S., Unifying clones with a generative programming technique: a case study, *Journal of Software Maintenance and Evolution: Research and Practice,* 18(4), 267–292, July–August 2006.

12. Jarzabek, S. and Seviora, R., Engineering components for ease of customization and evolution, *IEEE Proceedings — Software,* 147(6), December 2000, pp. 237–248, a special issue on Component-based Software Engineering.

13. van der Lingen, R. and van der Hoek, A., Experimental, pluggable infrastructure for modular configuration management policy composition, *Proceedings of the 26th International Conference on Software Engineering, ICSE'04, Edinburgh, U.K., May 2004.*

14. Milligan, T. and Bellagio, D., *What Is Software Configuration Management?,* Addison Wesley Professional, 2005.

15. Ommering, von R., Building product populations with software components, *International Conference on Software Engineering, ICSE'02,* May 2002, pp. 255–265.

16. Synergy/CM http://www.telelogic.com/products/synergy/.

17. Tichy, W., Design, implementation and evaluation of a revision control system, *6th International Conference on Software Engineering,* September 1982, pp. 48–67.

18. Tichy, W., Tools for software configuration management, *Proceedings of the International Workshop on Software Configuration Management,* Grassau, 1988, Teubner Verlag, pp. 1–20.

19. Nguyen, T.N., Munson, E.V., Boyland, J.T., and Thao, C., Architectural software configuration management in Molhado, *Proceedings of the International Conference Software maintenance, ICSM'2004,* Chicago, IL, September 2004, pp. 296–305.

Chapter 6

Limits of Conventional Techniques

Chapter Summary

In Chapter 2 through Chapter 5, we discussed static program analysis, reverse engineering, model-based design, and software configuration management (SCM) techniques. We commented on their strengths and limitations in addressing the challenges of software maintenance and long-term evolution.

In this chapter, we further highlight the difficulties of combating the problems of change with conventional techniques, in view of the maintenance and evolution challenges discussed in Chapter 1. We also briefly preview some of the remedies to fight these problems using unconventional approaches. With emphasis on the complexity inherent in software, we focus on the following problems: Poor visibility of past changes triggers much rework that could be avoided, should the knowledge of such changes be made available to developers. Each new change is reinvented afresh and implemented in its own way, despite possible similarities to past changes. By ignoring similarity of evolution patterns, we reinvent the way changes must be implemented, redoing the same kind of costly change impact analysis all over again. We blow up code size and complexity. The number of similar component versions explodes, degrading conceptual integrity of the program design. The overall complexity of an evolving program grows, making any future changes even harder.

This chapter motivates the mixed-strategy approach discussed in Part II, which applies a generative technique to address the problems mentioned earlier. The premise of mixed-strategy is that we can ease the aforementioned problems by preserving the knowledge of past changes in a form that enables us to effectively reuse this knowledge when implementing new changes, which is what the concept of reuse-based evolution is about.

6.1 Software Complexity Factor

Software complexity is the main factor affecting productivity of maintenance programmers. The three primary approaches to managing software complexity are componentization (divide and conquer), separation of concerns, and abstraction. In his famous paper "No Silver Bullet" [4], Brooks argues that whether we use a machine language or a high-level programming language, we cannot get rid of programs' essential complexities. The technological advances of the last few decades have not succeeded in proving Brooks wrong and, indeed, we do not think it will ever be possible to eliminate such complexity.

Indeed, it is difficult to find a general way to reduce program complexity beyond a certain threshold. Three main factors determine the essential complexity threshold: (1) the complexity of a problem and its solution at the concept level; (2) the complexity of a problem solution by means of a computer program; and (3) the complexity of mappings and interactions between the conceptual and program-level solutions.

The fact that conceptual and programmatic concerns cannot be cleanly separated one from another in program components is one of the important forces that constrains our efforts in using componentization in combating software complexity. Very often, we cannot make software conform to the rules of a LEGO model, which works so well for hardware construction [2,23]. This difficulty of achieving clean decomposability is an important difference between hardware and software.

Software components are less stable and interact in more complex ways than hardware components. They are often changed, rather than replaced, and therefore must be much more flexible than hardware components. Another important difference is that we never try to change hardware as often and in such drastic ways as software. Consequently, software architectures are softer — less stable and more intangible — than architectures in traditional engineering disciplines, and must be flexible to be practical. This fragile nature of software components and architectures determines, to a large extent, how well various techniques can effectively help in maintenance and evolution.

Programs that are not subject to frequent and unpredictable changes can be effectively componentized (e.g., some of the middleware service components). As the technology changes, such components are most often replaced by new ones (like an obsolete hardware device) rather than evolved. But stable or exchangeable components are not the source of our main software problems. What is really difficult to work with is software in unstable, poorly understood domains [2]. Any successful program operating in that kind of environment is bound to change often. Information hiding [21] and separation of concerns [9] are the two main mechanisms for containing changes. But again, if we could always localize and hide the impact of change into a small number of components, we would not have a problem with changing programs. Computing concerns (or aspects) are not easily separated either, although recently there have been a number of attempts to provide a suitable mechanism for separating these concerns [20,27].

Modern middleware component platforms (such as .NET™ or J2EE™) use standardized architectures, patterns, and APIs to enable reuse of common service components preimplemented in the platform infrastructure. Model-driven engineering can further hide the complexity induced by platforms providing domain-specific solutions available directly on a platform of our choice [25].

Still, componentization in system areas above the middleware level remains a problem. Software components have not become a commodity to the extent that optimistic forecasts of the late 1990s had predicted (see, for example, Gartner and Cutter Consortium reports).

However, the most serious limitation of componentization as a means of fighting software complexity is that as long as we compose, test, and maintain concrete components, we are bound to face complexity that is proportional to the system size. In a system of thousands of interacting components comprising millions of lines of code, the complexity of validating, testing, and controlling maintenance changes must eventually explode beyond our control. It is a matter of speculation to what extent we can reduce this complexity by composing already-implemented, concrete components. In the author's view, this complexity is part of Brook's essential complexity [4]. It can be helped, but cannot be substantially reduced.

The difficulty of cleanly separating concerns by means of decomposition necessarily hinders changeability. What comes in very handy in this context is the infinite malleability of software, much above any levels that are possible in hardware. Nothing else on the horizon seems more promising than malleability as a potential rescuer in solving the dilemma of easing software changes. Generative approaches [7] apply unconventional means of exploiting software malleability to lower the barrier of software complexity. Some of the well-known techniques attempt to bring Dijkstra's separation of concerns [9] from the concept level down to design and implementation levels. Aspect-oriented programming (AOP) [20], multidimensional separation of concerns (MDSOC) [27], and AHEAD [3] modularize concerns at extra, metalevel planes, beyond conventional software components. Program manipulation (such as aspect weaving in AOP) is then used to produce concrete components from a metalevel program representation. "Configuration knowledge" [7] defines mappings that separate problem domain concerns from the solution space.

Separation of concerns is also a step forward toward more generic program representations. Concerns that we manage to modularize in unconventional ways, as well as conventional modules of primary decomposition (in AOP), become more generic and reusable in multiple contexts, to some extent alleviating the problem of having to deal with a complexity proportional to the size of a physical program.

In Part II, we see how we can exploit the "soft" nature of software with the mixed-strategy approach powered by XVCL [28], a generative program manipulation technique based on frame concepts [2]. XVCL's primary goal is to unify similar program structures with generic, metalevel representations, and also to achieve a fair amount of separation of concerns, as much as it is practical. We comment further on generative approaches to addressing separation of concerns, as well as on an interesting relationship between separation of concerns and generic design principles in Chapter 14.

Other than componentization, we may try to reduce software complexity by raising the level of abstraction of a program representation. This works fine in narrow application domains; by constraining ourselves to a specific application domain, we can make assumptions about its semantics. A domain engineer encodes domain-specific knowledge into a generic, parameterized program solution. A developer, rather than working out all the details of the program solution, writes a concise, declarative problem description in a domain-specific language (DSL). A generator uses DSL specifications to instantiate parameters of a generic solution to produce a custom program. Problem specifications in DSL are much smaller and simpler than the instantiated, complete, and executable program solution. Although we do not reduce essential complexity of the overall program solution, such generation-based domain-specific programming environments shield a programmer from some of the essential complexities, which are now contained in the domain-specific code that is manipulated by a generator. DSL may take many different forms, depending on a domain, such as a formal text (e.g., BNF for a parser generator), visual interface (e.g., GUI), or models (in model-driven engineering approaches [25]).

Unfortunately, abstraction directly translates into productivity gains only in narrow application domains. Still, problems that can be helped with generators may recur in many programs, even in many domains. Abstraction can reduce complexities induced by programming platforms [25]. Finally, abstraction offers modeling notations, such as Unified Modeling Language (UML) [24], that play an important descriptive role.

6.2 Tackling Software Evolution Challenges

Evolution challenges, some of which are discussed in Chapter 1, are not new, and we believe there have been many attempts to address some of them with conventional techniques. There are, however, technical problems with that approach, as change capabilities of conventional techniques are not really geared to tackling evolution challenges. We comment on mature and commonly used techniques, such as parameterization features of programming languages, "design for change" with information hiding, object-oriented (OO) and component-based design, and

SCM. These techniques have been around for long enough for us to evaluate their actual impact on our ability to deal with changes.

Each technique provides a sound solution to some aspect of evolution. Still, collectively, these techniques are limited in effective evolution.

Historically, the main role of programming languages has been to provide abstractions to define code structures to be executed on a computer. Typical abstractions are classes, objects, functions/methods, function invocations, or messages. Change mechanisms have never become powerful enough to make changes visible and tractable. Change mechanisms continued to remain second-class citizens in modeling notations [24], development methodologies, interactive development environments (IDEs), and component platforms, which were necessarily influenced by language concepts.

Generic design aims at achieving nonredundancy by unifying differences among similar program concepts or structures for simplification purposes. Despite its importance in fighting software complexity, generic design capabilities of conventional programming languages and techniques are often insufficient to effectively unify the variety of software similarity patterns that we encounter during evolution and reuse [18]. Generics [14] (or templates in C++) can effectively unify type-parametric differences among classes/functions. Generics can hardly be considered a change mechanism, as very few changes in evolution practice are of type-parametric nature. Still, type parameterization has a role to play in building generic solutions and unifying similar program structures, as is required in reuse-based evolution. However, even in well-designed class libraries and application programs, we find similar program structure — classes and bigger patterns of collaborating components — with many differences that cannot be unified by generics. Up to 60 percent of code may be contained in similar classes that differ in generic-unfriendly ways. We refer to detailed studies in Chapter 9 and Chapter 10 and also in References 1, 16 to 18, 22, and 29.

Macros are a simple form of a generative technique, not strictly a conventional technique in the sense we use the term "conventional" in this book. We comment on macros here because of their popularity in mainstream programming. Macros handle changes/variations at the implementation level, by performing local code expansion at designated program points. Macros have been used for a variety of purposes (see [10], for a study of a popular cpp). They have also been used to manage evolutionary changes. Failing to utilize design concepts to manage changes, macros handling code variants related to one source of change become scattered through a system and difficult to trace. Macros related to different sources of change interact in chaotic ways. As programs with macros become more general, they also become increasingly more complex to work with [19].

To support evolution, we need global controls to explicate dependencies among modifications spread across the whole system (or even across system releases) related to a given source of change. Most of the macros lack such global controls. Although macros can handle simple, localized changes across component versions, generally they are not geared to unify a variety of similarity patterns that arise in evolution. Frame Technology™ [2] and XVCL [28] (based on frame concepts and described in Part II) are also realized by an expansion operation that performs "composition with adaptation" of generic, metalevel components. However, unlike macros, frame mechanisms are specifically meant to address the evolution challenges discussed in Chapter 1.

Inheritance can explicate certain types of changes via subclassing. It works fine if the impact of change is local, confined to a small number of classes, and, at the same time, big enough to justify the need for creating new subclasses. Unfortunately, quite often this is not the case, and a small change in requirements may lead to big changes in OO design and code, due to extensive subclassing. Even a small modification of one class method requires us to derive a new class, repeating almost the same code for the modified method. There is no formal way to group all the classes modified for the same purpose or point to the exact modification points. Although inheritance is critical for usability reasons, we are not aware of inheritance playing a significant role in managing day-to-day changes or long-term evolution. Inheritance is not a technique of choice to build generic design solutions, either. STL [26] — a hallmark of generic programming with C++ templates — has a flat class structure.

Design patterns [13] can ease future changes, and help in refactoring programs into more maintainable and often more generic representations. Design patterns have a role to play in unifying similarity patterns during evolution. Pattern-driven development becomes increasingly important in modern component platforms such as .NET™ and J2EE™. Component-based reuse is most effective when combined with architecture-centric, pattern-driven development. Patterns are basic means to achieve reuse of common service components. Standardized architectures together with patterns lead to beneficial uniformity of program solutions.

However, the visibility of pattern application in a program is somewhat informal and limited. Some patterns can be identified by using standard names for functions, data, classes, and files participating in a pattern instance. It is common to comment out pattern application. Similarly, the only way to know how pattern instances differ one from another is to comment out the differences. The benefits of using patterns for maintenance and evolution would be greatly increased if pattern applications, as well as similarities and differences among pattern instances, could be formally represented and amenable to some automation. Generative techniques open up such possibilities by capturing patterns at the extra metalevel plane [29].

In design for change with information hiding [21], we encapsulate changeable elements within program units such as functions, classes, components, or component layers. When change occurs, if the impact of change can be localized to a small number of program units, we substitute the encapsulated element with the new one, and as long as we do not affect interfaces, changing a program is easy. However, if we could always localize and hide the impact of change in a small number of components, we would not have problems with changing programs at all. Problems start when the impact of change is not local.

Many unexpected changes have nonlocal impact on a program, as our existing design may not cater to them. Aspects (crosscutting concerns) are examples of changes that cannot be localized. The previously mentioned tools, AOP [20] and MDSOC [27] are motivated by the observation that one modular decomposition cannot cater to all kinds of changes that may happen. They offer unconventional solutions to this problem. AOP caters to changes that can be realized by weaving aspects into program modules at specified joint points (or taking out aspects from program modules). Not all the changes are of the aforementioned kind. At times, modifications may occur at arbitrary points in a program; modifications required at different program points may be similar but not the same, or completely different; and modifications may affect the design (component interfaces or component configuration). To address these types of changes, we would need to bring in a new aspect whenever such changes occur. Such aspects could crosscut base code modules in arbitrary, unexpected ways, as well as crosscut one another. Chains of modifications could occur within certain aspects; we would need parameterized aspects, possibly with other aspects.

During evolution, we often have to keep component (class or function) versions before and after change. Components after change are needed in a new system, although components before change appear in earlier releases of the system that may be operational and still changing according to their own needs. Even if a change is small, a typical solution is to create a new component version. This may result in a huge number of component versions. A common approach is to use SCM tools [6] and keep the release history in an SCM's repository (we discuss Concurrent Versions System (CVS) in Chapter 5). Each such component (or component configuration) accommodates some combination of variant features. When it comes to implementing a new release of a system, we try to select either individual component versions or their configurations that "best match" the new system. Then, we customize them to fully meet the requirements of the new system. This selection/customization effort determines programmers' productivity. As it is not easy to distill the overall picture of similarities and differences across system releases from the SCM repository, selecting best-match components and customizing them may become expensive [8]. Various approaches have been proposed to extract and visualize information from the SCM repository to aid in evolution [11,12,15].

6.3   Conclusions

We discussed some of the difficulties in addressing evolution challenges with conventional techniques, the main ones being: poor visibility of past changes, the lack of a clear picture of similarities and differences among system releases at all system levels from architecture down to code details, and the lack of strong-enough generic design mechanisms. Conventional approaches, based on enumerating component versions, lead to explosion of similar component versions. The more component versions, the more difficult it is to see what is common and what is different among system releases, and how to reuse already implemented features in building new system releases. Poor visibility of past changes triggers much rework that could be avoided should the knowledge of the past changes be available to developers. Necessarily, ad hoc maintenance degrades the conceptual integrity of the program design. The overall complexity of an evolving program grows, making any future changes even harder.

References

1. Basit, H.A., Rajapakse, D.C., and Jarzabek, S., Beyond templates: a study of clones in the STL and some general implications, *International Conference Software Engineering, ICSE'05*, St. Louis, MO, May 2005, pp. 451–459.
2. Bassett, P., *Framing Software Reuse — Lessons from Real World*, Yourdon Press, Prentice Hall, Englewood Cliffs, NJ, 1997.
3. Batory, D., Sarvela, J.N., and Rauschmayer, A., Scaling step-wise refinement, *Proceedings of the International Conference on Software Engineering, ICSE'03*, May 2003, Portland, OR, pp. 187–197.
4. Brooks, F.P., No Silver Bullet, *Computer Magazine*, April 1986.
5. Clements, P. and Northrop, L., *Software Product Lines: Practices and Patterns*, Addison-Wesley, Boston, 2002.
6. Conradi, R. and Westfechtel, B., Version models for software configuration management, *ACM Computing Surveys*, 30(2), 232–282, 1998.
7. Czarnecki, K. and Eisenecker, U., *Generative Programming: Methods, Tools, and Applications*, Addison-Wesley, Boston, 2000.
8. Deelstra, S., Sinnema, M., and Bosch, J., Experiences in software product families: problems and issues during product derivation, *Proceedings of the Software Product Lines Conference, SPLC3*, Boston, MA, August 2004, LNCS 3154, Springer-Verlag, pp. 165–182.
9. Dijkstra, E.W., On the role of scientific thought, *Selected Writings on Computing: A Personal Perspective*, Springer-Verlag, New York, 1982, pp. 60–66.
10. Ernst, M., Badros, G., and Notkin, D., An empirical analysis of C preprocessor use, *IEEE Transactions on Software Engineering*, 1146–1170, December 2002.
11. Fischer, M., Pinzger, M., and Gall, H., Populating a release database from version control and bug tracking systems, *Proceedings of the International Conference Software Maintenance, ICSM'03*, September 2003, pp. 23–32.
12. Gall, H., Jazayeri, M., and Krajewski, J., CVS release history data for detecting logical couplings, *Proceedings of the International Workshop on Principles of Software Evolution, IWPSE'03*, September 2003, Helsinki, pp. 13–23.
13. Gamma, E., Helm, R., Johnson, R., and Vlissides, J., *Design Patterns — Elements of Reusable Object-Oriented Software*, Addison-Wesley, Boston, 1995.

14. Garcia, R., Jarvi, J., Lumsdaine, A., Siek, J. and Willcock, J., A comparative study of language support for generic programming, *Proceedings of the 18th Conference on Object-oriented Programming, Systems, Languages, and Applications*, 2003, pp. 115–134.

15. German, D., Hindle, A., and Jordan, N., Visualizing the evolution of software using softChange, *Proceedings of the 16th International Conference on Software Engineering and Knowledge Engineering, SEKE'04*, Banff, Canada, June 2004, pp. 1–6.

16. Jarzabek, S. and Li, S., Eliminating redundancies with a composition with adaptation meta-programming technique, *Proceedings of the ESEC-FSE'03, European Software Engineering Conference and Symposium on the Foundations of Software Engineering*, ACM Press, September 2003, Helsinki, pp. 237–246; paper received ACM Distinguished Paper award.

17. Jarzabek, S. and Li, S., Unifying clones with a generative programming technique: a case study, *Journal of Software Maintenance and Evolution: Research and Practice*, 18(4), 267–292, July–August 2006.

18. Jarzabek, S., Genericity — a missing in action key to software simplification and reuse, to appear in *13th Asia-Pacific Software Engineering Conference, APSEC'06*, IEEE Computer Society Press, December 6–8, 2006, Bangalore, India.

19. Karhinen, A., Ran, A., and Tallgren, T., Configuring designs for reuse, *Proceedings of the International Conference Software Engineering, ICSE'97*, Boston, pp. 701–710.

20. Kiczales, G., Lamping, J., Mendhekar, A., Maeda, C., Lopes, C., Loingtier, J-M., and Irwin, J., Aspect-oriented programming, *European Conference Object-Oriented Programming*, Finland, Springer-Verlag LNCS 1241, 1997, pp. 220–242.

21. Parnas, D., On the Criteria To Be Used in Decomposing Software into Modules, *Communications of the ACM*, 15(12), December 1972, pp.1053–1058.

22. Pettersson, U. and Jarzabek, S., Industrial experience with building a web portal product line using a lightweight, reactive approach, *ESEC-FSE'05, European Software Engineering Conference and ACM SIGSOFT Symposium on the Foundations of Software Engineering*, September 2005, Lisbon, pp. 326–335.

23. Ran, A., Software isn't built from LEGO blocks, *ACM Symposium on Software Reusability*, 1999, pp. 164–169.

24. Rumbaugh, J., Jacobson, I., and Booch, G., *The Unified Modeling Languages Reference Manual*, Addison-Wesley, 1999.

25. Schmidt, D., Model-Driven Engineering, *IEEE Computer*, February 2006, pp. 25–31.

26. SGI STL, http://www.sgi.com/tech/stl/.

27. Tarr, P., Ossher, H., Harrison, W., and Sutton, S., N degrees of separation: multidimensional separation of concerns, *Proceedings of the International Conference Software Engineering, ICSE'99*, Los Angeles, CA, 1999, pp. 107–119.

28. XVCL (XML-based variant configuration language) method and tool for managing software changes during evolution and reuse, http://fxvcl.sourceforge.net.

29. Yang, J. and Jarzabek, S., Applying a generative technique for enhanced reuse on J2EE platform, *4th International Conference on Generative Programming and Component Engineering, GPCE'05*, September 29–October 1, 2005, Tallinn, pp. 237–255.

Part II

REUSE-BASED SOFTWARE MAINTENANCE AND EVOLUTION

Although tools may help understand and maintain programs, certain problems related to change are inherently difficult to address. As Frederick Brooks pointed out in his seminal paper "No Silver Bullet" [1], programs are essentially complex and there is no easy way to get around that fact. The sheer size of programs makes programs complex and difficult to both understand and change. Software systems today can comprise tens of millions of lines of code (LOC), with thousands of interrelated components. MS Windows is approaching 100 million LOC, complexity that becomes difficult to handle with today's technology. We will surely be challenged by even larger and more complex software in the future.

The methods and tools described in Part I are necessarily exposed to the full complexity of a software system under maintenance. They are constrained by essential complexity, as eventually the changes must be applied at the program code level.

The mixed-strategy approach described in Part II attempts to break this limitation and let developers work with a program representation that reveals a simpler program face.

Typically, we try to reduce software complexity by raising the level of abstraction and by "divide and conquer" — componentization. Both abstraction and componentization have their limits in fighting complexity. Abstraction can hide some of the essential complexity from a programmer, and we must find a way to fill in missing details before a complete, executable program is produced from abstract program specifications. Today, we know how to automatically fill in these "missing details" using generators. Generator-based solutions can dramatically increase programmer productivity, but only in narrow application domains, whereby we can make assumptions about application domain semantics. Hardware-like componentization of software has its limits, too. Building software out of concrete components is difficult, and as long as we compose, validate, test, and maintain concrete components, we are bound to be exposed to the complexity proportional to the system size.

There is, however, a tremendous amount of similarity and repetition in software, a mostly unexploited opportunity for program simplification. Our studies suggest that with today's paradigms, repetitions are practically unavoidable and often comprise large parts of software. Software similarities can be of great help in fighting complexity, but as they remain implicit and dispersed, they add to program complexity. A key to turning similarities from a hardship to an effective tool for software simplification is a technology capable of representing similarity patterns in generic and adaptable form. Such nonredundant program representation can reduce the number of conceptual elements (components and interactions) in the solution space, reducing software complexity in terms of its understandability and changeability. By unifying similarity patterns, we can achieve simplifications proportional to the similarity prevalence rates, which are often proportional to the size of a software system. Validation at the level of a nonredundant representation, in terms of formal verification or testing, would be much easier and more effective than validation of concrete systems. Although this vision sounds promising, we believe the very nature of the problem calls for a solution beyond what today's programming paradigm allows us to do.

If the preceding problems cannot be solved at the program level, there are good reasons to see if we can tackle them in other ways. The mixed-strategy approach described in Part II allows us realize this vision with only modest extensions to conventional programming methods.

Mixed-strategy combines program code and its design into a unified representation. The emphasis is on design information that is useful in maintenance, and generally in program understanding, such as traces of changes spanning a program and evolution history.

Another important aspect of the mixed-strategy approach is systematic identification of similarity patterns in evolving software. Mixed-strategy provides mechanisms to unify similarity patterns with generic, adaptable program structures.

Mixed-strategy does not reduce the essential complexity of the program — this is impossible. It does not require us to change a program structure or any of the program properties, if we choose not to. But mixed-strategy representation contains information that makes a program easier to maintain than the program alone.

In Chapter 7, we motivate and outline a mixed-strategy approach to reuse-based evolution.

Chapter 8 is a step-by-step introduction to XVCL [2].

In Chapter 9, we discuss a software similarity phenomenon.

In Chapter 10, we show how mixed-strategy powered by XVCL can unify similarity patterns in programs with generic, adaptable structures. We discuss how such unification facilitates reuse-based evolution.

Chapter 11 and Chapter 12 describe a case study in evolution, using a facility reservation system (FRS) as an example.

In Chapter 13, we summarize experiences with mixed-strategy in other laboratory studies and industrial projects.

In Chapter 14, we compare XVCL to other generative techniques.

In Chapter 15, we describe strategies for adopting the mixed-strategy approach in software projects, and evaluate trade-offs involved in adopting mixed-strategy.

Conclusions in Chapter 16 end the book.

References

1. Brooks, F.P., No Silver Bullet, *Computer Magazine*, April 1986.
2. XVCL (XML-based variant configuration language) method and tool for managing software changes during evolution and reuse, http://fxvcl.sourceforge.net.

Chapter 7

The Mixed-Strategy
Approach: An Overview

Chapter Summary

Chapter 6 motivated the quest for effective solutions to software evolution beyond conventional techniques. Among many problems complicating evolution of programs, two are particularly acute, namely, poor visibility of changes, and explosion of look-alike component versions caused by weak generic design capabilities of conventional techniques. If similarities and differences among past releases remain implicit, it is difficult to reuse features already implemented in those releases when building a new release of an evolving software. Any changes affecting past releases must then be done on a case-by-case basis on each system release. In this chapter, we present the concepts of the mixed-strategy approach, which relies on clear exposition of similarities and differences among the software releases and leads to more effective reuse-based evolution. The purpose of this chapter is to build an intuitive understanding of the approach, which will help the reader to easily absorb technical details presented in subsequent chapters.

7.1   Concepts of Reuse-Based Evolution

The idea behind reuse-based evolution is to reuse the knowledge of past changes to effectively implement future changes. The essence of reuse-based evolution is clear visibility of changes, clear understanding of software similarities and differences at all granularity levels, and nonredundancy achieved by unifying similarity patterns of evolutionary changes with generic structures.

Reuse-based software evolution is a concept, or a principle, of how to address changes so that evolution is easier, faster, and cheaper. Different techniques can be used to realize reuse-based evolution. However, we have already hinted at some problems that haunt approaches that attempt to tackle evolutionary changes at the level of concrete programs. For example, if a software configuration management (SCM) [2] tool is used, we work with component versions and component configurations that occurred in various system releases with documented differences among them. We face the problems of explosion of look-alike components [4] and poor visibility of how changes affect software during evolution. The first problem is inherent in evolution of concrete components as we often need a component version before and after changes. The second problem can be eased with tools that automatically analyze the SCM repository and visualize the change history [5,6,8].

Although difficult at the level of concrete components, we can attempt to manage changes at an extra plane beyond a program itself. We explain using an analogy to the well-known technique of aspect-oriented programming (AOP) [10]. Computational aspects that crosscut modules (classes) of the primary program decomposition cannot be defined as self-contained modules using conventional object-oriented design techniques. AOP introduces a meta-level extra plane to create unconventional modules localizing crosscutting aspects, easing maintenance of both crosscutting aspects and program modules of primary decomposition.

In the mixed-strategy approach, we extend a conventional program with a meta-level extra plane to manage changes in evolving software. We represent programs in generic (nonredundant), adaptable form, capable of accommodating changes arising during evolution. Mixed-strategy representation also encompasses the knowledge of how to derive custom components of any system release from these generic forms. The main idea is to keep change specifications separate from code, but fully and formally integrated with code structures.

Consider the following evolution scenario: Rather than burying changes in the code, we keep change specifications visibly separated from the base code, for as long as it is useful to do so*. We integrate change into the base code permanently, when its visibility is not required anymore. Change specifications contain knowledge of

---

* A typical situation when it is beneficial to keep changes separate from code components is when different changes are needed in component versions used in systems released to different customers.

a complete chain of modifications — at architecture and code levels — linked to a particular source of change.

Change specifications are in both human- and machine-readable form, so that we can easily see and automatically produce a program before or after any given change. This book introduces a notation, an XML-based variant configuration language, XVCL for short, to realize the above scenario. XVCL allows us to express program changes of any conceivable type and granularity, at both architecture (components, interfaces, subsystems) and detail code levels. A tool called the XVCL processor interprets change specifications, and modifies a program accordingly.

> The idea behind the mixed-strategy approach is to use a programming language to express the syntax and semantics of a program — its component architecture and runtime behavior in terms of user interfaces, business logic, and a database — and then to impose XVCL on conventional program structures to express the syntax and semantics of change. The term "mixed-strategy approach" reflects this synergistic merger of conventional programming techniques and XVCL, to achieve separation of change, and other concerns that matter at program design time, from the definition of runtime program structures (such as functions, classes, or components).

XVCL change mechanisms are capable of managing multiple changes implemented over time. This includes reconciling change specifications that interact with each other, and building generic design solutions unifying similar threads of changes that emerge during evolution. The XVCL processor can selectively inject into or take out of the system changes implemented at different times during evolution.

Groups of similar changes are handled in a common way, by means of generic, customizable, mixed-strategy program representation. This generic representation is very flexible: the XVCL processor can instantiate it, based on change specifications, to create many variant forms that appear in our system (or even in many similar systems). System views at all abstraction levels become fully integrated with the knowledge of changes affecting them. The knowledge of similarities and differences (at all abstraction levels) remains explicit throughout evolution.

We gain the visibility of change patterns and the impact of changes on software architecture and code. From a mixed-strategy generic representation of an evolving program, we can derive any concrete component configuration required in a specific system release, by injecting changes relevant to that release.

During evolution, changes accumulate. We continuously refine a mixed-strategy representation so that similarity patterns of both changes and an evolving system itself are exposed and controlled, rather than being implicit and having multiplied in a large number of ad hoc instances.

7.2 Change-Design versus Design for Change

There is a difference between the change-design concept and design for change. Change specifications discussed in the preceding section are related to change-design.

Design for change is a design goal that we achieve by means of programming language constructs. Parnas [11] proposed an information-hiding technique to realize that goal. Object-oriented languages introduced classes with public interfaces and hidden private parts of class implementation to directly support design for change with information hiding. Component-based techniques pushed Parnas' ideas further, whereby we can access components via APIs without knowing the components' source code or even identity. Other conventional techniques that help achieve design for change are generics, inheritance, dynamic binding, and design patterns [7]. Model-based design described in Chapter 4 (Part I) is a powerful design for change technique in some cases. AOP [10] and MSDOC [12] simplify changes in certain types of crosscutting concerns.

The idea of change-design is to create a plane at which all changes become the first class citizens, can be designed and understood in synergy, but without conflicts, within a program structure. A programming language defines runtime component structure and takes care that all runtime quality goals are met, while the change-design mechanism takes care of maintenance and evolution concerns, such as changeability or genericity. The concept of reuse-based evolution motivates such separation, but does not prescribe any particular approach to achieving the separation.

7.3   Concepts of the Mixed-Strategy Approach

A mixed-strategy solution is built by separating program construction-time concerns (such as maintenance, evolution, or reuse concerns) from the actual program runtime structures (such as functions, classes, or components) implemented in one of the programming languages. Program construction-time concerns refer to knowledge of how various features have been implemented in system releases, visibility of past changes, changeability, traceability of information from requirements to code, genericity, crosscutting concerns — anything that helps during development, evolution, or reuse. Program runtime concerns refer to program behavior (user interface, computation logic, persistence, storage of data, etc.), componentization, underlying component platforms, and quality attributes such as performance, reliability, or availability.

The essence of mixed-strategy is that we use a conventional programming language (e.g., Java, C++, C, Perl, or PHP) and platforms (e.g., J2EE™ or .NET™) to deal with runtime concerns, and XVCL to deal with construction-time concerns. Conventional program technology defines the syntax and semantics of a program, while XVCL defines the syntax and semantics of change and other construction-time concerns. The overall representation that integrates conventional program with XVCL forms a mixed-strategy solution (Figure 7.1).

We consider all kinds of changes that arise during day-to-day maintenance, such as fixing bugs or enhancements of a program's functions, as well as the cumulative results of many changes over years of software evolution. Here is an intuitive

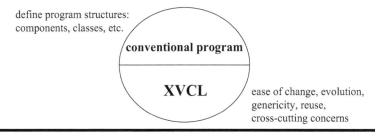

define program structures:
components, classes, etc.

conventional program

XVCL

ease of change, evolution,
genericity, reuse,
cross-cutting concerns

Figure 7.1   Mixed-strategy solution.

description of the mixed-strategy approach. As the program evolves, change specifications, recorded in XVCL, are imposed on a base program. A base program together with change specifications form a mixed-strategy representation that developers work with. This representation contains the evolution history — architecture and code for each of the releases, along with a complete trace of changes applied to generic components to obtain a given release. Generic components are built by applying XVCL to the base program. They are continuously refined during evolution, to accommodate changes relevant to various system releases. Therefore, the same mechanisms of XVCL are used for representing both change specifications and generic components that together form a mixed-strategy solution.

A unit of mixed-strategy representation decomposition is called an *x-frame*. Change specifications, generic components, and all the base code are contained in x-frames. Being unconstrained by the rules of the underlying programming language, x-frames can be small or big, coinciding with the natural granularity of change.

X-frames in a mixed-strategy representation are analogous to functional program abstractions, such as components, classes, methods, and functions in programming languages. However, the goals of mixed-strategy decomposition and those of conventional program decomposition are different:

■ The goal of mixed-strategy decomposition is to take care of construction-time concerns: To explicate changes, facilitate future changes via adaptation of generic components capable of accommodating variant features arising during evolution, unify similarity patterns in both evolutionary changes and in the structure of the base program.
■ The goal of conventional program decomposition is to ensure that runtime program behavior meets its functional and quality requirements. Here, the concerns are software architecture in terms of components and interfaces; software behavior that meets all its functional and quality requirements, such as of usability, performance, reliability, availability, and many others.

The goals of mixed-strategy and conventional decompositions are intimately interwoven, and complementary to each other. In conventional programming, these goals are often conflicting. Based on analysis of trade-offs, developers must compromise on less important goals so that they can ensure that more important ones are met.

> The benefit of mixed-strategy is that we can give full attention to construction-time concerns, optimizing them to required levels, without compromising any of the runtime program properties. Both construction-time and runtime properties may be optimized separately and independently of each other, without constraining each other. Mixed-strategy achieves separation of construction-time concerns from the actual program structures and their required qualities.

It is interesting to note that such separation of construction-time concerns from the issues concerning the structure and properties of the actual product is common in traditional engineering. It is a mark of the maturity of the engineering disciplines. Most often, each of the two areas of concern are even backed by scientific theories and well-established processes, standards, and tools. For example, the design of a car or a bridge involves a lot of mathematical calculations based on laws of physics and material sciences. On the other hand, car production or bridge building is based on management science, theories of manufacturing processes, and tools supporting the construction process.

The developer's mental model of software under evolution must encompass both x-frames and functional program abstractions (components, methods, and functions). Therefore, it is beneficial to have natural and transparent mappings between x-frames and program abstractions. For example, it is common that an x-frame corresponds to a subsystem, group of similar components, classes, methods, or interface definitions (e.g., in IDL).

The following properties of mixed-strategy are important for practical reasons:

- Traceability: This denotes full transparency of mappings between a mixed-strategy generic representation and a program itself. This ensures that virtual generic views never get disconnected from the base code. Failing to do so is a common pitfall of generators, and an important reason why abstractions disconnected from code are not trusted by programmers [3].
- The ability to organize generic structures in a hierarchical way: Examples are generic classes built from generic methods and generic components built from generic classes; generic component configurations built from generic components and patterns defining composition rules; and generic subsystems from generic component configurations. This ensures that similarities at all levels and of any granularity can by unified, interlinked, and the whole mixed-strategy solution space can be normalized for nonredundancy.
- The ability to express, easily and naturally, differences among similar program structures of arbitrary type and granularity: This ensures that any group of similar program structures can be unified with a generic representation, whenever this is required for simplification reasons, independent of differences among structures or members of a group. It helps to achieve the "small

change – small impact" effect, which is so difficult to achieve with conventional program abstractions such as procedures, classes, or components [1].

The overall mixed-strategy representation of a software system under evolution is a hierarchy of x-frames called an *x-framework*. An x-framework is a mixed-strategy counterpart of an evolution history stored in an SCM repository. It contains full details of software architecture and code for each release, generic structures representing similar, recurring patterns of design (e.g., a group of similar components), changes that lead to various releases, and other information that helps in systematic maintenance and evolution.

7.4 A Preview of the Mixed-Strategy Approach: An Example

We illustrate the main concepts with the facility reservation system (FRS) evolution example, discussed in Chapter 5 and illustrated in Figure 7.2.

FRS components are organized into three tiers, namely, the user interface, business logic, and database tiers. User interface components allow FRS administrators and reservation requestors to interact with the system. Business logic components accomplish various actions related to managing users, facilities, and reservations. The database stores data related to users, facilities, and reservations.

7.4.1 Evolving FRS with Mixed-Strategy Representation: The Big Picture

Mixed-strategy representation is built around a model of software system structure from subsystem, to component layer (e.g., user interface or business logic), to component, to class/procedure, and to class/procedure implementation details. Such a precise model of structure in a form that can be manipulated by the XVCL processor is necessary to deal with evolutionary changes affecting software at all of those levels.

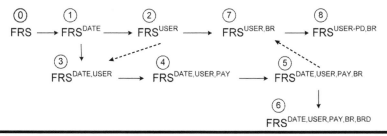

Figure 7.2   Stages in facility reservation system (FRS) evolution.

Rather than melding changes into code, we specify the impact of evolutionary changes on software in XVCL. Code structures affected by changes are continuously refined into generic mixed-strategy representation structures that can be easily adapted to changes arriving from various sources (e.g., changes relevant to various system releases). The goal is to reuse the same mixed-strategy structures in all system releases.

Figure 7.3 shows a sketch of an x-framework that represents five initial stages of FRS evolution. The x-framework contains full knowledge of how to build each FRS release from generic building blocks, shown as x-frames enclosed in the dashed rectangle. In Figure 7.3, we see a top-level view of FRS decomposition, with XVCL **<adapt>** commands showing how to compose FRS from its building blocks. Solid arrows correspond to **<adapt>** commands. Tick dashed arrows at the bottom show five FRS releases produced from the x-framework. Any of the topmost x-frames, called an SPC, contain SPeCifications of how to build a specific FRS release. For example, SPC-FRS^{DATE,USER} sets up parameters and controls, and contains definitions of other change specifications (e.g., unique features) required for FRS^{DATE,USER}. The XVCL processor interprets change specifications and propagates changes across the x-framework, producing custom component versions required in a given system release. Numbers attached to arrows identify stages of evolution and correspondence between SPC and respective FRS releases.

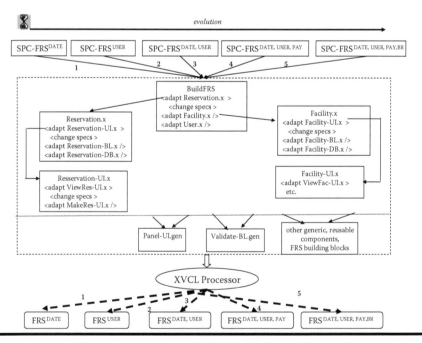

Figure 7.3   Facility reservation system (FRS) evolution with mixed-strategy.

Larger x-frames are composed from smaller x-frames, their building blocks. Composition relationship among x-frames, defined by <**adapt**> command, is shown as solid arrows in Figure 7.3. An arrow between two x-frames: X → Y is read as "X adapts Y," meaning that X controls adaptation of Y, while the composition takes place. Composition is the main organizing principle for an x-framework.

The XVCL processor traverses the x-framework, starting with the SPC, in depth-first order, interpreting any encountered XVCL commands. Whenever the XVCL processor encounters an <**adapt**> command, the interpretation of the current x-frame is suspended, and the interpretation of the x-frame designated by the <**adapt**> command begins. The XVCL processor emits "as is" code contained in x-frames visited during processing. Also, note that during processing, x-frames in an x-framework are never changed by the XVCL processor. Only the result of x-frame composition is emitted to the output.

Typically, x-frames at the bottom levels of an x-framework contain implementation of program components (or even classes or class methods). Above them are x-frames representing architecture-level elements (groups of components, interfaces, and subsystems). Toward the top of the x-framework, we often see x-frames whose only purpose is to specify customization, configuration, and composition rules for lower-level x-frames. Each x-frame specifies changes for the x-frames below, and receives changes from the upper-level x-frames. Therefore, x-frames are both active and passive. X-frames toward the bottom of an x-framework tend to be more generic, reusable, and adaptable to the needs of various FRS releases (e.g., x-frames below a dotted line in Figure 7.3).

In addition to composition relationship, an x-framework is further organized by a principle of separation of concerns. For example, x-frames with user interface components and x-frames with business logic are kept in separate partitions of an x-framework.

Although changes unique to a given release are contained in respective SPCs, change specifications related to features shared by a number of releases often become an integral part of the evolution knowledge. Such changes are embedded in x-frames below the SPC level, as shown in Figure 7.3.

Change specifications are formally linked to designated variation points in affected x-frames by means of XVCL commands embedded in x-frames. Changes specified in a higher-level x-frame override any changes contained in the adapted x-frames. This change propagation rule helps us achieve reusability of x-frames across system releases during evolution.

As shown in Figure 7.3, at each adaptation point (marked with an <**adapt**> command), we can specify (optional) changes to be applied to the adapted x-frame. These changes are propagated to all the x-frames reached in the adaptation chain, for example, from <**adapt** Reservation.x>, down to x-frames Reservation.x, Reservation-UI.x, ViewRes-UI, and any further adapted x-frames.

By reading change specifications and tracing change propagation across x-frames, we can see the exact similarities and differences among any two FRS releases, from the subsystem level to component and to component implantation details.

Applying XVCL to build a mixed-strategy representation is an incremental process. The mixed-strategy representation is continuously refined whenever an opportunity arises to simplify it, make it more generic, or more adaptable. Such refinements lead to a representation of the evolving system that is concise, conceptually clear, and easy to work with, in contrast to the usual decay of software structure in conventional maintenance. Refinements are essential to achieve the long-term benefits of mixed-strategy.

7.4.2 A Preview of Detailed Change Mechanisms

Composition rules defined by **<adapt>** commands form a macrostructure of an x-framework within which more detailed changes are specified. These changes can be specified at each **<adapt>** command, and they define customizations to be applied to the chain of x-frames that originates at that **<adapt>** command. XVCL change instruments include variables, expressions, and commands such as **<insert>**, **<break>**, **<select>**, or **<while>**. XVCL variables and expressions provide the parameterization mechanisms that make x-frames generic and, therefore, applicable to various releases. Typically, class or method names, data types, keywords, operators, or algorithmic fragments are represented as expressions that can then be instantiated by the XVCL processor, according to the context. We use **<select>** to direct processing into one or more of the many predefined branches (called options), based on the value of a variable. With **<insert>** we can modify x-frames at designated **<break>** points in arbitrary ways. A **<while>** command allows us to iterate over certain sections of an x-frame, with each iteration generating custom output. A typical use of **<while>** is in generating many similar concrete components needed in a software system from a generic x-frame playing the role of a template.

The usage of the preceding change mechanisms is informally illustrated in Figure 7.4. Solid arrows correspond to **<adapt>** commands, whereas dashed arrows link **<insert>** commands to matching **<break>** points. Suppose we find that there is a lot of similarity among modules in the following groups:

CreateRes, CreateFac, CreateUser
DeleteRes, DeleteFac, DeleteUser
UpdateRes, UpdateFac, UpdateUser

Despite similarities, there are also differences among modules in each group implied by the semantics of an operation (such as Create, Delete, or Update) and the entity (such as Reservation, Facility, or User). In addition, in the FRS evolution context, there are differences among modules in each group implied by specific features (such as DATE, USER, or PAY) implemented in a given FRS release.

A **<set>** command assigns a list of values to an XVCL variable. XVCL variables **oper** (set in BuildOperations.x) and **entity** (set in Operation.gen) are generic names

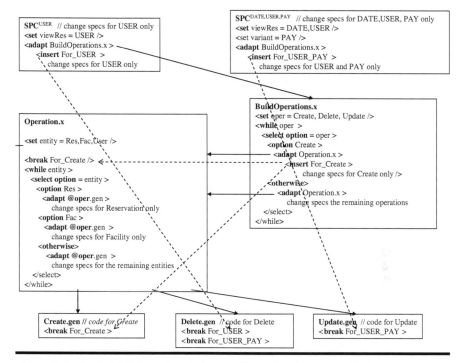

Figure 7.4   Basic XML-based variation configuration language (XVCL) mechanisms.

for operations and entities, respectively. As XVCL variables have global scope, they can coordinate chains of all the customizations related to the same source of variation or change that spans across multiple x-frames. During processing, values of variables propagate from an x-frame where the value of a variable is set down to all adapted x-frames. Thanks to this scoping rule, x-frames become generic and adaptable, with potential for reuse in many contexts.

Custom operations for specific entities (e.g., CreateRes, CreateFac, CreateUser) are obtained by adapting respective generic operation x-frames (e.g., Create.gen). X-frames BuildOperations.x and Operation.x navigate the process of building operations.

Changes specific to a certain group of operations (e.g., Create) are specified in x-frame BuildOperations.x. In the example, for operation Create, we insert Create-specific changes into matching **<break>**s named For_Create, placed in x-frames Operation.gen and Create.gen.

Changes specific to a certain operation for an entity (e.g., CreateRes) are specified in x-frame Operation.gen.

Changes specific to a given FRS release are specified in the respective SPC. For example, in SPC[USER] we **<insert>** USER-specific changes into matching the **<break>** named For_USER, placed in x-frame Delete.gen.

In each iteration of the <**while**> loop in BuildOperations.x, we generate operations Create for various entities. The i-th iteration of the loop uses the i-th value of a control variable **oper**, as assigned in the respective <**set**> command. The <**while**> loop in x-frame Operations.x adapts generic operations defined in x-frames in the following text, according to change specifications propagated from the upper-level x-frames.

Despite its simplicity, the preceding example communicates the essence of a mechanism that allows us to handle ad hoc variations related to specific operations, entities, and FRS releases without affecting other operations, entities, and FRS releases that should not be affected by these variations. Mechanisms for such selective injection of changes allow us to separate variants from common, generic structures, keeping generic structures reusable and easily adaptable.

With this general introduction, in the next chapter we describe main XVCL commands in greater detail, explaining their role in handling specific evolution problems.

7.5 The Role of Genericity in the Mixed-Strategy Approach

Genericity of program representation is the heart of the mixed-strategy approach to reuse-based evolution. We need generic program components that we can easily adapt to specific needs of various system releases. For example, features DATE and USER (view reservation by DATE and view reservations by USER) affect FRS components ViewRes-UI and ViewRes-BL. Different FRS releases may need either of them, both of them, or none. Components ViewRes-UI and ViewRes-BL must be generic to accommodate any required features combination.

Even in the case of a single program, by unifying similar, but also different, program structures with generic forms, we can achieve substantial simplifications leading to improved maintainability. The following simple argumentation supports this claim:

Suppose we have ten user interface forms $a_1, \ldots, a_{10}$ (e.g., data entry forms). Each form, say a_i, interacts with five business logic functions $b_{i,1}, \ldots, b_{i,5}$ (e.g., data validation rules or actions to be performed upon data entry at certain fields). We further assume that there is considerable similarity among the ten forms and business logic functions that each form needs.

If each form and each business logic function is implemented as a separate component, we have to manage $10 + 10*5 = 60$ components and 50 interactions [situation shown in Figure 7.5(a)].

Suppose we can unify business logic functions across ten forms, so that all ten forms use only five generic functions $B_1, \ldots, B_5$. We reduce the solution space to $10 + 5 = 15$ components and 50 interactions, with the slightly added complexity of a generic representation. The interactions have become easier to understand as each form interacts with components that have been merged into five groups rather than 50 distinct components [situation shown in Figure 7.5(b)].

Suppose we further unify ten user interface forms with one generic form A. We reduce the solution space to $1 + 5 = 6$ components and with five groups of interactions, each group consisting of ten specific interactions, plus the complexity of a generic representation [situation shown in Figure 7.5(c)].

Any form of validation at the level of generic representation depicted in Figure 7.5(b) or Figure 7.5(c) is bound to be much simpler and effective than validation at the level of concrete components [Figure 7.5(a)]. Similarly, any changes at the level of generic representation are easier to manage than at the level of concrete components, due to clearer visibility of change impact, reduced risk of update anomalies, and smaller number of distinct interfaces that have to be analyzed. Finally, generic representation of components and their configurations form natural units of reuse, potential building blocks of product line architectures.

Generic components along with specifications of adaptation changes retain and enhance a clear view of what is similar and what is different among system releases, and help us to avoid the problem of component version explosion. We need generic change specifications to avoid repeating the same or similar change specifications all over again. This further enhances the visibility of similarity patterns in the evolution history, simplifies change specifications, and further boosts reuse of knowledge accumulated during evolution.

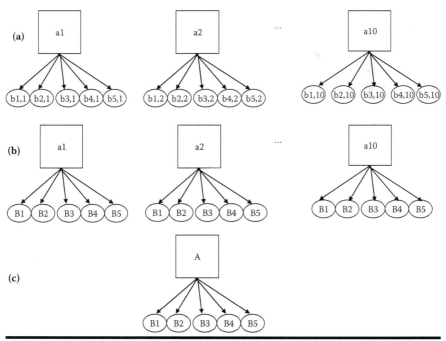

Figure 7.5   The impact of genericity on complexity.

7.6 Conclusions

In this chapter, we motivated the mixed-strategy approach and introduced its main concepts. We use a programming language to express the syntax and semantics of a program. We impose XVCL on program structures to express the syntax and semantics of change. A program along with the knowledge of evolutionary changes forms a mixed-strategy representation. Mixed-strategy achieves separation of construction-time concerns from runtime concerns; we can optimize construction-time and runtime properties separately and independently of each other, without constraining the other.

With mixed-strategy, we try to achieve (1) conceptual simplicity, (2) maximum changeability of software, (3) traceability of changes from requirements to system architecture and the base code, and (4) the visibility of similarities and differences among system releases. At the heart of the approach to achieve these engineering qualities is generic design that leads to nonredundant software representation.

An x-framework is created and then evolved by specifying changes related to various releases in XVCL, and by packaging components into generic x-frame structures capable of accommodating changes related to various releases. This is the essence of achieving reuse-based software evolution. Software evolution with XVCL is a continuous refinement of the x-framework.

XVCL aims at specifying changes at global and local scales, changes that have impact on system architecture, and small changes at the level of program statements. The ability to express a wide range of change specification and generic design issues in a simple, practical, and uniform way was the main philosophy for building the design of XVCL mechanisms. We emphasize the uniformity of solutions to a great extent in the mixed-strategy approach. Uniformity is one of the keys to simplicity, so much required in the inherently complex world of software evolution. Therefore, we keep the change mechanisms simple and favor uniformity of evolution pattern specifications over diversification, unless uniqueness of specifications is justified by the nature of a specific evolution pattern or engineering qualities to be met by its specifications.

Mixed-strategy represents commonalties and differences among releases of an evolving system, at any level of granularity, in both human- and machine-readable form. The precise understanding of commonalties and differences allows developers to make use of the knowledge of past changes to effectively implement future changes, which is the core idea behind reuse-based evolution.

References

1. Bassett, P., *Framing Software Reuse — Lessons from the Real World*, Yourdon Press, Prentice Hall, Englewood Cliffs, NJ, 1997.
2. Conradi, R. and Westfechtel, B., Version models for software configuration management, *ACM Computing Surveys*, 30(2), 232–282, 1998.

3. Cordy, J.R., Comprehending reality: practical challenges to software maintenance automation, *Proceedings of the 11th International Workshop on Program Comprehension, IWPC'03*, Portland, OR, May 2003, pp. 196–206 (keynote paper).

4. Deelstra, S., Sinnema, M., and Bosch, J., Experiences in software product families: problems and issues during product derivation, *Proceedings of the Software Product Lines Conference, SPLC3*, Boston, MA, August 2004, LNCS 3154, Springer-Verlag, pp. 165–182.

5. Fischer, M., Pinzger, M., and Gall, H., Populating a release database from version control and bug tracking systems, *Proceedings of the International Conference Software Maintenance, ICSM'03*, September 2003, pp. 23–32.

6. Gall, H., Jazayeri, M., and Krajewski, J., CVS Release history data for detecting logical couplings, *Proceedings of the International Workshop on Principles of Software Evolution, IWPSE'03*, September 2003, Helsinki, pp. 13–23.

7. Gamma, E., Helm, R., Johnson, R., and Vlissides, J., *Design Patterns — Elements of Reusable Object-Oriented Software*, Addison-Wesley, Menlo Park, NY, 1995.

8. German, D., Hindle, A., and Jordan, N., Visualizing the evolution of software using softChange, *Proceedings of the 16th International Conference on Software Engineering and Knowledge Engineering, SEKE'04*, Banff, Canada, June 2004, pp. 1–6.

9. Jarzabek, S., Basset, P., Zhang, H., and Zhang, W., XVCL: XML-based variant configuration language, *Proceedings of the International Conference on Software Engineering, ICSE'03*, IEEE Computer Society Press, May 2003, Portland, pp. 810–811, http://fxvcl.sourceforge.net.

10. Kiczales, G, Lamping, J., Mendhekar, A., Maeda, C., Lopes, C., Loingtier, J-M., and Irwin, J., Aspect-oriented programming, *European Conference Object-Oriented Programming*, Finland, Springer-Verlag LNCS 1241, 1997, pp. 220–242.

11. Parnas, D., On the Criteria to Be Used in Decomposing Software into Modules, *Communications of the ACM*, 15(12), December 1972, pp.1053–1058.

12. Tarr, P., Ossher, H., Harrison, W., and Sutton, S., N degrees of separation: multidimensional separation of concerns, *Proceedings of the International Conference Software Engineering, ICSE'99*, Los Angeles, 1999, pp. 107–119.

Chapter 8

Step-by-Step Introduction to XVCL

Chapter Summary

In this chapter, we introduce XML-based variant configuration language (XVCL) mechanisms to realize the mixed-strategy approach. First, we explain the rationale for XVCL in the context of maintenance changes and evolution. We introduce step-by-step XVCL commands in a series of examples, explaining their role in handling various types of changes and evolution situations. In Section 8.9, we summarize XVCL commands in a more formal and systematic way.

A notation described in this chapter is a simplified form of XVCL, which we use in the remaining part of the book. We use simplified, XML-free XVCL syntax to focus readers' attention on essentials. Appendix C defines XVCL in its XML form, and with all the details, many of which we omit from the presentation in this chapter.

First, we recapitulate the main points about building mixed-strategy solutions with XVCL. We start the detailed description of XVCL by explaining how XVCL allows us to achieve flexible composition to address large-granularity changes. Then, we show how XVCL commands allow us to specify small-granularity changes. At this point, we already have a complete set of change instruments to specify any modifications that programmers may conceivably want to do. Finally, we comment on how XVCL is used to unify similarity patterns in both base-program components and change specifications. The former allows us to avoid explosion of similar components, and the latter is essential in keeping change specifications as simple as possible. As we introduce XVCL conventions, we also comment on their role in addressing challenges of reuse-based evolution.

We would like the reader to note that the same small set of XVCL commands is used for all types of changes, from architecture (at subsystem or component level) down to statement-level modifications.

8.1   Salient Features of XVCL

XVCL complements conventional programming techniques. Developers still use one of the programming languages to define the behavioral core of their program solutions (e.g., user interfaces, business logic, or databases). However, when there are engineering benefits to capturing similarity patterns in generic form but conventional techniques do not allow us to do so, rather than using ad hoc solutions, we fall back on to XVCL mechanisms to deal with the problem.

Mixed-strategy partitioning is parallel to partitioning of a program along runtime software architecture boundaries, which includes subsystems, architectural descriptions, components, interfaces, classes, and implementation of all of these elements. The runtime architecture is built and expressed using conventional techniques and programming languages to meet the program's behavioral and quality requirements. The boundaries of mixed-strategy partitioning are solely dictated by the concerns of generic design, and are not restricted by the rules of a programming language or the semantics of a programming problem being solved.

The overall generic design solution is decomposed into a hierarchy of parameterized x-frames (denoted by capital letters in Figure 8.1). X-frames may represent program elements of an arbitrary kind, structure, or complexity, such as functions, classes, or architectural elements (interfaces, components, or subsystems). X-frames

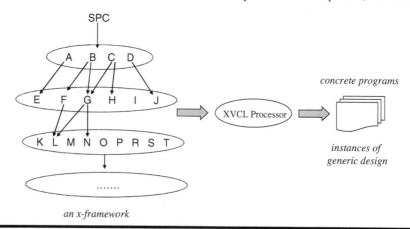

Figure 8.1   An overview of the mixed-strategy approach.

can be parameterized in fairly unrestrictive ways. Parameters range from simple values (such as strings) to types or other x-frames. Parameters mark variation points in x-frames.

Each x-frame in the hierarchy (e.g., G in Figure 8.1) defines a generic design solution in terms of lower-level x-frames (L and N), and also contributes to generic design solutions at the higher levels (B and C), as their building block.

The topmost x-frame, called SPC, SPeCifies global controls and parameters that allow the XVCL processor to synthesize a custom program from a generic x-framework. The XVCL processor interprets the SPC, traverses x-frame hierarchy accordingly, adapts visited x-frames, and emits the custom program. By varying specifications contained in the SPC, we can instantiate the same generic design in different ways, obtaining different custom programs.

In the evolution context, an x-framework contains information about systems released during evolution — commonalities and differences among system releases, changes that led to specific releases, and other design information that matters during evolution. Each system release is defined by an SPC, and the XVCL processor can produce a given release from the x-framework by interpreting its SPC.

A mixed-strategy representation unifies differences among software clones — similar program structures — with unique generic structures. Variations among similar program structures are specified as deltas from the generic structure and automatically propagated to the respective instances of a generic structure. Such unification of similarity patterns occurs within and across systems released during evolution.

From the XVCL window, a designer has a precise picture of program similarities (a generic structure) and differences among all the instances of a generic structure in a program. Any future changes are also done via generic structures. XVCL provides mechanisms to exercise full control over the cases when certain instances of a generic structure are to be treated differently from others. Unavoidably, redundant code may be emitted as a result, but that code is no longer the canonical specification of the solution. Nonredundant generic structures, together with their instantiating deltas, now play that role.

XVCL defines a number of mechanisms to achieve genericity and ease of adaptation. XVCL variables and expressions provide a basic parameterization mechanism to inject genericity into x-frames. Typically, names of entities (e.g., x-frames), architectural elements (such as interfaces and components), source files, classes, methods, data types, keywords, operators, or even short algorithmic fragments are represented as XVCL expressions, which can be then instantiated by the XVCL processor, according to the context. A <set> command assigns a value to an XVCL variable. During processing of x-frames, values of XVCL variables propagate from the x-frame where the value of a XVCL variable is set, down to lower-level x-frames. Although each x-frame usually can set default values for its XVCL variables, values assigned to XVCL variables in higher-level x-frames take precedence over the locally assigned default values. Thanks to this scoping mechanism, x-frames become generic and adaptable, with potential for reuse in many contexts. Other commands that help us design generic and adaptable x-frames include **<select>**, **<insert>** into **<break>**, and **<while>**. We use the **<select>** command to direct processing into one of the many predefined branches (called options), based on the value of an XVCL variable. With the **<insert>** command, we can modify x-frames at designated variation points — **<break>**s — in arbitrary ways. A **<while>** command allows us to iterate over certain sections of an x-frame, with each iteration generating custom output.

Similarity patterns occur at all the levels of abstraction, from software architecture to detailed class/component design and to code. Opportunities for program simplification or reuse by capturing similarity patterns in generic form exist at all those levels. To exploit those opportunities, the aforementioned XVCL mechanisms are uniformly applied at all levels of abstraction that are involved in formulation of a required generic design solution.

8.2 Flexible Composition of X-Frames

We introduce XVCL change mechanisms feature by feature, from the perspective of various program modifications developers typically implement. We hope such a presentation helps the reader appreciate the rationale behind various XVCL mechanisms and relate them to the usual tasks developers perform during maintenance.

For ease of reference, Figure 8.2 shows the main XVCL commands.

X-frame composition with adaptation may be the most fundamental and intuitive way to picture XVCL. We start with the composition part.

A popular approach to handling changes is by replacing or reconfiguring software components. Different component versions are usually stored in a repository of a software configuration management (SCM) tool [3] such as CVS. Of course, a new component that replaces an old one must fit into the context of the program. Components after replacement or reconfiguration must form a syntactically and semantically viable program. The #include command of a popular C preprocessor (cpp) [5] provides a simple form of file composition. Proteus Configuration Language (PCL) [7] offers more sophisticated rules for configuring files. Modern component platforms, such as J2EE™ or .NET™, allow us to plug in and plug out components conforming to interfaces providing the context definition. By interchanging components we can implement certain types of changes.

X-frames are units of mixed-strategy decomposition. The main criterion for decomposition is to preserve the history of an evolving software in a representation that is clear and easy to work with.

Specific releases of an evolving software (or any custom programs, in general) are built by composing x-frames. In XVCL, we compose x-frames by means of **<adapt>** commands. An x-frame may include any number of child x-frames. Flexible composition means that composition rules are not completely fixed. As the

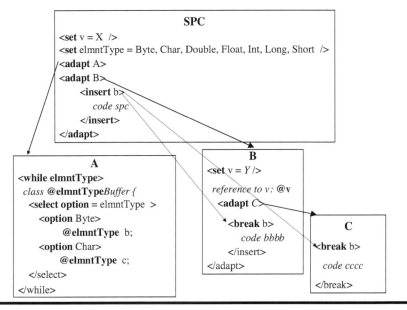

Figure 8.2   Main XML-based variant configuration language (XVCL) commands.

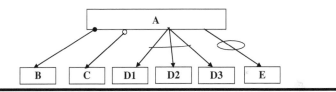

Figure 8.3   X-frame composition rules.

same x-frame is often customized in different ways depending on the reuse context, the exact composition rules may vary. For example, x-frame A may need x-frame B as its subcomponent in one context, but may not need B in some other context. Variations in composition rules may occur during the same run of the processor over an x-framework, or in separate runs, for different SPCs. Composition is the core of the XVCL customization mechanism that allows the same x-frames to be adapted in different ways, for reuse in many different contexts. Other fine-granularity XVCL customization mechanisms (such as parameterization, selection, or insertions at designated break points) are specified on top of x-frame composition rules (along adaptation paths) and in the x-frame body.

Suppose x-frames A, B, C, D1, D2, D3, and E have the composition structure depicted in Figure 8.3:

1. Mandatory composition: x-frame B is a mandatory part of A, meaning that in any context when we need x-frame A, B is also used.

2. Optional composition: x-frame C is an optional part of A, meaning that we may or may not need C to build A, depending on the context.
3. Alternative composition: x-frames D1, D2, and D3 are alternative parts of A, meaning that, depending on the context, we need exactly one of them to build A.
4. Multiple composition: x-frame E is used many times in the process of building A.

In the context of modeling evolving software, the preceding rules often have the following interpretation:

1. We need B to build A in any system release, that is, independently of changes affecting A.
2. In some system releases we need C to build A, but in other system releases we do not need C to build A; whether of not we need C to build A depends on specific changes affecting A.
3. Different system releases may need D1, D2, or D3 to build A; specific changes affecting A determine which of the three x-frames should be used to build A.
4. An x-frame E that is used many times to build A usually is a kind of template from which we generate many similar components needed in system releases. Depending on specific changes affecting A, we may need a different number of instances of E to build A.

Figure 8.3 shows one level of x-frame decomposition. In any real evolution situation, we normally decompose x-frames hierarchically, at many levels, as we saw in examples shown in Chapter 7. Such multilevel decomposition is necessary to achieving genericity (reusability) of x-frames across system releases, understanding of similarities and differences among system releases, and gaining a good grasp of changes affecting various system releases.

8.3   Defining Compositions with XVCL

Controls in XVCL are exercised by means of XVCL variables, so we briefly introduce variables first. An XVCL variable may be assigned values in any x-frame by the <**set**> command, for example: <**set** x = 1 />. Variable values are interpreted as character strings.

A variable that is assigned a list of values in the respective <**set**> command is called a multivalue variable, e.g., <**set** z = 1, 2, 3 />. Multivalue variables control loops that facilitate generation of many similar components; for example, in the multiple composition rule (rule 4 in the preceding list) discussed earlier.

When x-frames are interpreted by the XVCL processor, variables' values propagate from higher-level x-frames down to adapted x-frames. A value assigned to a variable in a higher-level x-frame takes precedence over any possible values assigned to the same variable in adapted x-frames. This variable-value-overriding rule has a role to play in achieving reusability of x-frames, so that the same x-frame may be flexibly adapted to the needs of different system releases.

8.3.1 Basic X-Frame Compositions

<adapt> commands mark points where x-frame compositions occur during XVCL processing. <adapt A> command is analogical to cpp's #include A [4]. Unlike #include, which includes a specified file "as is," <adapt> can customize a specified x-frame in different ways, at each of the many points at which x-frame A is needed.

We achieve mandatory composition of the x-frames A and B by putting command <adapt B> at the required composition point in A.

It is important to keep in mind that the XVCL processor never modifies x-frames. Instead, the processor emits the result of an x-frame composition and other processing to the output. We can imagine that the processor always works with a copy of an x-frame. Therefore, any reference to the same x-frame in subsequent processing always uses an original x-frame.

Optional composition is achieved by putting the <adapt> command inside the conditional <ifdef>. For example, the following <ifdef> command in x-frame A will conditionally compose B:

```
A:
<ifdef x>
        <adapt B />
</ifdef>
```

The decision whether or not to adapt B is made based on variable x; if variable x has been defined, then the body of <ifdef x> (i.e., <adapt B />) is processed and composition occurs; otherwise, composition does not occur.

(Using cpp, such versioning without creating another copy of a file, is achieved by #ifdef and #define macro commands. The scope of #define is a single file.)

Alternative composition is achieved by placing <adapt> commands under suitable <option>s of a <select> command. For example, the following <select> command composes one of the x-frames D1, D2, or D3 to build x-frame A, depending on the value of variable x:

```
A:
<select option = x>
    <option d1> <adapt D1 />
    <option d2> <adapt D2 />
    <option d3> <adapt D3 />
    <otherwise> error
</select>
```

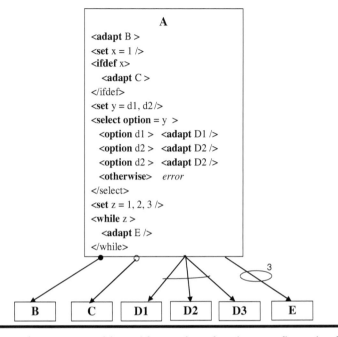

Figure 8.4 X-frame composition with XML-based variant configuration language (XVCL) commands.

Figure 8.4 shows the realization of compositions depicted in Figure 8.3 by XVCL commands placed in x-frame A.

Multiple compositions are achieved by putting an **<adapt>** command inside the **<while>** loop. For example, the following **<while>** loop in x-frame A **<adapt>**s x-frame E thrice:

A:
<set z = 1, 2, 3 />

Multivalue variable "z" controls the loop. The i-th iteration of the loop uses the i-th value of variable z. By changing the definition of variable z, we can change the number of loop iterations, and the number of times x-frame E is adapted in building A.

8.3.2 More Flexible X-Frame Composition with Parameters and Insertions

Parameterization can considerably enhance flexibility of x-frame compositions. This is done by representing the name of an adapted x-frame by a reference to an XVCL variable or expression, and by inserting <**adapt**> commands at designated composition points in the x-frames. With these extensions, our composition mechanism becomes powerful enough to define generic and flexible x-frame composition structures, such as are needed in modeling and representing complex software under long-term evolution.

We can represent the name of an adapted x-frame by a reference to an XVCL variable or expression, rather than by a constant given by a character string. A reference to an XVCL variable x, written as **@x**, may be placed anywhere in the x-frame body. When encountered during processing, the processor emits the current value of the variable on the output. The following example explains the basic mechanism. Line numbers are for ease of reference and do not play any formal role in x-frame definition.

B:
1. <**set** x = F />
2. **@x** // the processor emits F
3. <**adapt @x** /> // adapts x-frame F
4. <**set** x = FF />
5. <**adapt @x** /> // adapts x-frame FF
6. <**adapt** *yetOther***@x-***NEW* />

In line 3, the name of the adapted x-frame is given by reference to variable x: **@x.** The processor fetches the current value of variable x and <**adapt**>s x-frame F. In line 5, the processor adapts x-frame FF.

In line 6, reference **@x** is surrounded by text shown in italics (in this case, it is Java code). The processor concatenates the value of "x" with surrounding text "as is," and treats the result as the name of an x-frame to be adapted. Therefore, in line 6, the name of an adapted x-frame is yetOtherFF-NEW.

Figure 8.5 shows yet another situation, where x-frame B is adapted in the context of three different x-frames, namely A1, A2, and A3. When reused in the context of A1, x-frame B <**adapt**>s x-frame F; in the context of A2, x-frame B <**adapt**>s x-frame G; and, in the context of A3, x-frame B <**adapt**>s x-frame H. We say that value H is a default value of variable x, as it takes effect whenever x is not overridden by some <**set**> command in one of the higher-level x-frames. This example explains the reason why the value assigned to a variable in a higher-level x-frame overrides any possible values assigned to the same variable in adapted x-frames.

An example of flexible composition of Figure 8.5 also illustrates one of the mechanisms to address evolution challenges discussed in Chapter 1: x-frames F and

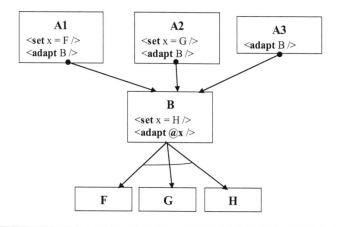

Figure 8.5   Context-sensitive composition (1).

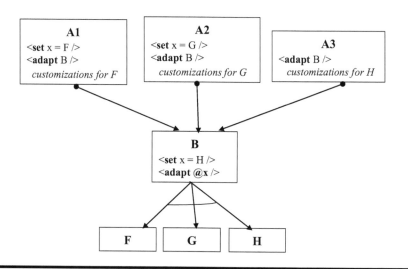

Figure 8.6   Context-sensitive composition (2).

G might provide implementation of some feature specific to system releases A1 and A2, respectively, although the default x-frame H might provide implementation of that feature for all the other releases (via x-frame A3).

Sometimes the impact of a variation (or change) on the base code is more diverse, and cannot be catered to by varying the names of adapted x-frames only, as was the case in our preceding example. Figure 8.6 and Figure 8.7 show solutions that cater to such situations. "Customizations" under each of the **<adapt>** commands apply selectively only to x-frames visited on a given adaptation path.

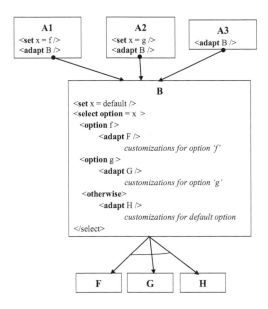

Figure 8.7   Context-sensitive composition (3).

We can also conduct multiple composition of x-frames by defining their names in a multivalue variable, and by placing parameterized **<adapt>** commands in a **<while>** loop, for example:

B:
<set x = F, G, H, I **/>**
<while x **>**
    <adapt @x /><
</while>

Consecutive iterations of the **<while>** loop **<adapt>** x-frames F, G, H, and I, respectively.

Insertion of **<adapt>** commands at designated variation points, called **<break>**s, gives us yet another way to vary composition rules.

We explain the basic rules for the **<insert>** into **<break>** XVCL construct first. Command **<insert>** is matched with corresponding **<break>**s by name. As the effect of **<insert>**, the processor replaces the original code contained in the matching **<break>**, called **<break>**'s default, by the modified code supplied by the matching **<insert>**. If there is no **<insert>** XVCL command matching a specific **<break>**, then the **<break>**'s default code is in force.

The net result of composition of x-frames in Figure 8.8 is the same as the situation depicted in Figure 8.5.

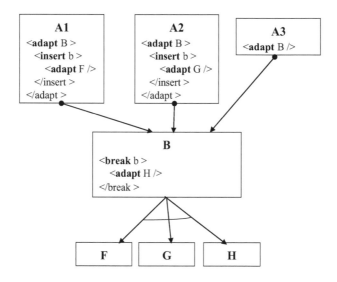

Figure 8.8 Context-sensitive composition with <insert> into <break>.

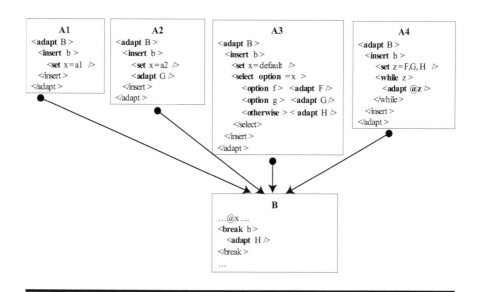

Figure 8.9 Yet another example of flexible composition.

An example of Figure 8.9 models the more diverse impact of change on x-frame B (any x-frames adapted by B), in the context of x-frames A1, A2, A3, and A4. This impact ranges from a single parameter x (in A1), to parameter x plus adaptation of x-frame G (in A2), to selection of an adapted x-frame based on the value of parameter x (in A3), to multiple composition of specified x-frames (in A4).

Methods illustrated in the earlier examples can be combined to achieve the desired properties of flexible composition structure. The main criteria to judge the quality of a solution is reusability across system releases, ease of extending, simplicity, and achieving "small change in requirements — small impact on an x-framework" effect.

Most often, x-frames represent large-granularity units of change (e.g., change at subsystem, component, or class levels). Flexible composition of x-frames described in this section addresses changes that match granularity of x-frames. By varying change specifications, the processor can compose the same composition structure (an x-framework) in different ways, emitting different custom code as required. Such a mechanism is sufficient to deal with large-granularity changes, but is not sufficient for small-granularity changes.

8.4   Specifying Small-Granularity Changes

The same XVCL commands that we used to define flexible composition are also used to specify small-granularity changes.

8.4.1 Parameterization

XVCL variables and expressions simply and conveniently address certain types of small changes. In the following example, we vary code emitted from x-frame B by means of a variable that takes different values in two different adaptations of x-frame X.

A:
1. <**set** x = modified code for **first** B >
2. <**adapt** B />
3. <**set** x = modified code for **second** B />
4. <**adapt** B />

For each reference @**x** in x-frame B adapted in line 2 (and in any x-frame adapted directly or indirectly from there), the processor uses the value "modified code for **first** B." For each reference @**x** in x-frame B adapted in line 4 (and in any x-frame adapted directly or indirectly from there), the processor uses the value "modified code for **second** B."

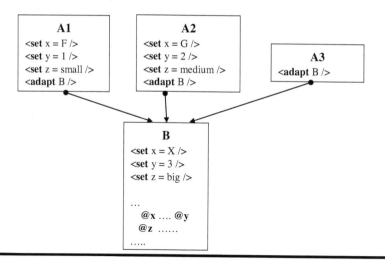

Figure 8.10   Context-sensitive parameterization.

In Figure 8.10, x-frame B is parameterized by variables x, y, and z. B also sets default values for those variables. When adapting x-frame B, x-frames A1 and A2 override defaults, whereas x-frame A3 accepts defaults (unless some other x-frame that adapted A3 set values for x, y, or z).

We discuss more about expressions in Section 8.9.

8.4.2 Selection

The command **<select>** is often used to select among the changes relevant to different system releases:

```
<set release = F3 />
<select option = release >
        <option F1> modification for release F1
        <option F2> modification for release F2
        <option F2> modification for release F3
        <otherwise> code for all other releases
</select>
```

<select> commands are used to deal with variant features arising during evolution that have become an integral part of the system evolution history. This usually means features that are shared by a number of released systems, or can be potentially useful to yet other systems to be released in the future. On the contrary, ad hoc enhancements of a single release should be handled in a nonintrusive way, usually by <**insert**>s into <**break**>s, so that they do not pollute or complicate the overall evolution history contained in an x-framework.

8.4.3 Insertions at Breakpoints

Small-granularity changes can be also specified as <**insert**>s into <**break**>s. The rules here are the same as in defining flexible compositions. The following example shows the basic case:

```
A:
<adapt B>
    <insert b>
        change at b for A
    </insert>
</adapt>
```

and the following breakpoint in x-frame B:

```
B:
...
<break b>
    default code at b
</break>
```

<**insert** b> overrides the "default code at b" contained in <**break** b> by the new code "change at b for A." Note that this change only occurs in B as adapted in the context of A. In other contexts in which B is needed, other changes or no changes at all could be specified. In the case of adapting B without any changes, the "default code at b" is in force.

<**insert**> commands are always attached to a specific <**adapt**>. In the example above, <**insert** b> applies to x-frame B and to all the x-frames reached in the chain of adaptations that originates at <**adapt** B>.

Here is a further illustration:

```
A:
<set x = B1 />
<adapt B>
    <insert b>
        bbbbb
    </insert>
</adapt>
<set x = B2 />
```

```
<adapt B>
   <insert b>
      BBBBB
      </insert>
</adapt>
```

B:
…
```
<break b>
   default code at b in B
</break>
<adapt C />
```

C:
```
<break b>
   default code at b in C
</break>
```

The first **<adapt** B> in x-frame A uses B1 as the value of variable x, and replaces **<break** b> in x-frames B and C with "bbbbb." The second **<adapt** B> in x-frame A will use B2 as the value of variable x, and replace **<break** b> in x-frames B and C with "BBBBB."

The scoping and overriding rules governing **<insert>**s and matching **<break>**s are analogical to **<set>** commands assigning values to variables and variable reference points: The first executed **<insert** b> wins — it overrides all the other **<insert** b> commands found in the processor execution sequence on the way to the matching **<break** b>. Therefore, any **<break>** can be affected by only one **<insert>**. The motivation for this scoping rule is the same as in the case of XVCL variables, namely, to keep lower-level x-frames generic and reusable in as many contexts as are practically needed in the evolution situation.

The **<insert>** command has two additional forms, namely, **<insert-before>** and **<insert-after>**, which insert changes before or after the designated **<break>**s, respectively.

A more detailed discussion of **<insert>**s into **<break>** will follow in Section 8.9.

8.5 Changes at Various Abstraction Levels

As we could see in the preceding two sections, the scale of change — its scope and granularity — exercised by **<select>**, **<insert>**, and other XVCL commands may vary. In one case, we can **<select>** or **<insert>** the whole component or subsystem, or modify components' interfaces, achieving changes at the architectural level. Even a change in the value of a single XVCL variable can determine a new context that triggers a new chain of customizations, and determines which x-frames should be composed and adapted. In other cases, the **<select>**ed or **<insert>**ed code may be just a couple of statements that modify algorithmic details of a certain component, and we may need an XVCL variable that may represent just names of classes, variables, operators, or keywords, in a generic form. Similarly, the **<while>** command can generate components, subsystems, or the application, or can be used to incorporate small changes in certain components.

Any program unit (such as file, interface definition, class, function, or even any part of them) that needs to be a separately represented for change specification purposes to adequately model evolution history, may become a unit of change specifications — an x-frame.

We build higher-level logical units of change specifications as grouping of lower-level units by means of **<adapt>** commands. By propagating variables across units, **<insert>**ing into **<break>**s, conditionals, and looping we achieve change specification goals at all levels of abstraction.

8.6 Defining Generic Structures and Generators

Genericity plays an important role in reuse-based evolution, and makes maintenance changes easier. It is important to achieve genericity in program components that we need to adapt to specific needs of various system releases. It is also important to unify similar program structures with generic forms within each release. Finally, change specifications should be normalized for nonredundancy (i.e., be generic).

XVCL mechanisms of parameterization, selection, and insertions contribute to building generic and flexible program representations to meet the above needs. The **<while>** loop helps us to design generators to produce custom instances of generic structures based on the specifications of their required properties.

Generic structures are a remedy for an explosion of component versions. Generics (or templates) are examples of conventional generic components whose instances (classes or functions) can differ in type parameters. Unlike type parameters, generic structures built with XVCL can capture any conceivable type of similarities and unify any type of differences among their instances.

A typical generic component and its instantiation mechanism are depicted in the following text. X-Frame Generic-x defines a common structure for a group of similar components and their variation points, that is, points at which a generic structure can be modified to produce a required custom instance. Variation points are marked with XVCL commands such as variable references, **<select>**, **<adapt>**, or **<break>**s. X-Frame A iterates over Generic-x. Each iteration produces a custom instance of Generic-x. X-Frame A specifies how to modify variation points in each iteration. Various **<option>**s of the **<select>** command define unique modifications required at variation points for a given instance. In the case of our example, instances x1 and x3 require unique modifications, whereas all the other instances require the same modifications (shown in option **otherwise**).

A:
```
<set x = x1, x2, x3, x4, x5>
<while x >
    <select x>
        <option x1>
            <adapt Generic-x>
                modification instructions for instance x1
        <option x3>
            <adapt Generic-x>
                modification instructions for instance x3
        <otherwise>
            <adapt Generic-x>
                modification instructions for the remaining instances x2, x4, x5
    </select>
</while>
```

Generic-x:

Common design and code for components x1–x5 are parameterized by: references to variable **@y**, **<break b>**, and **<adapt @x>**.

The mechanism is useful in forming concise generic highly parameterized and flexible design solutions.

The following example shows a slightly different design of a generator for class methods written in Java.

A:
```
<set x = foo />
<set z = 1, 2, 3 >
<set type = int, short, char />
<set arg = a, b, c />
<insert b>
        custom code
<insert />
<set size = 5 />
<adapt Generic-foo />
```

Generic-foo:
```
<while z, type, arg >
@type @x@z(@type @arg) {
```

```
// implementation of methods foo() can be customized at variation points by:
// references to variables:
    @x @z @type
// <break>s that can be overridden by custom code from higher-level frames:
    <break b>
        default code
    </break >
// <select> commands at which we can select among a number of options defin-
    ing custom code
    <select option = size />
        <option 3 > custom code for size 3
        <option 5 > custom code for size 5
        <otherwise > code for any other size
        </select >
// <adapt> commands:
<ifdef extra>
    <adapt Extra_Code />
</ifdef >
</while>
```

X-frame Generic-foo defines a common structure for methods foo() and variation points. X-Frame A sets parameters to instantiate variation points. The **<while>**
loop is controlled by three multivalue variables, namely, z, type, and arg. The t-th
iteration of the loop uses the i-th value of each of the control variables, namely, (1,
int, a), (2, short, b), and (3, char, c). In the case of a reference to a control variable in
the body of a loop, the processor emits a variable value of a current iteration. Each
iteration of the loop synthesizes a different header of Java class method, possibly
needed in different system releases.

Although in a very simple form, the preceding examples illustrate the main idea
of how we build XVCL generic structures and generators. A generic structure is a
template from which we can derive its variant forms.

We discuss more examples of generators in later chapters.

8.7 Capturing Change Traces and Similarity Patterns in Evolutionary Changes

The first step toward understanding evolutionary changes is to keep a record of the
whole chain of modifications related to a given source of change. The second step is
to unify similar components within and across released systems with generic components (discussed in the preceding section). The third step is to unify similarity
patterns in change specifications arising during evolution.

The "source of change" may just be any reason for changing software, such as fixing a bug, enhancing a single or a number of selected system releases with new features, or modification of a certain feature. In XVCL, variables have a global scope and their values propagate from the variable definition point (in the **<set>** command) to adapted x-frames. XVCL variables are a simple, yet effective, means to chain together detailed modifications across the x-framework related to a given source of change. Variation points are marked with XVCL commands such as **<adapt>**, **<ifdef>**, **<select>**, **<break>**, **<while>**, and others.

Using the **<select>** command alone may have shortcomings. First, it often happens that the same or similar modification must be done at multiple program points. Using **<select>** alone, we have to repeat the same change specifications in all the **<select>**s relevant to a particular change. Second, sometimes modifications may be similar but not the same. Using **<select>** alone, we have to specify such modifications as if they were totally different. If required modifications at different program points are similar, we should specify exactly what is common and what is different among them. This can result in shorter, easier-to-understand change specifications. Third, **<select>** is too coarse to show subtle modifications and to expose all the similarities between the original and the modified code.

The **<insert>** XVCL command used together with **<select>** provides necessary expressiveness and flexibility in structuring change specifications to overcome the aforementioned problems.

Similar modifications should be uniquely specified rather than scattered throughout change specifications. Having observed a recurring pattern of change specifications, we should try to unify possible differences in these change specifications so that similar modifications can be uniquely specified rather than scattered throughout the specifications. One way to achieve such unification is to **<insert>** common modifications into **<option>**s of a **<select>** command, rather than repeating them at each **<option>**. The following example illustrates the general structure of such a solution:

```
A:
<set x = x1, x2, x3, x4, x5>
<adapt X>
    <insert sameX>
        the same modification in scope of X
    </insert>
    <insert similar1>
        similar modification in the scope of X
    </insert>
    <insert similar2>
        yet other similar modification in the scope of X
    </insert>
<adapt />
```

X:
<while x >
  <select option = x >
    <option = x1> default
    <option = x2> **<break** sameX> … **</break>**
    <option = x3> … **<break** similar1> … **<break** similar2> **</break>**
    <otherwise> unique modification required in x4, x5
  </select>
</while>

Global modifications are under option x1, the same modifications in the scope of component X are under option x2, and similar modifications in the scope of component X are under **<otherwise>**.

Unrestricted parameterization is the essence of the preceding mechanism for unifying similar patterns of changes. Genericity is needed in both change specifications and component design. The same mechanism is used for both. In real programs, we find arbitrary similarities and differences. To deal with them, we need to build highly parameterized structures, with parameters ranging from simple values (such as integer or string) to subcomponent hierarchies. The **<insert>**ed code or **<select>** option may contain just simple code to cater to the former, and **<adapt @x>** or yet other nested **<select>** XVCL commands to cater to the latter. Indirect referencing to **<adapt>**ed components and **<break>**s further enhances genericity.

8.8 Handling Implementation Dependencies among Features

When one modification affects other modifications, things get necessarily more complicated. Typically, such a situation is handled by nested **<select>** (or **<ifdef>**) XVCL commands. In the following text, we sketch the situation of two features, F1 and F2, with two variants of F1 (F1.1 and F1.2) and four variants for feature F2 (F2.1–F2.4):

SPC:
<set F1 = F1.1>
<set F2 = F2.1, F2.3>
MakeRes-UI:
<select F1>
<option = F1.1>
<select F2>
<option = F2.1>
<option = F2.2>

```
<option = F2.3>
<option = F2.4 >
</select>
<option = F1.2>
<select F2>
   …
</select>
<otherwise>
</select>
```

XVCL cannot eliminate the inherent complexity of the problem. The question remains if we should specify all the combinations of interdependent variant features implemented in systems released during evolution or only some of them. The first solution will allow us to easily reuse existing variant features "as is." But as change specifications get more complex, it will inevitably become more difficult to customize features for specific systems and evolve the whole evolution architecture. It is necessary to carefully evaluate such trade-offs before making these important engineering decisions.

Emergence of implementation-dependent features (or changes, in general) often triggers the need for further decomposition and refinement of existing change specifications. One may be concerned about the increasing complexity of change specifications in view of interdependent features. We note that the problem of combining interdependent features is inherently complex. The alternative to change specifications is to enumerate component versions for each combination of features we are interested in, which is even more complex to work with than change specifications. A practical approach is to explicate only the most important feature combinations, leaving addressing the less important ones to the customization process.

8.9   Summary of XVCL Rules

We summarize the basic XVCL rules for ease of reference. At times, we also formalize the meaning of XVCL commands that were introduced in the previous sections in a very informal fashion. The reader can find a complete definition of XVCL in its XML syntax in Appendix C.

8.9.1   Basic XVCL Processing Rules

The processor traverses an x-framework in depth-first order, as dictated by **<adapt>**s embedded in x-frames. Processing starts at the topmost x-frame called SPC. The processor interprets XVCL commands embedded in visited x-frames, and emits a custom program into one or more files. XVCL commands in x-frames are processed in the sequence they appear in the x-frame. Whenever the processor encounters an <**adapt**> command, for example, <**adapt** B>, processing of the current x-frame, say, A, is suspended, and the processor starts processing x-frame B. Once processing of x-frame B has been completed, the processor resumes processing of x-frame A. The processing is completed when the processor reaches the end of the SPC.

Recursive adaptations are not allowed.

Customization commands are (optionally) specified for each <**adapt**> command. <**adapt** B> command instructs the processor to:

1. Process x-frame B and all x-frames adapted from B
2. Perform customizations of all the adapted x-frames as specified in the body of <**adapt** B>
3. Interpret any XVCL commands embedded in visited x-frames
4. Emit the result to the specified output file

For a given SPC, the processing flow is a trace that goes through the visited x-frames, starting with SPC. Suppose p1 and p2 are two, not necessarily distinct, points in the same or different x-frames. We say that:

> p1 **precedes** p2 (and p2 **follows** p1) if p1 appears before p2 in the processing flow. We use the notation p1 → p2 to indicate processing flow from p1 to p2.

Given an x-framework and SPC, for any two x-frames A and B, we say that:

■ A is an *ancestor* of B, if A <**adapt**>s (directly or indirectly) B in the processing flow defined by the SPC; we call B a *descendant* of A.
■ A is an *immediate ancestor* (or *parent*) of B, if A directly <**adapt**>s B in the processing flow defined by this SPC; we call B an *immediate descendant* (or *child*) of A. Note that for A to be a parent of B, A must contain an <**adapt**> command whose name attribute yields the name of x-frame B.

X-Frames are read-only. The processor creates and modifies a copy of the adapted x-frame and never changes the original x-frame.

8.9.2 XVCL Variables and Expressions

Generic names increase flexibility and adaptability of programs and play an important role in building generic, reusable programs. XVCL variables and expressions provide powerful means of creating generic names and controlling the x-framework customization process.

It should be noted that most of the elements in XVCL commands can be defined by XVCL expressions. This includes variable names and values in **<set>** commands, x-frame names in **<adapt>** commands, break names in **<insert>** and **<break>** commands, control variables in **<select>** and **<while>** commands, values in **<option>**s, etc. Only the name of an x-frame must be a defined by a constant.

An XVCL variable may be assigned values in any x-frame by the **<set>** command, for example: **<set** x = 1**>**. Variables are typeless. Variable values are interpreted as character strings.

A variable that is assigned a list of values in the respective **<set>** command is called a multivalue variable, e.g., **<set** x = F, G, H **>**. The main use of multivalue variables is in controlling loops. A reference to a multivalue variable in the loop yields the value of that variable in a given iteration

B:
<set x = F, G, H **/>**
<while x **>**
@x
<adapt @x /**>**
</while **>**

In the first iteration of the preceding loop, the processor outputs character "F" and **<adapt>**s x-frame F. In the second iteration, the processor outputs "G" and **<adapt>**s x-frame G. In the third iteration, the processor outputs "H" and **<adapt>**s x-frame H.

XVCL expressions are formed by variable references as follows:

A direct reference to variable C is written as **@C**. Each extra symbol "@" in the front of a variable name indicates a level of indirection. So:

@C means value-of (C)
@@C means value-of (value-of (C))
@@@C means value-of (value-of (value-of (C))), and so on.

Table 8.1   The Symbol Table with Variables

Name	Value
C	U
U	BU
BU	V
AV	W

The XVCL processor replaces references to variables by their values. Here, we should mention that the XVCL processor stores all the variables defined so far in the symbol table along with their current values, as assigned to variables in **<set>** and **<set**-multi> commands.

The processor reports an error for a reference to a variable that does not exist in the symbol table.

Table 8.1 gives an example of the symbol table we use in the examples.

For example, the value of **@C** is **U**, the value of **@@C** is **BU,** and the value of **@@@C** is **V.**

The name expressions are written as follows: ?@A@B@C?. The processor interprets this name expression as value-of ("A" | value-of ("B" | value-of (C))), where symbol '|' means text concatenation.

For example, referring to the Table 8.1, the evaluation of name expression, ?@A@B@C? is done as follows:

1. Get the value of variable C
   - The intermediate result is U
2. Concatenate B and U and get the value of variable BU
   - The intermediate result is V
3. Concatenate A and V and get the value of variable AV
   - The final result is W

After each evaluation step, the intermediate value computed is concatenated with the character string on the left to form a new variable name that is looked up in the symbol table. Evaluation of a name expression continues until the whole name expression is evaluated.

8.9.3 Variable Scoping and Propagation Rules

Variable scoping rules are the same for both single-value and multivalue variables.

Within an x-frame, each subsequent assignment of value to a variable overrides any previous **<set>**, which assigns value to that variable. Variable values propagate to adapted x-frames, as shown in Figure 8.11.

During processing, values of variables propagate through the whole adaptation chain of x-frames visited by the processor. The **<set>** command in the ancestor x-frame overrides **<set>** commands in all the subsequently processed descendent x-frames as shown in Figure 8.12. That is, once an x-frame **<set>**s the value of variable x, any further attempts to redefine that variable x in descendent x-frames will be ignored. The following example clarifies the variable propagation rule.

It is a good practice to make an x-frame **<set>** default values to variables it refers to. In case no ancestor x-frame **<set>**s value to a given variable, the default value is in force.

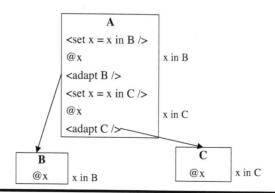

Figure 8.11   Variable value propagation.

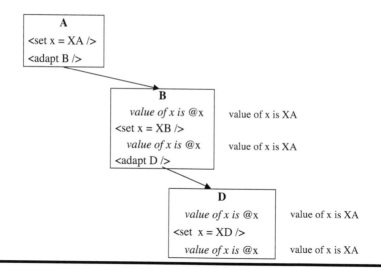

Figure 8.12   Variable value propagation along adaptation chains.

The processor treats a reference to an undefined variable as an error that terminates processing of an x-framework.

8.9.4 *The <select> Command*

The **<select>** Command is used to select zero or more of the predefined branches (**<option>**s) for further processing. **<select>** contains zero or more **<option>**s followed by an optional **<otherwise>**. For example:

```
<select option = x />
    <option a > option-body
    <option b > option-body
    <option c > option-body
    <otherwise> option-body
</select>
```

Options are selected based on the value of the control variable. If the control variable is undefined (that is it does not exist in the symbol table), the processor issues an error message and terminates processing.

An option-body may contain code written in one of the base languages and any XVCL commands.

The XVCL processor checks **<option>**s in sequential order and selects for processing **<option>**s as follows: the value of the control variable of **<select>** is compared against the values specified at each **<option>**. Each **<option>** whose value matches the value of the control variable is selected for processing in the order of its appearance in the **<select>** command. The processor processes each of the selected option clauses immediately upon selection. If none of the **<option>**s are selected, then **<otherwise>** is processed, if present.

A value specified in **<option>** may be an expression (for details refer to Appendix C).

8.9.5 *The <while> Command*

The **<while>** command iterates over its body. Multivalue variables listed in **<while>** are the loop's control variables. All control variables must have the same number of values. Each loop iteration uses the i-th value of each of its control variables; therefore, the number of iterations is equal to the number of values in each of the multivalue control variables.

The while-body may contain code and XVCL commands. Values of the loop's multivalue control variables can be referenced in the while-body. If used inside the **<while>** command, these multivalue variables behave like single-value variables and can be referenced just like a single-value variable.

A **<while>** loop in the following example generates three Java class methods foo, with some variants in the header and an empty body.

A:
```
<set z = 1, 2, 3 >
<set type = int, short, char />
<set arg = a, b, c />
<adapt Generic-foo />
```

Generic-foo:
<**while** z, type, arg >
@type @x@z(**@type @arg**) *{ }*
</while>

The loop is controlled by three multivalue variables, namely, z, type, and arg. The t-th iteration of the loop uses the i-th value of each of the control variables, namely (1, int, a), (2, short, b), and (3, char, c). In the case of a reference to a control variable in the body of a loop, the processor emits a variable value of the current iteration. Each iteration of the loop synthesizes a different header of Java class method, possibly needed in different system releases.

8.9.6 *<ifdef> and <ifndef> Commands*

These commands have the following syntax:

<**ifdef** x >
    if-body
</ifdef>
<**ifndef** x >
    if-body
</ifndef>

A variable specified in <**ifdef**> or <**ifndef**> is a control variable. If a control variable is defined (i.e., it exists in the symbol table), the processor processes the if-body of <**ifdef**> command. Otherwise, the if-body is ignored. The <**ifndef**> command acts in the opposite way — its if-body is processed only if a control variable is undefined.

The if-body may contain code and any XVCL commands.

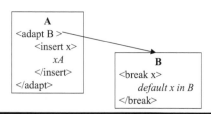

Figure 8.13   A basic rule for <insert> into <break>.

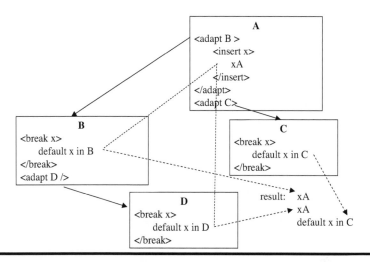

Figure 8.14 <insert> into multiple <break>s.

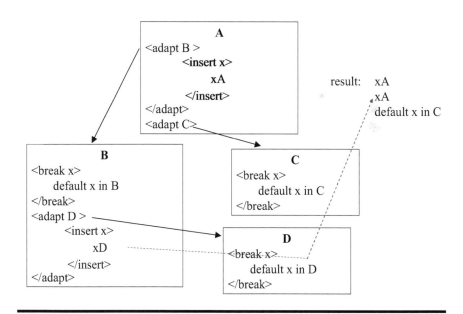

Figure 8.15 Upper-level <insert> overrides lower-level <insert>s.

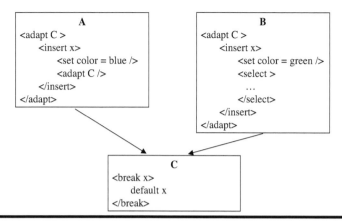

Figure 8.16 X-Frame C adapted with <insert>s in two contexts.

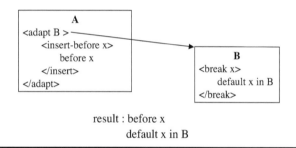

Figure 8.17 <insert-before>.

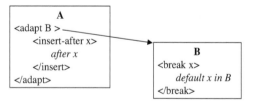

Figure 8.18 <insert-after>.

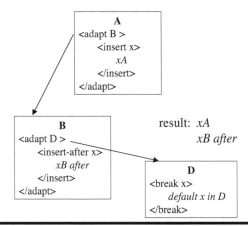

Figure 8.19 Cumulative result of <insert> and <insert-after>.

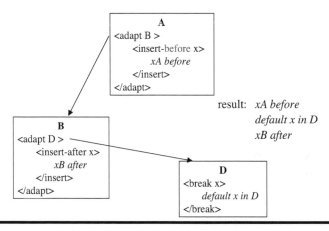

Figure 8.20 Cumulative result of <insert-before> and <insert-after>.

8.9.7 <insert> into <break> Command

The **<break>** command marks a variation point in an x-frame. The **<insert>** command replaces the contents of matching **<break>**s (e.g., default x in b in Figure 8.13) with new contents defined in **<insert>** (e.g., xA in Figure 8.13). If there is no **<insert>** matching a given **<break>**, the default contents contained in the **<break>** are processed. **<insert>** matches **<break>** by name.

<insert> commands can only be specified in the body of an **<adapt>** command. In Figure 8.13, **<insert x>** is specified for **<adapt B>**. **<insert>** propagates to all the subsequently adapted x-frames and may reach matching **<break>**s there (Figure 8.14). Note that **<insert x>** does not affect **<break x>** in x-frame C.

Only the **<insert>** command executed first in the processing flow matches (affects) a **<break>**.

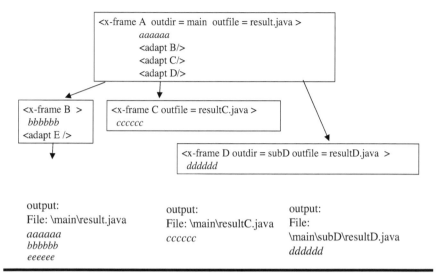

Figure 8.21   Attributes outdir and outfile

This first executed **<insert>** overrides **<insert>** commands that may appear in all the subsequently adapted x-frames, as illustrated in Figure 8.15.

This **<insert>** overriding rule, similar to the variable-value-overriding rule, has the purpose of making x-frames adaptable and reusable in multiple contexts (Figure 8.16).

Commands **<insert-before>** and **<insert-after>** are similar to **<insert>**.

The **<insert-before>** inserts its contents before the matching **<break>**s (Figure 8.17). The **<insert-after>** inserts its contents after the matching **<break>**s (Figure 8.18). Note that the **<insert-before>** and **<insert-after>** do not replace the **<break>**'s default contents.

Propagation and overriding rules for **<insert-before>** and **<insert-after>** are the same as for **<insert>**: the first **<insert-before>** overrides any subsequent ones, and as does the first **<insert-after>**.

Each of the **<insert>**, **<insert-before>**, and **<insert-after>** commands may match (affect) the same **<break>**, yielding an accumulative result, as shown in Figure 8.19 and Figure 8.20.

More rules governing **<insert>** into **<break>** are described in Appendix C.

8.9.8   *Attributes* Outdir *and* Outfile

Attributes **outdir** and **outfile** specify the directory name and the filename, respectively, to which the XVCL processor should emit the processing output. These attributes may be attached to an x-frame or to a specific **<adapt>** command. Values of **outdir** and **outfile** may be given by an expression.

Figure 8.21 illustrates how attributes **outdir** and **outfile** are used to direct the output to different files and directories.

Here is a more detailed explanation. We discuss attributes **outdir** and **outfile** for x-frames only. The case of attributes **outdir** and **outfile** of **<adapt>** command is similar, and for an explanation, refer to Appendix C.

8.9.8.1   *outdir* = dir-name

The value of attribute **outdir,** say *dir-name,* must be an XVCL expression (in the simplest case, it is just a constant). If the specified directory *dir-name* in attribute **outdir** does not exist, the processor creates one. The *dir-name* can be either an absolute path such as "c:\mydir\test" or a partial path, including the null path, for example the name "test" or "xvcl\test."

If *dir-name* is a partial path, the XVCL processor appends it to the output directory path of the current x-frame's parent. When the processor traverses back up the x-framework, it removes the directory paths that are appended at each level. This way, the directory structure may grow as the processor traverses down and shrink accordingly when the processor traverses back up the x-framework, placing outputs from various x-frames in different directories. For example, suppose the parent's output directory is "c:\mydir\." Defining "test" in the **outdir** attribute of the current x-frame will make the processor emit the output from the current x-frame into the file that will be placed in the "c:\mydir\test" directory. This feature is useful, for example, when the processor needs to emit Java code from different x-frames into different directories.

If *dir-name* is an absolute path, the processor emits output of the current x-frame into this directory. The current output directory is set to be this path and descendent x-frames can append their own partial paths to it. In this way, subsequently processed x-frames can create new output directories, as desired, if these do not exist.

If the **outdir** attribute is not defined in the current **<x-frame>**, then the parent's output directory path is used.

If no ancestor x-frame, including SPC, has defined an output path in the **outdir** attribute, the processor emits output from the current x-frame (as well as from all its ancestors) to the directory where the SPC is stored.

If the *dir-name* of SPC's **outdir** attribute is a partial path, for example, "test," then the processor appends "test" to the directory path where the SPC is stored and emits output from the SPC to that directory.

When both the **<adapt>** command in the parent x-frame and the adapted x-frame define the output directory path in their **outdir** attributes, the **<adapt>** command's output directory path is used.

For example, if x-frame X <adapt>s Y as follows:

<adapt Y outdir= c:\ancestor\ outfile = b.java />

and x-frame Y is defined as:

<x-frame Y outdir = c:\descendent\ />

then the output from x-frame Y will be emitted to the directory "c:\ancestor."

Value *dir-name* is often defined by an XVCL expression that involves variables. In such a case, an ancestor x-frame can override *dir-name*s in the descendant x-frames via variables that are **<set>** in ancestor x-frames and referenced in *dir-name* expressions in descendent x-frames.

8.9.8.2   *outfile* = file-name

This attribute specifies a file to which the processor emits the output from the current x-frame. The *file-name* must be an expression that yields a legal filename or absolute directory path including the filename. Partial (relative) paths are not allowed in the **outfile** attribute.

An extension (if any) is treated as an integral part of the filename. Although the processor does not check filename extensions or make any use of them, it is a good practice to use extension .xvcl for files containing x-frames.

When the processor emits output to file *file-name* for the first time in processing flow, and file *file-name* exists, the existing file is deleted before the output is emitted. If any subsequently processed x-frame emits output to the same file during the same run of the processor, the output is appended to the contents of that file.

A processor option –A allows the user to avoid deleting an existing file. If the processor is invoked with option –A, the processor appends the emitted output to file *file-name* even if the file *file-name* already existed before the processor was invoked.

If **outfile** is omitted, the processor checks the **outfile** attribute of the parent x-frame that adapts the current one as follows: if the **outfile** attribute is defined in the parent's command that adapts the current x-frame, that filename will be used. Otherwise, the parent's x-frame output file is used, if defined. If an output filename is not defined in any of the ancestor x-frames including SPC, the SPC's name is the *file-name*.

When both the parent's x-frame **<adapt>** command and the current x-frame define the output filename in their **outfile** attributes, the parent's <adapt> command's output filename is used. This is consistent with XVCL's variable scoping rules.

For example, if x-frame X <adapt>s Y as follows:

<adapt Y **outfile** = a.java />

and x-frame Y is defined as:

<x-frame Y **outfile** = b.java />

then the output from x-frame Y is emitted to the file "a.java."

8.9.9 Other Commands and Features

The <**remove** x /> command undefines a variable x by removing it from the symbol table. Removing a defined variable produces a warning message. The variable is removed if and only if the <remove> command appears in the x-frame that originally defined that variable (i.e., the x-frame that entered that variable into the symbol table). Otherwise, the command is ignored and a warning message is produced.

The <**message**> command displays a message on the screen. This command does not affect the output emitted by the XVCL processor. It is used for debugging purposes, for example, to check variable values to trap error situations.

There are a number of other XVCL features, such as the attribute **samelevel** of the <**adapt**> command, and defer-evaluation in the <**set**> command, as well as arithmetic expressions. These features are not often used and the reader can refer to Appendix C for details.

8.9.10 The XVCL Processor's Options

Processor options and environmental variables defined in a configuration file allow the user to tune the processing as follows:

-A option and variable optionA

Option –A allows the user to avoid deleting an existing file when the processor attempts to emit output to this file for the first time. When the processor is invoked with a option –A, for example,

java -jar xvcl.jar –A SPC

the processor appends emitted output to file *file-name* even if the file *file-name* already existed before the processor was invoked.

-T option and variable optionT

When the processor is invoked with a -T option, for example:

java -jar xvcl.jar –T SPC

the processor includes the comment line with the name of an x-frame as the first line in the output emitted from that x-frame.

The user should specify comment symbols in "begin-comment" and "end-comment" variables. The default for begin-comment is //. The default for end-comment is nil (nothing).

-B option and variable optionB

When the processor is invoked with a -B option, extra whitespaces (blank, space, etc.) normally emitted by the processor are removed.

8.10   Conclusions

In this chapter, we introduced a step-by-step description of XVCL mechanisms to realize the mixed-strategy approach. We used simplified, XML-free syntax to focus attention on essentials. Full specifications of XVCL are in Appendix C. In the initial sections, we introduced XVCL commands informally, in the context of various maintenance and evolution tasks. In the last section, we summarized XVCL commands in a more formal and systematic way.

The simplicity and uniformity of XVCL change instruments signifies a certain level of maturity of technology. It is not surprising if we recall that XVCL is based on principles of frame technology that emerged from the industrial maintenance battlefield, and have been refined in projects dealing with millions of lines of code.

We consider a current form of XVCL an assembly language of change specifications. XVCL's explicit and direct articulation is the source of its expressive power, but also the source of its weakness, as x-frames may become overly verbose. Currently, we address this problem with tools that reveal simplified, abstract views of x-frames. In the future, we hope to discover mixed-strategy abstractions that will allow us to define higher-level forms of XVCL, equally expressive but free of the current pitfalls.

References

1. Bassett, P., *Framing Software Reuse — Lessons from Real World*, Yourdon Press, Prentice Hall, 1997.
2. Clements, P. and Northrop, L., *Software Product Lines: Practices and Patterns*, Addison-Wesley, 2002.
3. Conradi, R. and Westfechtel, B., Version models for software configuration management, *ACM Computing Surveys*, 30(2), 232–282, 1998.
4. Eick, S.G., Graves, T.L., Karr, A.F., Marron, J.S., and Mockus, A., Does code decay? Assessing the evidence from change management data, *IEEE Transactions on Software Engineering*, 27(1), 1–12, January 2001.
5. Ernst, M., Badros, G., and Notkin, D., An empirical analysis of C preprocessor use, *IEEE Transactions on Software Engineering*, 28(12), 1146–1170, December 2002.
6. Karhinen, A., Ran, A., and Tallgren, T., Configuring designs for reuse, *Proceedings of the International Conference on Software Engineering, ICSE'97*, Boston, MA, pp. 701–710.
7. Sommerville, I. and Dean, G., PCL: a language for modeling evolving system architectures, *IEE Software Engineering Journal*, 111–121, 1996.

Chapter 9

Software Similarities: Symptoms and Causes

Chapter Summary

It is very much in the spirit of reuse-based evolution to identify and leverage all kinds of similarity patterns arising during evolution. Spotting patterns of evolutionary changes affecting software over time is essential to avoid complications during evolution. By *similarity patterns* we mean, for example, groups of similar components within a single released system or across released systems. In the first part of this chapter, we take a closer look at the software similarity phenomenon and the repetitions (software clones) it spawns. We make observations from empirical studies. We discuss one such study, the Java Buffer library, JDK 1.5, in detail. We briefly describe other studies, and comment on the main results.

In the second part of this chapter, we generalize findings from empirical studies. We trace the roots of the similarity problem and argue about the general nature of the problem's symptoms and causes.

In Chapter 10, we show how the mixed-strategy approach deals with unifying similarity patterns.

9.1   The Problem of Software Similarities and Cloning

Software similarity pattern is a concept denoting any recurring problem in analysis, design, or implementation spaces. *Software clones* are similar program structures that spawn from the fact that similarity exists.

We use terms *similarity patterns, similar program structures,* and *clones* interchangeably, depending on the context.

Similarity patterns create an opportunity for program simplification via generic design. The aim of *generic design* is to unify differences among similar program structures and represent a group of such structures in a unique, generic form. Most of the programming languages support type parameterization, called generics in Ada [1], Java JDK 1.5, and C# [36], and templates in C++ [61], to define generic classes or methods. Design patterns [25] and more recent techniques, such as aspect-oriented programming [37], also increase genericity of program solutions. Therefore, not all similarity patterns must necessarily lead to clones. Having observed similarities, skillful design may help us avoid some of the repetitions.

We define *clones* informally as program structures of considerable size that exhibit significant similarity. The actual size and similarity (which can be measured, for example, in terms of replicated lines of code) vary depending on the context. Clones may represent similar program structures of any kind and granularity.

Clones may or may not represent program structures that perform well-defined functions. We distinguish two types of clones, namely:

- *Simple clones:* the same or similar segments of contiguous code, such as class methods or fragments of method implementation
- *Structural clones*: patterns of interrelated components [6] (e.g., collaborating classes) representing design solutions repeatedly applied by programmers to solve similar problems and similar program modules or subsystems (so-called architecture-level patterns) comprising many components.

Most of the interesting clones, particularly structural clones, are similar but not identical. Changes among clones result from differences in intended behavior, and from dependencies on the specific program context in which clones are embedded (such as different names of referenced variables, methods called, or platform dependencies).

It is difficult to define the concept of similarity in precise, descriptive terms: similarity is a multifaceted phenomenon that escapes precise definition. The notion of similarity necessarily involves human judgment and, therefore, is subjective. Whether or not we consider two code structures as clones depends on what we want to do with them and for what purpose. For example, we might want to merely document instances of similar program structures for future maintenance or unify them with a single generic structure for the purpose of simplification. The reason for our interest in clones determines the type and size of similar program structures that we wish to consider clones.

We can characterize clones that are likely to meet our goals by measures such as the minimum size of clone candidates of interest, the percentage of common code among code structures [32], types of allowable parametric differences, or the Levenstein editing distance [44] among code structures. (The Levenstein editing distance is measured in terms of the number of editing operations required to convert one text fragment to another.) Finally, characterizations of clones may depend on the abstraction level of similarity patterns (design or code), and whether we use automatic or manual processes to identify clones in a program. Metrics are essential for automated detection of clones. On the other hand, manual analysis of design-level similarities is better done in a top-down manner, relying on concepts of the underlying application domain and a programming language.

Software clones have received much attention in research. Cloning has been studied in the context of reengineering [10], refactoring [24], and clone detection [10,32].

Poor design and ad hoc maintenance may induce clones. At times, cloning is done for a good cause. Programmers clone code for quick productivity gains and to speed up development and maintenance. Ad hoc cloning is a simple form of reuse, but it does not lead to systematic reuse (e.g., via software product lines [17]). Mayrand observes that cloning is a sign that good reuse processes are not in place [47]. Sometimes, cloning is done to increase the robustness of life-critical systems, for better performance, or to minimize dependencies among developers in large projects. Recurring problems of a similar structure in analysis and design spaces lead to structural clones. Analysis patterns [23] and design patterns [25] exemplify these situations. Programmers repeatedly apply so-called *mental macros* to solve various programming problems [10]. Mental macros reflect common programming wisdom or a programmer's specific experiences. With each application of a mental macro, a redundancy occurs, in a more or less explicit form. Architecture-centric and pattern-driven development encouraged by modern platforms (.NET™ and J2EE™) standardize program solutions, which leads to clones at all levels [70]. Similarities induced by standard ways of organizing software are beneficial, as it becomes easier to understand the code written by somebody else — similar problems are being solved in similar ways. Still, pattern-driven development may also pose certain complication for future maintenance and reuse due to fragmentation and scattering of code in application domain-specific areas. The issue is multifaceted, important, and interesting, and we revisit it later.

Finally, clones may be generated by tools. Rapid application development features of IDEs (integrated development environments) save programmer development time by generating code that can be inferred from simple programmer inputs (e.g., selections of menu items or clicking on a button in the IDE's user interface).

Many clones cannot be avoided [30]. Kim estimates that 34 percent of clones cannot be refactored [39]. In the example of the Buffer library discussed in this chapter, most of the 68 percent of code contained in simple and structural clones cannot be eliminated using object-oriented and other conventional methods without compromising other important design goals. In yet other studies, also summarized in this chapter, we found similar rates of incidence of cloned code, which is difficult to refactor with conventional methods.

We classify clones into the following categories:

1. *Desirable*: Such clones are useful at runtime (e.g., for performance or reliability) and cannot be eliminated from programs. Clones introduced deliberately by an implementation technique (e.g., by J2EE or .NET architecture and patterns) also belong to this category. We comment on these important types of clones in more detail later.
2. *Avoidable*: Such clones are caused by the programmer's carelessness. For example, similar code fragments introduced by poor design or an ad hoc "copy–paste–modify" practice during maintenance often fall into this category.
3. *Problematic*: These are the clones that are undesirable but are difficult to avoid using given design techniques, without compromising important design goals. As the name suggests, nothing definite can be said about problematic clones. They are relative to design techniques and design goals. Despite their hypothetical, imprecise, and floating nature, we find the concept useful in discussing cloning problems. Most of the clones discussed in the Buffer library case study belong to this category.

Although there are good reasons for creating certain clones, most of the clones, independent of the reasons why they occur, complicate programs. Cloning has received much attention because of its harmful impact on maintenance. Clones increase the risk of update anomalies and hinder program understanding during maintenance in at least two ways: (1) a programmer must maintain more code than he or she would have to maintain should the clones be removed, and (2) when one logical source of change affects many instances of a replicated program structure scattered throughout a program, to implement a change, a programmer must find and update all instances of the replicated structure. The situation is further complicated if a replicated structure must be changed in slightly different ways, depending on the context.

There are even deeper reasons to avoid repetitions: By multiplying similar program structures in variant forms, we hinder the conceptual integrity of the design, which Brooks calls "the most important consideration in system design" [13].

We may merely document clones for future maintenance; unify them by a macro or function, as is often done during reengineering [10]; refactor a program to avoid clones [24]; or apply generative techniques to eliminate clones at the extra plane level (such as mixed-strategy representation with XVCL), while leaving them in at the program code level [28,29,52,70]. At times, clone elimination at the program code level may be hindered by risks involved in changing programs [18] or by other design goals that conflict with refactorings [28,29].

To see how significant the problem of cloning is, let us look at the cloning rates (as percentages) reported in various surveys: 50–85 [46], 13–20 [2], 12.7 [10], and 6.4–7.5 [43]. Software examined in reengineering projects contained around 40 percent of cloned code [56]. It is important to note that these surveys did not consider design-level structural clones. Instead, they focused on simple clones (exact and similar code fragments), and in many cases addressed only clones found by automatic clone detection tools.

In our studies, we looked at the bigger picture, focusing on both simple clones and large-granularity, design-level structural clones. Then, cloning rates dramatically increased: In laboratory studies and two industrial projects, we found 50–90 percent cloning rates in well-designed programs, not affected by maintenance. Our studies covered a range of application domains (business systems, Web portals, command and control systems, and class libraries), programming languages (Java, C++, C#, ASP, JSP, PHP), and platforms (J2EE, .NET, Unix, Windows). For example, the extent of cloning in Java Buffer library was 68 percent [28,29] (described later in this chapter); in parts of STL (C++), over 50 percent [5]; in J2EE Web Portal, 61 percent [69]; and in certain ASP Web portal modules, up to 90 percent [52]. The last two results are from pilot projects by our industry partner ST Electronics. In many cases, repetitions occurred as there was no simple way of avoiding them with conventional methods without compromising other important design goals [30]. In the case of the J2EE Web Portal, the architecture and patterns induced cloning. However, we could effectively treat the similarities by unifying them with mixed-strategy generic structures. We measured the percentage of cloning by comparing the subject program against a nonredundant mixed-strategy representation of the same program in its original form.

Size reduction does not always lead to program simplification. However, in all our studies, we focused only on repetitions of significant engineering importance, meaning that they created reuse opportunities, induced extra conceptual complexity into a program, or were counterproductive for maintenance. In a survey of 17 Web applications we found 17–60 percent of code contained in clones [54] was the only exception, as in this study we were not able to conduct a qualitative analysis of the replicated code.

9.2 Software Similarities and Reuse

Avoiding repetition during development and in software products is the goal of software reuse. The main themes of software reuse are identifying similarities and differences (variabilities) in requirements (domain analysis [53]), architecture/design, and components [17]. With this understanding, we can attempt to build generic, adaptable, and therefore reusable program solutions. Current state of the art in reuse is based on architecture-centric, component-based approaches and product line concepts [17]. Having identified and scoped variant features (usually modeled as feature diagrams [33]), a product line architecture (PLA) is designed to accommodate variant features. With component-based design, genericity of a PLA is achieved by stabilizing component interfaces and localizing the impact of variant features to a small number of components. However, for variant features that have a crosscutting effect on PLA components, this goal cannot be easily achieved. A component affected by variant features explodes into numerous versions. Similarities among component versions cannot be easily spotted, and reuse opportunities offered by such similarities are often missed. Given thousands of variant features and complex feature interdependencies arising in industrial product lines, the cost of finding "best-matching" component configurations for reuse and the follow-up component customization, integration, and validation may become prohibitive for effective reuse [21].

With a mixed-strategy approach, we treat similarity patterns induced by variant features as first-class citizens, whether they have a crosscutting effect on components or not. Mixed-strategy generic structures unify similarity patterns at any granularity level and of any type – from a subsystem, to pattern of components, to component, to class, and to program statement in class implementation. For this reason, mixed-strategy often extends the scope and rates of reuse achievable by means of conventional techniques.

Architecture-centric, pattern-driven development is now supported by major platforms such as .NET™ and J2EE. Patterns lead to beneficial standardization of program solutions and are a basic means of achieving reuse of common service components. IDEs support application of major patterns, or programmers use manual copy–paste–modify to apply yet other patterns. Mixed-strategy can enhance the benefits of modern platforms by automating pattern application, and emphasizing the visibility of patterns in code. Pattern-driven design facilitates reuse of middleware service components, but tends to scatter application domain-specific code. With mixed-strategy, we can package and isolate otherwise scattered domain-specific code into reusable generic components. Such extensions improve development and maintenance productivity and allow reuse to penetrate application business logic and user interface system areas, not just middleware service component layers.

9.3 Software Similarities and Generic Design

Generic design [26,27] aims at achieving nonredundancy by unifying differences among similar program concepts or structures for the purpose of simplification. Yet, evidence abounds that programs are often polluted by redundant code [10,14,22,28,29,32,43,47]. The extent to which similar program structures deliberately spread through programs hint strongly that potentials of generic design may not be fully exploited. Particularly as we look at the bigger picture, moving beyond small-granularity duplications (e.g., similar code fragments often termed clones in the literature), we find increasing rates of code contained in similar design-level structures (e.g., similar classes or components, or patterns of collaborating classes or components). In our studies, in which we concentrated on similarity patterns at all levels, we often found around 60 percent of code repeated many times, in variant forms. Although not all such repetitions are necessarily bad, most of them complicate the program, hinder program understanding, and contribute a great deal to the high cost of day-to-day maintenance and long-term evolution.

There are three engineering benefits of generic design (and three reasons to avoid unnecessary repetitions): First, genericity is an important theme of software reuse, the goal being to recognize similarities to avoid repetitions across projects, processes, and products. Indeed, many repetitions merely indicate unexploited reuse opportunities. Second, repetitions hinder program understanding. Repeated similar program structures cause update anomalies complicating maintenance, according to research on reengineering, refactoring, and clone detection [6]. Third, by revealing design-level similarities, we reduce the number of distinct conceptual elements a programmer must deal with. We not only reduce the overall software complexity but also enhance conceptual integrity of a program, which Brooks calls "the most important consideration in system design" in his famous *The Mythical Man-Month*. Common sense suggests that developers should be able to express their design and code without unwanted repetitions, whenever they wish to do so.

Parameterization is a prime concept in generic design, almost as old as programming. Macros and preprocessing (such as cpp) are simple forms of parameterization that are still used today. Most of the programming languages provide type parameterization called generics (in Ada, Eiffel, Java, or C#) or templates (in C++). Despite benefits, type parameterization is not sufficient to unify the many similarity patterns that arise in class libraries and application programs.

In the following sections, we show examples and discuss the reasons why conventional programming techniques are not effective in achieving goals of generic design.

9.4 Software Similarities, Genericity, and Software Complexity

Consider a project collaboration Web portal (PCWP) such as that depicted in Figure 9.1. PCWP supports communication among team members. For this purpose, PCWP maintains information about staff, projects, who works on which projects, tasks assigned to various staff members, and other information that matters in collaboration.

PCWP consists of modules such as Staff, Project, or Task. For example, module Staff allows a user to create, delete, and modify data about staff members, assign staff members to projects, etc. CPG-Nuke allows its functionality to be extended by the addition of more modules.

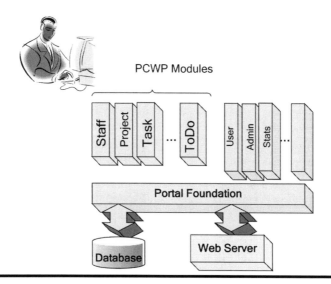

Figure 9.1 Project collaboration Web portal (PCWP).

PCWP modules are deployed on top of the portal foundation that implements common services reused by the portal modules. PCWP also reuses some of the standard modules such as Use, Admin, Statistics, History, and others.

PCWP may be implemented in many available Web technologies such as PHP™, ASP™, Ruby on Rails™, ASP.NET™, J2EE, or even just in Java™ and JavaScript™. Our argument is independent of the implementation language and platform.

For each module, there are operations, such as Create, Edit, Delete, Display, Find, or Copy. The design of each operation such as CreateStaff, CreateProject, UStaff, or EditProject involves a pattern of collaborating classes from the GUI, service, and database layers. Each box in Figure 9.2 represents a number of classes: GUI classes implement various forms to display or enter data; business logic classes implement data validation and actions specific to various operations or entities; entity classes define data access; and classes at the bottom contain table definitions.

Classes in corresponding boxes at each level display much similarity. Figure 9.2 shows two dimensions of DEMS similarity patterns: The first one results from the same operation applied to different entities, e.g., CreateStaff, CreateProject, ... , EditStaff, EditProject, ... , and others, as shown in Figure 9.2(a). The second similarity pattern results from different operations for a given module (e.g., CreateStaff, EditStaff, ... , CreateProject, EditProject, ... , and others, as shown in Figure 9.2(b).

However, there are also differences across classes for various operations, implied by the different meanings of various entities such as Staff, Project, Task: for example, operation CreateProject requires different types of data entry and data validation than CreateStaff. A user interface form for CreateStaff is displayed with empty

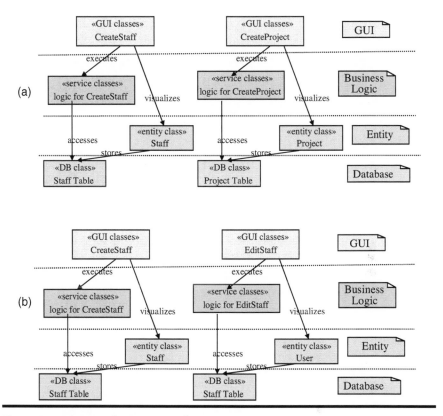

Figure 9.2 A recurring pattern of components.

data fields, whereas a form for EditStaff has to fetch data from the Staff table and display it in the proper data fields.

Suppose we are unable to find a way to unify differences among operations for different PCWP modules. Then we have to implement each operation such as CreateStaff, CreateProject, … , EditStaff, EditProject, etc., separately, ignoring much similarity that exists among operations.

To visualize the situation, let us assume we have ten modules and five operations. Then our program solution includes 10 * 5 = 50 patterns, as shown in Figure 9.2. If each box consists of only one class, then we have 50 * 4 = 200 classes and 200 interactions among classes. That is a conservative estimate, as in reality some of the boxes contain more than one class. This situation is shown in Figure 9.3(a).

Suppose we can unify differences among the same operation for different modules, so that the 10 modules use only five generic functions Create[M], Edit[M], etc. We reduce the solution space to 10 + 5 = 15 components and 50 interactions, with the slightly added complexity of a generic representation of operations. The interactions have become easier to understand as each form interacts with components

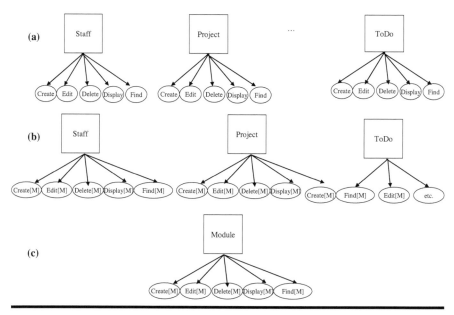

Figure 9.3 The impact of unifying similarities with generic structures on complexity.

that have been merged into five groups rather than 50 distinct components [situation shown in Figure 9.3(b)].

Suppose we further unify ten modules with one generic Module. We reduce the solution space to six (1 + 5) components with five groups of interactions, each group consisting of ten specific interactions, plus the complexity of a generic representation [situation shown in Figure 9.3(c)].

Any form of validation at the level of generic representation depicted in Figure 9.3(b) or Figure 9.3(c) is bound to be much simpler and more effective than validation at the level of concrete components [Figure 9.3(a)]. Similarly, any changes at the level of generic representation are easier to manage than at the level of concrete components owing to clearer visibility of change impact, reduced risk of update anomalies, and smaller number of distinct interfaces that have to be analyzed. Finally, generic representation of components and their configurations form natural units of reuse, potential building blocks of product line architectures [17].

Independent of an implementation technique (ASP, C#, J2EE, or PHP), it was not possible to represent operations for different modules in a generic form. This resulted in repetitions that increased the complexity of a program solution and contributed greatly to development and maintenance efforts. It also hindered reuse of similar program solutions across PCWP modules and the building of other Web portals.

A case study of a Buffer library illustrates typical problems in unifying similarity patterns with conventional programming techniques and explains the basis of the problem.

9.5 Similarity Patterns in the Buffer Library: An Example

9.5.1 An Overview of the Buffer Library

A buffer contains data in a linear sequence for reading and writing. A Buffer class library in our case study is a part of the java.nio.* packages of JDK 1.5. Depending on the purpose, programmers need buffers with specific features, for example, buffers holding elements of different types such as integer, float, or character, read-only or writable buffers, and so on. In particular, Java buffer classes are characterized by the following features:

Buffer data element types: Byte, Char, Int, Float, Double, Long, Short
Memory allocation scheme: Direct, Nondirect (Heap)
Byte ordering: Little_endian, Big_endian, Native, Nonnative.

Figure 9.4 shows some of the buffer classes covered in our study. A class name reflects a specific combination of features a given class implements. For example, class HeapIntBuffer implements a buffer of type integer (Int) with memory allocation scheme on the Heap. A generic form of a class name is a template: [MS][T]Buffer[AM][BO], where MS — memory scheme: Heap or Direct; T — type: Byte, Char, Int, Double, Float, Long, or Short; AM — access mode: W — writable (default) or R — read-only; BO — byte ordering: S — nonnative or U — native; B — BigEndian or L – LittleEndian. All the classes whose names do not include "R," by default are writable ('W'). VB — View Buffer is yet another feature

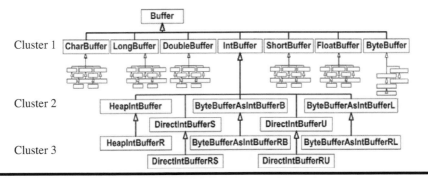

Figure 9.4   A fragment of the Buffer library.

that allows us to interpret byte buffer as Char, Int, Double, Float, Long, or Short (not shown in Figure 9.4).

Class subhierarchies are analogous to subhierarchies for classes IntBuffer, CharBuffer, LongBuffer, DoubleBuffer, ShortBuffer, and FloatBuffer, so for the sake of brevity we do not depict them in Figure 9.4. A class subhierarchy under ByteBuffer differs slightly from classes under other buffer element types, which we explain later.

Each legal feature combination — that is, a combination of features that a programmer may want — yields a class. As most feature combinations are legal, not surprisingly the number of classes explodes. This phenomenon was observed in other class libraries in early 1990s, and was termed the *feature combinatorics* problem [8,11].

All the buffer classes are derived from the top abstract class Buffer. Below class Buffer, we see a Cluster 1 of seven classes [T]Buffer that differ in buffer element data types T, where T stands for Char, Long, Double, and other element types. A programmer can directly use only [T]Buffer classes. Therefore, these classes contain many methods providing access to functionalities implemented in the classes below them.

Classes in Cluster 2, in addition to various element types, implement two memory allocation schemes and two byte orderings, in various combinations.

The direct memory allocation scheme allocates a contiguous memory block for a buffer and uses native access methods to read and write buffer elements, using a *native or nonnative byte ordering* scheme. In the nondirect memory allocation scheme, a buffer is accessed through Java array accessor methods.

For a variety of historical reasons, different CPU architectures use different native *byte ordering* conventions. For example, Intel microprocessors put the least significant byte into the lowest memory address (which is called Little_Endian ordering), whereas Sun UltraSPARC processors put the most significant byte first (which is called Big_Endian ordering). Byte ordering matters for buffers whose elements consist of multiple bytes, that is, all the element types but byte.

When using the direct memory allocation scheme, we must know if buffer elements are stored using native or nonnative byte ordering. When combining memory allocation and byte ordering features, we obtain 20 classes, as shown in Cluster 2 in Figure 9.4. For each [T]Buffer class, there is a Heap[T]Buffer counterpart class in Cluster 2 that implements the nondirect memory allocation scheme for that buffer. For each [T]Buffer class with the exception of ByteBuffer, there are also two classes implementing a direct memory allocation scheme with native (suffix "S") and nonnative (suffix "U") byte ordering. Their names are Direct[T]BufferS and Direct[T]BufferU, respectively. We have only one class DirectByteBuffer, as byte ordering does not matter for byte buffers. There are yet other classes in Cluster 2, but they are not important for our discussion here.

Classes whose names do not include the letter "R," by default represent writable buffers. In particular, all the buffers in Clusters 1 and 2 are writable. Twenty classes in Cluster 3 implement read-only variants of buffers, shown by the letter "R" in the class name.

9.5.2 Analysis Method and Experiment Summary

The experiment involved 74 classes that contained 6719 LOC (physical lines of code, without blanks or comments). At the time of the experiment, we did not have an automated clone detector. The small size and transparent design of the library made it possible to analyze classes manually in around four person-days. In software reuse, analysis of similarities and differences that aims at identifying reuse opportunities is called *domain analysis* [17,53]. Our analysis combined bottom-up examination of similarities and differences in the existing family of buffer classes, with elements of top-down domain analysis.

We gained a general understanding of buffer classes first. Based on that we hypothesized which classes were likely to be similar to each other, and therefore could be candidates for structural clones. To validate if our hypothesis was true, we further analyzed simple clones in each group of such classes — similar class methods and attribute declaration sections.

Classes that differ in only one feature we call *peer classes*. For example, classes IntBuffer, CharBuffer, and other classes in Cluster 1 form a group of peer classes. Another example is a group of Heap[T]Buffer classes. Our analysis often focused on various groups of peer classes to gain insights into a global and detailed impact of a specific feature on buffer classes.

Classes [T]Buffer (Cluster 1) differ only in the type of buffer element and were the most obvious candidates for structural clones. Yet other groups of classes that we thought could be similar are listed as follows:

1. [**T**]Buffer: Seven classes at Cluster 1 that differ in buffer element type, **T**: Byte, Char, Int, Double, Float, Long, Short
2. Heap[**T**]Buffer: Seven classes at Cluster 2, that differ in buffer element type, **T**
3. Heap[**T**]BufferR: Seven read-only classes at Cluster 3
4. Direct[**T**]Buffer[**S**|**U**]: Thirteen classes at Cluster 2 for combinations of buffer element type, **T**, with byte orderings: **S** – nonnative or **U** – native byte ordering (note that byte ordering is not relevant to buffer element type "byte")
5. Direct[**T**]BufferR[**S**|**U**]: Thirteen read-only classes at Cluster 3 for combinations of parameters **T**, **S**, and **U**, as above
6. ByteBufferAs[**T**]Buffer[**B**|**L**]: Twelve classes at Cluster 2 for combinations of buffer element type, **T**, with byte orderings: **B** – Big_Endian or **L** – Little_Endian
7. ByteBufferAs[**T**]BufferR[**B**|**L**]: Twelve read-only classes at Cluster 3 (not shown in Figure 9.4) for combinations of parameters **T**, **B**, and **L**, as above.

Examination of methods and attribute declarations in classes within each of the preceding groups confirmed that indeed there were many similarities among classes. But there were differences, too:

1. The same attributes or method signatures recurred with different data type parameters.
2. Fragments of constructor and method implementation recurred with different types, keywords, operators, or minor editing changes (additions or deletions).
3. Some methods with the same signature had different implementation in classes under the common parent class.
4. Certain classes in a group of otherwise similar classes had some extra methods or attributes as compared to other classes in that group.
5. Finally, certain classes in a group of otherwise similar classes differed in details of the "implements" clause.

Within each of the seven groups of similar classes, we identified unique and similar methods and sometimes yet smaller code fragments (e.g., fragments of method implementation or attribute declaration sections). In the following analysis, the term *code fragment* means any unit of similarity below the class level, such as a class method, constructor, declaration section, or a fragment of method or constructor implementation. A *simple clone* means a code fragment that recurs in the same or similar form in a number of places in class definitions. We paid attention only to similar code fragments that played a specific role in the Buffer domain or in class construction, and whose identification could enhance program understanding and help in eventual modifications.

9.5.3 Cluster 1: Analysis of [T]Buffer Classes

In seven [T]Buffer classes (Cluster 1), we found 30 simple clones, 28 of which recur in all the seven classes. For example, simple clones include:

- Two attribute definition sections recurring in the same form and one attribute definition section recurring with a slight change
- Two constructor definitions recurring with a slight change
- Four method definitions recurring in the same form
- Nineteen method definitions recurring with slight changes

Five classes, namely, IntBuffer, FloatBuffer, LongBuffer, ShortBuffer, and DoubleBuffer differ in type parameter and are otherwise identical.

Class ByteBuffer has 2 unique attribute declaration sections and 35 unique methods. Class CharBuffer has 13 unique methods.

Declarations of classes ByteBuffer and CharBuffer (shown in Figure 9.5 and Figure 9.6, respectively) differ only in the "implements" clause.

```
public abstract class ByteBuffer
   extends Buffer
   implements Comparable <ByteBuffer>
{
```

Figure 9.5   Declaration of class ByteBuffer.

```
public abstract class CharBuffer
   extends Buffer
   implements Comparable<ByteBuffer>,Appendable,CharSequence,Readable
{
```

Figure 9.6   Declaration of class CharBuffer.

The reader should refer to relevant entries in Table 9.2 for statistics of similarities in classes at Cluster 1.

9.5.4 Cluster 2: Analysis of Classes Heap[T]Buffer and Direct[T]Buffer[S|U]

Classes Heap[T]Buffer and Direct[T]Buffer[S|U] address memory allocation schemes (Heap or Direct), and byte ordering (S or U), in addition to the buffer element type (T). This new combination of features results in two new subclasses of ByteBuffer, and three new subclasses for each of the remaining classes in Cluster 1. Although the impact of various features visibly affects class implementation, there is still remarkable similarity among classes in Cluster 2.

We examine similarities in seven Heap[T]Buffer classes first. Eighteen simple clones recur in more than one class in the group, among which seventeen clones recur in all the seven classes.

Five classes, HeapIntBuffer, HeapFloatBuffer, HeapLongBuffer, HeapShortBuffer, and HeapDoubleBuffer, differ in type parameter and are otherwise identical.

Class HeapByteBuffer has 32 unique methods, whereas Class CharBuffer has 2 unique methods.

For example, method **put()** recurs in seven Heap[T]Buffer classes with small changes. Figure 9.7 and Figure 9.8 show method **put()** in classes HeapByteBuffer and HeapCharBuffer, respectively. Analogical methods **put()** recur in each of the remaining classes in this group.

```
//Writes the given byte into this buffer at the current position.
public ByteBuffer put(byte x) {
    hb[ix(nextPutIndex())] = x;
    return this;
}
```

Figure 9.7   Method put() in HeapByteBuffer class.

```
//Writes the given character into this buffer at the current position.
public CharBuffer put(char x) {
    hb[ix(nextPutIndex())] = x;
    return this;
}
```

Figure 9.8   Method put() in HeapCharBuffer class.

Twelve classes in the Direct[T]Buffer[S|U] group implement the direct memory allocation scheme. Classes in this group display much similarity. Twenty-three simple clones recur in either the same form or with slight changes in more than one class in the group, among which twenty-one fragments recur in all the twelve classes.

Five classes, DirectIntBufferS, DirectFloatBufferS, DirectLongBufferS, DirectShortBufferS, and DirectDoubleBufferS, differ in type parameter and otherwise are identical. Five classes, DirectIntBufferU, DirectFloatBuffeU, DirectLongBuffeU, DirectShortBuffeU, and DirectDoubleBuffeU, likewise. As before, these two subgroups of classes have no unique code fragments; that is, they are solely built with simple clones.

Class DirectByteBuffer has 44 unique methods, 3 unique constructors, and 1 unique attribute declaration section. Class DirectCharBufferS shares with DirectCharBufferU two cloned methods that do not appear in other classes in the group.

For example, method **slice()** is cloned in all the Direct[T]Buffer[S|U] classes with various combinations of values highlighted in bold. In Figure 9.9, we see method **slice()** from class DirectByteBuffer.

Method **order()** is cloned in 12 Direct[T]Buffer[S|U] classes, all but DirectByteBuffer. Figure 9.10 shows implementation of method **order()** in six classes Direct[T]BufferU, and Figure 9.11 shows implementation of method **order()** in six classes Direct[T]BufferS. Both implementations differ very little.

We did not find interesting similarities among groups Heap[T]Buffer and Direct[T]Buffer[S|U]. This is not surprising as most of the methods in those classes

```
/*Creates a new byte buffer containing a shared
subsequence of this buffer's content. */
public ByteBuffer slice() {
    int pos = this.position();
    int lim = this.limit();
    assert (pos <= lim);
    int rem = (pos <= lim ? lim - pos : 0);
    int off = (pos << 0);
    return new DirectByteBuffer(this, -1, 0, rem, rem, off);
}
```

Figure 9.9   Method slice() recurring with small changes in Direct[T]Buffer[S|U] classes.

```
public ByteOrder order() {
return ((ByteOrder.nativeOrder() != ByteOrder.BIG_ENDIAN)
    ? ByteOrder.LITTLE_ENDIAN : ByteOrder.BIG_ENDIAN);
}
```

Figure 9.10   Method order() in six Direct[T]BufferU classes.

```
public ByteOrder order() {
return ((ByteOrder.nativeOrder() == ByteOrder.BIG_ENDIAN)
    ? ByteOrder.LITTLE_ENDIAN : ByteOrder.BIG_ENDIAN);
}
```

Figure 9.11   Method order() in six Direct[T]BufferS classes.

deal with accessing buffer elements and depend highly on the specific memory allocation scheme.

We would like to turn the reader's attention to a striking symmetry in similarity situations in all the preceding class groups.

The reader should refer to relevant entries in Table 9.2 for statistics of similarities in classes in Cluster 2.

9.5.5 Cluster 3: Analysis of Read-Only Classes

In some applications, we need immutable, read-only buffers. This new feature brings in 20 new classes, namely, 7 Heap[T]BufferR classes and 13 Direct[T]BufferR[S|U] shown in Cluster 3 in Figure 9.4.

We examine the similarities in seven Heap[T]BufferR classes first. The results will not surprise the reader: we see 13 simple clones, of which 12 recur in all seven classes.

Five classes Heap[T]BufferR, where T is Int, Float, Long, Short, or Double, differ in type parameter and otherwise are identical.

Class HeapByteBufferR has 20 unique methods. Class CharBufferR has two unique methods.

13 classes in the Direct[T]BufferR[S|U] group display much similarity. There are 13 simple clones, of which 11 recur in all the 13 classes.

Five classes, DirectIntBufferRS, DirectFloatBufferRS, DirectLongBufferRS, DirectShortBufferRS, and DirectDoubleBufferRS differ in type parameter and otherwise are identical. Five classes DirectIntBufferRU, DirectFloatBuffeRU, DirectLongBuffeRU, DirectShortBuffeRU, and DirectDoubleBuffeRU, likewise.

Class DirectByteBufferR has 26 unique methods, and two unique constructors. Class DirectCharBufferR shares with DirectCharBufferRU two cloned methods that do not appear in other classes in the group. These two classes have no unique fragments.

We note that this time, simple clones also exist across horizontal classes such as HeapByteBufferR and HeapCharBufferR. There are many simple clones among the parent classes and subclasses, as well. Table 9.1 shows some examples.

Table 9.1 Similar Methods across Parent Classes and Their Subclasses

		Number of Similar Methods	
Parent Class	*Subclass*	S	C
HeapByteBuffer	HeapByteBufferR	1	8
HeapCharBuffer	HeapCharBufferR	2	3
HeapIntBuffer	HeapIntBufferR	1	2
……	…	…	…
DirectByteBuffer	DirectByteBufferR	3	8
DirectCharBufferU	DirectCharBufferRU	2	3
DirectCharBufferS	DirectCharBufferRS	2	3
DirectIntBufferU	DirectIntBufferRU	1	2
DirectIntBufferS	DirectIntBufferRS	1	2
……	……	……	……
……	……	……	……

Note: S = same content recurring in parent class and subclass; C = small change when recurring in parent class and subclass.

9.5.6 Analysis of the Remaining Buffer Classes

Here, we summarize results of similarity analysis in the remaining classes in the Buffer library. Two groups of classes, namely, ByteBufferAs[T]Buffer[B|L] and ByteBufferAs[T]BufferR[B|L], are derived from Cluster 1 classes. There are six classes in each group for types Char, Int, Float, Long, Short, or Double. For example, subclasses ByteBufferAsCharBufferB and ByteBufferAsCharBufferL allow us to view classes ByteBuffer as CharBuffer, using Big_Endian and Little_Endian ordering, respectively. Each of the Int, Double, Float, Long, and Short buffer classes has two analogical subclasses, ByteBufferAs[T]Buffer[B|L] and ByteBufferAs[T]BufferR[B|L].

Finally, a read-only class is derived from each of the ByteBufferAs[T]Buffer[B|L] and ByteBufferAs[T]BufferR[B|L] classes, yielding 12 more classes.

Each of the ByteBufferAs[T]Buffer[B|L] and ByteBufferAs[T]BufferR[B|L] class groups displays remarkable similarities. There are 19 simple clones recurring in all six ByteBufferAs[T]Buffer[B|L] classes. In addition, classes ByteBufferAsCharBufferB and ByteBufferAsCharBufferL have two unique methods.

There are 11 simple clones recurring in all six ByteBufferAs[T]BufferR[B|L] classes. In addition, classes ByteBufferAsCharBufferRB and ByteBufferAsCharBufferRL have two unique methods.

Method **ix**(int i) is cloned in ByteBufferAs[T]Buffer[B|L] classes with different values of the integer value shown in bold (Figure 9.12).

Method **order**() shown in Figure 9.13 is cloned in classes ByteBufferAs[T]BufferB, whereas method **order**() shown in Figure 9.14 is cloned in classes ByteBufferAs[T]BufferL.

The reader should refer to relevant entries in Table 9.2 or statistic of similarities in classes ByteBufferAs[T]Buffer[B|L] and ByteBufferAs[T]BufferR[B|L].

```
protected int ix(int i) {
  return (i << 1) + offset;
}
```

Figure 9.12   Method ix(int i).

```
public ByteOrder order() {
  return ByteOrder.BIG_ENDIAN;
}
```

Figure 9.13   Method order() in classes ByteBufferAs*BufferB.

```
public ByteOrder order() {
  return ByteOrder.BIG_ENDIAN;
}
```

Figure 9.14 Method order() in classes ByteBufferAs*BufferL.

Table 9.2 Buffer Library Statistics

Classes		Fragments — Recurring fragments (times)					Fragments — Unique	LOC
		2	6	7	12	13		
Cluster 1 7 classes [T]Buffer	same form		2	6			50	3720
	small changes			22				
Cluster 2 7 classes Heap[T]Buffer	same form		1	3			34	914
	small changes			14				
Cluster 2 13 classes Direct[T]Buffer[S|U]	same form	1				8	48	2428
	small changes	1			1	13		
Cluster 3 7 classes Heap[T]BufferR	same form		1	1			22	521
	small changes			11				
Cluster 3 13 classes Direct[T]BufferR[S|U]	same form	1				2	28	979
	small changes	1			1	9		
subtotal for 47 classes	same form	2	4	10		10	182	8562
	small changes	2		47	2	22		
other classes in Cluster 2 (12 classes)	same form	1			4		0	1014
	small changes	1			12			
other classes in Cluster 3 (12 classes)	same form	1			2		0	556
	small changes	1			9			
subtotal for other classes	same form	2			6		0	1570
	small changes	2			21			
total	same form	4	4	10	6	10	182	10132
	small changes	4		47	23	22		

9.5.7 Why Do Similar Classes Arise?

Usability is an important design goal for class libraries. To make buffer classes easy to use, designers decided to reveal to programmers only the top eight classes (Figure 9.4). Functionalities related to lower-level concrete classes can be accessed via special methods provided in the top eight classes. Conceptual clarity and good performance are yet other important design goals for the Buffer library. For conceptual clarity, designers did not multiply classes beyond what was absolutely needed. We see almost a one-to-one mapping between legal feature combinations and buffer classes. Although in many situations one could introduce a new abstract class or a suitable design pattern to avoid repetitions, such a solution would compromise these design goals.

Most of the similarity patterns in buffer classes are the result of feature combinations. As features cannot be implemented independently of each other in separate implementation units (e.g., class methods), program structures affected by feature combinations must appear in many variant forms, depending on the context. Whenever such program structure cannot be parameterized to unify the variant forms and placed in some upper-level class for reuse via inheritance, similar code structures must be replicated.

To observe the impact of feature combinations on buffer classes, we compared classes in various peer class groups (that is, classes differing in one feature only). For example, we compared classes that differed in element type (e.g., DirectCharBufferS and DirectIntBufferS), in byte ordering (e.g., DirectIntBufferS and DirectIntBufferU) and in access mode (e.g., DirectIntBufferS and DirectIntBufferRS).

A typical situation that leads to cloning is when some classes derived from the same parent A need a certain method (or data), and others derived from A do not need it. One solution could be to place such a method in a new parent class created for the purpose of abstracting a common method. However, creating many such classes would complicate the class hierarchy and hinder performance. Another solution could be to place such a method in the parent class. But then any attempt to invoke a method for a class that does not need it would result in a runtime error. To avoid such an error-prone solution, we would have to write extra code to disable the method in the classes that do not need it.

In yet other situations, a certain method may be needed in all the classes derived from the same parent, but in some of those classes the method may require different parameters, return type, or implementation than in other classes. Furthermore, implementations of such a method in different classes may refer to nonlocal attributes defined in the context of different classes. In the preceding cases, designers often choose to replicate a method in each class that needs it. Method **hasArray()** shown in Figure 9.15 illustrates a simple yet interesting case. This method is cloned in each of the seven [T]Buffer classes. Method **hasArray()** cannot be implemented in the parent class Buffer, as variable **hb** must be declared with a different type in

```
/* Tells whether or not this buffer is backed by
 an accessible byte array. */
public final boolean hasArray() {
return (hb != null) && !isReadOnly; }
```

Figure 9.15   Recurring method hasArray().

each of the seven classes. For example, in class ByteBuffer the type of variable **hb** is **byte** and in class IntBuffer, it is **int**.

We found some instances of methods defined in a parent class and then repeated in child classes. For example, the same method **_get()** is defined in classes HeapByteBuffer and HeapByteBufferR, and the same method **order()** is defined in classes HeapCharBuffer and HeapCharBufferR, HeapIntBuffer, and HeapIntBufferR, etc. Those clones may exist for performance reasons or due to the deficiency of the design.

Many repetitions arise owing to the inability to specify small variations in otherwise identical code fragments. For example, some attributes, methods, or even classes may differ only in data types, constants, keywords, or operators. Classes or methods that differ in type parameters are candidates for generics. JDK 1.5 supports generics, based on the earlier proposal JSR-14 [12]. However, generics have not been applied to unify similarity patterns described in our study. As generics are an important language-level feature to address problems of unifying similarities, we have done a detailed analysis of Java generics in the context of the Buffer library. Groups of classes that differ only in data type are obvious candidates for generics. There are three such groups comprising 21 classes, namely, [T]Buffer, Heap[T]Buffer, and Heap[T]BufferR. In each of these groups, classes corresponding to Byte and Char types differ in nontype parameters and are not generics-friendly. This leaves us with 15 generics-friendly classes whose unification with three generics eliminates 27 percent of code. There is, however, one problem with this solution. In Java, generic types cannot be primitive types such as Int or Char. This is a serious limitation, as one has to create corresponding wrapper classes just for the purpose of parameterization. Wrapper classes introduce extra complexity and hamper performance. Application of generics to 15 buffer classes is subject to this limitation.

Many simple clones differ in parameters representing constants, keywords, or algorithmic elements rather than data types. For example, method **slice()** is cloned 13 times in all the Direct[T]Buffer[S|U] classes with small changes highlighted in boldface in Figure 9.9. This happens when the impact of various features interacts in code fragments, affecting data type names, constant values, or details of algorithms. Generics are not meant to unify these kinds of differences in classes. We found other cases of similar but generics-unfriendly classes, and we refer the reader to further details of the generics solution (including code) to our case studies at the XVCL Web site [69]. In summary, it is unlikely that generics can help unify similarities patterns in software that exhibits a high degree of feature combinations such as the Buffer library.

It is interesting to note that small variations appear in otherwise identical code fragments across classes at the same level of inheritance hierarchy, as well as in classes at different levels of inheritance hierarchy. Programming languages do not have a proper mechanism to handle such variations at an adequate (that is, a sufficiently small) granularity level. Therefore, the impact of a small variation on a program may not be proportional to the size of the variation.

In summary, we observed substantial similarities within each of the seven group classes listed in Section 9.5.2. Table 9.2 shows the statistics of class methods and constructors, as well as smaller class-building blocks (e.g., attribute declaration sections or method implementation fragments), cloned in many classes. "Clusters" in the first column of Table 9.2 refer to classes shown in Figure 9.4. As we will see in Chapter 10, by unifying similarities with generic mixed-strategy solutions, we can collapse code size by 68 percent, reducing a program's conceptual complexity by rates proportional to the code size reduction.

9.5.8 Closing Comments on the Buffer Library Example

The Buffer library is a very special program. In other libraries, classes may serve distinct purposes, displaying less similarity than we observed in buffer classes. Application programs have a more monolithic structure than buffer classes, involve multitier architectures with user interface, business logic, and database layers, and today often rely on functionality provided by underlying component platforms (such as .NET™ or J2EE). Although this is all true, we believe the Buffer library allows us to observe in a pure and distilled form some common roots of software similarities and reasons why they may be difficult to unify with conventional programming techniques.

In particular, in other experiments, some of which we review in the following sections, we observed that feature combination was one of the major forces triggering similarity patterns that caused similar program structures to spread across programs under study. Ad hoc, irregular nature of variations among similar program structures made it difficult to unify the differences among these program structures with conventional generic design techniques. This difficulty was further magnified by the fact that programs had to meet other important design goals, and conventional generic design solutions, even if they existed, would require designers to compromise these goals; therefore, such solutions were not used.

9.6   Similarity Patterns and Clones in STL

The Standard Template Library (STL) [61] is a hallmark of powerful and elegant generic design. Because of light integration of templates with the C++ language core, template parameters are less restrictive than parameters of Java generics. Unlike Java generics, C++ templates also allow constants and primitive types to be passed as parameters. Not only does STL use the most advanced template features and design solutions (e.g., iterators), but it is also widely accepted in the research and industrial communities as a prime example of the generic programming methodology. Therefore, STL provides a good opportunity to strengthen observations made in the Buffer Library case study.

STL consists of containers (such as stack, set, or map), algorithms (such as sort or search), iterators, function objects, and adaptors. Algorithms and data structures commonly used in computer science are provided in the STL. There are plenty of algorithms that need to work with many different data structures. Without generic containers and algorithms, the STL's size and complexity would be enormous. Such a simple-minded solution would unwisely ignore similarities among data structures and also among algorithms applied to different data structures, which offer endless reuse opportunities. Redundant code arising from unexploited similarities would contribute much to the STL's size and complexity, hindering its evolution. All the components of STL have been heavily parameterized so that a single implementation of the container template can be used for all types of contained elements. In STL, generic solutions are mainly facilitated by templates and iterators.

Generic containers form the root of the STL. These are either sequence containers or associative containers. In sequence containers, all members are arranged in some order. In associative containers, the elements are accessed by some key and are not necessarily arranged in any order.

We selected associative containers for further detailed manual analysis because of their high level of cloning. An associative container is a variable-sized container that supports efficient retrieval of its elements based on keys. Containers are characterized by the following features:

Ordering: This could be either hashed or sorted. The elements of a "hashed" associative container are not guaranteed to be in any meaningful order. "Sorted" associative containers use an ordering relation on their keys.

Key type: This could be either simple or pair. In a "simple" associative container, elements are their own keys. A "pair" associative container associates a key with some other object.

Uniqueness: In a "unique" associative container each key in the container is unique, which need not be the case in a "multiple" associative container.

Any legal combination of these features yields a unique class template. For example, the container "set" represents an associative container where Storage = sorted, Uniqueness = unique, and Key type = simple. There is much similarity

```
template <class _Key, class _Compare, class _Alloc>
inline bool operator== (
    const set<_Key,_Compare,_Alloc>& __x,
    const set<_Key,_Compare,_Alloc>& __y) {
  return __x._M_t ==__y._M_t;
}
```

```
template <class _Key, class _Compare, class _Alloc>
inline bool operator< (
    const set<_Key,_Compare,_Alloc>& __x,
    const set<_Key,_Compare,_Alloc>& __y) {
  return __x._M_t <__y._M_t;
}
```

Figure 9.16   Cloned templates differing in operators.

across associative containers independently of the specific features they implement, which leads to clones.

We started the experiment by running automated clone detectors CCFinder [32] and Clone Miner [6] on STL. We further analyzed manually STL regions that showed high cloning rates, to identify possible design-level similarities. We found that containers displayed much similarity and code repetition. Four "sorted" associative containers and four "hashed" associative containers contained 57 percent of cloned code. Stacks and queues contained 37 percent of cloned code. Algorithms for set operations such as union, intersection, difference, and symmetric difference (along with their overloaded versions) contained 52 percent of cloned code.

There were many non-type-parametric differences among associative container group of templates. For example, certain otherwise similar methods differed in operators or algorithmic details. Figure 9.16 shows a simple example of cloned templates.

Other replicated templates differed in nonparametric ways (e.g., swapped lines of code or inserted lines of code). Although it is possible to treat many types of nonparametric differences using sophisticated forms of C++ template metaprogramming, often the resulting code becomes "cluttered and messy" [19]. We did not spot such solutions in STL, and believe their practical value needs to be further investigated.

The reader may find full details of the STL case study in Reference 5.

9.7   Similarity Patterns in Application Programs

9.7.1   Domain Entity Management Subsystem

We now discuss a similarity situation in a domain entity management subsystem (DEMS) written in C#. DEMS was a part of a command and control system developed by the author's industry collaborator, ST Electronics Pte Ltd (STEE). The system involved domain entities such as Task, User, or Resource. For each entity, the system implemented up to 10 operations, such as Create, Update, View, Delete, Find, or Copy.

DEMS was to serve a range of command and control applications, so it was meant to be easily adaptable and extensible. The intention was to make DEMS an integral part of the product line architecture for those applications. DEMS comprised 18,823 LOC of C# code, with 117 classes covering GUI, service, and database layers.

The project started by porting an existing DEMS written in Visual Basic into C#. At the same time, new variant features were considered to enhance reusability of the DEMS in a wider range of applications. In the process of rewriting the system, STEE analyzed similarity patterns to identify potential reuse opportunities. C# and .NET mechanisms were applied whenever possible to unify observed similarity patterns. The option of applying generics was taken into account based on the generics proposed for C# [36]. Similarities that could not be unified using conventional mechanisms and that were leading either to repetitions or to inefficiencies during customization of the DEMS for reuse in target applications were noted and documented. One of such similarity pattern is shown in Figure 9.17.

The design of each operation, say, CreateUser, involved a pattern of collaborating classes from GUI, service and database layers (Figure 9.17). The design of operation Create for other entities, e.g., CreateTask, was quite similar. Each box in Figure 9.17 represents a number of classes, with much similarity across classes implementing similar concepts for all the domain entities in their respective operations.

However, there were also differences across classes for various operations, caused by different meanings of domain entities: For example, operation CreateTask required different types of data entry and data validation than CreateUser.

Despite striking similarities, it was not possible to design a generic solution for groups of similar operations. To implement generic operations, one would have to first unify groups of classes in GUI, Service, Entity, and DB layers such

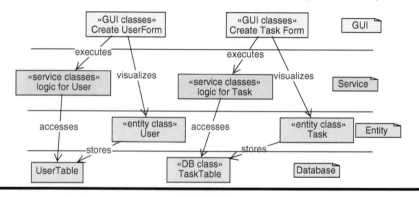

Figure 9.17   A recurring pattern of components.

as Create[entity-type]Form, Update[entity-type]Form, etc. However, the nature of variations across operations for different entity types was such that neither inheritance nor type parameters (such as in generics proposed for C#) could be used to implement operations in a generic way. Therefore, implementation of operations for different entities was replicated many times, with required variations. Structural clones, two of which we depicted in Figure 9.17, that arose from this similarity pattern contained an estimated 68 percent of DEMS code.

9.7.2 Similarity Patterns in Web Portals on J2EE Platform

The goal of this study was to evaluate J2EE (Java™ 2 Platform, Enterprise Edition) as a platform for Web portal (WP) product line development. An earlier project by STEE revealed 60 percent similarity rates in Active Server Pages (ASP) WPs, and in certain areas as high as 90 percent [52]. It was interesting to know the effectiveness of J2EE mechanisms in unifying various kinds of similarity patterns.

J2EE provides standardized architecture and supports reuse of common services via portlet technology. Unlike ASP, J2EE supports inheritance, generics, and other OO features via Java 1.5. We worked with a portal developed by STEE called CAP-WP. CAP-WP supported collaborative work and included 14 modules such as Staff, Project, or Task (Figure 9.18).

Figure 9.19 shows patterns of classes in CAP-WP that formed structural clones. CAP-WP is composed of a set of modules where each module is a portlet. There are 25 modules in CAP-WP. Each module contains all the code required to implement a particular core feature in CAP-WP (Forum, News, etc.). Each module follows standard design implied by the five-tier J2EE architecture model.

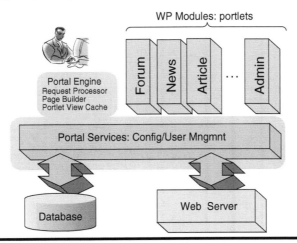

Figure 9.18   CAP-WP modules (portlets) and architecture.

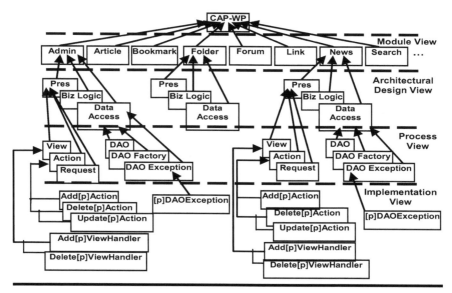

Figure 9.19   Similarities in CAP-WP.

We studied similarity patterns in the presentation layer (Pres), the business logic layer (Biz Logic), and the data access layer. Each layer of the architecture is subdivided into the various processes or functions (i.e., viewing of data) within that layer. Finally, each process is implemented by classes (Implementation View) of Figure 9.19. Parameter [p] in class names represents the module name (e.g., Article, Forum, or News).

We studied both intra- and intermodule similarities in CAP-WP design. The nature and degree of the similarities were different for the two cases. Within modules, we found 75 percent of code contained in exact clones and 20 percent of code contained in similar clones (leaving only 5 percent of the code unique). Analysis across modules revealed design-level similarities, with 40 percent of code contained in structural clones. Both intra- and intermodule similarities were important for clarity of the design; however, they could not be unified with generic design solutions expressed by J2EE mechanisms.

9.7.2.1   Interportlet Similarities

In particular, there was much similarity among various Implementation Layer classes implementing the same concepts in different portal modules (i.e., for different values of parameter [p]). For example, [p]ViewHandler classes for all 25 modules are very similar to each other. They all contain code shown in Figure 9.20, with variations indicated in underlined font, and slight changes in the contents of the method render 'Exception.' Such similar classes were common across the different CAP-WP modules.

```
class AddContentTypeViewHandler implements ViewHandler {

    private PortletConfig _config;

    public void init (PortletConfig config) {

        _config = config;

    }

    public void render (PortletRequest req, PortletResponse resp,

        AppResult [] result) throws ViewException {

                ......

    }

    public void renderException (PortletRequest req, PortletResponse resp,

        PortletException ex) throws ViewException {


        PortletContext context = _config.getPortletContext ();

        PortletRequestDispatcher disp = context.getNamedDispatcher ("ADMIN_ERROR");

        req.setAttribute (RequestKey.EXCEPTION, ex);

        req.setAttribute (RequestKey.ERROR_PAGE_TITLE, "Add Content Type Fail");

        try {

                                        disp.include (req, resp);

        }

        catch (Exception e) {

                                Log.error ("AddContentTypeViewHandler.renderException - Unable to

                render error page: " + e.getMessage ());

                                        throw new ViewException

                (ErrorCode.ERROR_CREATE_CONTENT_TYPE, e);

                                }

                        }
```

Figure 9.20   View handlers.

9.7.2.2   *Intraportlet Similarities*

Some of the CAP-WP modules have more than one view handler. For example, the Admin module has the following view handler classes: AddContentTypeViewHandler, UpdateContentTypeViewHandler, DeleteContentTypeViewHandler, and ViewContentType-ViewHandler. The structure of all these classes is similar to the one shown in Figure 9.20.

Also, classes implementing Add and Update operations for a given module are very similar to one another (for example, AddQueryRequestHandler and Update-QueryRequestHandler for the Query Management module). Here, the degree of similarity is even higher than in request handlers within the same module, for example, DeleteQueryRequestHandler.

The reader may find full details of this project in Reference 70.

9.7.3 Similarities in the Entity Bean Data Access Layer

Our final example shows explosion of look-alike Entity Beans triggered by feature combinations. We addressed variant features affecting Entity Beans depicted in Figure 9.21. The Domain Entity feature group represents database tables for different portal modules. Entity Beans receive query requests from the presentation or business logic layers, connect to the specified database (DBMS feature group in Figure 9.21) by the specified connectivity mechanism (Connection), receive query results, and pass them back to the caller in the required format (Input/Output parameter). As any combination of variant features shown in Figure 9.21 could be implemented in Entity Beans in some application, the number of required Entity Beans was huge. Although Entity Beans were similar across modules, there were differences among them, too. J2EE/EJB provided little support to abstract similarities among Entity Beans and to deal with the impact of variations in a generic way. Sometimes, we could implement "typical variant combinations" into components, allowing a developer to select variants needed in a WP using EJB mechanisms. However, using this method we covered only a small number of simple cases.

An alternative solution was to have a separate component version for each legal combination of features. But then we would end up with a huge number of look-alike components. Both solutions precluded systematic reuse. Consequently, a new application was basically built with components (and component configurations) that already appeared in some modules. These components could be reused in building new applications. As such, they required much manual work during customization. These experiences are in line with problems reported in industrial product lines, where many variant features and feature dependencies lead to thousands of component versions, hindering reuse.

Even though we did not create many look-alike components, Entity Beans still displayed much similarity that could not be unified by generic solutions. For example, many Entity Beans had similar interfaces and business logic related to handling tables. However, they differed in attributes and some other details. Unfortunately, we could not abstract commonalities among Entity Beans and parameterize them for reuse.

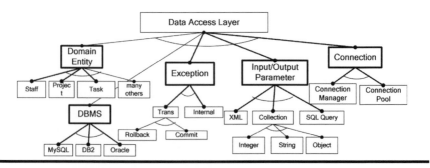

Figure 9.21   Variant features in data access layer

9.8   General Implications

Just as we cannot avoid the crosscutting impact of some of the computational aspects on modules [37,62], we cannot avoid repetitions stemming from certain similarity patterns.

What are similarity patterns and what do they represent?

Some similarity patterns can be observed at the level of software requirements. Others are the result of recurring design solutions of similar structure or can be induced by the underlying platform (e.g., by standardized architectures and patterns of J2EE or .NET). Design-level similarities, showing as patterns of classes or components, often represent domain-specific abstractions (e.g., operations on domain entities in DEMS; Figure 9.17). Generic structures unifying such similarities are particularly important as they describe how domain concepts are realized in the solution space. Such similarity patterns create opportunities for reuse within a given system, or even across similar systems. In the evolution context, instances of a generic structure in system releases show how the design and implementation of the same domain concept have been changing during system evolution.

Some similarity patterns do not have a corresponding functional abstraction suitable for its representation. Ad hoc, irregular nature of variations among similar program structures is another reason why it is difficult to unify the differences among similar program structures with conventional generic design techniques. Finally, software design is often constrained by multiple, sometimes competing design goals, such as development cost, usability, simplicity, performance, or reliability. A generic solution to unify similarity patterns will only be applied if it is natural and synergistic with all the other design goals that matter.

The feature combinatorics problem is the main reason why similar program structures in many variant forms arise and spread through the buffer classes. We observe the feature combination phenomenon within a single system (see DEMS or the Web portal examples) or class library (see the Buffer library or STL). We observe feature combinations across a family of similar systems forming a product line [17]. Finally, we observe feature combination across system releases arising from software evolution.

In all the preceding situations, a cost-effective solution to containing the impact of feature combination should rely on some kind of a structure representing the underlying similarity pattern in a generic form.

Differences among similar program structures, an effect of combining features, tend to be chaotic and are rarely confined to type parameters. Programs are designed under the constraints of the design goals (such as usability or performance), and the symptoms of the feature combinatorics problem must be considered in the context of those constraints. Therefore, it becomes difficult to define effective generic solutions unifying similarity patterns without compromising other design goals using conventional techniques.

Although not all such recurring similar program structures are necessarily bad, most of them hinder program understanding and contribute greatly to high maintenance cost [10,22,32]. There are a number of reasons why cloned structures increase program complexity, as perceived by programmers, hindering program understanding: Not only do clones blow up the size of a program, but they also increase the number of conceptual elements programmers must deal with, and hinder important relationships among program elements that must be understood whenever the program is to be changed. Whenever change happens to a cloned structure, a programmer must locate all its instances and analyze them in the appropriate context to see which clone instances are affected by the change and how. In that sense, cloned structures — untapped program similarity patterns, in general — increase the risk of update anomalies. Finally, design-level similarities recurring in multiple forms across a program hinder the conceptual integrity of the design, which Brooks calls "the most important consideration in system design" [13].

A more detailed examination is best done with reference to a nonredundant mixed-strategy program representation. We continue this discussion in Chapter 10.

9.9 Identifying Similarity Patterns and Automated Detection of Clones

The objective of domain analysis is to identify similarity patterns based on top-down analysis of an application domain. We can identify similarities within a program and across different programs in a domain. We further characterize differences among instances of similarity patterns. Feature diagrams are often used for that purpose [33]. Many similarity patterns become apparent only during architecture design, detailed design, and implementation.

To find clones in large legacy systems, some level of automated analysis is essential. Different techniques have been proposed to automate the finding of clones in existing programs. Most of the techniques focus on simple clones. We can broadly categorize clone detection techniques based on the program representation and the matching technique. For program representation, the different options are plain text [22], tokens [2,32], abstract syntax trees [10], program dependence graphs [41,42], and software metrics [40]. The different matching techniques include suffix tree based token matching [32], text fingerprints matching [31], metrics value comparisons [40], abstract syntax trees comparisons [10], dynamic pattern matching [40], and neural networks [20].

CCFinder [32] is easily configurable to read input in different programming languages like C, C+, Java, and COBOL. A suffix-tree matching algorithm is used for the discovery of clones. Some optimizations are applied to reduce the complexity of the token matching algorithm. These optimizations include the alignment of token sequences to begin at tokens that mark the beginning of a statement like

#, {, class, if, else, etc. Considering only these tokens as leading tokens reduces the resulting suffix tree size to one third. Another optimization is the removal of short, repeated code segments from the input source like case statements in switch-case constructs and constant declarations. Very large files are truncated and a "divide-and-conquer" strategy is applied to find duplicates in them.

Dup is another token-based clone detection tool [22]. It finds identical clones as well as strictly parameterized clones, i.e., clones that differ only in the systematic substitution of one set of parameter values for another. These parameters can be identifiers, constants, field names of structures, and macro names, but not keywords like While or If. The tool is text- and token-based, and the granularity of clones is line-based, where comments and white spaces are not considered. The algorithm used in this tool is based on a data structure called the parameterized suffix tree [3], which is a generalization of a suffix tree. Dup is developed in C and Lex, and only C code can be processed through Dup.

For finding maximal parameterized matching, Dup's lexical analyzer generates a string of one nonparameter symbol and zero or more parameter symbols for each line. The parameter and their positions are recorded in this parameterized string. This string is encoded in such a way that the first occurrence of each parameter is replaced by zero and every later occurrence is replaced by the distance in the string since the previous occurrence. Nonparameter symbols are left unchanged. This tokenization scheme ensures the strict parameterization requirement of Dup. The clones detected by Dup cannot cross file boundaries but can cross function boundaries.

With the experience gained from the clone analysis of different software, it was observed that some short repeated segments of code turn up as multiple clone classes that are not very useful [32]. In Dup, these fragments of code had to be removed by hand. In CCFinder, the first two repetitions are reported and the rest are ignored. Clone Miner [6] does not report these short repetitions as clone classes, but rather reports them separately as repetitions.

Clone detection tools typically produce much information that needs to be further analyzed, with programmer involvement, to filter useful clones. By useful clones, we mean clones that represent some significant program elements or concepts that play a role in program understanding and maintenance. Gemini [65] is a visualization tool that produces graphical views of the cloning situation (such as a clone scatter plot) to help a programmer find useful clones based on the CCFinder output. Kapser and Godfrey propose analysis through the sorting of clones into categories based on clone taxonomy and then displaying the clones in the form of an architectural landscape view [35]. This view is a graph where the edges are clone relations and the nodes are software artifacts such as files and methods. Reiger et al. use a duplication web to show the overview of cloning in a system. The nodes of the web represent files, and the edges represent a clone relation between the files [55]. They also use a clone scatter plot for an overview of cloning. This plot is a variation of the standard scatter plot in which they attempt to resolve the scaling problem of the original by applying logarithmic scales to the lines of code metric in files.

The aforementioned techniques are based on simple clone detection only. They do not address design-level similarities in the form of structural clones. Apparently, there is a gap between simple clone detection and useful design information, and visualization techniques may help us narrow down this gap only to some extent.

Clone Miner [6] applies a mixture of techniques to recover design-level similarities, the so-called structural clones discussed in this chapter. Clone Miner uses token-based techniques to find simple clones first. Then, Clone Miner applies data mining techniques to find configurations of simple clones that are likely to form higher-level similarity patterns. Similar to other clone detection tools, Clone Miner produces a great deal of information, not all of which represents useful design concepts. The follow-up visualization, filtering, and abstraction techniques, implemented in a clone analyzer, assist programmers in filtering useful structural clones from the Clone Miner output.

9.10 Conclusions

We discussed the problem of software similarities and the related problem of software clones. We traced the roots of the problem and discussed the general nature of the problem's symptoms and causes. We discussed feature combination as a common trigger of software similarities. Software is affected by multiple features. Similarities arise from feature combinations that have to be implemented in software modules such as classes or components. However, given the overall design goals, in many cases similarity patterns are difficult to avoid — refactored or otherwise unified — with conventional programming techniques. In some cases, such unification conflicted with other design goals. In yet other situations, such unification was not possible at all given the programming technology used. We supported our argument with examples from class library, application programs, and J2EE domains. Although not all the clones are necessarily bad, most of them hinder program understanding and contribute significantly to high maintenance cost.

References

1. ANSI and AJPO, Military Standard: Ada Programming Language, ANSI/MIL-STD-1815A-1983, February 17, 1983.
2. Baker, B.S., On finding duplication and near-duplication in large software systems, *Proceedings of the 2nd Working Conference on Reverse Engineering*, 1995, pp. 86–95.
3. Baker, B.S., Parameterized duplication in strings: algorithms and an application to software maintenance, *SIAM Journal of Computing*, October 1997.
4. Bassett, P., *Framing Software Reuse — Lessons from Real World*, Yourdon Press, Prentice Hall, Englewood Cliffs, NJ, 1997.

5. Basit, H.A., Rajapakse, D.C., and Jarzabek, S., Beyond templates: a study of clones in the STL and some general implications, *International Conference on Software Engineering, ICSE'05,* St. Louis, MO, May 2005, pp. 451–459.

6. Basit, A.H. and Jarzabek, S., Detecting higher-level similarity patterns in programs, *ESEC-FSE'05, European Software Engineering Conference and ACM SIGSOFT Symposium on the Foundations of Software Engineering,* ACM Press, September 2005, Lisbon, pp. 156–165.

7. Batory, D. and O'Malley, S., The design and implementation of hierarchical software systems with reusable components, *ACM Transactions on Software Engineering and Methodology,* 1(4), October 1992, pp. 355–398.

8. Batory, D., Singhai, V., Sirkin, M., and Thomas, J., Scalable software libraries, *ACM SIGSOFT'93: Symposium on the Foundations of Software Engineering,* Los Angeles, CA, December 1993, pp. 191–199.

9. Batory, D., Sarvela, J.N., and Rauschmayer, A., Scaling step-wise refinement, *Proceedings of the International Conference on Software Engineering, ICSE'03,* May 2003, Portland, OR, pp. 187–197.

10. Baxter, I., Yahin, A., Moura, L., Sant'Anna, M., and Bier, L., Clone detection using abstract syntax trees, *Proceedings of the International Conference on Software Maintenance,* 1998, pp. 368–377.

11. Biggerstaff, T., The library scaling problem and the limits of concrete component reuse, *3rd International Conference on Software Reuse, ICSR'94,* 1994, pp. 102–109.

12. Braha, G., Cohen, N., Kemper, C., Marx, S. et al., JSR 14: Add Generic Types to the Java Programming Language, http://www.jcp.org/en/jsr/.

13. Brooks, P.B., *The Mythical Man-Month,* Addison Wesley, 1995.

14. Burd, E. and Munro, M., Investigating the maintenance implications of the replication of code, *Proceedings of the IEEE International Conference on Software Maintenance (ICSM '97),* pp. 322–329.

15. Burd, E. and Bailey, J., Evaluating clone detection tools for use during preventative maintenance, *2nd IEEE International Workshop on Source Code Analysis and Manipulation (SCAM'02),* pp. 36–43.

16. Clarke, S., Harrison, W., Ossher, H., and Tarr, P., Subject-oriented design: toward improved alignment of requirements, design, and code, *Proceedings of the OOPSLA'99,* November 1999, Denver, CO, pp. 325–339.

17. Clements, P. and Northrop, L., Software product lines: practices and patterns, Addison-Wesley, Boston, 2002.

18. Cordy, J.R., Comprehending reality: practical challenges to software maintenance automation, *Proceedings of the 11th IEEE International Workshop on Program Comprehension, (IWPC 2003),* pp. 196–206.

19. Czarnecki, K. and Eisenecker, U., *Generative Programming: Methods, Tools, and Applications,* Addison-Wesley, 2000.

20. Davey, N., Barson, P., Field, S., Frank, R., and Tansley, D., The development of a software clone detector, *International Journal of Applied Software Technology,* 1(3–4), 219–236, 1995.

21. Deelstra, S., Sinnema, M., and Bosch, J., Experiences in software product families: problems and issues during product derivation, *Proceedings of the Software Product Lines Conference, SPLC3,* Boston, MA, August 2004, LNCS 3154, Springer-Verlag, pp. 165–182.

22. Ducasse, S., Rieger, M., and Demeyer, S., A language independent approach for detecting duplicated code, *International Conference on Software Maintenance, ICSM'99,* September 1999, Oxford, pp. 109–118.

23. Fowler, M., *Analysis Patterns: Reusable Object Models,* Addison-Wesley, 1997.

24. Fowler, M., *Refactoring — Improving the Design of Existing Code,* Addison-Wesley, 1999.

25. Gamma, E., Helm, R., Johnson, R., and Vlissides, J., *Design Patterns — Elements of Reusable Object-Oriented Software,* Addison-Wesley, 1995.

26. Garcia, R. et al., A comparative study of language support for generic programming, *Proceedings of the 18th ACM SIGPLAN Conference on Object-oriented Programming, Systems, Languages, and Applications,* 2003, pp. 115–134.

27. Goguen, J.A., Parameterized programming, *IEEE Transactions on Software Engineering,* SE-10(5), 528–543, September 1984.

28. Jarzabek, S. and Li, S., Eliminating redundancies with a "composition with adaptation" meta-programming technique, *Proceedings of the ESEC-FSE'03, European Software Engineering Conference and ACM SIGSOFT Symposium on the Foundations of Software Engineering,* September 2003, Helsinki, pp. 237–246.

29. Jarzabek, S. and Li, S., Unifying clones with a generative programming technique: a case study, *Journal of Software Maintenance and Evolution: Research and Practice,* 18(4), 267–292, July–August 2006.

30. Jarzabek, S., Genericity — a "missing in action" key to software simplification and reuse, to appear in *13th Asia-Pacific Software Engineering Conference, APSEC'06,* IEEE Computer Society Press, December 6–8, 2006, Bangalore, India.

31. Johnson, J.H., Substring matching for clone detection and change tracking, in *Proceedings of the International Conference on Software Maintenance (ICSM '94),* pp. 120–126.

32. Kamiya, T., Kusumoto, S., and Inoue, K., CCFinder: a multi-linguistic token-based code clone detection system for large scale source code, *IEEE Transactions Software Engineering,* 28(7), 654–670, 2002.

33. Kang, K. et al., Feature-Oriented Domain Analysis (FODA) Feasibility Study, Technical Report, CMU/SEI-90-TR-21, Software Engineering Institute, CMU, Pittsburgh, PA, November 1990.

34. Karhinen, A., Ran, A., and Tallgren, T., Configuring designs for reuse, *International Conference on Software Engineering, ICSE'97,* Boston, MA, 1997, pp. 701–710.

35. Kapser, C. and Godfrey, M., Improved tool support for the investigation of duplication in software, *International Conference on Software Maintenance, ICSM'05,* Budapest, September 2005, pp. 25–30.

36. Kennedy, A. and Syme, D., Design and implementation of generics for the .Net Common language runtime, *Proceedings of the ACM Conference on Programming Languages Design and Implementation (PLDI-01),* New York, June 2001, pp. 1–12.

37. Kiczales, G, Lamping, J., Mendhekar, A., Maeda, C., Lopes, C., Loingtier, J-M., and Irwin, J., Aspect-oriented programming, *European Conference on Object-Oriented Programming,* Finland, Springer-Verlag LNCS 1241, 1997, pp. 220–242.

38. Kiczales, G., Hilsdale, E., Hugunin, J. et al., An overview of AspectJ, *Proceedings of the of 15th European Conference on Object-Oriented Programming*, Budapest, Hungary, June 18–22, 2001, Lecture Notes in Computer Science, 2072, pp. 327–353.

39. Kim, M., Bergman, L., Lau, T., and Notkin, D., An ethnographic study of copy and paste programming practices in OOPL, *Proceedings of the International Symposium on Empirical Software Engineering*, ISESE'04, August 2004, Redondo Beach, CA, pp. 83–92.

40. Kontogiannis, K.A., De Mori, R., Merlo, E., Galler, M., and Bernstein, M., Pattern matching for clone and concept detection, *Journal of Automated Software Engineering*, 3, 770–108, 1996.

41. Komondoor, R. and Horwitz, S., Using slicing to identify duplication in source code, in *Proceedings of the 8th International Symposium on Static Analysis*, 2001, pp. 40–56.

42. Krinke, J., Identifying similar code with program dependence graphs, in *Proceedings of the Eight Working Conference on Reverse Engineering*, Stuttgart, Germany, October 2001, pp. 301–309.

43. Lague, B., Proulx, D., Mayrand, J., Merlo, E.M., Hudepohl, J., Assessing the benefits of incorporating function clone detection in a development process, *Proceedings of the International Conference on Software Maintenance (ICSM '97)*, Bari, Italy, October 1997, pp. 314–321.

44. Levenshtein, V.I., Binary codes capable of correcting deletions, insertions, and reversals, *Cybernetics and Control Theory*, 10(8), 707–710, 1966.

45. Loughran, N., Rashid, A., Zhang, W., and Jarzabek, S., Supporting product line evolution with framed aspects, *3rd AOSD Workshop on Aspects, Components, and Patterns for Infrastructure Software*, ACP4IS'04, March 22–26, 2004, Lancaster, U.K.

46. Maginnis, N., Specialist: Reusable Code Helps Increase Productivity, in *Computerworld*, November 1986.

47. Mayrand, J., Leblanc, C., and Merlo, E., Experiment on the automatic detection of function clones in a software system using metrics, in *Proceedings of the International Conference on Software Maintenance*, 1996, pp.244–253.

48. Meyer, B., *Object-Oriented Software Construction*, Prentice-Hall, London, 1988.

49. Musser, D. and Saini, A., *STL Tutorial and Reference Guide: C++ Programming with Standard Template Library*, Addison-Wesley, Reading, MA, 1996.

50. Neighbours, J., The Draco approach to constructing software from reusable components, *IEEE Transactions on Software Engineering*, SE-10(5), September 1984, pp. 564–574.

51. Parnas, D., On the criteria to be used in decomposing software into modules, *Communications of the ACM*, 15(12), December 1972, pp.1053–1058.

52. Pettersson, U. and Jarzabek, S., Industrial experience with building a web portal product line using a lightweight, reactive approach, *ESEC-FSE'05, European Software Engineering Conference and ACM SIGSOFT Symposium on the Foundations of Software Engineering*, ACM Press, September 2005, Lisbon, pp. 326–335.

53. Prieto-Diaz, R., Domain analysis for reusability, *Proceedings of the COMPSAC'87*, October 1987, Tokyo, Japan, pp. 23–29.

54. Rajapakse, D.C and Jarzabek, S., An investigation of cloning in Web portals, *International Conference on Web Engineering, ICWE'05*, July 2005, Sydney, pp. 252–262.

55. Rieger, M., Ducasse, S., and Lanza, M., Insights into system-wide code duplication, *Proceedings of the 11th Working Conference on Reverse Engineering (WCRE'04)*, 2004, pp. 100–109.
56. Sneed, H., private conversation.
57. Shaw, M. and Garlan, D., *Software Architecture: Perspectives on Emerging Discipline*, Prentice Hall, 1996.
58. Smaragdakis, Y. and Batory, D., Application generators, in *Software Engineering Volume of the Encyclopedia of Electrical and Electronics Engineering*, Webster, J., Ed., John Wiley and Sons, 2000.
59. Smyth, W.F., *Computing Patterns in Strings*, Pearson-Addison-Wesley.
60. Soe, M.S., Zhang, H., and Jarzabek, S., XVCL: a tutorial, *Proceedings of the 14th International Conference on Software Engineering and Knowledge Engineering, SEKE'02*, ACM Press, July 2002, Italy, pp. 341–349.
61. STL, http://www.sgi.com/tech/stl/.
62. Tarr, P., Ossher, H., Harrison, W., and Sutton, S., N degrees of separation: multi-dimensional separation of concerns, *Proceedings of the International Conference on Software Engineering, ICSE'99*, Los Angeles, CA, 1999, pp. 107–119.
63. Tarr, P. and Ossher, H., Hyper/J User and Installation Manual, http://www.research.ibm.com/hyperspace/, IBM, 2000.
64. Thompson, S., Higher Order + Polymorphic = Reusable, unpublished manuscript available from the Computing Laboratory, University of Kent, http://www.cs.ukc.ac.uk/pubs/1997.
65. Ueda, Y., Kamiya, T., Kusumoto, S., and Inoue, K., Gemini: maintenance support environment based on code clone analysis, *Proceedings of the 8th IEEE Symposium on Software Metrics*, 2002, pp. 67–76.
66. Wong, T.W., Jarzabek, S., Myat Swe, S., Shen, R., and Zhang, H.Y., XML implementation of frame processor, *Proceedings of the ACM Symposium on Software Reusability, SSR'01*, Toronto, Canada, May 2001, pp. 164–172.
67. Zhang, H.Y., Jarzabek, S., and Soe, M.S., XVCL approach to separating concerns in product family assets, *Proceedings of the Generative and Component-based Software Engineering (GCSE 2001)*, Erfurt, Germany, September 2001, pp. 36–47.
68. Zhang, H. and Jarzabek, S., An XVCL-based approach to software product line development, *Proceedings of the 15th International Conference on Software Engineering and Knowledge Engineering* (SEKE'03), San Francisco, CA, July 1–3, 2003.
69. XVCL (XML-based variant configuration language) method and tool for managing software changes during evolution and reuse, http://fxvcl.sourceforge.net.
70. Yang, J. and Jarzabek, S., Applying a generative technique for enhanced reuse on J2EE platform, *4th International Conference on Generative Programming and Component Engineering, GPCE'05*, September 29–October 1, 2005, Tallinn, Estonia, pp. 237–255.

Chapter 10

The Mixed-Strategy
Approach to
Generic Design

Chapter Summary

In Chapter 9 we discussed the software similarity phenomenon, and reasons why it often leads to software clones — program structures recurring within and across programs, in many variant forms, in many places. We find clones of different granularity levels, occurring at all levels of program abstraction, from the subsystem level to implementation, taking many forms, from similar program fragments to patterns of collaborating components. The reasons why repetitions occur are common. As the cloning problem must be viewed in the context of other design goals, many clones are difficult to avoid with conventional techniques for generic design.

As there is much similarity across systems released during evolution, effective treatment of clones is essential for managing software evolution in a cost-effective way. It is at the center of the mixed-strategy approach to reuse-based evolution.

In this chapter, we elaborate on the mixed-strategy approach to unifying similarity patterns with generic software representations. We build such representations by applying XVCL on top of conventional component design and code written in a programming language such as Java or C++. In a mixed-strategy solution, we represent each of the important similarity patterns in a unique, generic, but adaptable form, along with information necessary to obtain specific program structures, instances of the generic form. Mixed-strategy is capable of unifying a wide range of similarity situations we find in software, considerably enhancing the power of generic design of conventional methods.

To illustrate the approach, we discuss mixed-strategy solutions to similarity patterns found in the Buffer library. In Chapter 13, we analyze mixed-strategy solutions developed in yet other studies discussed in Chapter 9.

The reader should briefly revisit XVCL notation described in Chapter 7 and Chapter 8.

10.1 Buffer Library in Java/XVCL Mixed-Strategy Representation

We now describe and analyze a mixed-strategy representation for the Buffer library. As a mixed-strategy representation is a combination of Java and XVCL, we call it the Java/XVCL mixed-strategy solution. For the sake of comparison, we design a mixed-strategy representation so that the XVCL processor can produce original buffer classes from it.

The sketch of a Java/XVCL x-framework for buffer classes is shown on the left-hand side of Figure 10.1. Having identified similarity patterns, the Java/XVCL x-framework represents each significant similarity in a generic form as follows:

For each of the seven groups of similar classes, such as [T]Buffer or Heap[T]Buffer, we have x-frames to generate classes in a given group. A metaclass, e.g., [T]Buffer.gen, is an x-frame defining a common structure for classes in a given group. Metaclasses correspond by name to seven groups of similar classes. For example, x-frame [T]Buffer.gen defines a common structure of seven [T]Buffer classes, Heap[T]Buffer.gen – seven Heap[T]Buffer classes, and so on. In Figure 10.1, we show only two of the seven class groups and metaclass x-frames.

Each metaclass has a corresponding *class specification* x-frame. Class specification x-frames also correspond by name to seven groups of similar classes. For

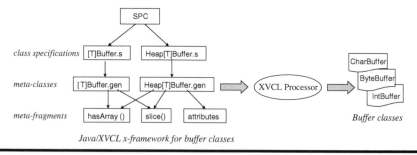

Java/XVCL x-framework for buffer classes

Figure 10.1   An overview of a Java/XVCL mixed-strategy solution to the Buffer library.

example, [T]Buffer.s specifies global parameters and controls to construct seven [T]Buffer classes.

Generic representation of smaller-granularity similarity patterns such as methods or attribute declaration sections appear as metafragments. Metafragments are reusable building blocks for classes. They are customized for reuse in different classes, as specified in earlier x-frames.

The topmost SPC x-frame specifies global parameters and controls to construct all the buffer classes.

The overall Java/XVCL x-framework has been "normalized" for nonredundancy to represent each of the meaningful similarity patterns in a generic way.

We now examine examples of generic solutions from the Java/XVCL buffer x-framework.

Program structures with type-parametric variations are the simplest form of similarity. Generics (or templates in C++) are language features meant for representing such program structures in a generic form. For example, five of the [T]Buffer classes of numeric element type, namely, IntBuffer, ShortBuffer, DoubleBuffer, FloatBuffer, and LongBuffer, differ only in the data-type definitions and type names in some of the method names (differences shown in blue color in Table 10.1).

Table 10.1 Excerpts from Classes ShortBuffer and DoubleBuffer

Class **Short**Buffer	Class **Double**Buffer

public abstract class **Short**Buffer
    extends Buffer
    implements Comparable
    {
    final **short**[] hb;
    final int offset;
    boolean isReadOnly; // Valid only
    for heap buffers
    ShortBuffer(int mark, int pos, int
    lim, int cap,
    short[] hb, int offset)
    {
    super(mark, pos, lim, cap);
    this.hb = hb;
    this.offset = offset;
    }
    ShortBuffer(int mark, int pos, int
    lim, int cap)
    {this(mark, pos, lim, cap, null, 0);
    }
    public static **Short**Buffer
    allocate(int capacity)
    {...
	public abstract class **Double**Buffer
	    extends Buffer
	    implements Comparable
	    {
	    final **double**[] hb;
	    final int offset;
	    boolean isReadOnly;
	    DoubleBuffer(int mark, int pos, int
	    lim, int cap,
	    double[] int offset)
	    {
	    super(mark, pos, lim, cap);
	    this.hb = hb;
	    this.offset = offset;
	    }
	    DoubleBuffer(int mark, int pos, int
	    lim, int cap) {
	    this(mark, pos, lim, cap, null, 0);
	    }
	    public static **Double**Buffer allocate(int
	    capacity) {
	    ...

```
* Creates a new byte buffer containing a shared  subsequence of this
buffer's content. */
public ByteBuffer slice() {
    int pos = this.position();
    int lim = this.limit();
    assert (pos <= lim);
    int rem = (pos <= lim ? lim - pos : 0);
    int off = (pos << 0);
return new DirectByteBuffer  (this, -1, 0, rem, rem,  off); }
```

Figure 10.2   Method slice() recurring with small changes in 13 Direct[T]Buffer[S|U] classes.

At times, parametric differences among similar program structures are not be confined to type names. For example, Figure 10.2 shows a method **slice()** that recurs 13 times in the Direct[T]Buffer[S|U] classes with various combinations of values highlighted in boldface. In Figure 10.2, we see method **slice()** from class DirectByteBuffer**.**

All kinds of parametric differences are easily unified with XVCL variables or expressions. An x-frame representing method **slice()** in a generic way is shown in Figure 10.3.

As XVCL expressions, especially references to XVCL variables, can be intermixed with Java code, for clarity we use italic font for Java code and bold font

Slice: // meta-method x-frame
/* Creates a new byte buffer containing a shared subsequence of this buffer's content. */
public **@elmtTYPE***Buffer slice()* {
    int pos = this.position();
    int lim = this.limit();
    assert (pos <= lim);
    int rem = (pos <= lim ? lim - pos : 0);
    int off = (pos << **@elmtSize***);*
        *return new Direct***@elmtTYPE***Buffer***@byteOrder*** *(this, -1, 0, rem, rem, off); }*

Figure 10.3   An x-frame for generic method slice().

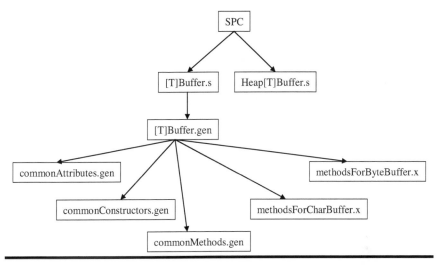

Figure 10.4   A fragment of an x-framework for generating seven [T]Buffer classes.

for XVCL expressions. References to XVCL variable **@elmtTYPE**, are replaced by the XVCL variable's value during processing. Variables referred to in x-frame **Slice** are assigned values in x-frames that adapt x-frame **Slice**, directly or indirectly. For example, the value of XVCL variable **byteOrder** is **<set>** to an empty string, "S" or "U." To produce method **slice()** for class DirectByteBuffer, we **<set>** the value of XVCL variable **elmtTYPE** to "Byte" and **byteOrder** to an empty string. From *Direct***@elmtTYPE***Buffer***@byteOrder** in Figure 10.3 the XVCL processor generates names for all the Direct[T]Buffer[S|U] classes such as DirectByteBuffer, DirectIntBufferU, and DirectIntBufferS.

Parameterization via XVCL variables and expressions plays an important role in building generic components. It provides the means for creating generic names and controlling the traversal and adaptation of x-frames.

Program structures participating in other similarity patterns differ from each other in more diverse ways than we have seen in the previous examples. For example, classes in each of the seven groups of similar classes differ in method signatures, method implementations, and attribute declarations. Some classes in a group may have extra methods that are not needed in other classes in the same group. Then, it becomes difficult to build a generic solution unifying such differences among similar program structures with simple parameters. Instead, we use the following technique to define a generic solution:

Suppose we have N similar program structures, e.g., seven [T]Buffer classes, that we wish to unify with a generic solution. We represent a common part of similar program structures as a generic adaptable x-frame [T]Buffer.gen that plays the role of a template. Then, we iterate over the [T]Buffer.gen N times, in each itera-

SPC

```
<set packageName = "java.nio" />
<set elmtTYPE=Byte,Char,Double,Float,Int,Long,Short />
<set elmttype=byte,char,double,float,int,long,short/ >
<set elmtSize =0,1,3,2,2,3,1 />
<while classGroup = [T]Buffer.s,Heap[T]Buffer.s, ... />
// values of classGroup are names of x-frames for seven groups of similar
buffer classes
    <adapt classGroup />
</while >
```

Figure 10.5   A fragment of SPC.

tion adapting the [T]Buffer.gen in a different way, to produce a required instance, a specific program structure.

Figure 10.4 shows x-frames used in generating seven [T]Buffer classes from a generic x-frame [T]Buffer.gen. Sections of common attributes, constructors, and methods used as building blocks of [T]Buffer classes are defined in generic x-frames adapted from [T]Buffer.gen. The names of these x-frames are commonAttributes.gen, commonConstructors.gen, and commonMethods.gen, respectively (Figure 10.4). These x-frames are shown as metafragments in Figure 10.1.

X-frame [T]Buffer.s iterates over [T]Buffer.gen seven times. For each iteration, [T]Buffer.s executes different XVCL customization commands to adapt [T]Buffer.gen and metafragments to generate a suitable [T]Buffer class.

The SPC of Figure 10.5 sets general parameters used in generating all the buffer classes. First, the SPC <set>s the value of XVCL variable **packageName** to "java.nio" and the value of XVCL variable **elmtTYPE** to <Byte,Char,Double,Float,Int, Long,Short>, the value of **elmttype** to <byte,char,double,float,int,long,short> and the value of **elmtSize** to <0,1,3,2,2,3,1>. XVCL variable **elmtSize** indicates the size of a buffer element:

$$2^{elmtSize} = \text{(the number of bytes per buffer element)}.$$

Command **<while>** is controlled by a variable whose values are names of x-frames specifying how to generate classes in each of the seven groups of similar classes (we listed only two out of the seven x-frame names).

In x-frame [T]Buffer.s (Figure 10.6), a **<while>** loop iterates over its body seven times, generating one of the seven [T]Buffer classes in each iteration. The loop is

[T]Buffer.s

```
<while elmtTYPE, elmttype, elmtSize >
   <select option = elmtTYPE >
      <option = Byte >
         <adapt [T]Buffer.gen >
            <insert moreMethods >
               <adapt methodsForByteBuffer.x />
         </adapt>
      <option = Char >
         <adapt [T]Buffer.gen >
            <insert moreMethods >
               <adapt methodsForCharBuffer.x />
            <insert-after extends-implements-clause >
               Appendable,CharSequence,Readable
            <insert toString >
               Public String toString()
               { return toString(
                  position(),limit()); }
         </adapt>
      <otherwise>
         <adapt [T]Buffer.gen />
   </select>
</while>
```

Figure 10.6 A fragment of specs to generate seven [T]Buffer classes

---

controlled by three multivalued variables, namely **elmtTYPE**, **elmttype**, *and* **elmt-Size**. In each iteration, one of the three variables accepts one value from their list, in the left-to-right order. Based on that value, the processor **<select>**s a suitable option (such as Byte, Char, or otherwise) and generates code for appropriate classes (ByteBuffer, CharBuffer, and all the remaining classes, respectively.) Generation is done by **<adapt>**ing the x-frame [T]Buffer.gen.

We now comment on x-frame [T]Buffer.gen (Figure 10.7). An expression **@elmtTYPE***Buffer.java* in the **outfile** attribute at the top of the x-frame [T]Buffer specifies the names of files where the XVCL processor is to emit the code for the respective classes. Rows below define the package name and the headers for each

[T]Buffer.gen *outfile*:@elmtTYPEBuffer.java

package **@packageName**;

public abstract class **@elmtTYPE***Buffer extends*

    *Buffer implements Comparable<***@elmtTYPE***Buffer>* **<break** *extends-implements-clause* **/>**

{ // attributes and methods here

<adapt commonAttributes.gen **/>**

<break moreAttributes **/>**

<adapt commonConstructors.gen **/>**

<break moreConstructors **/>**

<adapt commonMethods.gen **/>**

<break moreMethods **/>**

<break toString **>**

 public String toString() {

    StringBuffer sb = new StringBuffer();

    sb.append(getClass().getName());

    sb.append("[pos="+ position());

    sb.append(" lim="+ limit());

    sb.append(" cap="+ capacity()+"]");

    return sb.toString(); }

</break>

{

Figure 10.7 A fragment of generic x-frame [T]Buffer.

of the seven classes [T]Buffer in turn. Then, x-frame [T]Buffer defines a common structure of [T]Buffer classes in terms of attribute, contractor, and method definitions, with suitable **<break>**s for extensions.

Five numeric [T]Buffer classes differ only in parameters that are catered to by XVCL variables defined in the SPC. These five classes do not require any further adaptations of the common class representation provided by the x-frame [T]Buffer. gen. The five classes are generated in five iterations over the **<otherwise>** clause, where **<adapt** [T]Buffer.gen **/>** does not specify any further customization commands.

However, classes ByteBuffer and CharBuffer require some specific customizations of the template [T]Buffer.gen. These customizations are handled by **<insert>** into **<break>** commands.

```
public abstract class ByteBuffer
    extends Buffer
    implements Comparable <ByteBuffer>
{
```

Figure 10.8   Declaration of class ByteBuffer.

```
public abstract class CharBuffer
    extends Buffer
    implements Comparable<ByteBuffer>,Appendable,CharSequence,Readable
{
```

Figure 10.9   Declaration of class CharBuffer.

Class ByteBuffer needs 35 extra methods in addition to those found in other [T]Buffer classes. These extra methods are in x-frame methodsForByteBuffer.x and are <**insert**>ed at a suitable <**break**> point in [T]Buffer.gen.

Extra methods for class CharBuffer are <**insert**>ed in a similar way as in the case of ByteBuffer. However, class CharBuffer requires yet other customizations:

The <**insert-after**> under <**option**> Char extends the implements-clause in a way that is required only for class CharBuffer. Figure 10.8 and Figure 10.9 show the implements-clauses in ByteBuffer and CharBuffer classes, respectively.

Method **toString**() converts a buffer element to a character string. For Char-Buffer such conversion is trivial. For other buffer element types, implementation of **toString**() requires some interpretation. As six of the buffer classes need the same implementation of **toString**() whereas only one needs a different implementation, we define the more commonly used implementation as a default in x-frame [T]Buffer.gen (Figure 10.7). Method **toString**() for CharBuffer is handled by the last <**insert**> specified at the adaptation point in <**option**> Char (Figure 10.6). This <**insert**> overrides the default implementation of toString()-defined <**break**> in [T]Buffer.gen.

As already observed, inserting code and specifications at designated <**break**> points is also a simple yet powerful means of handling unexpected changes arising during software evolution. The implements-clause (Figure 10.8 and Figure 10.9) illustrates this point. As we add new features and the number of feature combination increases, we may need to specify more interfaces a given class implements. We often cater to such unexpected extensions with <**insert**> into <**break**> com-

commonConstructors.gen

// contains constructor definitions for all [T]Buffer classes

......//other constructors

@elmtTYPE Buffer(int mark, int pos,

      int lim, int cap,**@elmttype** [] hb, int offset)

  {

     super(mark, pos, lim, cap);

     this.hb = hb;

     this.offset = offset;

  }

......//other constructors

Figure 10.10 An excerpt from generic constructor definition x-frame.

mands. In the x-frame [T]Buffer (Figure 10.7), the **<break>** named extends-imple-ments-clause marks the point into which **<insert>** commands from higher-level x-frames can insert custom code. In particular, when generating class CharBuf-fer, we **<insert>** text "CharSequence" at the **<break>** extends-implements-clause. Note that the implements-clauses of other classes are not affected. In general, a **<break>** point can have a default content (Java code with XVCL commands) and higher-level x-frames can replace the default content or insert extra content after or before many **<break>** points in **<adapt>**ed x-frames. If no **<insert>** command from higher-level x-frames affects the **<break>** point, then the XVCL processor emits the <break>'s default content to the output.

Finally, we have a brief look at the bottom level of the x-framework hierar-chy, where we find so-called metafragments — x-frames representing generic class-building blocks. Excerpts from generic constructor and method definitions are shown in Figure 10.10 and Figure 10.11, respectively.

We have only highlighted the structure of the solution. Complete documenta-tion and XVCL code for the Buffer library case study can be found at our Web site [4], under "Case Studies." This study was also described in Reference 2 and Reference 3.

We would like to end this section by summarizing the process of designing the Java/XVCL buffer x-framework. We gained a general understanding of buffer classes first. Then, we identified groups of classes that we suspected would be similar. We examined methods and attribute declarations within each group that confirmed there was much similarity among classes. We designed x-frames for each group of classes, eliminating redundant code fragments as follows: For each group of similar fragments, we created a suitable metafragment. As for metafragments that appeared

commonMethods.gen

```
// contains method definitions for all [T]Buffer classes
......//other omitted methods
//Tells whether or not this buffer is equal to another object.
public boolean equals(Object ob){
    if (!(ob instanceof @elmtTYPEBuffer)) return false;
  @elmtTYPEBuffer that = (@elmtTYPEBuffer)ob;
    if (this.remaining() != that.remaining()) return false;
    int p = this.position();
    for (int i=this.limit()-1, j=that.limit()-1; i >= p;i--,j--) {
        byte v1 = this.get(i);
        byte v2 = that.get(j);
        if (v1 != v2) {
    if ((v1 != v1) && (v2 != v2))  // For float and double
    continue;
        return false;
      }
    }
    return true;
}
......//other methods
```

Figure 10.11 An excerpt from generic method definition x-frame.

in different contexts with changes, we parameterized them with XVCL variables, **<break>** points, **<select>**, **<insert>**, **<adapt>**, and other XVCL commands to cater to required variations. Then, we created a template x-frame (e.g., [T]Buffer.gen) for each of the seven groups of similar classes, along with a corresponding specification x-frame (e.g., [T]Buffer.s). Finally, we created an SPC with global controls of the generic Java/XVCL mixed-strategy representation of the Buffer library.

In this and other case studies in which we applied XVCL, the object-oriented structure of the programs to be generated has always been a starting point for building a metasolution. It is not surprising, as the structure of a mixed-strategy solution depends on and implicitly defines the intended structure of programs to be generated.

10.2 Evaluation of the Mixed-Strategy Buffer Library Solution

The Buffer library in the representation described in this chapter is meant for developers and maintainers of the Buffer library. The Java/XVCL x-framework contains target code in generic form, along with the information about how to derive concrete buffer classes from their respective generic representations. The framework also contains additional information that aids in understanding classes, and helps developers maintain Buffer classes. For example, it explicates the impact of various features on code.

Developers have full control over every detail of the class structure and code that the XVCL processor generates from the Java/XVCL x-framework. Programmers using the library need not be concerned about or even aware that the library is managed with XVCL. On the other hand, some programmers may also wish to incorporate elements of the XVCL technique into their mainstream programming work; especially, programmers working in unstable domains, where change is pervasive, may see good reasons to do so. In such cases, x-frames of the class library can be neatly integrated with programs using those libraries at the mixed-strategy.

To enable fair comparison, in this experiment, a class library generated from the Java/XVCL x-framework was no different from the original class library. In another study, we redesigned the x-framework to generate buffer classes optimized for performance, as required, for example, in embedded systems.

In the following sections, we conduct quantitative and qualitative analyses of the presented Java/XVCL mixed-strategy solution for the Buffer library. Our qualitative analysis includes an experiment (Section 10.2.3) in which we extend the Buffer library with a new type of buffer element (Complex), comparing the maintenance effort involved in each, the original and the mixed-strategy solutions. The reader can find a comprehensive evaluation of strengths and weaknesses of the mixed-strategy approach on general grounds in Chapter 14, once we have discussed other mixed-strategy projects.

10.2.1 Quantitative Comparison of Buffer Library Solutions

Table 10.2 and Figure 10.12 show the results of comparing the original Java Buffer classes with the Java/XVCL mixed-strategy solution.

Columns 1 and 4 show the number of conceptual elements in each of the solution spaces, Java and Java/XVCL, respectively. Columns 2 and 3 show sizes of the elements in Java solution, in terms of physical lines of Java code **with** and **without** comments, excluding blanks, respectively. Columns 5 and 6 show sizes of the elements in the Java/XVCL solution, in terms of physical lines of Java code and XVCL commands, **with** and **without** comments, excluding blanks, respectively.

Table 10.2 Original Java Buffer Library versus Java/XVCL Mixed-Strategy Solution

Classes	Original Java Buffer Library			Java/XVCL Mixed-Strategy Representation of Buffer Library		
	1	2	3	4	5	6
	# Class-Building Blocks	LOC[a]	Java Code[b]	# x-Frames	LOC[c]	Java Code[d]
[T]Buffer						
(7 classes)	258	3720	871	79	1400	320
Heap[T]Buffer						
(7 classes)	159	914	802	52	313	291
Direct[T]Buffer [S|U]						
(13 classes)	337	2428	2249	85	689	665
Heap[T]BufferR						
(7 classes)	112	521	444	35	226	209
Direct[T]Buffer R[S|U]						
(13 classes)	187	979	895	42	378	367
Subtotal						
(47 classes)	1053	8562	5261	293	3006	1852
Other classes						
(24 classes)	332	1570	1458	31	239	228
Total	1385	10132	6719	324	3245	2080

[a] Physical lines of Java code **with** comments, excluding blanks.

[b] Physical lines of Java code **without** comments, excluding blanks.

[c] Physical lines of Java code **with** comments and XVCL commands, excluding blanks.

[d] Physical lines of Java code and XVCL commands, **without** comments, excluding blanks.

A conceptual element in the Java program is a class or a program "fragment" such as a method or constructor, or even smaller code fragments representing the declaration section or a fragment of method or constructor implementation. We pay attention only to fragments that, in our understanding, play a specific role in the Buffer domain or in class construction, and therefore, are important for program understanding.

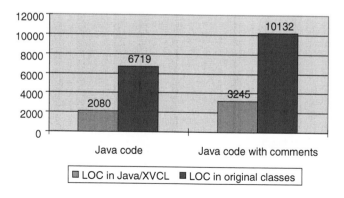

Figure 10.12   Buffer library: summary chart.

Figure 10.12 shows the overall code size of each solution. Unification of similarities with XVCL on top of Java code eliminates 68 percent of the code as compared to the original buffer classes. We observe a similar code reduction if we count code lines with comments. It is possible and useful to manage both executable code and comments with XVCL.

10.2.2 Qualitative Analysis of the Java/XVCL Solution

As we can see in Table 10.2, in the Java/XVCL solution a programmer deals with a smaller number of conceptual elements than in the original Java solution. Also, the sizes of conceptual elements in the Java/XVCL solution are smaller than those in the original Java solution. On the other hand, in the Java/XVCL solution developers have to deal with the added complexity of understanding generic representation.

The physical size is just one among many factors that collectively determine the complexity of a program solution in terms of its understandability, changeability, or maintainability. For example, by applying data compression techniques, we do not make a program any simpler for a programmer to understand. Likewise, unifying all possible similarity patterns in a program would complicate program understanding rather than simplify it. (Consider an extreme case in which we unify all references to a certain program variable or all occurrences of the letter "a" in a program!). Balance and common sense are irreplaceable in arriving at any good design solution.

Not only does such unification reduce the conceptual and physical size of the overall program solution, but it also emphasizes important relationships among program elements that matter to programmers trying to understand and modify the program. Instead of dealing with each class separately from others, we can understand classes in groups. Traceability allows us to see the exact differences among specific classes in a group, should we need this information. The same rule of genericity/traceability is applied below the class level to methods/constructors and to other meaningful program fragments (such as method implementation fragments). In the Java/XVCL x-framework, we can see what is similar and what is different at each level. The x-framework also interconnects all the levels of program definition, so that we can see important relationships among them: If we want to change one class, we can check if the change also affects other similar classes. If we want to change a class method, we can analyze the impact of change on all the classes that use that method in the same or similar form.

The preceding relationships are implicit in the Java buffer classes (and in most conventional programs in general). A programmer must recover them whenever he or she needs to understand a program during maintenance. The benefit of the Java/XVCL solution also lies in separating concerns: Defining a class architecture, to meet usability, performance, and other runtime concerns, is the domain and responsibility of a programming language. Design-time concerns — such as how classes are built, what is similar and different among them, and what it takes to change them — are delegated to the mixed-strategy.

10.2.3 Extending the Buffer Library: An Experiment in Maintenance

We now describe a small experiment comparing maintainability of the Java/XVCL buffer x-framework versus the original buffer classes. Suppose we need to extend the Buffer library with buffers of a new element type, say, complex number (Complex). Many classes must be implemented to address this new element type, but here we concentrate only on three of them, namely, ComplexBuffer, HeapComplexBuffer, and HeapComplexBufferR. We start by illustrating what it takes to extend our metasolution so that the XVCL processor can generate these three new classes.

A Complex buffer is similar to other numeric buffers, but as Complex is not a primitive type such as Int or Float, we must implement it first. A sample implementation of class Complex is given in Figure 10.13.

We represent a complex number as two double numbers: double re; double rm;. As each double occupies 2^3 bytes, the size of a Complex number is 2^4 bytes and the value of **elmtSize** for a Complex number is 4. To generate class ComplexBuffer, we need to add an extra iteration of <**while**> loop <**adapt**>ing x-frame [T]Buffer with values of XVCL variables **elmtTYPE**, **elmtype**, and **elmtSize** set to **Complex**, **Complex**, and **4**, respectively. Figure 10.14 shows a relevant part of the revised SPC. These changes in SPC are sufficient to generate classes HeapComplexBuffer and HeapComplexBufferR.

The new type Complex also affects definitions of methods **hashCode**() and **CompareTo**() in the x-frame commonMethods.gen (Figure 10.4 and Figure 10.11). XVCL code in Figure 10.15 shown in boldface results from addressing the new

```
//Complex.java
package.java.nio;
public class Complex extends Number
{
                    private double re =0;
                    private double im = 0;
public Complex (double re, double im) {
                        this.re = re;
                        this.im = im;
                    }
public int getReal() {
                        return re;
}
public int compareReal(Complex c) {//compare real parts
                        return re – c.getReal();
}
}
```

Figure 10.13   Class Complex.

SPC // modified SPC of Figure 5; modifications shown in **red**
<set packageName = "java.nio" >
<set elmtTYPE = Byte, Char, Double, Float, Int, Long, Short, **Complex**>
<set elmttype = byte, char, double, float, int, long, short, **Complex**>
<set elmtSize=<0, 1, 3, 2, 2, 3, 1, 4 >
 <while classGroup = [T]Buffer.s,Heap[T]Buffer.s, ... />
// values of classGroup are names of x-frames for seven groups of similar buffer classes
</while >

Figure 10.14   Modified SPC for class Complex.

commonMethod.gen
… // other methods
// Returns the current hash code of this buffer.
 public int hashCode() {
   int h = 1;
   int p = position();
   for (int i = limit() - 1; i >= p; i--)
<select option = elmtTYPE **>**
    <option = Complex **>** *h = 31 * h + ((Complex)get(i)).getReal();*
    <otherwise > *h = 31 * h + (int)get(i);*
</select>
return h }
// Compares this buffer to another object.
public int compareTo(Object ob) {
    @elmtTYPE*Buffer that = (***@elmtTYPE***Buffer)ob;*
    int n = this.position() + Math.min(this.remaining(), that.remaining());
    for (int i = this.position(), j = that.position(); i < n; i++, j++) {
      @elmtTYPE*Buffer v1 = this.get(i);*
      @elmtTYPE*Buffer v2 = that.get(j);*
       if (v1 == v2) continue;
     if ((v1 != v1) && (v2 != v2))   // For float and double
          continue;
<select option = elmtTYPE **>**
    <option = Complex **>** if (v1.compareReal(v2) < 0)
    <otherwise > if (v1 < v2)
</select>
               return -1;
          return +1;
  }
   return this.remaining() - that.remaining(); }
……// other methods

Figure 10.15   Modified methods hashCode() and CompareTo().

---

type Complex. In method **hashCode()** the buffer element must be cast to type Int in all classes but ComplexBuffer, in which the buffer element must be cast to type Complex. The **<select>** commands in methods **hashCode()** and **compareTo()** distinguish between these two situations.

This completes the description of modifications of the Java/XVCL x-framework to address class Complex. We generated sample classes from the modified x-framework and tested the result.

Now, let us try to address element type Complex in the original Java Buffer library, concentrating on the same three classes as before for the Java/XVCL solution. As **Complex** buffer is analogical to other numerical buffers, we could start with integer buffer and copy selected code from classes IntBuffer.java, HeapIntBuffer.java, and HeapIntBufferR.java to the three new classes. However, adaptation of the copied code is very tedious and error prone. For example, there are 42 places in class IntBuffer.java (which is only 124 lines) that must be changed from **Int** or **int** to **Complex.** This replacement cannot be done automatically, as not all occurrences of "Int" should be changed. Methods **hasCode()** and **compareTo()** mentioned before must be also changed. Adaptation of code from classes HeapIntBuffer.java and HeapIntBufferR.java for classes HeapComplexBuffer.java and HeapComplexBufferR.java, respectively, requires similar actions.

Table 10.3 compares changes of the original Buffer library with the Java/XVCL solution involved in adding element type Complex. For example, in the original Buffer library, implementing class ComplexBuffer.java based on the code of class IntBuffer requires 25 replacements of "int" by "Complex," which can be automated by an editing tool. A further 17 replacements of "int" to "Complex" must be done manually. On the other hand, in the Java/XVCL solution all the changes must be done manually, but only five modifications are required.

This experiment is small, but it gives a flavor of the types of changes required in each case.

10.3 Conclusions

We described the principle of generic design with a mixed-strategy approach, using a Buffer library as an example. We analyzed engineering qualities of the Java/XVCL mixed-strategy solution in quantitative and qualitative terms, and by conducting a controlled experiment.

A Java/XVCL mixed-strategy solution compressed the physical and conceptual solution size as compared to the original Java Buffer library. It also emphasized relationships among program elements that matter to programmers trying to understand and modify the program. Finally, it enhanced the conceptual integrity of the design, which Brooks calls "the most important consideration in system design" [1].

The Mixed-Strategy Approach to Generic Design ■ 235

Table 10.3 The Impact of Addressing Type Complex in the Original Buffer Library versus Java/XVCL Solution

New Classes	Copied Classes	Changes in Original Buffer Library			Changes in Java/XVCL Solution		
		Type of Changes	Number	Type	Type of Changes	Number	Type
ComplexBuffer	IntBuffer	Text:					
Int — Complex	25	Automatic	Values of multivariables	3	Manual		
		Text:					
Int — Complex	17	Manual					
		Specific changes	2	Manual	Specific changes	2	Manual
HeapComplexBuffer	HeapIntBuffer	Text:					
Int — Complex	21	Automatic	Values of multivariables	3	Manual		
		Text:					
Int — Complex	10	Manual					
HeapComplexBufferR	HeapIntBufferR	Text:					
Int — Complex	16	Automatic	Values of multivariables	3	Manual		
		Text:					
Int — Complex	5	Manual					

References

1. Brooks, P.B., *The Mythical Man-Month*, Addison Wesley, Boston, 1995.
2. Jarzabek, S. and Li, S., Eliminating redundancies with a "composition with adaptation" meta-programming technique, *Proceedings of the ESEC-FSE'03, European Software Engineering Conference and ACM SIGSOFT Symposium on the Foundations of Software Engineering*, September 2003, Helsinki, pp. 237–246.
3. Jarzabek, S. and Li, S., Unifying clones with a generative programming technique: a case study, *Journal of Software Maintenance and Evolution: Research and Practice*, 18(4), 267–292, July–August 2006.
4. XVCL (XML-based variant configuration language) method and tool for managing software changes during evolution and reuse, xvcl.comp.nus.edu.sg.

Chapter 11

Evolution with the Mixed-Strategy Approach

Chapter Summary

In this chapter, we walk the reader through steps of FRS evolution with the mixed-strategy approach. We show how the techniques described in previous chapters address the evolution challenges described in Chapter 1, helping us realize the reuse-based evolution concept. We use XVCL techniques explained in the previous chapters. We follow an FRS evolution scenario discussed in Chapter 5 in the context of evolution with CVS. Therefore, the reader should briefly review Chapter 1, Chapter 5, and Chapter 7 before reading this chapter.

11.1   Introduction

Software evolution is a succession of changes that result in a number of similar systems being released to various customers. Each system release shares certain common features with other releases, but also differs from them in user requirements or design-related details. Some new evolutionary changes (e.g., enhancements or upgrades) should uniformly apply to all the past releases, whereas other changes may apply only to some of the releases, without affecting other releases that do not need them. Handling those nuances in an effective way is the challenge of reuse-based software evolution. Knowing exactly what is common to all the releases and what is unique to each release is the essence and a prerequisite for effective evolution, and reuse-based evolution in particular.

Now we recapitulate how the mixed-strategy approach tackles challenges of reuse-based software evolution:

As the purpose of an x-framework is to help us evolve system components, it is both natural and necessary to consider the main assumptions of an FRS component architecture first. These assumptions shape and constrain the x-framework. Therefore, we first plan overall software system structure at all levels of abstraction and granularity, from subsystem, to component layer (e.g., user interface or business logic), to component, to class, and to class implementation details. A precise model of a software component architecture is a prerequisite to applying XVCL. A software component architecture is a backbone structure around which we form a mixed-strategy representation of an evolving software, the so-called x-framework.

In the case of FRS, a first-cut FRS x-framework is built by turning FRS components into x-frames with XVCL.

Rather than directly modifying code components in response to evolutionary changes, we use XVCL to specify the impact of changes on code structures. An x-framework that emerges in the process of software evolution contains both code structures and the knowledge of evolutionary changes. Code structures affected by changes are continuously transformed into generic x-frames that can be easily adapted to changes arriving from various sources (e.g., changes relevant to various system releases). The goal is to reuse the same x-frames, after suitable adaptations, in all system releases. The XVCL processor generates each release R by interpreting an x-framework, and applying customizations required for that release, recorded in SPC^R.

An x-framework explicates similarities and differences among systems released during evolution. An x-framework maps variant features (and also any changes such as enhancements of user requirements and changes in design decisions or underlying technology) into a chain of x-frame modifications required for implementation of that feature or change. X-frames are designed to be generic and adaptable, and to accommodate features in various combinations. Threads of modifications required for various features arising during evolution are visibly recorded in the form of change specifications in relation to generic x-frames, but in separation from them. Change specifications are formally linked to designated variation points in x-frames below.

An x-framework is continuously refined during evolution, thus x-frames remain generic and adaptable, serving as a base for evolution of the released systems.

The aim of an x-framework is to avoid the explosion of component versions, to enhance the visibility of changes across released systems, to capture similarity patterns of changes and program structures arising during evolution, and to automate change propagation across complex program structures.

A software component architecture is described by a set of components that interact with one another through well-defined interfaces (connectors) to deliver the

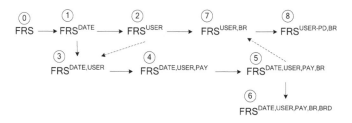

Figure 11.1   Stages of facility reservation system (FRS) evolution.

required system behavior. In this chapter, we focus on an FRS x-framework for components. We extend an FRS x-framework to address connectors in Chapter 12.

11.2   Stages of FRS Evolution

In Chapter 5, we discussed evolution of FRS with CVS. Here, we assume the same FRS component architecture as in Chapter 5 and an evolution scenario with extensions as shown in Figure 11.1. We summarize the main assumptions, referring the reader to Chapter 5 for other details.

We summarize the meaning of various FRS features for ease of reference. There are a couple of new features (highlighted in bold) as compared to Chapter 5.

- VIEW-RES = {FAC, RES-ID, DATE, USER} a group of reservation viewing methods:
  - FAC: view reservations by facility
  - RES-ID: view reservations by reservation ID
  - DATE: view reservations by date
  - USER: view reservations by user
  - USER-PD: view reservations by user for a preferred date
- **PREF: making reservation with or without preferred facility**
- BR: block reservation – making reservations in bulk:
  - **MF – block reservation of multiple facilities**
  - **MTS – block reservations at multiple time slots**
- PAY = {RC, CC, BC, FCD}: a group of features related to payment for reserving facilities:
  - **RC: reservation charges**
  - **CC: cancellation charges**
  - **BC: bill construction**
  - **FCD: frequent-customer discount**
  - BRD: discount for block reservations
  - PD: view reservations for a preferred date
  - BR: block reservation — making reservations in bulk

- MF: block reservation of multiple facilities
- MTS: block reservations at multiple time slots

Stage 1: Suppose one of our customers requests a new feature, to view reservations by date (DATE, for short). Having implemented the required enhancement, we have two versions of the FRS in use, namely, the original FRS and the enhanced system FRS^{DATE}.

Stage 2: After some time, yet another customer would like to view reservations by user (USER). Having implemented this new enhancement, we have three versions of the FRS in use: the original FRS, FRS^{DATE}, and FRS^{USER}.

Stage 3: We also realize that the new features may be generally useful for other customers and yet another version FRS^{DATE,USER} may make perfect sense to some of them.

Stage 3a: We extend FRS^{DATE,USER} with the ability to make reservation with or without a preferred facility: FRS^{DATE,USER,PREF}

Stage 4: Sometime later, a new customer wants an FRS that supports the concept of payment for reservations (PAY). **This includes computing and displaying reservation charges (RC), cancellation charges (CC), bill construction (BC), and frequent-customer discount (FCD)**. The name PAY refers to all such payment features. FRS^{DATE,USER,PAY} results from that enhancement.

Stage 4a: We extend FRS^{DATE,USER,PAY} with the ability to make reservation with or without a preferred facility: FRS^{DATE,USER,PAY,PREF}

Stage 5: Another customer would like to make block reservations (BR), as well as support for payment (FRS$^{DATE,USER,\ PAY,BR}$)

Stage 6: We include a block reservation discount (FRS^{DATE,USER,PAY,BR,BRD}).

Stage 7: We need an FRS with existing features USER and BR (FRS^{USER,BR}).

Stage 8: A customer asks us to customize the USER feature to view reservations made for only preferred range of dates ((FRS$^{USER-PD,BR}$).

We now explain how this evolution scenario is handled with the mixed-strategy approach.

11.3   An Overview of the FRS X-Framework

An FRS x-framework is to represent FRS releases, and the knowledge of evolutionary changes that led to various releases. It should also help developers selectively include specific features (after possible adaptations) into specific FRS releases.

Specifications of customizations unique to a given FRS release are contained in the topmost x-frame, called an SPC. Figure 11.2 shows SPCs for various FRS releases at the top. To produce a specific FRS release, say FRS^{DATE,USER}, we write an

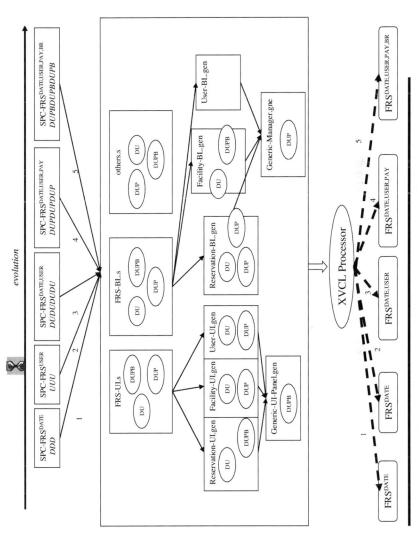

Figure 11.2 Facility reservation system (FRS) evolution with mixed-strategy.

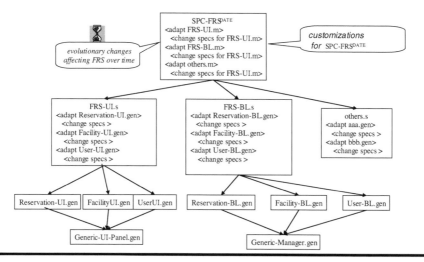

Figure 11.3   A facility reservation system (FRS) x-framework: architecture-level view.

SPC-FRS^{DATE,USER} describing features specific to that release as changes (deltas) of the generic x-frames.

In Figure 11.2, numbers attached to arrows identify stages of evolution and correspondence between SPC and respective FRS releases. Ovals in x-frames are variation points at which x-frames can be customized to accommodate feature combinations to be implemented in various releases. These variation points are marked with letters to indicate traceability between feature specifications and feature implementation (D – DATE, U – USER, etc.).

Figure 11.2 and Figure 11.3 show a macrostructure of an FRS x-framework. X-frames shown in figures correspond to subsystems (such as Reservation, Facility, or User), and groupings of user interface, business logic, and database components.

Changes are described and propagated across x-frames by means of XVCL commands embedded in x-frames. Each x-frame specifies changes for the lower-lever x-frames, and receives changes from the upper-level x-frames. Therefore, x-frames are both active and passive. As shown in Figure 11.3, at each adaptation point we can specify (optional) changes to be applied to the adapted x-frame. These changes are also propagated to x-frames below in the hierarchy (e.g., change specifications from the SPC level for FRS-UI.m apply also to Reservation-UI.gen, Facility-UI.gen, User-UI.gen, and Generic-UI-Panel.gen).

With this introduction, we now illustrate how change specifications are used to handle some of the evolution problems discussed in previous sections.

11.4 Development of a New System Release

We contrast the development life cycle for a new system release in the mixed-strategy approach with evolution supported by CVS (Chapter 5).

In CVS, we have the following development life cycle for a new system release, S^{NEW}:

1. Analyze requirements for S^{NEW}.
2. Understand similarities and differences between S^{NEW} and earlier releases.
3. Select from the CVS repository configurations of component versions "best matching" S^{NEW}. We call this S^{NEW} component the *baseline*.
4. Customize the selected component baseline to fully meet requirements of S^{NEW}.
5. Test and integrate customized components to obtain S^{NEW}.
6. Validate S^{NEW} to see if it meets its requirements.

In the mixed-strategy approach, we use x-framework as a basis for building a new system release, S^{NEW}, as follows:

1. Analyze requirements for S^{NEW}.
2. Understand similarities and differences between S^{NEW} and earlier releases.
3. Any new feature that is unique to the current release is implemented in specification x-frames, outside the reusable x-framework core. Such features may be incorporated into the x-framework core once their general value for the system under evolution has been confirmed.
4. Any new feature that can benefit yet other system releases is implemented into the reusable x-framework core.
5. Any new feature f^{new} that is similar to an already implemented feature f^{old} is implemented by following the pattern of f^{old}, reusing x-frames already implemented in the x-framework
6. Brand-new features must be carefully implemented taking into account functional and implementation dependencies among features. This is the most knowledge-intensive part of building S^{NEW}.
7. This development scenario is executed incrementally. After each partial implementation of new features, the XVCL processor generates FRS, which is compiled and tested.
8. An x-framework is refined during feature implementation, and also upon completion of a new system release. The refinements normalize the x-framework for nonredundancy: each significant repetition of program structures or repetitions of change specification patterns signifies an opportunity for enhancing the genericity and engineering qualities of an x-framework for future evolution.

1. class ViewRes extends FRSPanels implements ActionListener
2. { …
3. ViewRes(FRSClient client) // constructor
4. { …
5. // menu items for selecting a required res. viewing method:
6. viewResMethodList = new List ();
7. viewResMethodList.addItem ("Facility"); // view res. by facility
8. viewResMethodList.addItem ("Reservation ID"); // view res. by ID
9. // actions for res. viewing methods:
10. public void actionPerformed (ActionEvent ev) {
11. Object source = ev.getSource();
12. if (source == viewButton) {
13.   if (viewResMethodList.getSelectedItem() == "Facility") { … }
14. else if (viewResMethodList.getSelectedItem() == "Reservation ID")   {...}
15. // event handling:
16. …details not shown
17. }

Figure 11.4   Java class *ViewRes* to handle reservation viewing methods.

11.5   Specifying Changes for FRS^{DATE}

In the initial FRS, a user can view reservations by facility (FAC) and reservation ID (RES-ID). Java class *ViewRes* defines the functionality for building the menu for viewing reservations. This class also displays the available retrieval methods for reservations and elicits the user's choice of retrieval method. Based on the user's choice of a retrieval method, the class *ViewRes* calls the appropriate method from the corresponding business logic component. Figure 11.4 shows fragments of class *ViewRes* implementation. Code lines 5–8 display menu items for selecting reservation viewing methods (by Facility and by Reservation ID, in this case). Code lines 9–14 define actions to be executed upon selecting various reservation viewing methods. Event handling, if any, is defined below line 15.

Suppose at Stage 1 of evolution (Figure 11.1), we implement DATE feature for one customer only, and we do not know yet if DATE will be useful for other customers or not. In such a case, change should be nonintrusive to the existing FRS components used in the original FRS release. Therefore, we instrument class *ViewRes* with XVCL to cater to DATE, and place it in an x-frame ViewRes-UI.gen (Figure 11.5).

X-frame ViewRes-UI.gen defines three variation points (**<break>** commands) at which we can modify class *ViewRes* to cater to viewing reservations by DATE. The three **<break>**s allow us to add a menu item, action, and even handling code

ViewRes-UI.gen: handles variant reservation viewing methods

```
class ViewRes extends FRSPanels implements ActionListener
{ ...
ViewRes(FRSClient client) // constructor
   {    ...
// menu items for selecting a required res. viewing method:
viewResMethodList = new List ();
viewResMethodList.addItem ("Facility"); // view res. by
facility
viewResMethodList.addItem ("Reservation ID"); // view res.
by ID
<break viewResBy-Menu-UI /> // code to extend menu with
view reservations by DATE can be inserted here
   }
// actions for res. viewing methods:
public void actionPerformed (ActionEvent ev) {
Object source = ev.getSource();
if (source == viewButton) {
   if (viewResMethodList.getSelectedItem() == "Facility") {
... }
   else if (viewResMethodList.getSelectedItem() ==
"Reservation ID")      {...}
<break viewResBy-Action-UI > // code for new action to
view reservations by DATE can be inserted here
// event handling:
...details not shown
<break   viewResBy-EventHandling-UI />  // code for new
event handler to view reservations by DATE can be inserted
here
}
```

Figure 11.5   X-frame ViewRes-UI.gen.

for a new reservation viewing method. The reader should note that if no **<insert>** commands from upper-level x-frames affect **<break>**s, no action is required to obtain the original class *ViewRes* shown in Figure 11.4 to view reservations by Facility and Reservation ID. As **<break>** commands do not contain any default code, the XVCL processor simply ignores them when emitting output. In that sense the change is nonintrusive.

```
<adapt ViewRes-UI.gen >
  <insert  viewResBy-Menu-UI >
    viewResMethodList.addItem ("Date");
   </insert>
  <insert viewResBy-Action-UI >
    else if (viewResMethodList.getSelectedItem() ==
"Date") { … }
   </insert>
</adapt>
```

Figure 11.6   Customizations for FRSDATE**.**

Figure 11.6 shows customizations required to update the x-frame ViewRes-UI.gen for FRS[DATE].

Similar solutions are designed in subhierarchies FRS-BL and others to add the business logic, database access code, and other changes needed to accommodate the DATE feature, without affecting the original FRS.

This trivial evolution stage tells us something about the general way in which XVCL handles changes: X-frame ViewRes-UI.gen is a simple generic component that allows us to avoid creating two specialized, very similar variants of class *ViewRes*, for the original FRS and for FES[DATE]. Instead, we can produce custom class *ViewRes* from a generic ViewRes-UI.gen.

As we go through subsequent evolutionary stages, consistent application of this approach allows us to avoid explosion of component versions, which is the first challenge of evolution (Chapter 1). In addition, x-frames preserve the visibility of new feature implementation and make similarities and differences among two releases of FRS visible and tractable, which are the fifth and sixth challenges of evolution, as discussed in Chapter 1.

11.6   Specifying Changes for FRS[USER] and FRS[DATE,USER]

When implementing FRS[USER], it is helpful to observe that viewing reservations by USER may affect FRS components in a similar way as did viewing reservations by DATE. By following the same pattern, implementation of a new but similar enhancement is faster and more reliable than reinventing a new implementation from scratch. In this case, no changes are needed for x-frame ViewRes-UI.gen, and customizations are also easy (Figure 11.7).

We can now build FRS[DATE,USER] by combining customizations as shown in Figure 11.8.

```
<adapt ViewRes-UI.gen >
  <insert viewResBy-Menu-UI >
    viewResMethodList.addItem ("User");
   </insert>
  <insert viewResBy-Action-UI >
    else if (viewResMethodList.getSelectedItem() ==
"User")   { ... }
  </insert>
</adapt>
```

Figure 11.7   Customizations for FRS^USER.

```
<adapt ViewRes-UI.gen >
  <insert viewResBy-Menu-UI >
    viewResMethodList.addItem ("Date");
    viewResMethodList.addItem ("User");
   </insert>
  <insert viewResBy-Action-UI >
    else if (viewResMethodList.getSelectedItem() ==
"Date")   { ... }
    else if (viewResMethodList.getSelectedItem() ==
"User")   { ... }
  </insert>
```

Figure 11.8   Customizations for FRS^DATE,USER.

Figure 11.9 shows a custom class *ViewRes* to view reservations by the facility, reservation ID, date, and user.

However, there is a better way of dealing with a group of variant features such as reservation viewing methods. We may come to the conclusion that in the future we may have more features of that kind, and we may want to mix them in various combinations in any given FRS. Furthermore, we may also want to upgrade some of the already-released FRSs with some of those features.

For that, we decide to make features DATE and USER an integral part of the FRS x-framework. Instead of specifying all the changes in an SPC, outside of the FRS components, we embed the core functionality related to the new features in the FRS x-frames, but in a customizable form. We refine our initial ad hoc solution by creating a generic mechanism to handle all the viewing reservation methods in the same way, as shown in Figure 11.10.

```
class ViewRes extends FRSPanels implements ActionListener
{ ...
ViewRes(FRSClient client) // constructor
{   ...
// menu items for selecting a required res. viewing method:
viewResMethodList = new List ();
viewResMethodList.addItem ("Facility"); // view res. by facility
viewResMethodList.addItem ("Reservation ID"); // view res. by ID
```
viewResMethodList.addItem ("Date");
viewResMethodList.addItem ("User");

```
// actions for res. viewing methods:
public void actionPerformed (ActionEvent ev) {
Object source = ev.getSource();
if (source == viewButton) {
  if (viewResMethodList.getSelectedItem() == "Facility") { ... }
    else if (viewResMethodList.getSelectedItem() == "Reservation ID")     {...}
```
  else if (viewResMethodList.getSelectedItem() == "Date")   { ... }
  else if (viewResMethodList.getSelectedItem() == "User")   { ... }

```
// event handling:
...details not shown
}
```

Figure 11.9 Java class *ViewRes* **to handle two extra reservation viewing methods.**

Instead of inserting code related to variant features, x-frame ViewRes-UI.gen predefined options correspond to variant features. XVCL variable viewRes specifies variant features required in a given FRS release, and controls the selection of relevant code.

We build similar mechanisms into all the other x-frames affected by reservation viewing methods. For example, building the menu from which a user can select the required method to view reservations is shown in Figure 11.11. The shaded part of

```
// customizations for FRS^{DATE, USER} to view reservation by
date and user
<set viewRes = Date, Use>
<adapt ViewRes-UI.gen />
ViewRes-UI.gen:
class ViewRes extends FRSPanels implements ActionListener
{ …
ViewRes(FRSClient client) // constructor
  {    ...
// menu items for selecting a required res. viewing method:
viewResMethodList = new List ();
viewResMethodList.addItem ("Facility"); // view res. by
facility
viewResMethodList.addItem ("Reservation ID"); // view res.
by ID
<while viewRes >
      viewResMethodList.addItem ("@viewRes");
</while>
// actions for res. viewing methods:
public void actionPerformed (ActionEvent ev) {
Object source = ev.getSource();
if (source == viewButton) {
  if (viewResMethodList.getSelectedItem() == "Facility") {
… }
    else if (viewResMethodList.getSelectedItem() ==
"Reservation ID")     {...}
<while viewRes>
  else if (viewResMethodList.getSelectedItem() == "@
viewRes");
  <select option viewRes >
    <option Date>
      { code for Date }
    <option User >
      { code for User }
  <select />
</while>
… other Java code here
// event handling:
<while viewRes>
      code to extend event handlers here
</while>
```

Figure 11.10   X-frame with generic mechanism for viewing reservations.

```
<set viewRes = Date, Use>
<set availMenuPos = 3>
System.out.println(1, "View Reservations by Reservation
ID");
System.out.println(2, "View Reservations by Facility");
<while viewRes>
  System.out.println(@availMenuPos, "View Reservations by
@viewRes" />);
  <set availMenuPos = @availMenuPos + 1 />
</while>
```

Figure 11.11   Building a menu for viewing reservations.

the <**set**> command in the last line of the XVCL processor evaluates the right-hand-side arithmetic expression before assigning a new value to variable availMenuPos.

The XVCL processor evaluates any well-formed arithmetic expression and uses the result in further processing (e.g., assigns its value to a variable or emits on output). Although arithmetic computations are rarely needed in designing mixed-strategy representations, at times they are useful, and in the future we plan to provide more refined support for XVCL computations. The reader can find the exact rules for current XVCL support for arithmetic computations in Appendix C.

A couple of comments on the solution shown in Figure 11.10 and Figure 11.11, versus the solution with <**insert**>s into <**break**>s of Figure 11.8: Even though part of the change specifications are now embedded in x-frames, the solution enhances their genericity in the sense that now the x-frames can be reused in a wider range of situations. We achieve this without multiplying x-frames. The solution still maintains the visibility of changes and does not compromise traceability of changes: Modifications related to one source of change are linked via XVCL variables that control generation loops and other mechanisms for selecting variant features (such as DATE or USER). At the same time, the solution becomes more readable than the one with <**insert**>s into <**break**>s because related functionalities are kept close to each other. Uniform navigation over changes using a single variable *viewRes* is clearer than inserts into multiple breakpoints.

In our example, we could handle variant features DATE or USER with XVCL variables <**while**> and <**select**>. We have shown only a user interface component. To complete the x-framework, we would have to instrument business logic and database access components affected by DATE and USER in a similar way. In other cases, variant features may have a more profound impact on FRS, its component implementation, and the underlying architecture.

```
// customizations for creating reservation with or without
preferred facility in mind
<set PREF = YES, NO>
<adapt CreateRes-UI>
<adapt CreateRes-BL>
CreateRes-UI:
<while PREF>
   <select option PREF>
     <option = YES >
       ...
     <option = NO >
       ...
     <otherwise>
       <message "error" />
   </select>
</while>
CreateRes-BL:
<while PREF>
   <select option PREF>
     <option = YES >
       ...
     <option = NO >
       ...
     <otherwise>
       <message "error" />
   </select>
</while>
```

Figure 11.12   Catering to preferred facility feature (PREF).

11.7   Specifying Changes for FRS$^{\text{DATE,USER,PREF}}$

Mutually implementation-independent features, such as DATE and USER, are relatively easy to handle, as the impacts of changes can be neatly separated from one another. Still, the modifications required to bring in certain features may be much more complex than we saw in the case of DATE and USER. When a new feature has a bigger impact on existing components, we use either **<ifdef>** or **<select>** to specify required changes. For example, the impact of feature PREF, which requires two scenarios for making reservations — with preferred facility (PF) and without preferred facility (NO-PF) — on components for creating a new reservation, namely, CreateRes-UI and CreateRes-BL, is shown in Figure 11.12.

Command <**message**> makes the XVCL processor output an error message in case variable PREF is assigned an invalid value.

Suppose customer A is using FRS^{DATE,USER} and is not interested in the new PREF feature, whereas customer B is using FRS^{DATE,USER,PREF}. For FRS^{DATE,USER}, we specify <**set** PREF = NO /> to obtain the original behavior, which is creating reservations without preferred facility. For customer B, <**set** PREF = YES,NO /> will yield an FRS with options to create reservations with or without preferred facility, whereas <**set** PREF = YES /> will yield an FRS with the option to create reservations with preferred facility only.

Both customers A and B may be interested in future upgrades of FRS. These upgrades may be available to their FRSs without any conflicts with already-implemented feature PREF.

11.8   Specifying Changes for FRS^{DATE,USER,PAY}

Payment for reservations includes features PAY = {RC, CC, BC, FCD}, where:

- RC: reservation charges
- CC: cancellation charges
- BC: bill construction
- FCD: Frequent-customer discount

Most of the FRS components are affected by PAY. Also, features DATE and USER are implementation dependent on PAY. To address PAY, first we implement a Java class that defines the business logic for calculating reservation charges and other PAY-related computations. We wrap the payment logic into a new x-frame Payment.gen. We introduce a new XVCL variable called *pay* to indicate whether the payment option is needed in the FRS (value of *pay* is YES) or not (value of *pay* is NO). If the value of *pay* is defined, then the whole chain of actions will be triggered throughout the FRS x-frames to cater to the payment feature. For example, the x-frame Payment.gen is included into the FRS by:

```
<set pay = any value />
<ifdef pay>
<adapt Payment.gen>
</ifdef>
```

Payment features include RC, CC, BC, and FCD. At the point of Payment. gen adaptation, we indicate which particular payment features are required, using a multivalue variable *payFeatures*, as shown in Figure 11.13.

```
<ifdef pay>
  <adapt Payment.gen>
    <insert  set-pay-features>
      <set payFeatures = RC, BC, FCD>
      </insert>
</select>
```

Figure 11.13   Defining required payment for reservations (PAY) features.

Note that command <**break** set-pay-features> is placed in x-frame Payment.gen to mark a variation point at which a specified <**set**> command is to be executed.

The following code creates the facility and reservation tables with a column labeled "Cost":

<**ifdef** pay >
    include = "Cost DOUBLE,";
</ifdef >

In an x-frame Facility-UI.gen (not shown here), we use <**ifdef**> to include code to allow the user to enter the cost of the facility. The cost is then passed to the add and modify facility methods to update the database. The method call for modifying facilities is changed in the same way, as shown in the following text:

<**ifde** pay>
    double cost = getCost();
</ifdef >
id = fm.addFacility(name);

In x-frames that have to do with making or displaying reservations, the PAY feature is dealt with in a similar way, by means of <**ifdef**> or <**select**> commands including PAY-related functionality. For example, in Facility modules, we instrument class methods to add, modify, and retrieve facilities to cater to the optional "cost" of facility reservation. In CreateRes-BL, we include the code for attribute "Cost" and a method for retrieval of the cost.

X-frames related to all the components affected by the PAY feature (such as components in Reservation-UI and Reservation-BL groups) are modified in a similar way. Although the impact of change triggered by the PAY feature is more significant than before for DATE, USER, or PREF features, the same mechanism is used to specify the impact of the PAY feature on FRS components. We still preserve the qualities that matter during evolution, namely, avoiding explosion of component versions, the visibility of similarities and differences among releases of FRS for different customers, and traceability of changes.

```
// customizations for selected PAY features:
<set PREF = PF>
<set payFeatures = RC, CC>
CreateRes-UI:
<select PREF>
  <option = YES>
    <select pay>
      <option = YES>
          <select payFeatures>
            <option = RC>
                code for RC
            <option = CC>
                code for CC
            <option = BC>
                code for BC
            <option = FCD>
          </select> // payFeatures
      <option = NO>
        code for no payment
    </select> // pay
  <option = NO>
    <select pay>
        <option = YES>
          <select payFeatures>
            <option = RC>
                code for RC
            <option = CC>
              code for CC
            <option = BC>
              code for BC
            <option = FCD>
          </select> // payFeatures
        <option = NO>
          code for no payment
    </select> // pay
</select> // PREF
```

Figure 11.14 Implementation-dependent features.

```
<while blkResTypes >
  <select blkResTypes>
    <option = MF>
      code for reserving multiple facilities
    <option = MTS>
      code for reserving multiple time slots
  </select>
</while>
```

Figure 11.15   Selecting a type of block reservation.

11.9   Specifying Changes for FRS^{DATE,USER,PREF,PAY}

Now we wish to combine features PAY and PREF, while preserving the qualities of the FRS x-framework. As PREF is implementation dependent on PAY, any FRS component affected by PREF and PAY features must be sensitive to these implementation dependencies. This is achieved by nested **<select>**s as shown in the example of Figure 11.14 for x-frame CreateRes-UI.m.

As the complexity of the feature combination problem increases, change specification also becomes more complex and we may have multiple scoping levels and branching in change specifications. XVCL Workbench becomes very helpful in developing and analyzing mixed-strategy solutions. XVCL Workbench includes a Smart Editor that understands XVCL rules and can display abstract views of mixed-strategy specifications. Analysis features of the Workbench further aid in analyzing change specifications for understanding. We describe the XVCL Workbench in more detail in later chapters.

Emergence of mutually implementation-dependent features (or any mutually implementation-dependent changes, in general) often triggers the need for further decomposition and refinement of existing change specifications of our mixed-strategy representation.

One may be concerned about the increasing complexity of change specifications in view of interdependent features. We note that the problem of combining interdependent features is inherently complex. The alternative to changing specifications is enumerating component versions for each combination of interest, which is even more complex to work with than change specifications. A practical approach is to explicate only the most important feature combinations, leaving addressing less important ones to the customization process.

11.10   Specifying Changes for FRS^{DATE,USER,PAY,BR}

FRS feature block reservation (BR) allows users to reserve multiple facilities (MFs) for the same time slot, or the same facility for multiple time slots (MTSs). This is the case of implementing a completely new feature into a new FRS release. The effort to implement a new feature is proportional to the complexity of the feature itself, and to the extent of implementation dependencies between the new feature and other features already implemented. In the case of this FRS release, BR is implementation dependent on PAY.

As before, we introduce a variable *blockRes* to indicate whether a block reservation option is needed in the FRS (*blockRes* is then defined) or not (*blockRes* is then undefined). We also introduce a multivalue variable *blkResTypes,* whose values indicate the required type of block reservation, namely, MF (multiple facilities) and MTS (multiple time slots).

A new x-frame called BlockRes-BL.gen is created to define the block reservation logic. This new x-frame is conditionally included into the CreateRes-BL.gen depending on the variable *blockRes*:

```
<ifdef blockRes>
    <adapt BlockRes-BL.gen >
</select>
```

As BR depends on PAY, we have to further instrument x-frame BlockRes-BL.gen to accept logic to calculate the charges for reserved facilities (Figure 11.16).

X-frames for components in a group Reservation-UI are also modified to include an option for selecting and deleting block reservations.

Further modifications to this release of FRS include the following: An x-frame Payment.gen is instrumented to accommodate block reservation. A vector of values must be used to store the cost of each reservation. The total number of reservations

```
<select pay>
  <option = YES >
    Payment p = new Payment();
       ...
    p.calculateCost(cost, start, end);
    int id = rm.addReservation(user, facility, start, end,
p);
  <option = NO >
    int id = rm.addReservation(user, facility, start,
end);
</select>
```

Figure 11.16   Features block reservations (BR) with PAY.

```
<ifdef blockers >
  <select option = DISCOUNT >
    <option = YES>
        cost = ...
//add charges to a vector when system includes block
reservations
          (this.charges).add(new Double(cost*count));
    <option = NO>
      this.charges = cost*count;
  </select>
</ifdef >
```

Figure 11.17   Addressing block reservation discount (BRD)

in a given block must be also stored. Methods are added to calculate the total cost of all the block reservations.

11.11   Specifying Changes for FRS^{DATE,USER,PAY,BR,BRD}

Block reservation discount (BRD) is an extra option for the FRS and affects both PAY and BR. The BRD feature is controlled by the variable *brd*. X-frame Payment. gen is modified for different calculations owing to block reservation discount. This is only done if block reservation is included in the first place. Again, nested commands are used to achieve the desired result (Figure 11.17).

Modification of an x-frame BlockRes-BL.gen to inform the user that a block reservation discount is included in the charges in done in a similar way.

11.12   Specifying Changes for FRS^{USER,BR}

The complexity of implementing a completely new feature cannot be reduced below a certain threshold. However, once implemented, we would like to minimize the effort of propagating the new feature to other releases that can also benefit from it. XVCL mechanisms are meant to simplify reuse of features, in their variant forms, across system releases. Construction of FRS^{USER,BR} shows the flexibility of the previously described change specifications in this respect. All that is required to build FRS^{USER,BR} is to enable or disable features via relevant variables:

```
<set blockRes = any value />
<set blkResTypes = MF />
```

Suppose we need only block reservation of multiple facilities. Even though many new features have been implemented in the previous releases, the unwanted features are simply disabled by not defining variables that control them.

11.13 Specifying Changes for FRS^USER-PD,BR

Construction of this FRS^USER-PD,BR requires us to slightly modify existing features. USER-PD allows users to view reservations by user, for a preferred date. This new feature may be needed in just one release, so we should be able to handle it with minimum impact on existing x-frames. An XVCL variable *userPd* and XVCL commands <**insert**> and <**break**> handle such small modifications in a simple, visible, and nonintrusive way. At places where extra code is needed to implement this variant, we place <**break**>s. The extra code needed is specified in matching <**insert**>s placed in the SPC for that release. This solution keeps the change separate from the code that is common to other releases. As only a customer of the FRS^USER-PD,BR release needs the feature USER-PD, the preceding method plays its role well.

11.14 Conclusions

We described FRS evolution using the mixed-strategy approach. We illustrated how the mixed-strategy approach helps alleviate the evolution problems discussed in Chapter 1, realizing reuse-based evolution.

CVS and XVCL differ in how they represent and use the evolution history (refer to Chapter 5). CVS stores component versions along with deltas among versions. XVCL, on the other hand, attempts to represent component versions in a generic form, and records the process of recreating required component versions from the generic form. The overall evolution history in the mixed-strategy representation contains knowledge of how to recreate any system release, as a hierarchical composition of component versions. Variations specific to each release are specified as deltas with respect to generic (common) representation at the level of each component version that forms the release.

XVCL does not support conflict resolution and does not have any features for collaborative work (such as check-in or check-out facilities to assist parallel development). CVS and XVCL complement each other, and we have found only synergy and no conflicts in using them together. Using mixed-strategy, there is less information to be stored in CVS.

The mixed-strategy approach mitigates the evolution problems discussed in Chapter 1 as follows:

> *Explosion of component versions*: Rather than storing component versions, mixed-strategy can produce any component version (and component version con-

figuration) from a relatively small number of generic x-frames, based on specification of required features.

Reuse of features, selective propagation of new features, and visibility of feature implementation: Change specifications enhance the visibility of how variant features are implemented. Subtle differences in feature implementation in various system releases can be traced. This helps in reuse of features already implemented in past releases when building new system releases. The mechanism that we use to build generic components is also useful in treatment of similar features. Adding new similar features is therefore simplified. Finally, an x-framework give us full control over propagation of features (and any changes in general) to selected system releases, without affecting other releases that do not need those features. When feature dependencies are involved, we can clearly see the relationship between features, and how they affect one another. One example of such a situation was illustrated when building release $FRS^{DATE,USER,PAY,BR}$.

Selecting and customizing baseline components: As we enhance the visibility of similarities and differences in systems released over evolution, selecting "best-matching" components and customizing them when building a new system release, S^{NEW}, is greatly simplified. An x-framework is continuously refined during evolution to unify similar components appearing in various system releases with generic ones (to avoid explosion of similar component versions) and to unify patterns of similar change specifications.

Addressing changes only at the code level, without paying attention to the design, is a common reason why software structure decays during evolution, and why future changes are even more difficult to implement. In mixed-strategy, we avoid this problem by chaining together the whole thread of feature-related modifications affecting software at all decomposition levels, from subsystem, to component layer (e.g., user interface or business logic), to component interface (e.g., in IDL), to every detail of component implementation. Modifications at all levels are formally linked together, and can be analyzed and executed by the XVCL processor.

Chapter 12

Scaling Up the Mixed-Strategy Approach

Chapter Summary

In this chapter, we show a more complete picture of the software evolution life cycle, including analysis, design of an x-framework, and its use during software evolution. We sketch a mixed-strategy evolution support environment (MESE). We describe techniques for organizing x-frameworks for large systems, and illustrate a process of deriving new system releases by x-framework customization in more detail. We extend our working example of a facility reservation system (FRS) to describe these more advanced concepts.

The reader may choose to skip this chapter at first reading.

12.1　Introduction

The more successful a software system, the longer its lifetime, and the wider the range of customers. Evolution of a successful system may result in a large number of system releases and component versions that differ in many variant user-related features or design-related details. The explosion of variant features, their combinations in various releases, the complicated dependencies among them, and the impact of variant features on system component architecture and code are among the main challenges of long-term evolution. Understanding of the overall situation during the evolution, and dealing with specific problems using mixed strategy together with other proven approaches is the subject of this chapter. We focus on enhancing the visibility of change impacts at all levels, from requirements, to software architecture, to code components.

We start this chapter by describing notations for modeling variant features implemented into various system releases during evolution (Section 12.2). In Section 12.3, we describe the concept of a mixed-strategy evolution support environment (MESE, for short). We use XVCL to record change specifications and to turn system components into generic adaptable x-frames capable of accommodating new features and changes arising during evolution. These x-frames organized into an x-framework form the core of the MESE. It is an x-framework that facilitates reuse-based evolution and ensures that the information arising during evolution is readable and organized for reuse in building new system releases. MESE also contains a customization decision tree that captures information about variant features implemented in various system releases, and forms a bridge between those features and an x-framework. We describe organizational principles for an x-framework, and illustrate its usage in development of new system releases.

We continue our FRS example, introduced in Chapter 5, where we discussed evolution of FRS with CVS, and then in Chapter 11, where we discussed evolution of FRS with mixed strategy. We ask the reader to briefly review FRS requirements and evolution stages described in the introductory part of Chapter 5.

12.2   Modeling Features Arising during Evolution

For a more comprehensive coverage, in this section we consider a number of other FRS variant features, as follows:

1. Reservations may be done by a requester, or through a middleman, who is usually a staff member of the institution. For example, in hotel room reservation, the hotel staff will use the system to reserve rooms for the customers.
2. Notification: Upon creating, modifying, or canceling a reservation, requesters receive a notification confirming the action. Notifications are only sent if the requester is making a reservation through a middleman. Notifications can be sent through e-mail, fax, a printed letter, or a telephone call. A copy of the bill for reservation charges may be also included in the notification, if any.
3. The ability to deal with different physical facilities and different rules for making reservations.
4. FRS supports exactly one of the following Delete Facility (DF) options:
   a. Delete Later (DL): If the facility has existing reservations, the facility will be deleted later, after all the reservations have been fulfilled. No new reservations will be taken for the facility.

    b. Brute Force Delete (BFD): The facility is deleted, along with any reservations for the facility.

    c. Do Not Delete (DND): If there are existing reservations, the facility is not to be deleted.

5. FRS supports exactly one of the Delete Reservation (DR) options:

    a. Physical Deletion: a reservation record is permanently removed from the database.

    b. Logical Deletion: a reservation record marked as deleted is not removed from the database (e.g., for the purpose of reporting).

6. Conflict Resolution (CR): In the event that a user is unable to make or modify his or her reservation due to a clash with an existing reservation, FRS will aid the user in conflict resolution. Any of the following options may be available when faced with conflicting reservations:

    a. Propose Another Facility (PAF): FRS searches the list of facilities available during the chosen time period. The user is then offered a list of suitable facilities as an alternative. He or she may then select another facility from the list and continue with the reservation.

    b. Propose Another Time (PAT): FRS searches for the timings when the chosen facility is available. The user may then select another time period and continue with the reservation.

    c. Repeat Selection (RS): The user can choose to abandon the current reservation attempt, and make a fresh reservation with another facility and time slot.

    d. Reservation Queue (RQ): If the user does not wish to select another facility or timing, his or her reservation is placed on a waiting list. If an existing reservation for the facility is cancelled, the reservation made by the first user in the queue comes into effect, and the rest of the queue is moved up accordingly.

7. Membership: Users can choose to pay a membership fee to enjoy special privileges such as membership discounts or priority, when reserving facilities.

    a. Life Members: Users pay a more substantial one-time fee to become a life member. They do not have to renew their membership.

    b. Honorary Members: Users pay a smaller fee to become an honorary member, but have to renew their membership on a yearly basis.

8. More Payment options:

    a. Basic Charge: This is the standard fee every user has to pay for the use of the facility. The basic charge for each facility may differ. Facilities are usually charged by the hour or by the day.

    b. Deposit: Deposits are used as a method to discourage users from canceling reservations. Upon making a reservation, a user pays a percentage of the total amount payable as a deposit. The remaining amount is paid at the time of usage. If the user cancels his reservation, the deposit is forfeited.

c. Penalty Charge: A penalty charge is imposed whenever a user cancels or modifies a reservation.

d. Tax: The total amount payable for each user is inclusive of tax. Tax is calculated from and added to the amount each user has to pay. Examples of tax include government tax and service tax of the institution.

e. Surcharge: Surcharge is an extra charge users have to pay at certain times of the year when demand for the facility is high. For example, during public or school holidays, there is holiday surcharge when reserving seats on a plane flight.

f. Refund: If the institution is unable to fulfill an existing reservation, for example, due to failure of the facility, the user will receive a refund of the amount he has paid.

g. Discount: Types of discounts available are membership discount and block reservation discount.

    i. Membership Discount (MD): This is only applicable to users who are members.

    ii. Block Reservation Discount (BRD): Users who make block reservations will be entitled to a discount, proportionate to the number of reservations made.

9. FRS user interface: This may be a graphical user interface (GUI) or a simple command line interface.

10. FRS architectures: Client/server, 3-tier, and distributed component architecture.

11. Platforms: Unix or Windows.

12. User permissions: There is a high level of variability in the nature of permissions granted to various users. In some FRSs, permissions are given across the board to a whole group of users. In other FRSs, there may be a need to individually specify the permissions that each user has. This is further complicated by the presence of middlemen in some FRSs. Some FRSs may require a middleman to vet certain user actions, such as adding reservations. In other FRSs, users may be able to make reservations directly without any middlemen or through a specific middleman. Typically simpler, but less general, default alternatives related to reservation permissions are described as follows:

RES_PERM–ALT1: Any user can manage reservations for any facility.

RES_PERM–ALT2: Specific users can manage reservations for any facility.

RES_PERM–ALT3: Specific users can manage reservations for specific facilities.

RES_PERM–ALT4: FRS allows specific users to manage reservations for specific facilities.

Understanding a requirement space of an evolving system is by no means a trivial problem. We use a modeling technique of feature diagrams [3,7,12] developed in software product line research to model common and variant features across FRS releases. Whenever possible, we give each feature a unique name, for example,

DATE or USER, for ease of reference. We also give names to groups of related features, for example: VIEW-RES = {FAC, RES-ID, DATE, USER}.

We classify features as follows:

- Mandatory features: These appear in all the released systems. For example, a feature FAC, "the ability to view reservations by facility," is a mandatory feature for all FRSs.
- Variant features: These are relevant only to certain systems released during evolution. Variant features are further qualified as optional, alternative, and or-features.
    - Optional features may or may not appear in a system release. An example of an optional feature is any of the payment group of FRS features (PAY).
    - An alternative feature means that we need choose exactly one from a group of given features for any given system release. For example, FRS may have either GUI or command line interface.
    - An or-feature [3] means that we may choose any number from a group of given features (or none at all) for any given system release. For example, features {DATE, USER} are or-features, as different releases of FRS may support viewing reservation by DATE or USER (or none or both of those features).

In textual descriptions, we use the naming convention proposed by Tracz [12]: we add a suffix "–OPT" to the feature's name for optional features, suffix "–ALTn" to indicate alternative features, and suffix "-ORn" to indicate or-features. If the number of alternatives cannot be determined, the suffixes "–ALT" and "-OR" are used. A feature without a suffix is considered to be mandatory.

12.2.1 Feature Diagrams

In a feature diagram, features are organized into a tree structure. Different types of variant features are depicted using distinct graphical symbols, as shown in Figure 12.1.

Figure 12.2 depicts some of the variant features that we find in the FRS releases. Under "Functional Features" we find the Reservation-Mngmt feature group with Create, Delete, View-Res (reservation viewing methods), and optional Notification and Block Reservation features. Note that in feature diagrams we can skip suffixes (OPT, ALT, and OR) as they are implied by graphical conventions of the feature model.

"Permissions" option under the "Reservation-Mngmt" feature group shows the permission defaults mentioned in point 12 of the FRS feature description.

Obviously, for a sizable system with many features arising during evolution, we cannot describe all the features in one diagram. It is convenient to split a feature

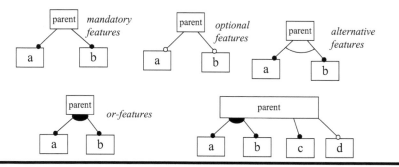

Figure 12.1   Feature modeling conventions.

diagram into a number of component diagrams that remain logically interconnected via consistent use of names of feature nodes. We show a series of FRS feature diagrams in the following diagrams (Figure 12.3–Figure 12.11).

Dashed arrows in Figure 12.9 indicate dependencies among features.

Feature diagrams play an important descriptive role in our method for change specification. A customization decision tree (CDT) extends feature diagrams with customization scripts.

12.2.2 Describing Feature Dependencies

Variant features can appear in different configurations in any given system release. However, only certain configurations of features are legal. For example, reservation charges (RC) only make sense if requesters pay for facilities (PAY option).

We say that feature f_2 is functionally dependent on feature f_1 (in short notation $f_1 \xrightarrow{f} f_2$) if feature f_2 can't exist without f_1. That is, f_1 is a prerequisite for f_2 (see Chapter 1).

Feature diagrams indicate some of the functional dependencies among features. For example, the following feature dependencies (among many others) are explicitly shown in FRS feature diagrams:

Conflict-Resolution $\xrightarrow{f}$ Repeat-Selection
Notification $\xrightarrow{f}$ Fax
Notification $\xrightarrow{f}$ Email

However, there are often extra semantic relationships among variant features that cannot be directly modeled by feature diagrams. For example, e-mail notification confirming deletion of a reservation only makes sense if reservations are done by a middleman.

Therefore, it is essential to complement feature diagrams with specification of feature dependencies. In column 1 of Table 12.1, types of functional feature

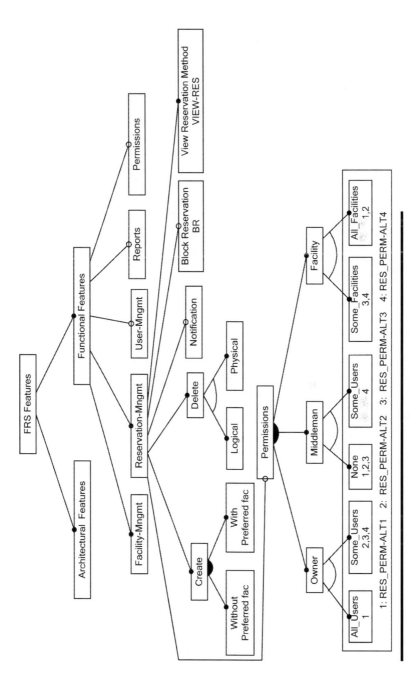

Figure 12.2   Facility reservation system (FRS) feature diagram (1).

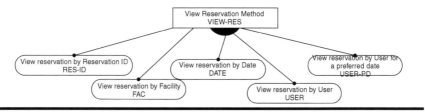

Figure 12.3   View reservation method.

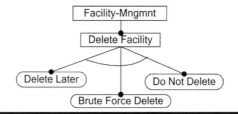

Figure 12.4   Delete facility method.

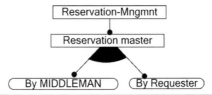

Figure 12.5   Reservation method.

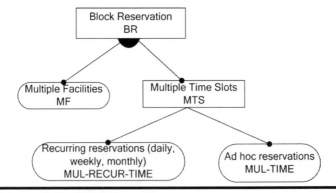

Figure 12.6   Block reservation.

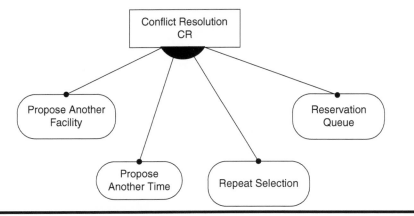

Figure 12.7   Reservation conflict resolution.

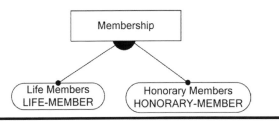

Figure 12.8   Membership.

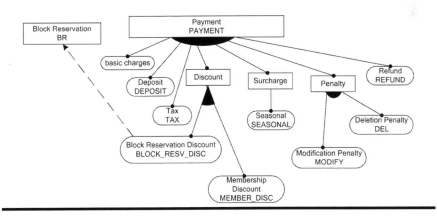

Figure 12.9   Payment.

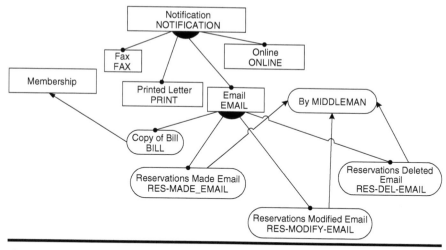

Figure 12.10   Notification.

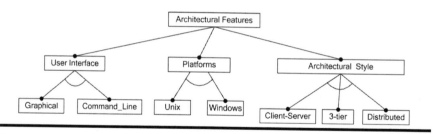

Figure 12.11   Architectural features.

dependencies that are useful are listed. Column 2 of the same table shows a symbolic notation for a given type of feature dependency.

Feature diagrams do not capture the meaning of product line requirements. To convey the domain's semantics, we must use other notations such as Unified Modeling Language (UML) [10]. However, most of the conventional notations cater to modeling for a single system and provide only limited support for modeling variants (such as extension or inclusion points in use cases or class inheritance). Jacobson, Griss, and Jonsson [5] formulated the problem of incorporating variants into any modeling notation and analysis component (i.e., any reusable analysis element). Variants are exploited at variation points in analysis components. A variation point identifies one or more locations at which the variation will occur. An analysis component is customized (specialized) by attaching one or several variants to its variation points. Authors describe a number of variability mechanisms for modeling variants and customizing components, such as inheritance, macros, templates, parameterization, and frames. They discuss different ways of describing variants in UML notations in particular use cases.

Table 12.1 Types of Functional Dependencies among Features

Notation	What It Means
$f_1 \xrightarrow{f} f_2$	f_2 is functionally dependent on f_1
$f_1 \xleftrightarrow{f} f_2$	f_1 and f_2 are mutually dependent on each other; that is, any system that has f_1 must also have f_2 and vice versa
$f_1 \xrightarrow{f} ! f_2$	f_2 is functionally independent of f_1
$f_1 \xleftrightarrow{f} ! f_2$	f_1 and f_2 are functionally independent of each other
$< f_2 \mid f_3 \mid \dots \mid f_N > \xrightarrow{f} f_1$	f_1 is functionally dependent on one of the features $f_2, f_3, \dots, f_N$; that is, any system that has f_1 must have one of the features $f_2, f_3, \dots, f_N$;
$< f_2 \& f_3 \& \dots \& f_N > \xrightarrow{f} f_1$	f_1 is functionally dependent on all the features $f_2, f_3, \dots, f_N$; that is, any system that has f_1 must have all of the features $f_2, f_3, \dots, f_N$;
$[f1, f2, \dots, f_N]$	Any system must have all the features f1, f2, $\dots$, f_N or none of them

In our projects, we model variants using feature diagrams first and then use UML notations extended with provisions for modeling variants, to enhance the semantics of variants. Modeling variants in extended UML and integrating different model views into a cohesive picture is a difficult task, especially when the number of legal combinations of interdependent variants increases. We attempted to tackle this problem with tools that help trace variant dependencies and produce customized views of a domain model for given variant configuration. We refer the reader to other papers for details of our domain modeling method [6] and focus this chapter on handling variants in a product line architecture.

12.3 A Mixed-Strategy Evolution Support Environment (MESE)

Figure 12.12 depicts the main elements of an MESE. An MESE includes an x-framework and two global structures, namely, a requirements model of an evolving software, and a customization decision tree (CDT)[1]. As described in previous chapters, an x-framework is a generic representation of a system under evolution. It contains both specification of changes related to various system releases, expressed in XVCL, and x-frames — generic building blocks — from which system releases are constructed.

The role of a requirements model is to grasp a range of features implemented into systems released to customers during evolution. A CDT is a bridge between

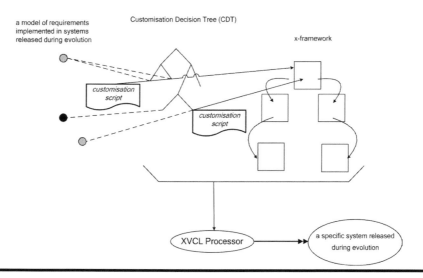

a model of requirements
implemented in systems
released during evolution

Customisation Decision Tree (CDT)

x-framework

customisation
script

customisation
script

XVCL Processor

a specific system released
during evolution

Figure 12.12   The conceptual structure of a mixed-strategy evolution support environment (MESE).

requirements model and an x-framework: a CDT shows how variant features are reflected in the x-framework, and what customizations are required to incorporate variant features into the x-framework.

A requirements model includes UML diagrams extended with provisions for modeling variant features [6]. UML diagrams add semantics to purely syntactic specifications of features in feature diagrams.

A CDT is a feature diagram annotated with customization information. A CDT shows how an x-framework can be customized to accommodate required variant features. Dotted lines in Figure 12.12 link features to corresponding customization options in a CDT.

For each variant feature, there is a customization script written in XVCL that specifies the customizations of an x-framework required to meet a given variant. The XVCL processor interprets these scripts and composes, after possible adaptations, x-frames to build a specific release of a system. A double arrow represents activities, such as testing and compilation.

Customizations to accommodate anticipated variant features are automated, can be repeated on demand, but still may be subject to human analysis and modification. This is important when developers need to extend an x-framework with an unexpected new feature. Developers start by inspecting other similar features under the related option in a CDT (there is always one at some level of a CDT) to find out how they are implemented. Developers should at least obtain certain clues as to how implement a new feature consistently with an x-framework rationale and structure. Once a customization script for a new feature is written, a CDT is extended to reflect a new feature.

There are many technical scenarios to realize the above concept of an evolution support environment, and XVCL is one of them. We believe Figure 12.12 reflects fundamental elements that appear in any reuse-based software evolution situation. Of course, these elements will appear in different, not necessarily explicit, forms, depending on the software development method and technology used. For example, in most companies there is no explicit model describing features arising during evolution, nor explicit mappings of those features to system releases; links between variant features and related customizations remain undocumented; most often, we have a manual customization process instead of a generator, with emphasis on management of already customized components. The actual representation of an x-framework may also range from program files instrumented with conditional compilation commands to object-oriented (OO) frameworks and component frameworks, to mention just a few possibilities.

12.4   An FRS Architecture with Connectors

A software architecture is described by a set of components that interact with each other through well-defined interfaces (connectors) to deliver the required system behavior [11]. In the FRS architecture described in Chapter 5 and Chapter 11, we did not separate connectors from components themselves. Consequently, x-frames in our FRS x-framework represented FRS components, their aggregations and building blocks, but not connectors.

The FRS architecture is extended so that connectors are defined separately from components. Variability in components and connectors must be managed during evolution; therefore, they both have explicit representation in the x-framework. In the following sections, we show how we represent connectors as x-frames, and then extend the FRS x-framework to explicitly represent both generic components and connectors.

In Chapter 11, we described mandatory FRS components. We start by extending the FRS architecture with optional components arising during evolution. Figure 12.13 depicts a logical view of component packages (both mandatory and optional), and connectors that make up an FRS architecture. Table 12.2 describes connector types and Table 12.3 describes connector instances reflected in Figure 12.13.

12.5   Generic Connectors in the FRS X-Framework

We now comment on connector representation in the FRS x-framework. The FRS client and server components communicate via method invocation calls. The nature of these calls is specified by interface definition language (IDL) declarations (Object Management Group, http://www.omg.org/). IDLs are commonly used to specify

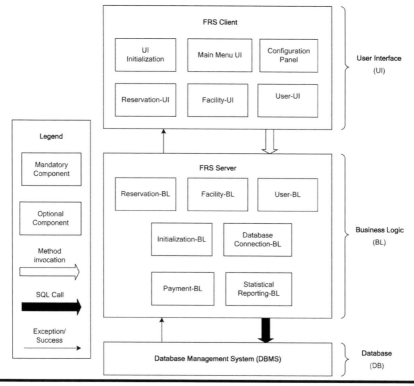

Figure 12.13   Facility reservation system (FRS) runtime component architecture.

Table 12.2   Description of Connector Types

Connector Type	Description
	A method invocation over an object request broker (ORB); the ORB establishes a client/server relationship between a user interface component that invokes a method and a business logic component that implements the method; the ORB intercepts the method invocation and locates the business logic component that implements it
	An SQL call, implemented using a Java database connection (JDBC) to open database connectivity (ODBC) bridge
	Either an exception or success message

Table 12.3   Description of Connector Instances

Connector	Description
FRS UI to FRS BL	Method invocations triggered by UI events; for example, pressing a button or selecting a menu item to add or delete a facility
FRS BL to FRS UI	Data (such as reservation, user, or facility data) returned as a result of a method invocation, error message, or exception
FRS BL to Database	SQL call to retrieve data from a database
Database to FRS BL	Data retrieved from the database returned as a result of an SQL call

the interfaces of the architecture components in an abstract fashion. A sample set of IDL declarations for the FRS x-framework is shown in Figure 12.14. IDL specifications are compiled to Java to produce code for intercomponent communication either within a single physical machine or over an object request broker (ORB).

The IDL specifications include constants, exceptions, type declarations that define various data structures and types used, interface declarations that define operation signatures for method invocations, and a single module declaration that contains IDL declarations for client/server connectors. We use the term metaconnector to mean an x-frame that contains connector definitions in IDL. Table 12.4 lists types of metaconnectors. We discuss further details of metaconnectors and the structure of an x-framework in the following sections, together with the x-framework customization process.

12.6   Comments on X-Framework Organization Principles

Many variant features arising during evolution affect components and connectors at all levels of the component hierarchy and in all three architecture tiers. We discuss a specific example in Section 12.10. When designing an x-framework, we analyze the impact of variant features on components and connectors and turn them into generic, adaptable x-frames.

An x-framework is created and then evolved by specifying changes related to various releases, and by packaging components and connectors into generic x-frame structures capable of accommodating changes related to various releases. This is the essence of achieving reuse-based software evolution. Software evolution with XVCL is a continuous refinement of the x-framework.

Software architecture consists of components (of various granularity and types) and connectors. Much of an x-framework is built around software architecture elements. For large systems, it is essential to organize an x-framework in such a way

```
module FRSModule { // Start of module declaration
   typedef long FacNo; // This is a type declaration
   typedef long ResNo;
   struct TimeDateStruct {
      string date;
      string time;
   };
   struct FacStruct {
      FacNo facID;
   };
   typedef sequence<FacStruct> FacSeq;
   struct ResStruct {
      FacNo facID;
      TimeDateStruct start;
      TimeDateStruct end;
   };
interface FRSInterface { // This is a interface declaration
      ResNo     addReservation (in FacNo facID, in ResStruct resData);
      ResStruct getReservation (in ResNo resID);
      boolean   cancelReservation (in ResNo resID);
      FacNo     addFacility (in FacStruct facData);
      FacStruct getFacility (in FacNo facID);
      boolean   removeFacility (in FacNo facID);
   };
}; // End of module declaration
```

Figure 12.14 Sample connector description in interface definition language (IDL).

Table 12.4 Types of Metaconnectors

Name	Description
FRS_Mod_Decl.c	Contains a single module declaration of IDL for a client/server connector; contains declarations for mandatory features; during customizations, the x-frame processor will include additional declarations related to required variant features
FRS_Const_Decl.c	Contains any number of constant declarations
FRS_EXCEP_DECL.c	Contains a basic exception declaration that is used by the FRS for generic error reporting
FRS_Type_Decl.c	Contains type declarations used in interface declarations
FRS_Int_Decl.c	Contains interface declarations (i.e., operation signatures) for a client/server connector

that information related to different architectural elements can be easily located and manipulated.

Separation of concerns is a guiding principle for organizing x-frames within an x-framework. We organize x-frames along a number of different dimensions:

First, we separate x-frames used for building components (metacomponents) from those that are used to build connectors (metaconnectors). For conceptual clarity, when building a new system release, we customize an x-framework in three distinctive steps, namely (1) selecting metacomponents and metaconnectors; (2) customization of metacomponents and metaconnectors; and (3) assembling resulting components and connectors into a custom software system that forms a required release.

Second, we put x-frames related to different computational aspects into separate partitions of an x-framework. For example, we keep x-frames related to the user interface, business logic, and the database in separate partitions of an x-framework.

Third, we organize x-frames into layers of abstraction. By the nature of a mixed-strategy, x-frames representing large-granularity system components are located in upper parts of an x-framework. Upper-level x-frames often contain more XVCL specifications (controls and compositions), whereas lower-level x-frames contain parameterized code. X-frames toward the bottom of the x-framework tend to be more context-free and reusable, whereas upper-level x-frames tend to be more specific to the context of a given system release.

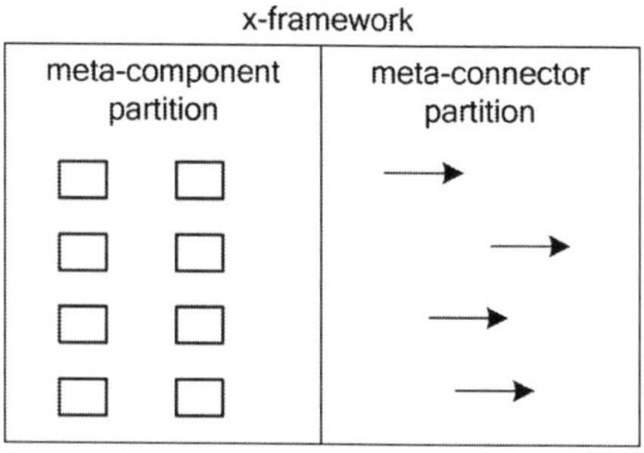

x-framework

Figure 12.15   Component and connector partitions of an x-framework.

12.7   An Overview of the X-Framework Customization Process

The structure of the FRS x-framework is derived from the FRS software architecture: the core of the FRS x-framework comprises components and connectors of the FRS architecture turned into x-frames and metaconnectors, respectively. Meta-component and metaconnector x-frames are placed in two different partitions of an x-framework (Figure 12.15).

Each of the two partitions of the x-framework contains its own specification x-frames describing how to build system components and connectors, respectively.

Developers build a new system release by customizing, or sometimes extending, an x-framework. In product line terminology, we often say that a system, a product line member, is derived from product line architecture [4]. As reuse-based evolution in many ways resembles the product line situation (in particular, an x-framework for evolution is an analog of product line architecture [2]), we use both the terms derivation and customization to mean the process of building/maintaining system release during evolution.

Any new system release required by a customer may need some combination of features already implemented in past releases (with possible modifications), as well as some new features. Feature models provide an overview of all the features implemented in various releases during evolution. Such features are catered to in an x-framework. Therefore, we start by inspecting the "model of requirements" (in the top right corner of the MESE depicted in Figure 12.12) to find features that have already been implemented in past releases. These features are mapped into nodes of a CDT (at the top of Figure 12.16, and also shown in Figure 12.12). A customization script attached to a CDT node gives us clues about how to customize an x-framework to accommodate a given feature into components and connectors of a system release that we wish to build.

Then, a new system release may require new features, unique to the system under construction. Implementing completely new features must necessarily involve more effort, that is, proportional to the feature complexity and to the extent

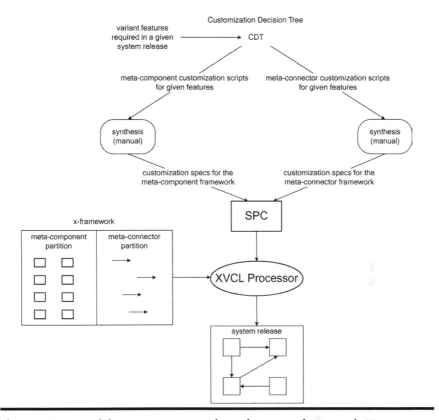

Figure 12.16   Deriving a new system release from an x-framework (1).

of implementation-dependencies among the new and existing features. As we discussed earlier, initially, such new features are usually implemented in a nonintrusive way, that is, with minimum changes done to the x-framework. Once a new feature has a confirmed value for other releases, we integrate the new feature into the x-framework. We illustrated this strategy when discussing evolution stages in Chapter 11 (e.g., addressing DATE and USER).

As shown on the left-hand-side and right-hand-side branches of Figure 12.16, customization scripts for various features related to metacomponents and metaconnectors are then synthesized to form an SPC from which the XVCL processor can produce a new system release, as shown at the bottom of Figure 12.16.

The MESE provides the basic information (such as mappings among features and customization scripts) to help developers customize the x-framework to accommodate known, existing features. It also helps in features modifications and in implementing new features that are similar to some existing ones. The process of synthesizing an SPC is manual, aided by the CDT. The XVCL processor automates the x-framework customization process once an SPC has been synthesized.

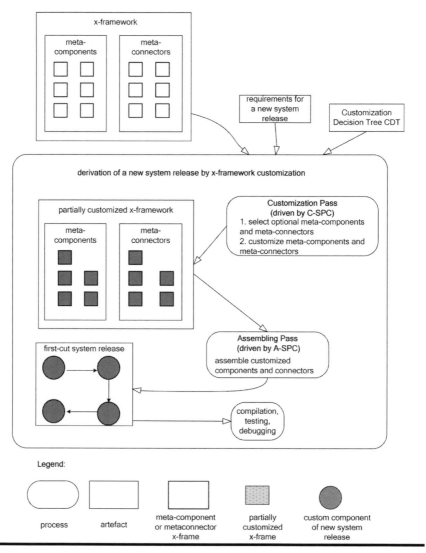

Figure 12.17 Deriving a new system release from an x-framework (2).

12.8 Customization and Assembly Passes over an X-Framework

For a large x-framework, it is convenient to split the overall process of deriving a new system release from an x-framework into customization and assembling passes (Figure 12.17). Customization SPC (C-SPC) and Assembling SPC (A-SPC) are two specification x-frames that navigate the customization and assembling passes, respectively. Although metacomponents and metaconnectors play different roles in an x-framework, from the customization and assembly pass points of view, their processing looks the same.

Having selected required features for the new system release, we build a first cut of the new release by following the steps listed below:

Customization Pass (guided by C-SPC):
1. Deciding which runtime components should be included into the new system release
2. Selection of relevant x-frames (in the x-frame branch of the x-framework)
3. Customizing internal workings of x-frames to accommodate required features
4. Selection of relevant metaconnectors (in the metaconnector branch of the x-framework)
5. Customizing connectors affected by required features
   Assembling Pass (guided by A-SPC):
6. Assembling system components into a working system release

By selecting and customizing metacomponents, we built components specialized for the new system release. By selecting and customizing metaconnectors, we obtain IDL definitions for intercomponent communication specialized for the new system release. Finally, we assemble components with the help of the A-SPCs. After compilation of IDL specifications into Java and linking them with Java components, the overall result is the source code for the first cut new system release. The first cut system must be then extended with any features that have not been implemented in the x-framework.

The usual follow-up activities, such as compilation, testing, and debugging, complete the x-framework customization process. Figure 12.17 provides a snapshot of the main activities involved in deriving a new system release by customizing an x-framework.

During the customization pass, the XVCL processor process interprets C-SPC, and applies customizations to metacomponents and metaconnectors accordingly. These customizations accommodate all the variant features and new features required in a new system release we wish to build.

The purpose of the follow-up assembling pass is to generate source code for a system release, in our case — Java code. To execute the assembling pass, the XVCL processor executes the A-SPCs on the x-framework produced by the customization pass. An A-SPC typically contains <**adapt**> commands to include proper x-frames into the output file. If required for clarity, it is possible to define multiple A-SPCs, one for every major component or subsystem.

Customization and assembly passes are coordinated by an SPC (not shown in Figure 12.17), which always plays the role of top-level control.

If a system release needs some brand new features, not implemented yet in the x-framework, C-SPCs, A-SPCs, as well as top level SPC and elements of an x-framework may need to be modified accordingly, to produce the desired effect.

12.9   Using the Customization Decision Tree (CDT)

Reuse-based evolution supported by XVCL relies on a clear mapping between features and the specific mechanisms for x-frame customization and assembly required to implement given features. We use a graphical notation and tool called a customization decision tree (CDT) to keep track of those mappings (a CDT is shown as one of the inputs to the x-framework customization process in Figure 12.17). Also refer to Figure 12.12, where a CDT is shown in the context of the MESE. A CDT depicts the possible ways in which an x-framework can be customized. Nodes in a CDT, called customization options, correspond to features implemented in system releases. A CDT is a hierarchical structure of customization options. Each CDT node is annotated with a corresponding feature and a C-SPC describing how to customize an x-framework to address a given feature. As the same feature may appear in more than one customization option, we give unique names to customization options and mark them with names of relevant features.

For each feature to be included in a new system release, we consult a CDT to find out if a given feature has been implemented in the x-framework. If we find the feature, the CDT will provide us with the C-SPC that tells the x-frame processor how to customize the x-framework to meet that feature. If we do not find a given feature in the CDT, then it means that the feature has not been implemented in the past system releases. This situation is addressed by implementing the new feature in change specifications, with minimum impact on the x-framework, or by extending the x-framework (in case the new feature should also be available for other system releases).

A CDT described in the previous text is partly based on a configuration decision diagram [12] and design decision tree (DDT) [8]. Our CDT is similar to a DDT in that both allow system engineers to cope with ad hoc change requests, and both map existing features to an existing design. They differ, however, in graphical notation and in the information that is stored in the trees. While DDTs span the gap between features and design decisions, our CDTs go one step further by including actual implementation decision information as well. It is often the case that systems once developed will inevitably have to be modified to meet new features. System engineers can use the CDT to find out how best to meet the requirements of a new feature.

12.10   Using MESE to Customize and Evolve the FRS X-Framework: An Example

We refer the reader to the FRS evolution depicted in Figure 11.1, Chapter 11. For simplicity of explanation, we use the evolution Stage 1, building FRS^{DATE}, to illustrate the customization of the FRS x-framework. We use evolution Stage 3, building FRS$^{\text{DATE,USER}}$, to illustrate a simple case of x-framework evolution and comment on more complex evolution in Stage 5, building FRS$^{\text{DATE,USER,PAY}}$. We focus on the user interface components and connectors.

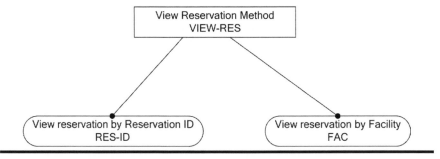

Figure 12.18   Customization decision tree (CDT) options before FRS^{DATE}.

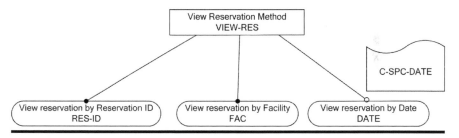

Figure 12.19   Customization decision tree (CDT) with new option DATE.

12.10.1 *Building System Release FRS^{DATE}*

The initial FRS supports reservation viewing by reservation ID (RES-ID) and by facility (FAC), as shown in the CDT of Figure 12.18. Those two mandatory features have been implemented into the FRS x-framework, in the component ViewRes-UI.

We examine implementation of features RES-ID and FAC in component ViewRes-UI and try to implement feature DATE in a similar way. Under the list of available view reservation methods, we add an additional choice DATE (Figure 12.19). We build x-frame ViewRes-UI.gen as discussed in Chapter 11. Finally, we update the CDT with a new customization option DATE under "View Reservation Method" grouping.

A customization script C-SPC-DATE (Figure 12.20) specifies how to accommodate feature DATE in x-frames. Our example shows only adaptation of x-frame viewResBy-Menu-UI (Figure 12.21).

X-frame ViewRes-UI.gen defines three variation points (**<break>** commands) at which we can modify class *ViewRes* to cater to viewing reservations by DATE.

12.10.2 *Building System Release FRS^{DATE,USER}*

USER is a new feature. We do not find the USER feature in the CDT, but we find a similar feature DATE. We study the C-SPC-DATE to understand how the

```
<adapt ViewRes-UI.gen >
  <insert  viewResBy-Menu-UI >
    viewResMethodList.addItem ("Date");
   </insert>
  <insert viewResBy-Action-UI >
    else if (viewResMethodList.getSelectedItem() ==
"Date") { … }
  </insert>
</adapt>
```

Figure 12.20   Customization script: C-SPC-DATE for FRS^{DATE}.

new feature USER should be implemented. The C-SPC-DATE reveals that x-frame ViewRes-UI.gen must be selected and customized. We could use the C-SPC-DATE as a template to implement C-SPC-USER in a similar way. However, we note that it is better to implement a generic mechanism to deal with various reservation viewing methods. Therefore, we decide to refine the x-frame ViewRes-UI.gen as shown in Figure 12.22. C-SPC-DATE-USER is shown in Figure 12.23.

The CDT is refined as shown in Figure 12.24.

To customize metaconnectors for features USER, we proceed as follows (customization for DATE is analogical to USER and we do not discuss it here): We find sections in type declaration IDL ((FRS_Type_Decl) and interface declaration (FRS_Int_Decl) that contain definitions for existing view reservation methods, by facility and reservation ID. We build two metaconnectors around type and interface declarations, namely, FRS_Type_Decl.c and FRS_Int_Decl.c, instrumenting them to accommodate definitions for features DATE and USER. We write a new C-SPC-USER, shown in Figure 12.25, that selects these metaconnectors, and inserts appropriate type and interface declarations for the new feature USER. In particular, we need type declarations for a data structure that the FRS server will use to reply to requests by the client to retrieve reservations for a particular user. We use <**adapt**> and <**insert-after**> commands to select the type declaration x-frame and insert these type declarations into it. We also require interface declarations for declaring operations that will allow the FRS client to obtain a list of registered users and reservation data. We again use <**adapt**> and <**insert-after**> commands to customize the interface declaration x-frame accordingly. We annotate the new type and interface declarations with the name of the new feature. Finally, we update USER customization option in the CDT under the "View Reservation Methods" grouping, including relevant C-SPC-USER for both the x-frame and metaconnector customizations. Figure 12.25 shows the contents of the C-SPC-USER. Figure 12.26 and Figure 12.27 show customized type declaration and interface declaration connectors, respectively.

The preceding connectors are also appropriate for the reservation permission requirement. The Permission feature states that FRS is to grant specific users the

```
ViewRes-UI.gen:  handles variant reservation viewing
methods
class ViewRes extends FRSPanels implements ActionListener
{ …
ViewRes(FRSClient client) // constructor
    {    . . .
// menu items for selecting a required res. viewing method:
viewResMethodList = new List ();
viewResMethodList.addItem ("Facility"); // view res. by
facility
viewResMethodList.addItem ("Reservation ID"); // view res.
by ID
<break viewResBy-Menu-UI /> // code to extend menu with
view reservations by DATE can be inserted here
    }
// actions for res. viewing methods:
public void actionPerformed (ActionEvent ev) {
Object source = ev.getSource();
if (source == viewButton) {
    if (viewResMethodList.getSelectedItem() == "Facility") {
… }
    else if (viewResMethodList.getSelectedItem() ==
"Reservation ID")     {...}
<break viewResBy-Action-UI > // code for new action to
view reservations by DATE can be inserted here
// event handling:
…details not shown
<break   viewResBy-EventHandling-UI /> // code for new
event handler to view reservations by DATE can be inserted
here
}
```

Figure 12.21   X-frame ViewRes-UI.gen adapted by C-SPC-DATE.

permission to make reservations for any facility. This feature is defined in the feature diagram of Figure 12.2 and has a corresponding node in the CDT. We deal with the permission feature in the metaconnectors as follows: the C-SPC selects and customizes the type and interface declaration x-frames. In particular, the C-SPC augments the type declaration x-frame with a data structure for keeping track of permission-related information. It also inserts a number of operation signatures (e.g., addPermission) into the interface declaration x-frame. These operation signatures will allow (authorized) users to manage permissions. After customizations, we obtain IDL type and interface declarations shown in Figure 12.26 and Figure 12.27, respectively.

```
ViewRes-UI.gen:
class ViewRes extends FRSPanels implements ActionListener
{ …
ViewRes(FRSClient client) // constructor
   {    ...
// menu items for selecting a required res. viewing method:
viewResMethodList = new List ();
viewResMethodList.addItem ("Facility"); // view res. by
facility
viewResMethodList.addItem ("Reservation ID"); // view res.
by ID
<while viewRes >
      viewResMethodList.addItem ("@viewRes");
</while>


// actions for res. viewing methods:
public void actionPerformed (ActionEvent ev) {
Object source = ev.getSource();
if (source == viewButton) {
  if (viewResMethodList.getSelectedItem() == "Facility") {
… }
    else if (viewResMethodList.getSelectedItem() ==
"Reservation ID")      {...}
<while viewRes>
  else if (viewResMethodList.getSelectedItem() == "@
viewRes");
  <select option viewRes >
    <option Date>
      { code for Date }
    <option User >
      { code for User }
  <select />
</while>
… other Java code here

// event handling:
<while viewRes>
      code to extend event handlers here
</while>
```

Figure 12.22   X-frame with generic mechanism for viewing reservations.

```
// customizations for FRS^{DATE,USER}  to view reservation by
date and user
<set viewRes = Date, Use>
<adapt ViewRes-UI.gen />
```

Figure 12.23 C-SPC-DATE-USER.

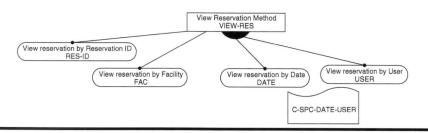

Figure 12.24 Customization decision tree (CDT) with option DATE and USER added.

```
C-SPC-USER-CONNECTOR.c:
<adapt  FRS_Type_Decl.m >
  <insert-after Type_Decl  >
typedef sequence<UserNo> UserNoSeq;
typedef sequence<ResNo> ResNoSeq;
struct UserSummaryStruct {
// Data structure to store retrieved reservations by user
UserNo    userID;
ResNoSeq resNoSeq; //One user may have many reservations
};
typedef sequence<UserSummaryStruct> UserSumSeq;
  </insert-after>
</adapt>
<adapt FRS_Int_Decl.m>
  <insert-after  FRS_Interface
UserNoSeq  getUser ();
UserSumSeq getUserReservations (in UserNo userID);
  </insert-after >
</adapt>
```

Figure 12.25 C-SPC-USER: customizations of a connector for feature USER.

```
FRS_Type_Decl:
typedef long FacNo;
typedef long ResNo;
...
struct ResStruct {

FacNo facID;
TimeDateStruct start;
TimeDateStruct end;
};
typedef long PermNo; // RES_PERM-ALT2
struct PermStruct { // RES_PERM-ALT2
    PermNo permID;
    UserNo permOwnerID;
};
typedef sequence<UserNo> UserNoSeq;
typedef sequence<ResNo> ResNoSeq;
struct UserSummaryStruct {
    UserNo   userID;
    ResNoSeq resNoSeq; // One user may have made many
reservations
};
typedef sequence<UserSummaryStruct> UserSumSeq;
```

Figure 12.26   Type declaration connector.

```
FRS_Int_Decl:
interface FRSInterface {
    ResNo      addReservation (in FacNo facID, in ResStruct
resData);
    ResStruct getReservation (in ResNo resID);
    boolean   cancelReservation (in ResNo resID);
    FacNo      addFacility (in FacStruct facData);
    FacStruct getFacility (in FacNo facID);
    boolean   removeFacility (in FacNo facID);
PermNo
addPermission (in UserNo permOwnerID); //RES_PERM

PermStruct viewPermission (in PermNo permID); //RES_PERM

boolean    removePermission (in PermNo permID); //RES_PERM
    UserNoSeq  getUser ();
    UserSumSeq getUserReservations (in UserNo userID);
} ;
```

Figure 12.27   Interface declaration connector.

12.11 Assembly Pass

The purpose of the assembly pass is to assemble already customized components into a working system release. Figure 12.28 shows an A-SPC for the FRS user interface. Other A-SPCs, not shown here, would produce sources for the business logic and database tiers. For example, by including the customized ViewRes-UI.gen x-frame in this assembly, we ensure that the resulting source code file satisfies the required variant reservation viewing methods.

Figure 12.29 shows an A-SPC for the connector x-framework. This A-SPC contains XVCL commands for assembling metaconnectors required for the IDL declaration file. The assembly is achieved using the **<adapt>** command. The exception, constant, type, and interface declaration x-frames are assembled within a single module declaration. In this example, the type and interface declaration x-frames have been customized, although the constant and exception x-frames have not been customized. The end result of generation is a single declaration file (Figure 12.30) that contains the declarations appropriate for the retrieval method requirement and the permission requirement.

A-SPC-Components..m // assembles customized FRS components

<adapt FRS_UI.gen **/>**

<adapt FRS_Panels.gen **/>**

<adapt FRS_Main_Menu.x **/>**

<adapt C-SPC-DATE-USER // customized ViewRes-UI.gen for DATE and USER

<break Codegen_Additional_Classes>

Figure 12.28   Assembling facility reservation system (FRS) components.

A-SPC-Connectors.c // assembles customized FRS connectors

module FRSModule {

<adapt FRS_Const_Decl.c>

<adapt FRS_Except_Decl.c>

<adapt FRS_Type_Decl.c>

<adapt FRS_Int_Decl.c>

< break Codegen_Additional_Classes

};

Figure 12.29   An A-SPC for the metaconnector x-framework.

```
FRS_MOD_DECL.c
module FRSModule { // Start of Module Declaration
// Start of Constant Declarations
...
// End of Constant Declarations
// Start of Exception Declarations
...
// End of Exception Declarations
// Start of Type Declarations
...
typedef long PermNo; // (RES_PERM-ALT2)
struct PermStruct { // (RES_PERM-ALT2)
    PermNo permID;
    UserNo permOwnerID;
typedef sequence<UserNo> UserNoSeq;
typedef sequence<ResNo> ResNoSeq;
struct UserSummaryStruct {
    UserNo    userID;
    ResNoSeq resNoSeq; // One user may have made many reservations
};
typedef sequence<UserSummaryStruct> UserSumSeq;
};
...
// End of Type Declarations

// Start of Interface Declarations
interface FRSInterface {
    ResNo       addReservation(in FacNo facID, in ResStruct
resData);
    ResStruct getReservation (in ResNo resID);
    boolean    cancelReservation (in ResNo resID);
    FacNo       addFacility (in FacStruct facData);
    FacStruct getFacility (in FacNo facID);
    boolean    removeFacility (in FacNo facID);
    PermNo       addPermission (in UserNo permOwnerID); //
(RES_PERM-ALT2)
    PermStruct viewPermission (in PermNo permID); //
(RES_PERM-ALT2)
    boolean    removePermission (in PermNo permID); //
(RES_PERM-ALT2)
    UserNoSeq  getUser ();
    UserSumSeq getUserReservations (in UserNo userID);
...
};
...
// End of Interface Declarations
}; // End of Module Declaration
```

Figure 12.30 Interface definition language (IDL) declaration for client/server connector produced by *A-SPC-Connectors.m.*

12.12 Related Work on Product Line Research

Reuse-based evolution has much in common with a software product line approach to reuse [2]. In a product line approach, we develop and maintain a family of similar software products from a common core of reusable software assets called product line architecture (PLA). In reuse-based evolution, we also tap into opportunities hidden in similarity among systems release during evolution. An x-framework for reuse-based evolution is an analog of a PLA.

Looking at evolution from the reuse angle, many techniques developed in product line research become useful in evolution situations. In particular, we use feature diagrams [7] to model the range of variant features implemented into the systems released during evolution. We also use elements of domain analysis to understand the requirements of a system under evolution.

From the mixed-strategy point of view, there is not much difference between reusability and maintainability. Both qualities are achieved by the same means identifying similarity patterns and unifying them with generic, adaptable XVCL structures. A structure of an x-framework for a product line is no different from an x-framework for reuse-based evolution. XVCL was successfully applied in both situations.

12.13 Conclusions

In this chapter, we illustrated the following aspects of the mixed-strategy approach: (1) we structured the x-framework customization into three distinct steps, namely, selecting architecture components and connectors, customization of component code and connector specifications, and assembling components and connectors into a working custom software system that meets required variant features; (2) application of a single customization mechanism, XVCL, for customizations at all levels and for system assembly; and (3) clear separation of computational aspects (components) from component interfaces (connectors). We emphasized the x-framework construction and customization processes, and only briefly touched on the domain-modeling problems.

The core of the FRS x-framework was formed by architecture components and connectors turned into generic, adaptable x-frames. We organized the x-framework according to the principle of separation of concerns. We mapped variant features into sequences of customization activities on the x-framework. For simplicity and better control, we split customization of the FRS x-framework into three distinct steps listed earlier. The XVCL processor automated the customization and assembly processes.

We described a mixed-strategy evolution support environment (MESE) based on the earlier concepts and showed how it facilitates x-framework customization and evolution. MESE creates formal links between a domain model and the process of an x-framework customization process. The CDT captures the relationship between software requirements configurations and an architecture customization process that leads to satisfying these requirements.

The major difficulty is to understand the impact of variant features on an x-framework and on the process of customizing it. Ideally, a software developer would define only novel requirements for a new system release, and an automated engineering environment would actively guide him or her in producing a required system. MESE described in this chapter is a step in this direction.

References

1. Cheong, Y.C. and Jarzabek, S., Frame-based method for customizing X-frameworks, *Proceedings of the Symposium on Software Reusability, SSR'99*, Los Angeles, CA, 1999, pp. 103–112.
2. Clements, P. and Northrop, L., *Software Product Lines: Practices and Patterns*, Addison-Wesley, Boston, 2002.
3. Czarnecki, K. and Eisenecker, U., *Generative Programming: Methods, Tools, and Applications*, Addison-Wesley, 2000.
4. Deelstra, S., Sinnema, M., and Bosch, J., Experiences in software product families: problems and issues during product derivation, *Proceedings of the Software Product Lines Conference, SPLC3*, Boston, MA, August 2004, LNCS 3154, Springer-Verlag, pp. 165–182.
5. Jacobson, I., Griss, M., and Jonsson, P., *Software Reuse. Architecture, Process and Organization for Business Success*, ACM Press, 1997.
6. Jarzabek, S. and Zhang, H., XML-based method and tool for handling variant features in domain models, *Proceedings of the of 5th IEEE International Symposium on Requirements Engineering, RE'01,* Toronto, Canada, August 2001, pp. 166–173.
7. Kang, K., Cohen, S.G., Hess, J.A., Novak, W.E., and Peterson, A.S., Feature-Oriented Domain Analysis (FODA) Feasibility Study, Technical Report, CMU/SEI-90-TR-21, Software Engineering Institute, Carnegie Mellon University, Pittsburgh, PA, 1990.
8. Karhinen, A. and Kuusela, J., Structuring design decisions for evolution, *Proceedings of the 2nd International Workshop on Development and Evolution of Software Architectures for Product Families*, Lecture Notes in Computer Science, Springer-Verlag, 1995.
9. Karhinen, A., Ran, A., and Tallgren, T., Configuring designs for reuse, *Proceedings of the 1997 International Conference on Software Engineering, ICSE'97,* Boston, MA, 1997, pp. 701–710.
10. Rumbaugh, J., Jacobson, I., and Booch, G., *The Unified Modeling Language, Reference Manual*, Addison-Wesley, 1999.
11. Shaw, M. and Garlan, D., *Software Architecture: Perspectives on an Emerging Discipline*, Prentice-Hall, 1996.
12. Tracz, W., DSSA (Domain-Specific Software Architecture) pedagogical example, *ACM Software Engineering Notes*, 49–62, 1995.

13. Zhang, H., Jarzabek, S., and Myat Swe, S., XVCL approach to separating concerns in product line assets, *Proceedings of 3rd International Conference on Generative and Component-Based Software Engineering*, LNCS, Springer Verlag, September 2001, Erfurt, Germany, pp. 36–47.

Chapter 13

The Mixed-Strategy Approach in Other Projects

Chapter Summary

We summarize experiences from other projects in which we applied mixed-strategy. We observed similar benefits in terms of maintainability and reusability, as in the Buffer library experiment described in Chapter 8 and Chapter 9, and the facility reservation system (FRS). Also, the structure of x-frameworks was similar in all the projects. XML-based variant configuration language (XVCL) addresses issues such as changeability, evolution, and reuse by applying the same underlying principles of genericity and adaptability, with relatively simple mechanisms. Mixed-strategy focuses on unifying software similarity patterns that cannot be unified with conventional techniques alone. In Chapter 9, we hinted at common reasons why similarity patterns arise, and common problems that make it difficult to come up with generic solutions with conventional programming techniques. As the mixed-strategy approach deals with similarities at the root level, the uniform structure of solutions across very different program domains should not be very surprising.

13.1   STL in C++/XVCL

We discussed similarity patterns in the standard template library (STL) in Chapter 9.

Having identified clones in STL with the automated clone detector CCFinder [8], we manually analyzed parts of the STL affected by clones. We analyzed the reasons why similar functions and templates occurred, and then we designed x-frames for each group of similar templates/functions, in a similar way as we designed x-frames for groups of similar classes in the Buffer library. In this case, a mixed-strategy solution was formed by imposing XVCL on C++ templates/functions that displayed much similarity, but also nonparametric differences that could not be unified by the template mechanism.

In STL, iterators proved very effective in separating algorithmic details from the data structures on which they operated. We did not find significant clones in algorithms. However, containers displayed a high degree of similarity in structure and a large amount of repeated code. Four "sorted" associative containers and four "hashed" associative containers could be unified into two generic C++/XVCL containers, achieving 57 percent reduction in the related code. Stack and queue contained 37 percent of the cloned code. Algorithms for set union, intersection, difference, and symmetric difference (along with their overloaded versions) formed a set of eight clones that could be unified by a generic C++/XVCL set operation, eliminating 52 percent of code.

The feature combinatorics problem is a challenge for many class libraries: as we combine features, classes grow in number and become polluted by redundancies. At times, even the sheer size of a library may become an issue. This certainly would be the case of the STL, and templates helped designers control the situation. Still, as our experiment showed, there was room for improvement.

13.2   DEMS in C#/XVCL

We discussed similarity patterns in domain entity management subsystem (DEMS) in Chapter 9.

We unified similarities in DEMS with XVCL at two levels: At the detailed level, similar classes in the GUI, service and entity tiers were unified with suitable x-frames. Then, patterns of collaborating components (such as those shown in Figure 9.17 in Section 9.7.1) were unified with higher-level x-frames. For example, all the Create operations for different entities could be generated from a single x-frame Create[entity-type]. Similar classes participating in operation implementation could also be unified by suitable x-frames.

Figure 13.1 shows an outline of a C#/XVCL x-framework for DEMS. Each group formed by the same operation applied to different entities, (e.g., *CreateUser*, *CreateTask*, …) has been represented by one generic operation parameterized by domain entities (e.g., Create.gen). Similarities among different operations for the

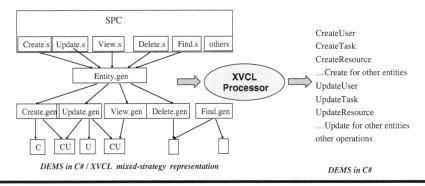

DEMS in C# / XVCL mixed-strategy representation   *DEMS in C#*

Figure 13.1   Hierarchical unification of similarities in domain entity management subsystem (DEMS).

same entity (e.g., *CreateUser, UpdateUser, …*) have been unified with bottom level x-frames representing generic classes, which are the building blocks for DEMS operations. This is indicated by x-frames referenced from more than one operation (e.g., generic classes labeled with CU are reused in construction of Create and Update for various entities). X-frame Entity.gen defines the common, adaptable structure for DEMS modules. This includes DEMS architecture, that is, the organization of component patterns implementing various operations, together with any other functions supported by DEMS not discussed in this example. The SPC contains global controls and parameter settings for the overall process of generating DEMS modules for various domain entities and operations acting on them.

This simplified description does not address classes belonging to the four system layers, namely user interface, business logic, database access, and database structure definition.

The C#/XVCL mixed-strategy representation contains C# code needed to produce all the DEMS operations, and also information helpful in maintenance/reuse, such as the record of similarities and differences among operations for different entities. In most programs, their system structures, such as in Figure 13.1, are implicit and must be expressed in the form of an external documentation. Mixed-strategy makes such views explicit and an integral part of a formal program representation. Mixed-strategy contains both code and the knowledge of program design, integrated into one representation.

The C#/XVCL solution compressed the size of the original C# entity management subsystem by 68 percent, which also led to improved maintainability. For example, it was eight times faster to create a new domain entity in the C#/XVCL solution as compared to the C# solution alone. Typical enhancements of the subsystem (such as a change of business rules for domain entities or adding/deleting a new entity or operation) required fewer modifications with smaller impact in the C#/XVCL solution as compared to its C# counterpart. For example, to add a new domain entity in the C#/XVCL solution required writing 133 LOC and took 2 man-hours, although the same enhancement in C# required writing 1440 LOC and took 16 man-hours. Finally, it was quite easy to reuse the C#/XVCL solution in other similar command and control systems.

The reader should note that adding more operations and entities to DEMS in C# increases the complexity by a constant value, independently of the similarity of new operations/entities to existing ones. In mixed-strategy, C#/XVCL, complexity grows proportionally to the level of novelty that a new operation/entity brings. New operations and entities that differ little from existing ones require little new code to be written.

13.3   Web Portal Product Line in ASP/XVCL

STEE (ST Electronics Pte Ltd) applied the mixed-strategy approach to evolve a simple ASP Web portal (WP) developed for personal use into a family of WP business products [9], called a software product line [3]. Although sharing a common core, implemented as an x-framework, the individual products differed from each other in many requirements. From the ASP/XVCL x-framework, STEE produced over 20 WP product variants that now serve customers from a variety of business sectors such as hospitals or e-learning. So far, this has been the largest (in scale) application of the mixed-strategy approach in an industrial setting. In the following text, we outline the main story line of this project and discuss the benefits.

It started with a personal ASP WP developed by Ulf Pettersson of STTE. The personal portal facilitated information sharing via management of users, HTML content, images, and video clips. It also included access statistics, news and announcements, weather animations, and posting/feedback facilities. The personal portal was then extended in the company environment to form a team collaboration portal (TCP) shown in Figure 13.2. TCP supported a wide range of functionalities and scenarios commonly useful in collaborative environments. For example, TCP had a Staff module to manage information about staff working on projects, a Project module to manage information about projects, and a Task module so that project tasks could be assigned to staff. It also supported means for staff to provide feedback about the progress of a project, and monitoring facilities for managers to monitor the progress and identify possible sources of problems. Finally, TCP included a range of generally useful features such as News, Forum, Statistics, and Polls.

Initially used in one division of STEE, a number of TCP variants were then developed and released to other STEE divisions.

During the SARS crisis in May 2003, STEE developed a WP to facilitate analysis of people movements in hospitals. This WP was to register people movement within a hospital to facilitate tracing of people who could have been in contact with SARS infected persons. Under great time pressure (five days), two people transformed the TCP into a people tracking portal, and integrated this portal with an

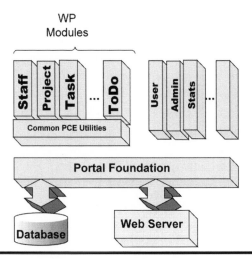

Figure 13.2   Team collaboration portal (TCP).

external radio frequency identification (RFID) tracking system at two hospitals. Some key entity modules in the people tracking portal were: zone, visitor, and visitor movement (including movement and contact analysis). With this deployment, the portal actually turned into a business product (even though from a business perspective, this was more of a community service).

Several other WP variants were later developed and released to various customers. At this stage, maintenance of existing WP products was getting very difficult due to the many product variants. Even though development of new portal modules could be done with reasonable ease (typically, 500–1500 code lines each), the constantly growing need for enhancements to existing portals and development of new portals resulted in increasing difficulty to maintain the WP family.

Although STEE applied state-of-the-art model-based design and component-based reuse techniques, and a single team was maintaining most of the WPs, it was not possible to maintain them from a single code base for the following reasons:

1. Specific adaptations were often required in areas of business logic and almost always in the area of user interface. To address such customer specific variations, the underlying component platforms and conventional design techniques proved ineffective in defining generic solutions to avoid explosion of many similar components. Because of these difficulties, the reuse of CAP solutions was limited to functional areas where variations were few and could be easily managed with conventional design techniques, although for other areas cut–paste–modify was applied, resulting in explosion of similar components.

2. Most of the enhancements (new WP features) were only needed in some of the WPs, whereas other already-released WPs were not allowed to be affected by these enhancements. However, such selective injection of features (one of the challenges of reuse-based evolution discussed in Chapter 1) was impos-

sible to achieve using conventional techniques: Should such enhancements be implemented into reusable components, they would be propagated to all the WPs, which was not a viable solution. The portals were deployed in a turnkey project manner rather than a product manner. As a result, some portals were in a frozen state where only critical defects would be corrected, and feature enhancements were thus not wanted. Therefore, new enhancements had to be implemented into those WP releases that needed them, resulting in increasing cost of maintenance.

3. Even though some entity modules were required in multiple portals, there were specific variations that applied to each individual portal, resulting in difficulties in maintaining a single code base.

A new business opportunity occurred, and the team was given seven days to develop an e-learning demonstration portal that required about 20 new modules. With the existing design and code volume required for each portal module, it was deemed impossible to achieve both design and implementation within a week.

At this point, mixed-strategy was adopted to take over the control of the common core of WPs to facilitate efficient evolution of existing portals and creation of new ones. Figure 13.3 shows the main steps in the evolution of WP products. The numbers attached to transition arrows show evolution steps. Mixed-strategy reuse-based evolution occurs on the right-hand side of the diagram. In Step 4, a common core of the existing WPs was identified and redesigned into an x-framework. Any further maintenance of existing portals and development of new ones was done by customizing the ASP/XVCL x-framework. As new WPs were developed, the

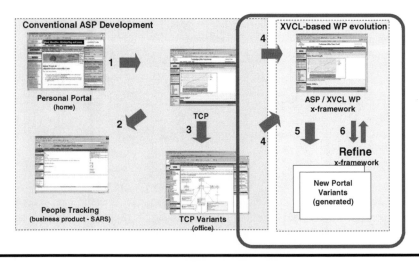

Figure 13.3   Evolution from personal Web portal (WP) to 20 WP business products.

x-framework was continuously refined so that other portals could benefit from new features.

The benefits of a mixed-strategy ASP/XVCL solution for TCP were the following:

- Short time (less than two weeks) and small effort (two persons) to transform the TCP into the first version of a mixed-strategy ASP/XVCL solution.
- High productivity in building new portals from the ASP/XVCL solution. Based on the ASP/XVCL solution, ST Electronics could build new portal modules by writing as little as ten percent of unique custom code, although the rest of code could be reused. This code reduction translated into an estimated eightfold reduction of effort required to build new portals.
- Significant reduction of maintenance effort when enhancing individual portals. The overall managed code lines for nine portals were 22 percent less than for the original single portal.
- Wide range of portals differing in a large number of interdependent features supported by the ASP/XVCL solution.

The reader can find full details of this project in Reference 9.

13.4 CAP-WP in J2EE™/XVCL

The J2EE/XVCL mixed-strategy solution unified both inter- and intramodule similarity patterns in CAP-WP discussed in Chapter 9. This solution represented each similarity pattern with a unique generic mixed-strategy structure, as shown in Figure 13.4.

Not only did such unification reduce the solution size by 61 percent, but, most importantly, it increased the clarity of the portal's conceptual structure as per-

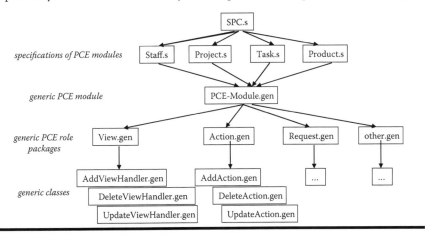

Figure 13.4   J2EE/XVCL CAP-WP x-framework.

ceived by developers. In particular, it reduced the number of conceptual elements a programmer had to deal with and enhanced the visibility of relationships among program elements that mattered during changes: Rather than maintaining multiple variant code structures delocalized across the CAP-WP, in the mixed-strategy J2EE/XVCL solution a programmer dealt with one generic structure, with full visibility of customizations required to produce instances of variant structures, as well as their exact locations. Nonredundancy of the J2EE/XVCL CAP-WP, achieved by generic mixed-strategy structures unifying similarity patterns, reduced the risk of update anomalies.

13.5 Role-Playing Games (RPG) for Mobile Phones

Mobile games have become an important trend in the mobile phone industry. In role-playing games (RPG), the players take the roles of fictional characters and participate in an interactive story. Figure 13.5 shows four RPGs called DigGem, Hunt, Jump, and Feeding.

At some abstraction level, all RPGs share a similar conceptual model. However, RPGs also differ from one another in certain functional requirements. RPGs are further differentiated by the properties of a specific mobile device platform on which they run, and which affect the RPGs' design and implementation. This includes mobile devices with high-resolution colorful displays and up to 80M memory, low-end devices with smaller mono displays and less than 100kB memory, the new J2ME MIDP2.0 compliant mobile devices, and MIDP1.0-enabled older ones.

The challenge is that RPGs must perform well across all these different devices. A simple-minded solution is to ignore similarities among RPGs and to develop a separate product for each combination of an RPG and a target mobile device. However, such a solution is costly to develop and maintain.

This project involved RPGs on the J2ME platform. RPGs were redesigned into a J2ME/XVCL x-framework that defined a common core for a range of RPGs and mobile devices. Not only did the mixed-strategy approach achieve development/maintenance productivity gains, but also enabled sharing common successful

Figure 13.5 Four role-playing games (RPGs).

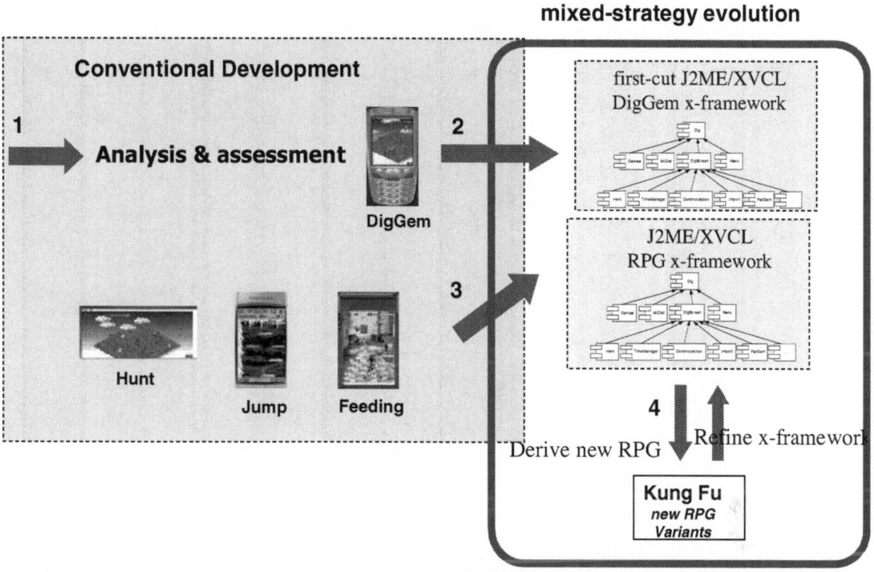

Figure 13.6 **Evolution of role-playing games (RPGs) with the mixed-strategy approach.**

optimization strategies across a range of RPGs. This considerably enhanced performance of all the RPGs.

The transition from ad hoc evolution of RPGs to mixed-strategy reuse-based evolution involved steps shown in Figure 13.6.

Having completed analysis of the RPG domain (Step 1), a first-cut J2ME/XVCL x-framework was built based on one selected RPG, namely DigGem (Step 2). The first-cut x-framework was then refined with features of the other three RPGs, as well as with optimization strategies found in all four RPGs (Step 3). From this point, any enhancements of the four RPGs were done via the J2ME/XVCL x-framework. New RPGs, such as Kung Fu, were developed by customization and extensions of the J2ME/XVCL x-framework (Figure 13.7).

The following benefits were observed in this project:

1. Improved productivity in building new RPGs: reduced effort to develop a new game from 88 man-days (in J2ME) to 28 man-days (in mixed-strategy J2ME/XVCL).
2. Enhanced conceptual clarity, uniformity, and integrity of the design of RPGs.
3. Improved performance, as all the RPGs shared best-design solutions and optimizations; for example, the size of the RPGs was reduced by 26 percent on average.
4. Improved productivity in maintenance, as much maintenance could be done via J2ME/XVCL x-framework using XVCL's capability to selectively

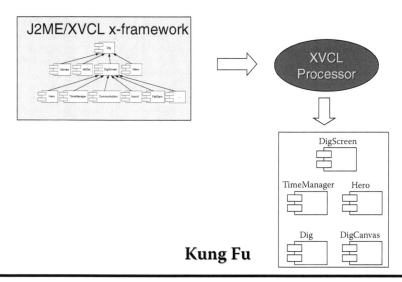

Figure 13.7   Deriving new releases of role-playing games (RPGs) from the J2ME/XVCL x-framework.

propagate new features into RPGs that needed them, without affecting other RPGs that did not need new features.

13.6   Conclusions

We described the structure of solutions in a range of projects with the mixed-strategy approach. We evaluated the engineering qualities of presented solutions. The following are some preliminary observations and evaluation:

The structure of a mixed-strategy solution follows a similar pattern: Similar program structures are unified with generic structures built with XVCL. Unification occurs at multiple levels, with lower-level generic structures serving as building blocks for higher-level ones.

The main strength of the mixed-strategy approach is its ability to define powerful generic design solutions. Because of its low-level mechanisms which deal with changes, XVCL is capable of unifying any kind of similar structures, of any granularity, and independently of the nature of differences among them.

We believe mixed-strategy program representation offers some interesting engineering benefits. In particular, it (1) reduces the code size, yet contains 100 percent of the information necessary to produce the original buffer classes; (2) defines program solution using fewer conceptual elements than those in the actual program; (3) represents design information that matters during maintenance in a form that is understandable for programmers and amenable to automation by the XVCL processor; and (4) enhances the conceptual integrity of the design, which Brooks calls "the most important consideration in system design" [2].

In this chapter, we substantiated the preceding observations with empirical and analytical arguments. The idea behind the mixed-strategy approach is general and can be applied to any program that exhibits a lot of similarity, independently of an application domain or a programming language.

However, applying and adopting techniques like XVCL does not come for free. Adopting a new technique always brings some overhead, and XVCL is no different. It is essential to understand and evaluate the trade-offs involved. We conduct a comprehensive evaluation of the strengths and weaknesses of the approach in the next chapter.

References

1. Basit, H.A., Rajapakse, D.C., and Jarzabek, S., Beyond templates: a study of clones in the STL and some general implications, *International Conference on Software Engineering, ICSE'05*, St. Louis, MO, May 2005, pp. 451–459.
2. Brooks, P.B., *The Mythical Man-Month*, Addison-Wesley, 1995.
3. Clements, P. and Northrop, L., *Software Product Lines: Practices and Patterns*, Addison-Wesley, 2002.
4. Czarnecki, K. and Eisenecker, U., *Generative Programming: Methods, Tools, and Applications*, Addison-Wesley, 2000.
5. Deelstra, S., Sinnema, M., and Bosch, J., Experiences in software product families: problems and issues during product derivation, *Proceedings of the Software Product Lines Conference, SPLC3*, Boston, MA, August 2004, LNCS 3154, Springer-Verlag, pp. 165–182.
6. Jarzabek, S. and Li, S., Eliminating redundancies with a "composition with adaptation" meta-programming technique, *Proceedings of the ESEC-FSE'03, European Software Engineering Conference and ACM SIGSOFT Symposium on the Foundations of Software Engineering*, September 2003, Helsinki, pp. 237–246.
7. Jarzabek, S. and Li, S., Unifying clones with a generative programming technique: a case study, *Journal of Software Maintenance and Evolution: Research and Practice*, 18(4), 267–292, July–August 2006.
8. Kamiya, T., Kusumoto, S., and Inoue, K., CCFinder: a multi-linguistic token-based code clone detection system for large scale source code, *IEEE Transactions on Software Engineering*, 28(7), 2002, pp. 654–670.
9. Pettersson, U. and Jarzabek, S., Industrial experience with building a web portal product line using a lightweight, reactive approach, *ESEC-FSE'05, European Software Engineering Conference and ACM SIGSOFT Symposium on the Foundations of Software Engineering*, ACM Press, September 2005, Lisbon, pp. 326–335.
10. Yang, J. and Jarzabek, S., Applying a generative technique for enhanced reuse on J2EE platform, *4th International Confernce on Generative Programming and Component Engineering, GPCE'05*, September 29–October 1, 2005, pp. 237–255.

Chapter 14

Other Techniques Related to XVCL

Chapter Summary

In this chapter, we discuss other techniques, both conventional and unconventional, comparing them to XVCL. We primarily focus on engineering goals that are typically achieved using various techniques, but also comment on the actual mechanisms underlying the discussed techniques. Generic design, componentization, reuse, separation of concerns, and enhancing the visibility of changes are among the leading themes of reuse-based evolution, and also the main forces that motivated XVCL. Therefore, we discuss other techniques around those themes, relating them to XVCL. Conventional techniques include type parameterization [17], other forms of parameterization such as higher-order functions [39], modular decomposition with information hiding [29], inheritance with dynamic binding, design patterns [16], and mechanisms supported by modern component platforms (such as J2EE™ or .NET™). Unconventional techniques include generative approaches [12].

14.1 Frame Technology

XVCL has its roots in Frame Technology™ by Netron, Inc. [3]. A number of frame-based systems have been implemented in both industrial and academic institutions [15]. We believe any system based on frame principles can achieve similar engineering benefits in areas of maintenance, evolution, and reuse as those demonstrated with XVCL in this book, independently of a specific syntactic representation that different systems may use. Whether or not similar engineering benefits can be achieved by other technical approaches remains an open question. We are not aware of reports demonstrating capabilities of other techniques to tackle evolution challenges discussed in Chapter 1, particularly in the area of unifying software similarity patterns.

Frame Technology™ has been extensively applied to maintain multimillion-line COBOL-based information systems and to build reuse frameworks in companies [3]. An independent assessment by QSM Associates, Inc., showed that frames could achieve up to 90 percent reuse, reduce project costs by over 84 percent, and their time to market by 70 percent, when compared to industry norms [3]. We are in the lucky situation that the basic principles of XVCL have been already tested in practice, though in a different setting than ours. Our contribution is that we refined frame concepts into a general-purpose technique of XVCL [41]. We also demonstrated that XVCL can enhance modern programming paradigms in areas of maintainability and reusability, and formulated a mixed-strategy approach to guide developers in exploiting frame benefits in their projects.

14.2   Conventional Techniques

The search for effective generic programming and design techniques to unify software similarities has a long history. Most often, we try to achieve genericity through parameterization, whose general forms were proposed by Goguen in 1983 [18]. Programming languages such as Ada [1], Eiffel [27], C++, Java JDK 1.5, and C# support some form of generics. Generics use type parameters to unify groups of similar classes. In C++, type parameterization is called *templates* and can also be applied to unify similar unattached functions. Garcia et al. [17] compare generics in six programming languages. Generics show limitations when we need to unify similar classes or functions that differ in non-type parameters. We discussed difficulties in applying Java generics to unify differences among buffer classes in Chapter 10. C++ templates are more powerful than other generics owing to light integration of templates with the C++ language core. Unlike Java generics, C++ templates also allow constants and primitive types to be passed as parameters. STL [28,36], a hallmark of powerful generic programming, achieves much genericity via type parameterization. STL implements type-safe polymorphic containers. Still, repetitions exist in areas of associative containers [2] which, despite many similarities, cannot be easily unified with templates.

Static C++ template metaprogramming techniques can deal with complicated forms of parameterization, achieving remarkable results in building adaptable software [12]. As such, unconventional usage of templates may lead to overly complex software representations. The engineering qualities of the solution should be consciously evaluated when the technique is applied.

Some limitations of type parameterization can be alleviated with function parameters (e.g., higher-order functions [39] or pointers to functions in C++).

Modularization with information hiding [29] is also a simple form of generic design. Here, a similarity pattern is reflected by the module's application program interface (API). A hidden implementation plays the role of a parameter that makes a module generic. Instantiation of such a "generic module" is done by defining a specific data representation, and implementing API operations in terms of the chosen data representation.

XVCL provides parameterization that is not restricted by the rules of programming languages, which are used together with XVCL to form mixed-strategy solutions. The type and granularity of similar program structures unified by generic representations built with XVCL is unrestricted, too. They may range from small-granularity similar code fragments (such as class methods), to classes, to components, to patterns of collaborating components, and to large-granularity architecture-level code formations (e.g., subsystems). Domain analysis [31] is essential in identifying such high-level, large-granularity patterns of similarity. Mixed-strategy generic solutions unifying such similarity patterns are most beneficial for a programmer's productivity as they can significantly reduce the size and complexity of the program representation.

Macro systems are one of the oldest attempts to generalize programs. Macros are a simple form of a generative technique [12], not strictly a conventional technique in the sense we use the term "conventional" in this book. We comment on macros in this section because of their common use in mainstream programming. Macro systems work on the principle of code expansion according to a certain set of rules. A macro-processor replaces macros found in a program with text that defines a given macro. This text may contain code and also invocations of other macros, allowing one macro to invoke other macros. Macros may have parameters that are instantiated in the process of macro expansion. Macros handle variant features only at the implementation level, which causes well-known problems when trying to tackle more complex change situations with macros [22]. We believe (in the context of software evolution challenges discussed in Chapter 1) macros can play an important supporting role, but it may be difficult to attack the core of the problems with macro-based solutions.

XVCL also works on the principle of code expansion according to a certain set of rules. Some of the XVCL commands (such as <**set**>, <**adapt**>, <**ifdef**>, or <**select**>) have close counterparts in macro systems: <**adapt**> corresponds to macro invocation, <**set**> corresponds to setting macro variables, and <**ifdef**> and <**select**> play similar roles to macros defining conditional compilation. Other XVCL features do not have a macro counterpart or are less carefully defined in macro systems. They include XVCL's ability to define customizations for generic x-frames at their adaptation points, or to propagate customizations across an x-framework, whereby globally defined customizations override customization defined locally. XVCL allows us to place logical groupings of change specification commands in dedicated x-frames that are easy to identify, and propagate them from there — in variant forms — to any program component that needs be changed, without affecting components which do not need that change. We refer the reader to Reference 3, pp. 116–120, which explains the details of technical differences between frame principles and macros. It is the right collection of mechanisms and rules (described in Chapter 8), rather than the fundamental principle of operation, that gives XVCL its unique power to solve engineering problems posed by software evolution and reuse.

Software configuration management (SCM) systems have been applied to handle variant features in software [10,38]. For each legal combination of features, an SCM tool maintains a separate component version — a situation analogous to multiplying similar classes in the Buffer library. SCM tools are strong in handling variants at the file level, but weak in handling small, interdependent variants spread over many components. File-level variations may not neatly map into design concepts. In XVCL, we capture component variability specifications separately from the components themselves, producing custom components with a required combination of variant features on demand. We discussed CVS in the context of evolution in Chapter 5. We then contrasted the CVS approach with XVCL in Chapter 11.

Software architectures [33] and architectural styles and patterns [9] help developers avoid repeatedly designing the same solution by providing component plug-in plug-out capability. Reuse via a software product line approach is often supported by stabilizing software component architecture [9]. Component-based reuse is most effective when combined with architecture-centric, pattern-driven development, which is now supported by the major platforms such as .NET and J2EE. Component platforms provide an infrastructure for reuse of predefined common services. Patterns are basic means to achieve reuse of common service components. Standardized architectures, together with patterns, lead to beneficial uniformity of program solutions. Interactive development environments support application of major patterns, or programmers use manual copy–paste–modify to apply to yet other patterns.

XVCL can enhance the benefits of modern platforms by automating pattern application, emphasizing the visibility of patterns in code, and helping to avoid explosion of similar components and component patterns by unifying them with generic representations. Pattern-driven design facilitates reuse of middleware service components, but tends to scatter application domain-specific code. With XVCL, we can package and isolate otherwise scattered domain-specific code into reusable generic components. Such extensions improve development and maintenance productivity, and also allow reuse to penetrate application business logic and user interface system areas, in addition to middleware service component layers.

It is interesting to note that component platforms hide implementation of some of the functionality that would normally be scattered across program components. These are called crosscutting concerns, and are discussed in more detail in the next section. Component platforms provide transparent access to them via APIs. In J2EE, containers provide a general mechanism to access services via APIs whose implementation would otherwise lead to crosscutting concerns. Examples of such services include transaction management, persistence, security, authentication/authorization, and session management depending on the container used [26]. Without J2EE infrastructure or the support of an unconventional technique, such as aspect-oriented programming (AOP) [23], these concerns would have a crosscutting effect.

14.3 Generation Techniques

Generators [34] produce custom programs from problem specifications in domain-specific languages. Domain-specific languages can be developed in well-understood and stable domains. As problem specifications can be very compact, generators can yield high productivity gains in domains formalized by generation solutions. Most generators easily accommodate changes that can be expressed in the scope of a domain-specific language, but do not provide explicit support for changes beyond that. A common pitfall of generators, in the context of maintenance and evolution, is that any modification of the generated code causes disconnection of the code from the abstract specifications from which the code has been generated. From that point onward, the generated code has to be maintained by hand.

XVCL is an application-domain- and programming-language-independent technique. It does not rely on any form of abstract specifications that would not be transparently linked to code. Every detail of an x-framework can be exposed to a developer, who also has full control over every detail of the transformations performed by the XVCL processor. The XVCL processor does not inject any hidden code into a custom program produced from the x-framework. Specifications of custom changes are visible, and their impact on a custom program produced, as well as on the processing, can be traced to every detail. Custom code produced from an x-framework never gets disconnected from it.

XVCL shows the most benefit in domains where frequent, unexpected changes occur at both large- and small-granularity levels. In such domains, it is usually difficult to formalize enough abstractions to build generators. In the case where generation solutions exist for certain subdomains, subsystems serviced by generators can be integrated with other subsystems controlled by XVCL. XVCL can also be used to implement generators. A simple example of that was demonstrated in Chapter 10, where we produced many class variants from a small number of x-frames [19,20]. In other projects described in Chapter 13, we produced modules of Web portals from module templates [30,42], patterns of collaborating components implementing various combinations of domain entities, such as User, Task, or Resource, and operations applied to those entities, such as Create or Update, from a small number of pattern templates.

Generators for domain-specific languages can be made to emit x-frameworks, permitting the automatic recustomization of regenerated code. In this way, the system's high-level abstractions remain connected to the executable code throughout its maintenance and evolution. Such solutions have been developed at Netron for Frame Technology™.

14.4 Separation of Concerns and Its Relation to Generic Design

An important class of generative techniques [12] focuses on separation of concerns, a principle introduced by Dijkstra [14] to the software domain in early 1980s. These techniques attempt to bring separation of concerns from the concept level down to the design and implementation levels. Aspect-oriented programming (AOP) [23,24], MDSOC from IBM [37], and AHEAD [5] are the most widely published among such techniques. Separation of concerns helps in maintainability, long-term evolution, and is also conducive to building more generic, reusable software. Although we did not come across applications of techniques based on separation of concerns to solve evolution problems, such as the ones that we studied in this book, both the principle and techniques that help in its realization are most relevant to this book's theme.

A concern can be any area of interest in a program solution, pertinent to functional features, quality requirements, software architecture, detail design, or implementation. The idea of separation of concerns is to break a program into distinct concerns to deal with them separately. As we do so, we try to limit interactions between concerns as much as it is possible. The motivation for separation of concerns is to better cope with complexity, and to achieve the required engineering quality factors such as robustness, adaptability, maintainability, and reusability.

One modular program decomposition cannot give equal importance to localization of all the computational concerns. Therefore, any modular decomposition of a given program can be nicely aligned with only some of the concerns. Such concerns can be localized to a single module (a component, class, or function) or a group of modules (e.g., component layer), exposing an API to its clients. The details of a concern implementation become hidden behind the API [29].

However, other concerns that are not aligned with a given modular decomposition necessarily crosscut modules of primary decomposition (in AOP) and other concerns. Separation of crosscutting concerns, if possible at all, requires unconventional solutions. Generative techniques attempt to separate concerns at a metalevel extra plane. Techniques differ in the nature of that extra plane and in mechanisms used to transform a metalevel representation into concrete components.

As we discussed in Chapter 6, problem domain concerns become intimately and unavoidably interwoven with problem solution concerns in program components.

We also commented on limitations of software componentization induced by that fact. The "configuration knowledge" technique [12] uses unconventional means to achieve separation of these two important concerns, by explicating mappings between the problem domain and the solution spaces.

Other techniques focus on different kinds of concerns, trying to combat their crosscutting effect, to allow for their independent treatment (e.g., maintenance and reuse), and to facilitate composition of concerns.

In AOP, various computational aspects are programmed separately and weaved into the base of conventional program modules of primary decomposition (e.g., classes). Aspect code is weaved into program modules at join points that are specified in a descriptive way. AOP can simply and elegantly separate a range of programming aspects such as synchronization, persistence, security transaction management, or authentication/authorization. Because of such separation, aspects can be easily modified and also added to or deleted from program modules, which automatically become more generic and reusable in different contexts. AOP can be extended to allow for parametric differences among aspect code weaved at different join points [25].

The feature-oriented programming AHEAD technique [5], based on GenVoca [3], attempts to elevate separation of concerns to the level of user-level requirements. Features represent software requirements, but can also refer to any other computational concerns. Features are defined separately as mathematical functions. Programs are produced by refining features and composing them in different combinations. Legal combinations of features are described by a GenVoca grammar. AHEAD models software as a mathematical structure of nested equations, making it possible to study formal properties of refinements and resulting programs.

The trust of the MDSOC approach [37] is separation of concerns to overcome a "tyranny of a dominant decomposition" of programs into functional modules. Among other goals, MDSOC attempts to achieve better alignment of requirements, design, and code [8]. Hyperslices are metalevel abstractions that encapsulate specific concerns and can be composed in various configurations to form custom programs. Hyperslices are written in the underlying programming language and can be composed by merging or overriding program units by name and in many other ways. Compositions yield programs with modified or extended behavior. Unlike in AOP, it is typical for hyperslices to represent functional units.

Situations where concerns occur in programs in many different combinations lead to explosion of look-alike program components. Termed as the "feature combinatorics" problem, the phenomenon was first observed in class libraries [4,6]. Both class libraries and application programs are affected by the symptoms of the "feature combinatorics" problem (as illustrated in Chapter 9 and Chapter 13). Thousands of component versions may be produced in industrial projects as a result of the growing number of features and their mutual dependencies [13]. Program representations that successfully achieve separation of some of the concerns also become more generic, helping to combat explosion of look-alike component versions.

Like AOP, MDSOC, or AHEAD, XVCL offers a mechanism to define alternative program decompositions using unconventional means, at the metalevel extra plane. This extra plane is a mixed-strategy representation formed by XVCL, applied together with programming languages. Although groups of interrelated x-frames often correspond to concerns, analysis of similarity patterns, and design of generic mixed-strategy representations unifying similarity patterns, drive the process of developing a mixed-strategy solution.

XVCL's mechanisms cater to both generic design and separation of concerns. There is an interesting relation between these two principles, which we explain in the following text.

As already noted, program representations that achieve separation of concerns also become more generic, parameterized by other concerns. However, we often observe that concerns become so tightly coupled with one another (or with modules of primary decomposition) that their physical separation becomes unthinkable. For example, performance concern in some real-time systems has a pervasive impact on many design decisions. Although we can conceptualize performance concern (e.g., by documenting design decisions that have to do with performance), "physical" separation of performance concern from functional modules or other concerns that interact with performance may not be feasible. In other systems, where performance strategies are simpler, it may be possible to localize the performance concern in certain modules, or separate it by means of AOP.

We believe many concerns in application domain-specific areas, often referred to as features [5,21], are inseparable, just as performance concern is inseparable in time-critical systems. This was the case of features in the Buffer library (Chapter 9 and Chapter 10), STL, Web portals (ASP and J2EE), DEMS (Chapter 13), and other projects. Situations in which concerns become difficult to separate are important, as they shed light on requirements for techniques to achieve separation of concerns, and possible limits of what we can practically expect from such techniques.

We found that generic design can be a natural extension of separation of concern into the areas where separation of concerns tends to show its limits.

For example, it is difficult to observe the exact impact of features in the Buffer library on class implementation (Chapter 9 and Chapter 10). Here, features are buffer element type, memory allocation scheme, byte ordering, and access mode. Separation of concerns only succeeds in a small number of classes that differ in numeric buffer element types, and then is achieved by type parameterization, which is also a generic design solution. If we continue with similarity analysis from the point where separation of concerns becomes difficult, we can achieve further simplifications. In our analysis described in Chapter 9, we came up with the following seven groups, each containing similar classes:

1. [**T**]Buffer: Seven classes at Level 1 that differ in buffer element type, **T**: Byte, Char, Int, Double, Float, Long, Short
2. Heap[**T**]Buffer: Seven classes at Level 2, that differ in buffer element type, **T**

3. Heap[**T**]BufferR: Seven read-only classes at Level 3
4. Direct[**T**]Buffer[**S|U**]: Thirteen classes at Level 2 for combinations of buffer element type, **T**, with byte orderings: **S** — nonnative or **U** — native byte ordering (note that byte ordering is not relevant to buffer element type "Byte")
5. Direct[**T**]BufferR[**S|U**]: Thirteen read-only classes at Level 3 for combinations of parameters **T**, **S**, and **U**, as above
6. ByteBufferAs[**T**]Buffer[**B|L**]: Twelve classes at Level 2 for combinations of buffer element type, **T**, with byte orderings: **B** — Big_Endian or **L** — Little_Endian
7. ByteBufferAs[**T**]BufferR[**B|L**]: Twelve read-only classes at Level 3 for combinations of parameters **T**, **B**, and **L**, as above.

We can unify classes in each group with a generic mixed-strategy Java/XVCL representation (Chapter 10). The preceding seven groups of similar classes are clearly organized around concerns: each group is characterized by concerns that vary across classes in a group, and yet other concerns that are fixed. Mixed-strategy representation improves the visibility of concerns, owing to groupings of similar classes into groups, but here the separation of concerns is less systematic, only as much as is practically possible. Therefore, focusing on unifying similarity patterns with generic design representations, we also do selective and imperfect separation of concerns.

The concept of similarity is less formal than a concept of cleanly separated concern. It is easier to find similarities than to spot the exact impact of concerns. Focusing on similarities is more pragmatic, as we do not even have to fully understand the exact nature of a given concern or complex interactions among the concerns. Instead, we stay at the level of observing the symptoms of net effect of concern interactions. We can use a clone detector [2] together with top-down domain analysis to zoom into similarity areas that are significant.

Experiences from other projects confirm these observations. We believe the principles of separation of concerns and generic design are intimately interrelated and can be applied in a synergistic way.

At the level of actual mechanisms, unlike in other approaches, XVCL's compositions are defined in an operational way and take place at designated program points marked with <**adapt**>, <**break**>, and other XVCL commands. Concerns encapsulated in x-frames, in areas where separation of concerns with XVCL is feasible, are unconstrained, in the sense that they may overlap with one another or form concern hierarchies, as one concern may contain other concerns. XVCL's concerns can be parameterized (e.g., via XVCL expressions or <**select**> commands), which further enhances the programmer's ability to define variations in code at any level of granularity that is required, from a single program statement to a component or subsystem. It is the right collection of mechanisms and rules (described in Chapter 8) that gives XVCL its unique power to solve engineering problems posed by software evolution and reuse.

XVCL is a lower-level language than AOP, hyperspaces, or AHEAD. It is an assembly language of program manipulation and synthesis. XVCL's explicit and direct articulation is the source of its expressive power, but also the source of its weakness, as x-frames may become overly verbose. Currently, we address this problem with tools that reveal simplified, abstract views of x-frames. In the future, we hope to discover mixed-strategy abstractions that will allow us to define higher-level forms of XVCL, equally expressive but free of current pitfalls.

14.5 Conclusions

Each technique has its own merits, and allows developers to meet specific engineering goals, in specific situations. For different types of problems, AOP, MDSOC, AHEAD, or XVCL may yield the simplest, and most elegant and useful solution. It is essential to understand the strengths and limitations of a technique, trade-offs involved in its application, and possibly ways of using techniques in a synergistic combination to best meet the engineering goals at hand.

References

1. ANSI and AJPO Military Standard: Ada Programming Language, ANSI/MIL-STD-1815A-1983, February 17.
2. Basit, H.A., Rajapakse, D.C., and Jarzabek, S., Beyond templates: a study of clones in the STL and some general implications, *International Conference Software Engineering, ICSE'05*, St. Louis, MO, May 2005, pp. 451–459.
3. Bassett, P., *Framing Software Reuse — Lessons From Real World*, Yourdon Press, Prentice Hall, 1997.
4. Batory, D., Singhai, V., Sirkin, M., and Thomas, J., Scalable software libraries, *ACM SIGSOFT'93: Symposium on the Foundations of Software Engineering*, Los Angeles, CA, December 1993, pp. 191–199.
5. Batory, D., Sarvela, J.N., and Rauschmayer, A., Scaling step-wise refinement, *Proceedings of the International Conference on Software Engineering, ICSE'03*, May 2003, Portland, OR, pp. 187–197.
6. Biggerstaff, T., The library scaling problem and the limits of concrete component reuse, *3rd International Conference on Software Reuse, ICSR'94*, 1994, pp. 102–109.
7. Brooks, P.B., *The Mythical Man-Month*, Addison-Wesley, 1995.
8. Clarke, S., Harrison, W., Ossher, H., and Tarr, P., Subject-oriented design: toward improved alignment of requirements, design, and code, *Proceedings of the 14th Conference on Object-Oriented Programming, Systems, Languages, and Applications OOPSLA'99*, Denver, CO, November 1999, pp. 325–339.
9. Clements, P. and Northrop, L., *Software Product Lines: Practices and Patterns*, Addison-Wesley, 2002.
10. Conradi, R. and Westfechtel, B., Version models for software configuration management, *ACM Computing Surveys*, 30(2), 232–282, 1998.

11. Cordy, J.R., Comprehending reality: practical challenges to software maintenance automation, *Proceedings of the 11th IEEE International Workshop on Program Comprehension, (IWPC 2003)*, pp. 196–206.

12. Czarnecki, K. and Eisenecker, U., *Generative Programming: Methods, Tools, and Applications*, Addison-Wesley, 2000.

13. Deelstra, S., Sinnema, M., and Bosch, J., Experiences in software product families: problems and issues during product derivation, *Proceedings of the Software Product Lines Conference, SPLC3*, Boston, MA, August 2004, LNCS 3154, Springer-Verlag, pp. 165–182.

14. Dijkstra, E.W., On the role of scientific thought, *Selected Writings on Computing: A Personal Perspective*, Springer-Verlag, New York, 1982, pp. 60–66.

15. Emrich, M., Generative programming using frame technology, Diploma thesis, University of Applied Sciences Kaiserslautern, Department of Computer Science and Micro-System Engineering, July 29, 2003.

16. Gamma, E., Helm, R., Johnson, R., and Vlissides, J., *Design Patterns — Elements of Reusable Object-Oriented Software*, Addison-Wesley, 1995.

17. Garcia, R., Jarvi, J., Lumsdaine, A., Siek, J., and Willcock, J., A comparative study of language support for generic programming, *Proceedings of the 18th Conference on Object-Oriented Programming, Systems, Languages, and Applications*, 2003, pp. 115–134.

18. Goguen, J.A., Parameterized programming, *IEEE Transactions on Software Engineering*, SE-10(5), 528–543, September 1984.

19. Jarzabek, S. and Li, S., Eliminating redundancies with a "composition with adaptation" meta-programming technique, *Proceedings of the ESEC-FSE'03, European Software Engineering Conference and ACM SIGSOFT Symposium on the Foundations of Software Engineering*, September 2003, Helsinki, pp. 237–246.

20. Jarzabek, S. and Li, S., Unifying clones with a generative programming technique: a case study, *Journal of Software Maintenance and Evolution: Research and Practice*, 18(4), July–August 2006, pp. 267–292.

21. Kang, K. et al., Feature-Oriented Domain Analysis (FODA) Feasibility Study, Technical Report, CMU/SEI-90-TR-21, Software Engineering Institute, CMU, Pittsburgh, November 1990.

22. Karhinen, A., Ran, A., and Tallgren, T., Configuring designs for reuse, *Proceedings of the International Conference on Software Engineering, ICSE'97*, Boston, MA, 1997, pp. 701–710.

23. Kiczales, G, Lamping, J., Mendhekar, A., Maeda, C., Lopes, C., Loingtier, J-M., and Irwin, J., Aspect-oriented programming, *European Conference on Object-Oriented Programming*, Finland, Springer-Verlag LNCS 1241, 1997, pp. 220–242.

24. Kiczales, G., Hilsdale, E., Hugunin, J., Kersten, M., Palm, J., and Griswold, W., An overview of AspectJ, *Proceedings of 15th European Conference on Object-Oriented Programming*, Budapest, Hungary, June 18–22, 2001, Lecture Notes in Computer Science, 2072, pp. 327–353.

25. Loughran, N., Rashid, A., Zhang, W., and Jarzabek, S., Supporting product line evolution with framed aspects, *3rd AOSD Workshop on Aspects, Components, and Patterns for Infrastructure Software, ACP4IS'04*, March 22–26, 2004, Lancaster, U.K.

26. Mesbah, A. and van Deursen, A., Crosscutting concerns in J2EE applications, *Proceedings of the 7th IEEE International Symposium on Web Site Evolution, WSE'05*, Budapest, Hungary, September 2005, pp. 14–21.

27. Meyer, B., *Object-Oriented Software Construction*, Prentice-Hall, London, 1988.

28. Musser, D. and Saini, A., *STL Tutorial and Reference Guide: C++ Programming with Standard Template Library*, Addison-Wesley, Reading, MA.

29. Parnas, D., On the Criteria To Be Used in Decomposing Software into Modules, *Communications of the ACM*, 15(12), December 1972, pp.1053–1058.

30. Pettersson, U. and Jarzabek, S., Industrial experience with building a Web portal product line using a lightweight, reactive approach, *ESEC-FSE'05, European Software Engineering Conference and ACM SIGSOFT Symposium on the Foundations of Software Engineering*, ACM Press, September 2005, Lisbon, pp. 326–335.

31. Prieto-Diaz, R., Domain analysis for reusability, *Proceedings of the COMPSAC'87*, October 1987, Tokyo, Japan, pp. 23–29.

32. Rajapakse, D. and Jarzabek, S., An investigation of cloning in Web portals, *International Conference on Web Engineering, ICWE'05*, July 2005, Sydney, pp. 252–262.

33. Shaw, M. and Garlan, D., *Software Architecture: Perspectives on Emerging Discipline*, Prentice Hall, 1996.

34. Smaragdakis, Y. and Batory, D., Application generators, in *Software Engineering volume of the Encyclopedia of Electrical and Electronics Engineering*, Webster, J., Ed., John Wiley and Sons, 2000.

35. Soe, M.S., Zhang, H., and Jarzabek, S., XVCL: a tutorial, *Proceedings of the 14th International Conference on Software Engineering and Knowledge Engineering, SEKE'02*, ACM Press, July 2002, Italy, pp. 341–349.

36. STL, http://www.sgi.com/tech/stl/.

37. Tarr, P., Ossher, H., Harrison, W., and Sutton, S., N degrees of separation: multidimensional separation of concerns, *Proceedings of the International Conference on Software Engineering, ICSE'99*, Los Angeles, CA, 1999, pp. 107–119.

38. Tichy, W., Tools for software configuration management, *Proceedings of the International Workshop on Software Configuration Management*, Grassau, 1988, Teubner Verlag, pp. 1–20.

39. Thompson, S., Higher Order + Polymorphic = Reusable, unpublished manuscript available from the Computing Laboratory, University of Kent, http://www.cs.ukc.ac.uk/pubs/1997.

40. Zhang, H.Y., Jarzabek, S., and Soe, M.S., XVCL approach to separating concerns in product family assets, *Proceedings of the Generative and Component-based Software Engineering (GCSE 2001)*, Erfurt, Germany, September 2001, pp. 36–47.

41. XVCL (XML-based variant configuration language) method and tool for managing software changes during evolution and reuse, http://fxvcl.sourceforge.net.

42. Yang, J. and Jarzabek, S., Applying a generative technique for enhanced reuse on J2EE platform, *4th International Conference on Generative Programming and Component Engineering, GPCE'05*, September 29–October 1, 2005, Tallinn, pp. 237–255.

Chapter 15

Evaluation of the Mixed-Strategy Approach

Chapter Summary

We start by summarizing the salient features of the mixed-strategy approach and describing a typical project application scenario. Then, we evaluate trade-offs involved in adopting this approach.

15.1 Summary of the Mixed-Strategy Approach

Mixed-strategy supports generic design and enhances software changeability. The main motivation for building a mixed-strategy solution is to exploit opportunities offered by similarity patterns. By doing this, we gain extra levels of changeability, which matters in maintenance, and genericity, which matters in reuse. From the mixed-strategy perspective, there is no difference between maintainability and reusability. Change specifications and generic design mechanisms address these two important software engineering goals, which are difficult to achieve in practice, in a unified, simple, yet effective way.

Mixed-strategy is meant for developers and maintainers of complex, evolving software systems. It is applied on top of conventional programs, in synergy with design techniques supported with current programming paradigms and component platforms (such as .NET™ or J2EE™). The main idea behind mixed-strategy is to separate concerns related to genericity and changeability, from the concerns of how programs are designed and implemented in terms of class/component architecture, platforms used, or required program runtime characteristics. By extending programs with XVCL, we deal with issues of generic design and change, without conflicts with — and in separation from — other programming concerns.

The main benefit of mixed-strategy is to avoid implementing similar concepts repeatedly, and to ease changes. The expected return on investment in applying mixed-strategy is from savings on program maintenance, long-term evolution, or better reuse.

15.2   The Mixed-Strategy Process

The design of a software component architecture, and at least partial implementation of components, is a prerequisite for building a mixed-strategy solution. The reason for that is that although some of the similarity patterns are inherent in an application domain, many others become evident as we design and implement a program. Furthermore, the intended architecture and components of programs to be supported by a mixed-strategy solution influence the structure of that solution. Therefore, the architecture must be envisioned first.

In the following text, we describe how we designed a mixed-strategy solution for buffer classes, and then outline a project scenario for reengineering an existing program into a mixed-strategy solution. To make the process description more meaningful, we have annotated specific process steps with remarks on methodological guidelines.

15.2.1   Arriving at the Mixed-Strategy Solution for the Buffer Library

To build a Java/XVCL generic representation for the Buffer library, we first gained a general understanding of buffer classes by manual domain analysis [20]. At the time of the first experiment, no clone detection tools were available to us. Owing to the small size of the library and its clear design, manual analysis was relatively simple. We aimed at design-level similarities (structural clones) and similar code fragments (simple clones). We identified groups of classes that we suspected would be similar. We examined methods and attribute declarations within each group which confirmed that there was much similarity among classes. We designed metacomponents for each group of classes, eliminating redundant code fragments as follows: For each group of similar fragments, we created a suitable metafragment. As for metafragments that appeared in different contexts with changes, we parameterized them with metavariables, <**break**> points, <**select**>, <**insert**>, <**adapt**>, and other XVCL commands to cater to required variations. Finally, we incorporated suitable adaptation commands to the corresponding metaclasses and SPC. It took ten days for one person, with no prior knowledge of the Buffer library but with good knowledge of XVCL, to complete the job.

15.2.2 Reengineering of the Existing Program into a Mixed-Strategy Representation

The objectives were to simplify a library/program by enhancing its genericity and changeability; enhance visibility and automate adaptive changes involved in customization of generic solutions; reuse similar design solutions within the scope of a library or program; and design generic program solutions for possible reuse in other programs. To do this, the following steps were required:

1. Apply one of the clone detection tools [3,4,11,17] to identify the extent of cloning in the subject program.

   Remark: Most current clone detectors find only similar code fragments differing in parametric ways (e.g., in variable names, keywords, or operators). This is not enough to identify design-level similarities (e.g., similar classes in the Buffer library). Clone Miner [3] applies data mining heuristics to infer possible design-level similarities.

2. Analyze the application domain to identify design-level similarity patterns.

   Remark: Design-level similarity patterns result in recurring program structures that may involve a number of collaborating classes. Unification of such structures is very beneficial for maintainability. It is essential to complement bottom-up semiautomated analysis of clones with manual top-down domain analysis: the top-down domain analysis and the bottom-up analysis of clones feed each other with useful inputs.

3. Analyze the subject program to identify design-level program structures that exhibit significant similarity.

   Remark: Typically, there will be much cloning among such structures. Other structures may implement similar analysis or design concepts with variants.

4. Identify program areas that are heavily maintained and select critical areas for reengineering.

5. Reengineer the subject program incrementally to form a mixed-strategy solution. In each iteration, build a partial mixed-strategy generic solution to unify selected groups of similar program structures.

   Remark: A mixed-strategy solution must be carefully designed, and iterations must be planned accordingly to minimize the effort of refining the solution (refining the solution is analogous to refactoring of a conventional program [12]). Although some rework is unavoidable, we found that focusing on design-level, large-granularity similarity patterns (as opposed to simple clones) leads to relatively stable mixed-strategy solutions. Smaller-granularity similarities are then dealt in the context of generic solutions for design-level similarities.

6. Future maintenance is done via the mixed-strategy solution, which never becomes disconnected from the base code.

15.3 Trade-Offs Involved in Applying the Mixed-Strategy Approach

Adopting and applying techniques such as XVCL does not come for free. Bringing in a new technique necessarily entails cost and involves trade-offs. Therefore, to be attractive, a new technique must solve some important engineering problems that cannot be solved otherwise, providing benefits that outweigh the cost. In the attempt to meet this challenge, XVCL provides strong capabilities for designing generic, highly adaptable structures, with full automation and visibility of adaptive changes at the architecture, detailed-design, and code levels. The source of XVCL's expressive power is that mixed-strategy representation is unrestricted by the rules of the underlying programming language. The inherent dangers of moving beyond the level strictly controlled by a programming language are mitigated by maintaining 100 percent integration between mixed-strategy representation and program structures, and by keeping XVCL simple.

In this section, we evaluate the trade-offs involved in applying the mixed-strategy approach.

15.3.1 Strengths

A mixed-strategy representation displays a clear view of commonalities and differences among program structures within or across programs. XVCL generic structures can unify a similarity patterns at any abstraction level, from design to code, and of any granularity — from a subsystem, to component, to class, and to program statement in class implementation. We can specify almost arbitrary differences among similar program structures. This enhanced genericity is due to the unrestricted parameterization mechanism, which, unlike conventional generics [13], is decoupled from the language core: The overall generic design solution is decomposed into a hierarchy of parameterized metacomponents called x-frames. Mixed-strategy representation partitioning is parallel to partitioning of a program along component boundaries (at the architecture level) and class, function/method, and statement boundaries (at the program level). The boundaries of mixed-strategy partitioning are not restricted by rules of a programming language or the semantics of a programming problem being solved. The boundaries are solely dictated by the concerns of generic design.

We can achieve genericity at the level of mixed-strategy representation, if it is so required for ease of maintenance, and still keep clones in executable programs, which is often unavoidable [8,14–16,19].

Mixed-strategy representation is also operational: The XVCL processor instantiates generic structures and automates the process of deriving specific, custom programs from the generic representation, based on the specification of the required properties of the program that is needed.

An important principle of XVCL design is clean separation of various sources of change affecting a program. Each source of change (e.g., a combination of features in our earlier examples) can be traced to codes affected by this change. Non-redundancy of a mixed-strategy representation reduces the number of points at which affected classes must be modified. Changes done to one x-frame consistently propagate to all the contexts in which the x-frame is adapted. If the impact of change is not uniform in all such contexts, the exceptions can be handled at the specific adaptation point, without directly modifying the code fragment involved. X-frames explicitly reflect the impact of change on program elements. The traceability information is helpful in program understanding and maintenance.

The mixed-strategy approach shows its strength when addressing changes (or variant features in a product line) that have a global impact on a system. The impact of such variants cannot be localized into a single component identified through conventional modularization approaches such as object-oriented analysis and design. We accommodate these variants into metacomponents by parameterizing components for change, and by designing lower-level metacomponents that absorb the impact of variants. As is often the case, changes (or variant features) affect many metacomponents. The XVCL processor automatically propagates changes to all the affected components, saving programmers the trouble of manually repeating routine changes.

The need for genericity and change arises in any application domain. Mixed-strategy concepts apply to any domain and any programming language. XVCL distills these concepts into a minimum set of domain-independent and language-independent rules that, in a very simplified way, can be described as a "composition with adaptation" mechanism, capable of selecting software building blocks and composing them after suitable adaptations. Depending on the level of abstraction and the goal of generic design, a "software building block" may mean a subsystem, a component, component interface, class, function, or any other element that is useful in software construction. These concepts are universal, and in one form or another appear in any application domain and implementation technique.

The XVCL solution is transparent — a programmer can intervene in any detail of the transition from the metalevel to programs. This allows XVCL to circumvent the problem of the techniques based on abstractions disconnected from the base code, which maintenance programmers find difficult to work with [8].

XVCL complements rather than competes with programming language constructs and conventional design techniques: a developer using his or her favorite programming language and design technique can fall back on XVCL to tackle problems that cannot be easily solved at the program level. Therefore, the XVCL solution can be neatly integrated into other programming methodologies and environments.

15.3.2 Weaknesses and How They Are Addressed

Despite those benefits, two-level design — in terms of programming language and XVCL — has its difficulties. Mixed-strategy introduces extra steps into the conventional software development process and requires developers to embed usual program solutions into generic design structures. Therefore, the development of a mixed-strategy solution takes longer than the development of a conventional program, which is generally expected for the design of generic, reusable solutions. The feedback from our industry partner indicates that, in practice, the benefit of being able to deal with complexity at two levels outweighs the cost of the added complexity [14]: the learning curve and development effort of an XVCL solution can be reasonable even for large programs (provided an XVCL expert is also familiar with the application domain and the program itself). At the same time, the return on investment may be quick and substantial. In the case of the Buffer library study, it took at most ten days for a skilled XVCL developer with no prior knowledge of the Buffer library to analyze buffer classes and develop a Java/XVCL mixed-strategy solution. We are collecting further empirical evidence to better assess the trade-offs involved.

It is more difficult to understand a generic mixed-strategy representation than a concrete program. It is also difficult to validate a mixed-strategy representation, as we can derive many concrete programs from it. These problems can be mitigated by skillful design and by tools. The mixed-strategy representation can be organized into a layered architecture, based on the usual principles of the abstraction and separation of concerns. "Good design" can minimize the scope of a metaprogram that has to be analyzed at any time. As lower-level x-frames become stable and reliable over time, potential errors tend to be located only in the topmost, context-specific, and still fragile metacomponents. In a mixed-strategy representation, patterns of similar, recurring program structures (such as groups of similar buffer classes) are represented in a generic way. A single x-frame provides a window into multiple program structures (pattern instances), that can be obtained from a generic solution.

Could we do better by raising the level of abstraction of XVCL? We consider the current form of XVCL an assembly language of change specifications. XVCL contains the minimum constructs to specify any type of changes, but specifications can get tedious and overly complex. We have considered adopting specified composition points, such as joint points in aspect-oriented programming [18], in addition to composition points explicitly marked with <**break**> commands. This can simplify specification of changes in certain cases. However, at this point we do not know how to raise the level of abstraction without compromising the expressive

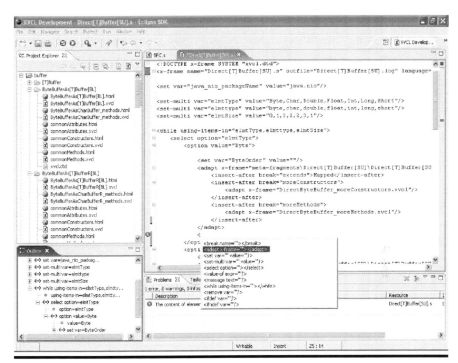

Figure 15.1   A snapshot of the XVCL Workbench.

power of the current change mechanism. In the future, we hope to discover meta-level abstractions that will allow us to define higher-level forms of XVCL, equally expressive but free of current pitfalls. Domain-specific abstract specifications are certainly useful and application generators exemplify neat solutions that can be obtained in that way. Although the approach works fine in narrow application domains, it does not scale to general programming paradigms in which we cannot make assumptions about the semantics of the underlying domain. Abstract specifications are intellectually appealing, but they can get easily disconnected from the actual code. In the case of change specification, such discontinuity is undesirable for practical reasons [8].

As applying mixed-strategy is not an "all-win" situation, it is essential to apply qualitative and quantitative evaluations of the results. This can be done by (1) conducting controlled experiments in which two teams perform the same program modifications using traditional and mixed-strategy approaches; (2) comparing the productivity index achieved with mixed-strategy against an industry productivity index (such as described in Reference 1); (3) analytical argumentation; and (4) metrics-based evaluation of equivalent program solutions developed using different techniques. The limitation of method 1 is that differences in productivity among programmers participating in experiments may significantly influence the results. Method 2 can be used for mature technologies for which much experimental data

326 ■ *Effective Software Maintenance and Evolution*

is already available (for example, original frames from Netron, Inc., have been assessed in that way [1]). Method 3 is always required, as it explains the rationale for the expected benefits of the technique and its pitfalls.

We use analytical argumentation, metrics (e.g., physical size and conceptual complexity), and controlled experiments (e.g., to evaluate effort involved in changes) to assess mixed-strategy solutions.

15.4   XVCL Workbench

Tools may considerably simplify application of mixed-strategy. In our laboratory, we are developing an XVCL IDE called XVCL Workbench that helps in editing, visualizing, debugging, and static analysis of x-frameworks (Figure 15.1). XVCL Workbench helps developers to browse and analyze x-frameworks (in the Project Explorer window) and x-frames (in the Outline Window) structures in XML-free format. The upper right-hand window shows an x-frame in raw XML format. In the future, a developer will be able to query properties of x-frames, and run the processor in debugging mode. XVCL Workbench is implemented as a plug-in to the Eclipse platform.

References

1. Bassett, P., Framing *Software Reuse — Lessons from the Real World*, Yourdon Press, Prentice Hall, Englewood Cliffs, NJ, 1997.
2. Basit, H.A., Rajapakse, D.C., and Jarzabek, S., Beyond templates: a study of clones in the STL and some general implications, *International Conference on Software Engineering, ICSE'05*, St. Louis, MO, May 2005, pp. 451–459.
3. Basit, A.H. and Jarzabek, S., Detecting higher-level similarity patterns in programs, *ESEC-FSE'05, European Software Engineering Conference and ACM SIGSOFT Symposium on the Foundations of Software Engineering*, ACM Press, September 2005, Lisbon, pp. 156–165.
4. Baxter, I., Yahin, A., Moura, L., Sant'Anna, M., and Bier, L., Clone detection using abstract syntax trees, *Proceedings of the International Conference on Software Maintenance 1998*, pp. 368–377.
5. Bosch, J., *Design and Use of Software Architectures — Adopting and Evolving a Product-Line Approach*, Addison-Welsey, Harlow, UK, 2000.
6. Brooks, P.B., The *Mythical Man-Month*, Addison-Welsey, Boston, 1995.
7. Clements, P. and Northrop, L., *Software Product Lines: Practices and Patterns*, Addison-Welsey, Boston, 2002.
8. Cordy, J.R., Comprehending reality: practical challenges to software maintenance automation, *Proceedings of the 11th IEEE International Workshop on Program Comprehension*, (IWPC 2003), pp. 196–206.

9. Czarnecki, K. and Eisenecker, U., *Generative Programming: Methods, Tools, and Applications*, Addison-Wesley, 2000.

10. Deelstra, S., Sinnema, M., and Bosch, J., Experiences in software product families: problems and issues during product derivation, *Proceedings of the Software Product Lines Conference, SPLC3*, Boston, MA, August 200.

11. Ducasse, S., Rieger, M., and Demeyer, S., A language independent approach for detecting duplicated code, *International Conference on Software Maintenance, ICSM'99*, September 1999, Oxford, pp. 109–118.

12. Fowler, M., *Refactoring — Improving the Design of Existing Code*, Addison-Wesley, 1999.

13. Garcia, R., Jarvi, J., Lumsdaine, A., Siek, J., and Willcock, J., A comparative study of language support for generic programming, *Proceedings of the 18th ACM SIGPLAN Conference on Object-oriented Programming, Systems, Languages, and Applications*, 2003, pp. 115–134.

14. Jarzabek, S. and Li, S., Eliminating redundancies with a "composition with adaptation" meta-programming technique, *Proceedings of the ESEC-FSE'03, European Software Engineering Conference and ACM SIGSOFT Symposium on the Foundations of Software Engineering*, September 2003, Helsinki, pp. 237–246.

15. Jarzabek, S. and Li, S., Unifying clones with a generative programming technique: a case study, *Journal of Software Maintenance and Evolution: Research and Practice*, 18(4), 267–292, July–August 2006.

16. Jarzabek, S., Genericity — a "missing in action" key to software simplification and reuse, to appear in *13th Asia-Pacific Software Engineering Conference, APSEC'06*, IEEE Computer Society Press, December 6–8, 2006, Bangalore, India.

17. Kamiya, T., Kusumoto, S., and Inoue, K., CCFinder: a multi-linguistic token-based code clone detection system for large scale source code, *IEEE Transactions on Software Engineering*, 28(7), 2002, pp. 654–670.

18. Kiczales, G., Lamping, J., Mendhekar, A., Maeda, C., Lopes, C., Loingtier, J-M., and Irwin, J., Aspect-oriented programming, *European Conference on Object-Oriented Programming*, Finland, Springer-Verlag LNCS 1241, 1997, pp. 220–242.

19. Kim, M., Bergman, L., Lau, T., and Notkin, D., An Ethnographic study of copy and paste programming practices in OOPL, *Proceedings of the International Symposium on Empirical Software Engineering, ISESE'04*, August 2004, Redondo Beach, CA, pp. 83–92.

20. Pettersson, U. and Jarzabek, S., Industrial experience with building a web portal product line using a lightweight, reactive approach, *ESEC-FSE'05, European Software Engineering Conference and ACM SIGSOFT Symposium on the Foundations of Software Engineering*, ACM Press, September 2005, Lisbon, pp. 326–335.

21. XVCL (XML-based variant configuration language) method and tool for managing software changes during evolution and reuse, http://fxvcl.sourceforge.net.

22. Yang, J. and Jarzabek, S., Applying a generative technique for enhanced reuse on J2EE platform, *4th International Conference on Generative Programming and Component Engineering, GPCE'05*, September 29–October 1, 2005, Tallinn, Estonia, pp. 237–255.

Chapter 16

Conclusions

The mixed-strategy approach to software maintenance and evolution emphasizes reuse of knowledge of past changes to implement new changes. Explicit representation of this knowledge in executable form is hardly possible at the level of contemporary programs. Mixed-strategy uses the generative technique of XVCL to facilitate explicit handling of design-level alternatives in a visible executable form. The name "mixed-strategy" is appropriate because it relies on conventional program languages and design techniques to define a core of program solutions, falling back on XVCL to handle issues related to changes and to the overall control over component versions and system releases produced during evolution. Reuse-based evolution is achieved by systematically identifying software similarity patterns and unifying them with generic, adaptable mixed-strategy software representations.

The mixed-strategy approach addresses design issues that are poorly supported by today's programming paradigms. We believe that the full potential of this simple yet powerful approach is yet to be discovered.

Appendix A: Summary of *PQL* Grammar Rules

Lexical tokens are written in capital letters (e.g., LETTER, INTEGER, STRING). Keywords are between *apostrophes* (e.g., 'procedure'). Nonterminals are in small letters.

Meta symbols:
    a* — repetition 0 or more times of "a"
    a+ —- repetition 1 or more times of "a"
    a | b   — a or b
    brackets (and) — used for grouping

Lexical rules:
    LETTER : A-Z | a-z — capital or small letter
    DIGIT : 0-9
    IDENT : LETTER (LETTER | DIGIT)* — procedure names and variables
        are strings of letters and digits, starting with a letter
    INTEGER : DIGIT+
    STRING : ' " ' (LETTER | DIGIT)+ ' " '
    CONST : STRING | INTEGER

Auxiliary grammar rules:
    tuple : elem | '<' elem (',' elem)* '>'
    elem : synonym | attrRef
    synonym, attrName: IDENT
    entRef : synonym | '_' | STRING
    stmtRef : synonym | '_' | INTEGER
    lineRef : synonym | '_' | INTEGER

Grammar rules for select clause:

select-cl : declaration* **Select** result (with-cl | suchthat-cl | pattern-cl)*

declaration : IDENT synonym (',' synonym)* ';'

result : tuple | 'BOOLEAN'

with-cl : **with** attrCond

suchthat-cl : **such that** relCond

pattern-cl : **pattern** patternCond

attrCond : attrCompare ('**and**' attrCompare) *

attrCompare : attrRef '=' ref

attrRef : synonym '.' attrName

ref : CONST | attrRef

relCond : relRef ('**and**' relRef) *

relRef : ModifiesP | ModifiesS | UsesP | UsesS | Calls | CallsT |
        Parent | ParentT | Follows | FollowsT | Next | NextT | Affects | AffectsT

ModifiesP : 'Modifies' '('entRef ',' entRef ')'

ModifiesS : 'Modifies' '('stmtRef ',' entRef ')'

UsesP : 'Uses' '('entRef ',' entRef ')'

UsesS : 'Uses' '('stmtRef ',' entRef ')'

Calls : 'Calls' '('entRef ',' entRef ')'

CallsT : 'Calls*' '('entRef ',' entRef ')'

Parent : 'Parent' '('stmtRef ',' stmtRef ')'

ParentT : 'Parent*' '('stmtRef ',' stmtRef ')'

Follows : 'Follows' '('stmtRef ',' stmtRef ')'

FolowsT : 'Follows*' '('stmtRef ',' stmtRef ')'

Next : 'Next' '(' lineRef ',' lineRef ')'

NextT : 'Next*' '(' lineRef ',' lineRef ')'

Affects : 'Affects' '('stmtRef ',' stmtRef ')'

AffectsT : 'Affects*' '('stmtRef ',' stmtRef ')'

patternCond : pattern ('**and**' pattern)*

pattern : assign | while | if

assign : synonym '(' entRef ',' sub-expression | '_' ')'

    // 'synonym' above must be of type 'assign'

    // sub-expression is described in the query examples

if : synonym '(' entRef ',' '_' ',' '_' ')'

    // 'synonym' above must be of type 'if'

while : synonym '(' entRef ',' '_' ')'

    // 'synonym' above must be of type 'while'

Appendix B: Program Design Models for COBOL85

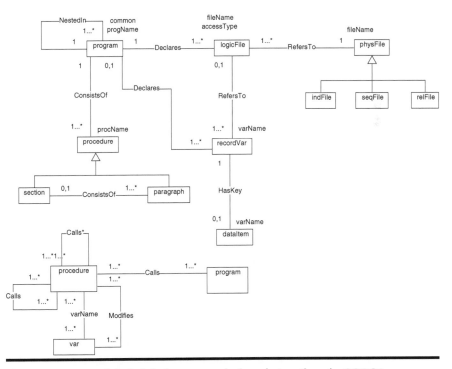

Figure B.1   A model of global program design abstractions in COBOL.

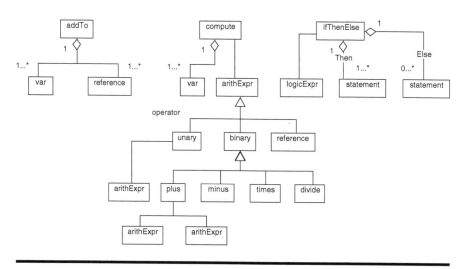

Figure B.2   A model of abstract syntax structure for COBOL statements.

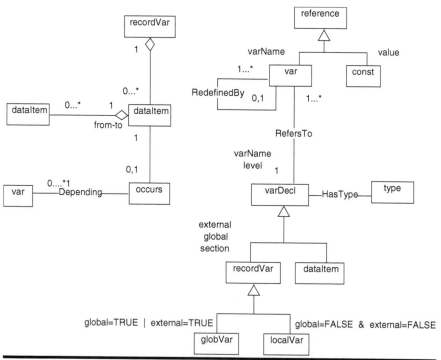

Figure B.3   A model of abstract syntax structure for COBOL records and references.

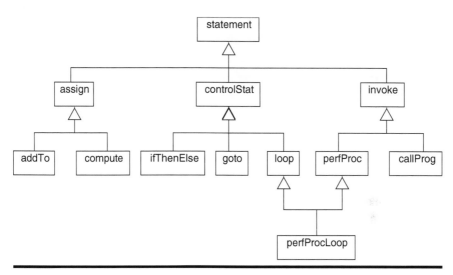

Figure B.4 Classification of COBOL statements.

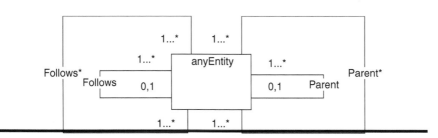

Figure B.5 Program nesting structure definition.

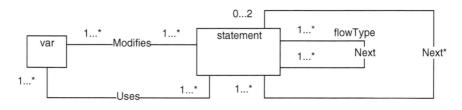

Figure B.6   Detailed program design (a).

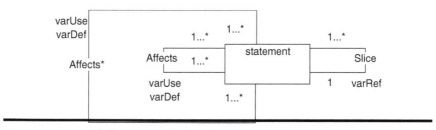

Figure B.7   Detailed program design (b).

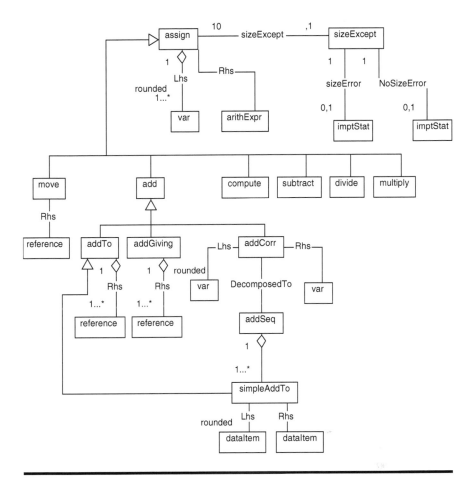

Figure B.8   COBOL assignments statements.

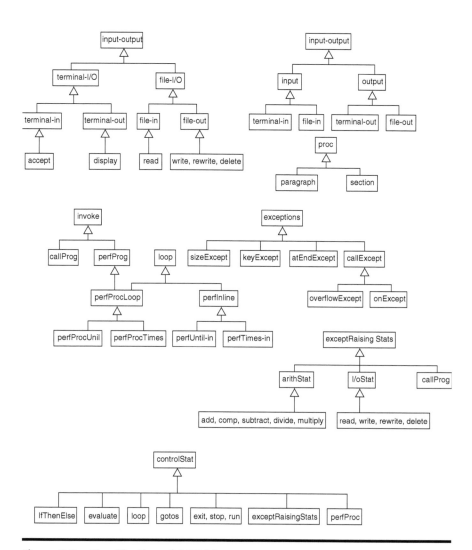

Figure B.9 Classification of COBOL statements.

Appendix C: XVCL Specifications — A Reference Manual

C.1 XVCL Overview

When developing an XML-based variant configuration language (XVCL) solution, we partition a problem description (e.g., a software program) into generic, adaptable metacomponents called *x-frames*. Each x-frame contains a fragment of the problem description called *textual content*. The textual content is written in a base language, which can be a programming language such as Java, a natural language such as English, or any other language. Although the base language is Java for the examples presented in this manual, we stress that the basic principle of applying XVCL to managing variants in problems described in other base languages remains the same.

Textual content in x-frames is instrumented with XVCL commands for change. XVCL commands mark the anticipated variation points (also called "hot spots") in x-frames, injecting flexibility into their textual contents. XVCL can be seen as a metalanguage whose commands direct adaptation of x-frames. The x-frame adaptation process includes x-frame composition and customization.

X-frames related by <**adapt**> commands form an x-framework. If you use XVCL to support software product lines, then an x-framework will form your product line architecture. The specification x-frame, SPC for short, specifies what variant requirements you need in a specific system, a product line member. The SPC specifies how to adapt the x-framework to accommodate required variants.

The SPC becomes the root of an x-framework. During x-frame processing, the XVCL processor interprets the XVCL commands contained in the SPC, traverses an x-framework, performs adaptation by executing XVCL commands embedded in x-frames, and emits code components for a specific system, a member of the product line.

C.1.1 Defining the Processing Flow

The XVCL processor starts processing with an SPC. XVCL commands in the SPC, and in each subsequently **<adapt>**ed x-frame, are processed in the sequence they appear in the x-frame. Whenever the processor encounters an **<adapt>** command in the currently processed x-frame, processing of the current x-frame is suspended and the processor will start processing the **<adapt>**ed x-frame. Once processing of the **<adapt>**ed x-frame is completed, the processor resumes processing of the current x-frame. When the XVCL processor reaches the end of the SPC, the processing is completed. Figure C.1a and Figure C.1b illustrate an x-framework and the processing flow.

As the XVCL processor reads through x-frames and interprets XVCL commands, it also emits the output according to the semantics of the XVCL commands, as described in this document.

The only exception to the preceding processing flow is when the processor interprets insert commands in **<adapt>** bodies, as explained in Section C.7.

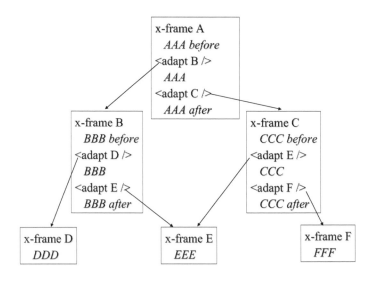

Figure C.1a   An x-framework (B, C, D, E, and F) and SPC (A).

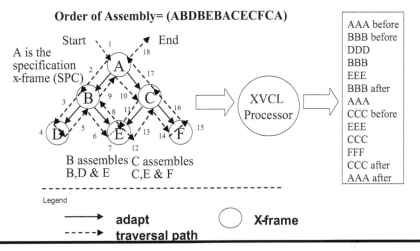

Figure C.1b   Processing an x-framework.

For a given SPC, the processing flow is a trace that goes through the content of visited x-frames (starting with SPC). Suppose p1 and p2 are two points — not necessarily distinct — in the same or different x-frames. We say that:

> p1 **precedes** p2 (and p2 **follows** p1) if p1 appears before p2 in the processing flow. We use notation: p1 → p2 to indicate processing flow from p1 to p2.

C.1.2 An Ancestor-Descendant X-Frame Hierarchy

Given an x-framework and an SPC, for any two x-frames X and Y, we say that:

- X is an *ancestor* of Y, if X <**adapt**>s (directly or indirectly) Y in the processing flow defined by the SPC; we call Y a *descendant* of X.
- X is an *immediate ancestor* (or *parent*) of Y, if X directly <**adapt**>s Y in the processing flow defined by this SPC; we call Y an *immediate descendant* (or *child*) of X. Note that for X to be a parent of Y, X must contain an <**adapt**> command whose name attribute yields the name of x-frame Y.

In Figure C.1, x-frame A is an ancestor of all other x-frames. X-frame E has two immediate ancestors, namely, x-frames B and C.

C.2 Preliminary Definitions

Textual content can be any text that is intended to be customized by XVCL commands. This text may include anything including symbols that XML reserves for its

```
<x-frame name="abc">
  <!-x-frame body -- >
</x-frame>
```

Figure C.2   The structure of an x-frame.

own use, namely, .<., .>. ,.&., double quote ("), and single quote ('). These symbols are not interpreted as XVCL commands by the processor 2.10 or later. For compatibility with earlier versions, you can still keep those symbols in CDATA sections. The processor ignores XVCL commands if they are written inside CDATA sections.

XVCL commands are XVCL commands that are not written inside CDATA sections and are meant to be interpreted by the processor.

XVCL reserved characters or symbols are characters such as "|", "?", and "@" that are reserved for use in the XVCL language. XVCL uses "?" and "@" characters in expressions and the "|" character in the **<select>** command. The effect of using them in the attributes of XVCL commands will be explained in relevant sections throughout the document.

Variable name is a mixture of any characters except "?", "@", and ",".

C.3 Rules for Writing Well-Formed X-Frames

In the rest of this document, we assume that the reader has a basic understanding of XML.* XVCL is a dialect of XML, so the usual XML rules apply to XVCL. In addition, well-formed x-frames must obey rules that are specific to XVCL.

XVCL commands are written as XML tags. Although the syntax structure and semantics of the textual content do not matter, XVCL commands must follow the rules of the XVCL language.

C.3.1 The X-Frame Structure

Each x-frame is stored in a separate file. All the x-frames (including SPC) have the code skeleton structure shown in Figure C.2.

```
<x-frame name="abc">
<!-x-frame body -- >
</x-frame>
```

Each file contains exactly one x-frame. The processor does not check or use the x-frame name, only the name of the file that contains an x-frame. But it is a good

---

* For more information on XML please refer to www.w3c.org/TR/REC-xml.

practice to give the same name to both the x-frame and the file that contains it. It is also a good practice to add "xvcl" extensions to a file that contains an x-frame, but the processor does not check that either.

Each x-frame has exactly one x-frame body enclosed within x-frame start and closing tags, as indicated in Figure C.1. The x-frame body is the textual content of an x-frame instrumented with XVCL commands for flexibility. Each x-frame contains one root tag called **<x-frame>**, enclosing all other XVCL command tags, except **<x-frame>**.

The preceding also implies that x-frames cannot be nested.

The line <!-- the body of x-frame -- > is a comment.

C.3.2 Well-Formed XVCL Commands

As in XML, each XVCL command start tag must have its corresponding closing tag such as:

```
<x-frame name=".." >
...
</x-frame>
```

Tagged structures must be properly nested, i.e., they are not allowed to overlap with one other.

XVCL tags are case sensitive; that is, the case of the start tag and its corresponding end tag must be the same. So, if we write, for example:

```
<break> </BREAK>
```

the XVCL processor will report an error.

XVCL commands may include attributes to provide the additional processing information. Attributes are written inside the angle brackets of the command tag. The attributes may appear in any order. In the following example, we define a breakpoint named "break_a": the **<break>** command tag has the attribute "name," which is assigned a value "break_a."

```
<break name="break_a" >
...
</break>
```

An empty tag (i.e., one with no contents between the begin tag and end tag) can be written as <tag />. For example, the empty tag for **<break>** can be written as:

```
<break name="break_a"/>
```

Here are examples illustrating these rules.

```
<x-frame name="A">
 <adapt x-frame = "B">
 </adapt>
</x-frame>
```

The above x-frame is well formed because it has only one root element <x-frame> and the tags do not overlap.

```
<x-frame name="A">
 <adapt x-frame= "B">
</x-frame>
 </adapt>
```

The above x-frame is not well formed because the tags overlap.

```
<x-frame name="A">
 <adapt x-frame="B">
 </adapt>
```

The above x-frame is not well formed because the end tag of <x-frame> is missing.

```
<x-frame name="A">
<adapt x-frame = "B">
</adapt>
</x-frame name= "A">
```

The above x-frame is not well formed because the </x-frame> tag must not contain an attribute.

```
<x-frame name="A">
 <value-of var />
</x-frame>
```

The above x-frame is not well formed because the attribute **var** in the <value-of> tag does not have a value assigned to it.

```
<x-frame name="A">
 <value-of <value-of var="x"/> />
</x-frame >
```

The above x-frame is not well formed because the <value-of> tag contains another angle brackets in it.

```
<x-frame name="A">
 <adapt x-frame="B"/>
</X-FRAME >
```

The above x-frame is not well formed because the start and end tags of <x-frame> do not match each other.

C.3.3 Validity Checking

XVCL is supported by a processor that traverses an x-framework according to specifications contained in the SPC and interprets XVCL commands embedded in visited x-frames. The main task of the XVCL processor is to customize and assemble the customized result of x-frames. But before that, the XVCL processor checks the validity of the x-frame file to ensure it obeys XVCL grammar rules. An XVCL file is valid if it conforms to the rules mentioned in its corresponding DTD. The DTD defines XVCL command syntax, command attributes, and valid command nesting rules. (The DTD is case sensitive, which means that the case of the commands in XVCL files must appear exactly as in the DTD).

By default, all XVCL commands are in lowercase letters; that is, the XVCL processor will only understand commands written in lowercase letters. However, the developer could change the cases of the command declarations in DTD to any desired case. When changing the case sensitivity, the developer should not change the format (grammar rules) of the DTD, because this may change the processing structure of XVCL processor and may lead to undesired results.

C.4 Notations for Defining XVCL Commands

In the following sections, we define XVCL commands. For each command, we first specify the command's syntax structure and then describe the meaning of the command and the role of its attributes.

We use the following Extended BNF conventions to specify the syntax structure of XVCL commands.

C.4.1 Metasymbols

Definition symbol is :=, e.g., A := B.

Short form may be used if all the left-hand-side symbols are defined in the same way, e.g., A, B, C := D.

Alternative symbol is |, e.g., A:= B | C | D

Repetition (0 or more times) symbol is *, e.g., A := B*

Repetition (1 or more times) symbol is +, e.g., A := B+

Grouping is symbolized by round brackets (and), e.g., A := (B | C)*

An optional part of command definition is symbolized by square brackets [ ]

C.4.2 Nonterminal Symbols

Nonterminals are written using a mixture of lower and uppercase letters, digits, and the symbol -. For readability, nonterminals representing command attribute values are written in *italic*, e.g., *dir-name*.

All other nonterminals are written in regular font, e.g., x-frame.

C.4.3 Terminal Symbols

Terminals represent keywords (command names and command attribute names), identifiers, special symbols, etc. For readability, keywords are written in **bold.** Special symbols such as ", <, >, etc., are written without quotation symbols — as long as this does not lead to ambiguities. Other terminals are written in capital letters such as IDENT, STRING, etc. Terminals representing command attribute values are written in *italics*, e.g., *X-FRAME-NAME*.

C.5 Comments in XVCL

XVCL comments are written between <!-- and -->. A comment can occupy a single line:

<!-- This is a single line comment in XVCL -->

or may spread over many lines:

<!-- This is a
multiline comment in XVCL   -->

C.6 <x-frame> Command

C.6.1   Syntax

x-frame :=   **<x-frame name** = *"X-FRAME-NAME"* [**outdir** = *"dir-name"*]

[**outfile** = *"file-name"*] [**language** = *"language-name"*]>
x-frame-body
</x-frame>
X-FRAME-NAME   := STRING – character string is a mixture of any char-
    acters but "?", "@", and ",".
dir-name, file-name, language-name := Expression
Expression   := defined later in this document
x-frame-body := (textual-content | break | adapt | set |
set-multi | select | ifdef | ifndef | value-of | message | while | remove)*

C.6.2   Command Description

The <x-frame> command defines the start and end of an x-frame. <x-frame> is
the root tag of an x-frame. An x-frame body contains all other XVCL commands
(except <x-frame>) intermixed with textual content.

C.6.3   Attribute Definition

name = *"X-FRAME-NAME"*

This attribute specifies the name of the x-frame. *X-FRAME-NAME* must be a
STRING.
    In the <adapt> command, we specify the name of a file containing the <adapt>ed
x-frame rather than *X-FRAME-NAME*. Therefore, the processor does not check or
use *X-FRAME-NAME*. But it is a good practice to give the same name to both the
X-FRAME-NAME and the file that contains it.

outdir = *"dir-name"*

This attribute specifies a directory in which the XVCL processor will store the file with
the output emitted from the current x-frame. The *dir-name* must be an expression.
    If the specified directory does not exist, the XVCL processor will create one.
The *dir-name* can be either an absolute path like "c:\mydir\test" or a partial path,
including the null path, for example, the name "test" or "xvcl\test."

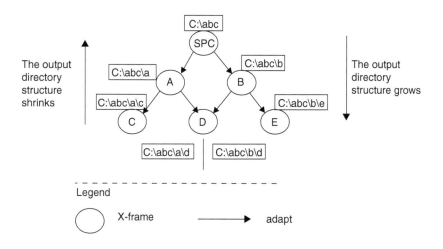

Figure C.3   An example of the output directory structure

If *dir-name* is a partial path, the XVCL processor will append it to the output directory path of the current x-frame's parent. When the processor traverses back up the x-framework, it removes the directory paths that are appended at each level. This way, the directory structure may grow as the processor traverses down and shrink accordingly when the processor traverses back up the x-framework, placing outputs from various x-frames in different directories. For example, suppose the parent's output directory is "c:\mydir\." Defining "test" in the **outdir** attribute of the current x-frame will make the XVCL processor emit the output from the current x-frame into a file that will be placed in "c:\mydir\test" directory. This feature is useful, for example, when the XVCL processor needs to emit Java code from different x-frames into different directories.

If *dir-name* is an absolute path, the XVCL processor emits the output of the current x-frame into this directory. The current output directory is set to be this path and descendant x-frames can append their own partial paths to it. In this way, subsequently processed x-frames can create new output directories as desired if these do not exist. Figure C.3 shows the output directory structure created by the XVCL processor, assuming that SPC's **outdir** attribute is defined as "c:\abc" and the descendant x-frames A, B, C, D, and E define their **outdir** attributes as "a," "b," "c," "d," and "e," respectively.

If the **outdir** attribute is not defined in the current <x-frame>, then the parent's output directory path will be used.

If no ancestor x-frame, including the SPC, has defined an output path in the **outdir** attribute, the processor will emit output from the current x-frame (as well as from all its ancestors) to a directory in which the SPC is stored.

If the *dir-name* of the SPC's **outdir** attribute is a partial path, for example, "test," then the processor will append "test" to the directory path where the SPC is stored and emit output from the SPC to that directory.

When both the <adapt> command in the parent x-frame and the adapted <x-frame> command define the output directory path in their **outdir** attributes, the <adapt> command's output directory path will be used.

For example, if x-frame X <adapt>s Y as follows:

```
<adapt x-frame="Y.xvcl" outdir="c:\ancestor\"
outfile="b.java"/>
```

and x-frame Y is defined as:

```
<x-frame name="Y" outdir="c:\descendent\"/>
```

then the output from x-frame Y will be emitted to the directory "c:\ancestor\b.java."

Value *dir-name* is often defined by an XVCL expression that involves variables. In such a case, an ancestor x-frame can override *dir-name*s in the descendant x-frames via variables that are <set> in ancestor x-frames and referenced in *dir-name* expressions in descendant x-frames.

outfile = *"file-name"*

This attribute specifies a file to which the XVCL processor will emit the output from the current x-frame. The *file-name* must be an expression that yields a legal filename or absolute directory path including the filename. Partial (relative) paths are not allowed in the **outfile** attribute.

An extension (if any) is treated as an integral part of the filename.

When the processor emits output to file *file-name* for the first time in processing flow and file *file-name* exists, the existing file is deleted before the output is emitted. If any subsequently processed x-frame emits output to the same file during the same run of the processor, the output is appended to the contents of that file.

If **outfile** is omitted, the processor checks the **outfile** attribute of the parent x-frame that <adapt>s the current one as follows: If the **outfile** attribute is defined in the parent's command that <adapt>s the current x-frame, that filename will be used. Otherwise, the parent's <x-frame> command's output file will be used, if defined. If an output filename is not defined in any of the ancestor x-frames including the SPC, the SPC's name will used as the *file-name*.

When both the parent's x-frame <adapt> command and the current <x-frame> command define the output filename in their **outfile** attributes, the parent's <adapt> command's output filename will be used. This is consistent with XVCL's variable scoping rules (see Section C.8.7).

For example, if x-frame X <adapt>s Y as follows:

```
<adapt x-frame="Y.xvcl" outfile="a.java"/>
```

and x-frame Y is defined as:

```
<x-frame name="Y" outfile="b.java"/>
```

then the output from x-frame Y will be emitted to the file "a.java".

language = *"language-name"*

This attribute specifies the base language in which the textual content of the x-frame is written (e.g., text, java, xmi, vb, etc.).

Currently, this attribute is ignored by the XVCL processor. It merely gives a hint to the developer as to how to interpret the textual content. In future, we envision that the processing of x-frames may be tailored to the needs of different base languages via this attribute.

C.7 Definition of <adapt>, <insert>, <insert-before>, and <insert-after> Commands

Commands <adapt>, <insert>, <insert-before>, and <insert-after> are always used together, which is why we define them in one section.

C.7.1 Syntax

adapt	::= **<adapt x-frame=**"*file-name*" [**outdir=**"*dir-name*"] [**outfile=**"*file-name*"] [**samelevel=**"*yes-no*"] [**once=**"*yes-no*"]> adapt-body </**adapt**>
file-name	::= Expression
yes-no	::= Expression
adapt-body	::= (insert | insert-before | insert-after)*
insert	::= **<insert break=**"*break-name*"> Insert-Content </**insert**>
break-name	::= Expression
insert-before	::= **<insert-before break=**"*break-name*"> Insert-Content </**insert-before**>
insert-after	::= **<insert-after break=**"*break-name*"> Insert-Content </**insert-after**>
Insert-Content	::= (textual-content | break | adapt | set | set-multi | select |

		ifdef | ifndef | value-of | message | while | remove)*
break	::=	**<break name=**"*break-name*"**>**
		Break-Content
		</break>
Break-Content	::=	(textual-content | adapt | set | set-multi | select | ifdef | ifndef |
		value-of | message | while | remove)*

C.7.2 Command Description

<adapt>

The <adapt> command instructs the processor to:

- Process the x-frame specified as the value of the **x-frame** attribute, *file-name*
- Process all the descendant x-frames of the preceding x-frame
- Perform customizations of visited x-frames as specified in the body of the <adapt> command (subject to the rules described further in this section)
- Emit the output to the specified output file

Note that all the x-frames are read-only; that is, when the x-frame is adapted, the processor does not make changes on the original x-frame. Rather, it reads the content of the x-frame and performs necessary operations in memory before writing it to the output file.

An x-frame is not allowed to <adapt> itself or any of its ancestor x-frames; that is, recursive adaptations are not allowed.

The *file-name* of the <adapt>ed x-frame given in attribute **x-frame** must be an expression.

<insert>, <insert-before>, and <insert-after>

The body of an <adapt> command may contain zero or more <insert>, <insert-before>, and <insert-after> commands. As many rules are the same for all three commands <insert>, <insert-before>, and <insert-after>, for brevity of the description, we shall use term **insert-xxx** to refer to any of the three commands.

The **insert-xxx** commands modify <adapt>ed x-frames at breakpoints identified by matching <break> commands. This matching between **insert-xxx** and <break> commands is established by values of attribute **break** of **insert-xxx** and **name** of <break> commands. The exact matching rules will be described later in the section.

The <insert> command replaces the Break-Content inside its matching <break> commands with its Insert-Content.

The <insert-before> command inserts its Insert-Content before the matching <break> commands.

The <insert-after> command inserts its Insert-Content after the matching <break> commands.

Note that the <insert-before> and <insert-after> commands do not replace the Break-Content inside its matching <break> commands.

The **insert-xxx** commands can only appear inside the body of <adapt> commands. There is no limit to how many **insert-xxx** commands can be contained in one <adapt> command.

The body of an <adapt> command may contain multiple **insert-xxx** commands referring to the same *break-name*. Similarly, **insert-xxx** commands referring to the same *break-name* may exist in many different <adapt> commands, placed in many x-frames.

<break>

The <break> command marks a place in the x-frame (called a breakpoint) at which the x-frame can be customized by an <insert>, <insert-before>, or <insert-after> command declared in the ancestor x-frames.

Details of How These Commands Work Together

The **insert-xxx** commands are matched with subsequently processed <break> commands in the descendant x-frames via the *break-name* defined in the **break** attribute of these commands. In addition to the *break-name*, scoping rules are used to determine which **insert-xxx** commands match which <break> commands. We describe the matching process later in this section.

The following are the details of how insertions are processed:

- If an <insert-before> command matches the <break> command, then the Insert-Content of the <insert-before> command will be processed as if it were inserted just before the matching <break> in the x-frame.
- If an <insert> command matches a <break> command, then the Insert-Content of the <insert > command will be processed as if it replaced the Break-Content of the <break> command. (If the Insert-Content of the <insert > command is empty, it is equivalent to deleting the Break-Content of the <break> command.)
- If no <insert> command matches a particular <break> command, the processor will process its Break-Content.
- The <insert-after> works analogous to <insert-before>.

For all the **insert-xxx** commands, the inserted Insert-Content will be processed as if the Insert-Content had originally appeared at the insertion point in the target x-frame.

If multiple <insert> commands within the body of the same <adapt> command refer to the same <break>, then the Insert-Content of all those commands is concatenated before the insertion is made at the matching <break> command. The same applies to <insert-before> and <insert-after> commands. This is illustrated in the following example.

X-Frame A

```
<adapt x-frame="B.xvcl">
 <insert-before break="x">
 xAB before
 </insert-before>
 <insert break="x">
 xAB
 </insert>
 <insert-after break="x">          xAB is concatenated with xAB
 xAB after
 </insert-after>                   again
 <insert break="x">
 xAB again
 </insert>
</adapt>
```

Result
```
before break in B
xAB before
xAB        } concatenated Insert-Content from <insert?
xAB again  } commands into <break>
xAB after
after break in B
```

Comments

Declaring multiple **insert-xxx** commands to the same breakpoint within the same <adapt> command will result in concatenation of the contents of all the <insert>s, before any insertion is conducted. That is to say, these <insert> declarations will be regarded as one <insert> if the target breakpoint is the same.

X-Frame B

```
  before break in B
<break name="x">
  break-content
</break>
    after break in B
```

Referring to the preceding example, x-frame A has two <insert>s with the body "xAB" and "xAB again" that are defined to insert into break x in x-frame B. The first <insert>'s "xAB" with the second <insert>'s "xAB again" are concatenated as if there was only one <insert> containing:

xAB

xAB again

Scoping Rule for Matching Insert-xxx Commands with <break>s

If <insert> commands refer to the same <break> by *break-name* from within multiple x-frames, only the <insert> command that is executed first in the processing flow will match this <break>. The remaining <insert> commands referring to the same <break> in other x-frames are ignored.

The following example illustrates matching between <insert> commands and <break>s. The same rule applies to <insert-before> and <insert-after> commands.

X-Frame A

```
<adapt x-frame="B.xvcl">
 <insert break="x">
 xAB
 </insert>
</adapt>
<break name="x"/> // this <break> will be ignored.
```

X-Frame B

```
<adapt x-frame="D.xvcl">
 <insert break="x"> // this <insert> will be overridden
by insert in x-frame A
xBD
 </insert>
</adapt>
```

X-Frame D

```
<break name="x">
 break-content
</break>
```

Result

xAB

Comments

In the preceding example, x-frames A and B declare <insert>s for <break> x. However, x-frame B's <insert> command is overridden by x-frame A's <insert> command because x-frame B is the descendant of x-frame A.

It is also important to note that the <break> command in x-frame A is not affected by the <insert> command. This is because the <insert> commands only affect the adapted x-frame and its descendant x-frames.

Multiple Insertions

If there is more than one <break> command with the same name, all the **insert-xxx** commands matching that <break> will make insertions to all those <break>s. This is called *multiple insertions*. This rule is illustrated in the following example.

X-Frame A

```
<adapt x-frame="B.xvcl">
<insert-before break="x">
 xAB before
</insert-before>
<insert break="x">
 xAB
</insert>
<insert-after break="x">
xAB after
</insert-after>
</adapt>
```

X-Frame B

```
<adapt x-frame="D.xvcl">
</adapt>
before break in B
<break name="x">
break-content
</break>
after break in B
```

X-Frame D

```
before break in D
<break name="x">
content.
</break>
after break in D
```

Result
```
before break in D
xAB before
xABxAB after
after break in D
before break in B
xAB before
xABxAB after
after break in B
```
Comments

If there are many <break>s with the same name in the descendant x-frames, the insert-xxx commands make insertions to all the matching <break>s.

A note on nested <break>s

Nested <break>s are not allowed. Though nested <break>s make sense at the first glance, they lead to more problems than they solve. For example, we might attempt to <insert> into an inner <break> that had been deleted by some other command. The following example demonstrates this:

Suppose x-frame A adapts x-frame B, and x-frame B adapts x-frame C. Further, x-frame A contains the <insert> command for <break> y and x-frame B contains the <insert> command for <break> x and in x-frame C, we have the following nested <break>s:

```
<break name="x">
   <break name="y">
   </break>
</break>
```

In the preceding situation, x-frame A's <insert> command will not be able to insert to **<break>** y, as it has been already superseded by the <insert> command in x-frame B.

C.7.3 Attribute Definition for <insert-before>, <insert>, and <insert-after> Commands

break =*"break-name"*

This attribute specifies the name of the <break> where the Insert-Content of **insert-xxx** should be inserted. The *break-name* must be an expression.

C.7.4 Attribute Definition for <break> Command

name =*"break-name"*

This attribute specifies the name of a breakpoint. The *break-name* must be an expression.

C.7.5 Attribute Definition for <adapt> Command

x-frame =*"file-name"*

This attribute specifies the name of the file containing the x-frame to be <adapt>ed. The *file-name* should be an expression that yields an absolute path including file-name, a relative path, or just a filename.

The processor looks for a specified file in the "designated directory." The processor uses the following rules to determine the "designated directory":

1. The designated directory for the SPC is the directory where the SPC x-frame is located.
2. Suppose x-frame A, with designated directory C:\dir_A\, contains the command <adapt x-frame="B"/>
   a. If B is just a filename, then the processor looks for file B in C:\dir_A\; the designated directory of B also becomes C:\dir_A\
   b. If B is an absolute path, say C:\dir_B\b.xvcl, then the processor looks for file C:\dir_B\b.xvcl; the designated directory of B becomes C:\dir_B\
   c. If B is a relative path, say, dir_B\b.xvcl, then the processor looks for file C:\dir_A\dir_B\b.xvcl, where C:\dir_A\ is a designated directory of x-frame A; the designated directory of B becomes C:\dir_A\dir_B\

If the file extension is omitted, the processor will first look for an exact match, and, if it is not found, for a file named *file-name* with ".xvcl" extension. Otherwise, the processor will use the specified filename and the extension.

outdir ="*dir-name*"

This attribute specifies a directory in which the XVCL processor will store the file with the output emitted from the <adapt>ed x-frame. The definition for this attribute is the same as that for the **outdir** attribute of the <x-frame> command (see Section C.6.3). The *dir-name* must be an expression.

outfile ="*file-name*"

This attribute specifies a file into which the XVCL processor will emit the output from the <adapt>ed x-frame. The definition for this attribute is the same as the **outfile** attribute of the <x-frame> command (see Section C.6.3). The *file-name* must be an expression.

samelevel ="*yes-no*"

This attribute specifies whether or not to raise the variables declared in the adapted <x-frame> to the current x-frame (that is one that contains the <adapt> command). The *yes-no* must be an expression that yields value "yes" or "no." If omitted, the default value is "no."

If the value is "yes," variables whose values are <set> (or <set-multi>) in the adapted x-frame are raised to the current x-frame. In other words, those variables behave as if they were <set> (or <set-multi>) at the place of <adapt> command in the current x-frame. Having raised the variables, the usual variable scoping rules will be applied to determine values of referenced variables (Section C.8.7).

The following example illustrates this concept:

Suppose in **x-frame A** we have:

```
<set var="x" value="XA"/>
<adapt x-frame="B" samelevel="yes"/> // the variable x
will be reset to "XB" here
<value-of expr="?@x?/> // the value of x is "XB"
```

and in **x-frame B**:

```
<set var="x" value="XB"/>
```

The result of evaluation of <value-of expr="?@x?"/> is "XB." For details about setting variables and their associated rules, please refer to Section C.10.

The following example further illustrates the effects of attribute **samelevel**.

X-Frame A

```
<set var="x" value="XA1"/>
 value of variable x is <value-of expr="?@x?"/> // value
of x is XA1
<adapt x-frame="B.xvcl" samelevel="yes"/>
value of variable x is reset to <value-of expr="?@x?"/>
// value of x is XB1
value of variable y is <value-of expr="?@y?"/> // value
of y is YB1
 <adapt x-frame="C.xvcl"/>
```

X-Frame B

```
<set var="y" value="YB1"/>
<set var="x" value="XB1"/>
```

X-Frame C

```
Because of same level, in x-frame C we have:
value of variable x is <value-of expr="?@x?"/>
value of variable y is <value-of expr="?@y?"/>
```

Result:

`value of variable x is XA1`

`value of variable x is reset to XB1`

`value of variable y is YB1`

Because of same level, in x-frame C we have:

`value of variable x is XB1`

`value of variable y YB1`

Comments:

The net effect of raising variables is the same as if all the <set> commands from x-frame B appeared in x-frame A at B's adaptation point. Thus, the value of x is reset to XB1. When adapting x-frame C in x-frame A, variable x with the new value XB1, together with variable y with value XY1, will be passed down to x-frame C.

---

once = *"yes-no"*

This attribute specifies whether or not the subsequent <adapt>s of the <adapt>ed x-frame should be ignored (value "yes") or not (value "no"). The *yes-no* must be an expression that yields value "yes" or "no." The default value is "no."

Note that if the value of attribute **once** is "no" (which is the usual case), the named x-frame can be adapted many times during processing of an x-framework.

C.8 Variables and Expressions

Generic names increase flexibility and adaptability of programs and play an important role in building generic, reusable programs. XVCL variables and expressions provide powerful means of creating generic names and controlling the x-framework customization process.

XVCL expressions include STRING constants, name expressions (direct and indirect references to variables and chains of variable references), string expressions (concatenations of name expressions and STRINGs), and arithmetic expressions. We use the term XVCL expression (or expression for short) to mean STRING, name expression, string expression, or arithmetic expression.

C.8.1 Syntax

Expression	::=	Name-Expression | String-Expression | Arithmetical-Expression
Name-Expression	::=	?@ (STRING | @)* VAR-NAME ?
String-Expression	::=	(Name-Expression | STRING) +

| VAR-NAME | ::= a mixture of any characters but "?", "@", and "," |
| STRING | ::= a mixture of any characters but "?", "@", and "," |

C.8.2 References to Variables

A direct reference to variable C is written as: @C:

Each extra symbol '@' in the front of a variable name indicates a level of indirection. So:

@@C means value-of (value-of (C))

@@@C means value-of (value-of (value-of (C))), and so on.

The XVCL processor replaces references to variables by their values. Here, we should mention, that the XVCL processor stores all the variables defined so far in the symbol table along with their current values, as assigned to variables in <set> and <set-multi> commands (see Section C.10 and Section C.11). Table C.1 shows the symbol table we shall use in the examples.

For example, the value of **@@C** is **BU**, and the value of **@@@C** is **V**.

A reference to a variable not in the symbol table is considered an error in all situations.

Table C.1   The Symbol Table with Variables

Name	Value
A	X
X	Y
Y	Z
C	U
U	BU
BU	V
AV	W
AT	S
V	T
R	B?@@A?B?@C?
BG	H
BYBU	G
E	?@F?
F	?@G?
G	L

C.8.3 Name Expressions

We shall introduce name expressions first and then explain string expressions. A simple name expression may contain just a variable reference, such as: ?@C? or ?@@C? (A name expression must be enclosed between question mark symbols.)

More complex (but more useful) name expressions can be written as: ?@A@B@C?. In that case, the value of such a name expression is computed from right to left as follows:

value-of (A | value-of (B | value-of (C)))

where symbol "|" means string concatenation. Note that only C is treated as a variable name, whereas A and B are treated as strings.

For example, referring to Table C.1, the evaluation of name expression, ?@A@B@C? is done as follows:

1. Get the value of variable C.
   - The intermediate result is U.
2. Concatenate B and U and get the value of variable BU.
   - The intermediate result is V.
3. Concatenate A and V and get the value of variable AV
   - The final result is W.

After each evaluation step, the intermediate value computed is concatenated with the character string on the left to form a new variable name that is looked up in the symbol table. Evaluation of a name expression continues until the whole name expression is evaluated.

The following examples illustrate evaluation of name expressions. For detailed steps please refer to the previous example.

Example C.1

The evaluation of name expression ?@@A? is as follows:

1. Get the value of A, which is X.
2. Get the value of X, which is Y.

So, the final result of the evaluation is Y.

Example C.2

The evaluation of name expression ?@A@@B@C? is as follows:

1. Get the value of C, which is U.
2. Get the value of BU, which is V.
3. Get the value of V, which is T.
4. Get the value of AT, which is S

So, the final result of the evaluation is S.

Deferred evaluation

A name expression may include references to variables whose evaluation is deferred. Such variables are <set> (or <set-multi>) with the value of the defer-evaluation attribute "yes," for example:

```
<set var="E" value=" ?@F?" defer-evaluation="yes"/>
<set var="F" value=" ?@G?" defer-evaluation="yes"/>
```

An expression defining the value of a deferred variable is evaluated at the variable reference point rather than at the point where the variable is <set>. For the preceding <set> commands, entries for variables E and F are indicated in Table C.1.

The following examples below illustrate how deferred evaluation affects evaluation of name expressions.

Example C.3

Suppose we have:

```
<set var="E" value=" ?@F?" defer-evaluation="yes"/>
<set var="F" value=" ?@G?" defer-evaluation="yes"/>
```

and the symbol table as shown in Table C.1.

Evaluation of the name expression ?@E? is as follows:

1. Get the value of variable E.
   - The result is ?@F? whose evaluation is deferred.
2. Get the value of variable F.
   - The result is ?@G? whose evaluation is also deferred.
3. Get the value of G.
   - The final result is L.

In the preceding example, we have two deferred evaluations chained together. The chain of deferred evaluations may be of any length.

Referenced variable names created at each intermediate evaluation step must represent variables that exist in the symbol table, otherwise the XVCL processor reports an error. All such variables must have been defined in <set> or <set-multi> commands before a given name expression is evaluated.

Deferred evaluation is further explained in Sections C.10.3.

C.8.4 String Expressions

String expressions may contain any number of name expressions intermixed with character strings.

To evaluate a string expression, we evaluate the name expressions from the left to the right of the string expression, replace name expressions with their respective values, and concatenate with character strings at the point of replacement.

In the following text, we illustrate evaluation of string expressions with examples, assuming variable values indicated in Table C.1.

Example C.4

We evaluate string expression ?@A@B@C?P?@X? as follows:

1. Evaluate name expression ?@A@B@C?
   - The result is W.
2. Replace ?@A@B@C? with W.
   - The partially evaluated string expression becomes WP?@X?
3. Evaluate name expression ?@X?
   - The result is Y.
4. Replace ?@X? with Y.
   - The final result is WPY.

Example C.5

The evaluation of a string expression "**B?@@A?B?@C?**" is as follows:

1. Evaluate the value of ?@@A?
   - The result is Y.
2. Replace ?@@A? with Y.
   - The partially evaluated string expression now becomes BYB?@C?
3. Evaluate the value of ?@C?
   - The result is U.
4. Replace ?@C? with U.
   - The final result is BYBU.

Example C.6 (with deferred evaluation)

Suppose we have:

```
<set var="R" value=" B?@@A?B?@C?" defer-evaluation="yes"/>
```

The evaluation of the name expression ?@B@@R? is as follows:

1. Get the value of R.
   - The result is B?@@A?B?@C?
2. Evaluate the value of B?@@A?B?@C? as shown in Example C.5.
   - The result is BYBU.
3. Replace @R with BYBU.
   - The partially evaluated name expression now becomes ?@B@ BYBU?
4. Get the value of variable BYBU.
   - The result is G.
5. Replace @BYBU with G.
   - The partially evaluated name expression now becomes ?@BG?
6. Get the value of BG.
   - The final result is H.

C.8.5 Evaluation of Arithmetic Expressions

If an expression is a well-formed arithmetic expression, it will be accepted as such and the XVCL processor will evaluate its value.

A well-formed arithmetic expression is formed with the following five operators +, -, /, *, and ^ (power). The operands can be either integers or decimals. Strings should represent integer or decimal numbers. References of variables and expressions must yield an integer or decimal number.

All decimal answers are rounded down to the nearest whole number.

The XVCL processor will report an error if a division by zero occurs.

Nested parenthesis can be used in expressions to indicated the grouping of operators and operands as in the following examples:

Suppose we have the following set commands:

```
<set var="x" value= "6"/>
<set var="y" value= "4"/>
```

Example 1: (?@x? +?@y?)/5
Example 2: (3 * (1.2 + 3.4))/4

In Example 1, the values of variable x and y are added, which yields 10, and the result is divided by 5, yielding 2.

In Example 2, the result is 3.

Note that any attribute of an XVCL command can accept arithmetic expressions. However, arithmetic expressions should not be used in the <while> and <select> commands' attributes. Otherwise, they will be calculated and the resulting values will be passed to attributes of those commands.

If the arithmetic expression is not valid (e.g., arithmetic expressions that contain strings), the processor will regard the whole arithmetic expression as a string and emit it to the output. For example, if the arithmetic expression "(a + 3) * c" is encountered, the processor cannot evaluate it, as it is not a valid arithmetic expression. So "(a + 3) * c" is regarded as a string and emitted to its output.

Scientific calculations such as mod, tan, cos, etc., are not supported, as XVCL is not intended to be a programming language.

C.8.6 How Are Expressions Used?

Expressions (Name Expression, String Expression, and Arithmetic Expression), rather than character strings, are commonly used in attributes of XVCL commands (except the name attribute of the <x-frame> command) to denote x-frame names to be adapted, pathnames, variable values, variable names, break names, etc. An example of using a name expression in <adapt> command follows:

```
<adapt x-frame="?@x-frame-name?" outdir="?@dir-name?"
outfile="?@fine-name?" >
```

C.8.7 Variable Scoping Rules

Variable scoping rules are the same for both single-value and multivalue variables. The <set> command in the ancestor x-frame takes precedence over <set> commands in its descendant x-frames. That is, once an x-frame A sets the value of variable x, <set> commands that <set> the same variable x in descendant x-frames (if any) will not take effect. However, the subsequent <set> commands in x-frame A can reset the value of variable x. This is illustrated in the following example. (Note that we use the "//" java comment style to explain the codes inside x-frames. They are there to help the reader to understand the code.)

X-Frame A

```
<set var="x" value="XA1"/> // value of x is set to XA1
 <adapt x-frame="B.xvcl"/> // value of x is XA1 in x-
frame B and its descendants
 <set var="x" value="XA2"/> // value of x is reset to XA2
 <adapt x-frame="C.xvcl"/> // value of x is XA in x-frame
C and its descendants
value of variable x in x-frame A is <value-of expr="?@
x?"/>
```

X-Frame B

```
value of variable x is <value-of expr="?@x?"/> in x-frame B
<adapt x-frame="E.xvcl"/>
```

X-Frame C

```
value of variable x is <value-of expr="?@x?"/> in x-frame C
<adapt x-frame="E.xvcl"/>
```

X-Frame E

```
value of variable x is <value-of expr="?@x?"/> in x-frame E
```

Result

```
value of variable x is XA1 in x-frame B
value of variable x is XA1 in x-frame E
value of variable x is XA2 in x-frame C
value of variable x is XA2 in x-frame E
final value of variable x in x-frame A is XA2
```

Comments

Note that x-frame E is adapted by x-frame B and x-frame C. When x-frame E is adapted by x-frame B, the value of variable x in x-frame E is XA1, which is passed down by x-frame B. When x-frame E is adapted from x-frame C, the value of variable x in x-frame E becomes XA2. This is because the previous value XA1 of variable x in x-frame A is reset again just before x-frame B is adapted again.

Variables become undefined as soon as the processing returns to the parent of the x-frame that effectively set those variables.

Note that variables that are set within <insert> commands become undefined when the x-frame containing the <break> returns the processing to its parent x-frame. This is illustrated in the following example.

X-Frame A

```
<adapt x-frame="B.xvcl">
 <insert break="x">
 <set var="VA" value="XA" />
 </insert >
</adapt>
<!-- <value-of expr="?@VA?"/> -- >// variable VA is out
of scope here
```

X-Frame B

```
<set var="VA" value="XB" />
value of VA before break x is <value-of expr="?@VA?"/> in
x-frame B // here VA is
 //XB
<break name="x"/> // the insert content, <set> command in
x-frame A is inserted
value of VA after break x is <value-of expr="?@VA?"/> in
x-frame B // here VA is
 //XA
<adapt x-frame="D.xvcl"/>
```

X-Frame D

```
value of aa is <value-of expr="?@VA?"/> in x-frame D
```

Result

```
value of VA before break x is XB in x-frame B
value of VA after break x is XA in x-frame B
value of VA is XA in x-frame D
```

Comments

The <set> command in x-frame A is inserted to the break x in x-frame B. X-frame B also has the <set> command that sets the variable VA to XB. The value of VA is XB before the <break> x in x-frame B. After the <break> x in x-frame B, the value of VA becomes XA because the <insert> command in x-frame A has inserted the <set> command that sets the variable VA's value to XA.

When <set> commands are inserted into a <break>, these commands behave as if they are written in the place of <break> command. It is very important to note that any XVCL commands that are inserted to break x will be processed as if they are originally written at the insertion point in the target x-frame.

In the case of the <insert-before> command, <set> will behave as if it is originally written just before the <break> x in x-frame B, whereas in the case of <insert-after> the <set> command will behave as if it is originally written just after the <break> x in x-frame B.

The variable scoping rules are important for reuse. To be reused in many contexts, x-frames are heavily parameterized by variables and expressions. Typically, names of adapted x-frames, break points, etc., are represented by expressions rather than STRINGs. X-frames use <set> (and <set-multi>) commands to define default values for variables. Ancestor x-frames can override the defaults, if necessary, adapting an x-frame to the specific reuse context.

C.9 <value-of> Command

C.9.1 Syntax

value-of : = <value-of expr= "Expression" />

C.9.2 Command Definition

The value of the expression is evaluated and emitted to the output. The evaluated result replaces the command. Expressions are described in Section C.8.

For example,

```
<set var="name" value="John"/>
My name is <value-of expr="?@name?"/>.
```

The result after processing will be:

```
My name is John.
```

The same result can be produced by including "My name is" to the **expr** attribute, which forms a string expression as in the following example:

```
<value-of expr="My name is ?@name?."/>
```

The <value-of> command is an empty tag and cannot contain any content between its start tag and end tag.

C.9.3 Attribute Definition

expr = *"Expression"*

This attribute specifies an expression to be evaluated (see Section C.8).

C.10 <set> Command

C.10.1 Syntax

set	:=	**<set var=**"*single-var-name*" **value=**"*value*" [**defer-evaluation=**"*yes-no*"]/>
single-var-name	:=	Expression
value	:=	Expression
yes-no	:=	Expression

C.10.2 Command Definition

The <set> command assigns a *"value"* defined in **value** attribute to single-value variable *"single-var-name"* defined in **var** attribute.

The <set> command is an empty tag and cannot contain any content between its start tag and end tag.

When a variable is <set> for the first time, say in x-frame A, the variable is entered into the symbol table along with its value. For any subsequent command in the same x-frame that <set>s the value of the same variable, the processor updates the value of the variable in the symbol table.

Suppose the processor executes the following <set> command in x-frame A:

```
<set var="x" value ="X1"/>
```

If variable x is not in the symbol table, variable x is entered along with its value X1. Suppose another <set> command in the same x-frame is subsequently executed:

```
<set var="x" value="X2"/>
```

This time the processor will just update the value of x to X2.

The <set> commands in A's descendant x-frames will normally be ignored and the variable is removed from the symbol table once the processing of an x-frame that inserted the variable to the symbol table is completed. But there are exceptions to this rule. We refer the reader to Section C.8.7 on variable scoping, Section C.7.5 on attribute **samelevel**, and Section C.15 on the <remove> command for further details.

C.10.3 Attribute Definition

var =*"single-var-name"*

This attribute specifies the name of a single-value variable. The *single-var-name* must be an expression that yields a legal variable name. A legal variable name is a mixture of any characters except "?", "@", and ",".

value =*"value"*

This attribute specifies the value of the variable. The *"value"* must be an expression.

The evaluation of the variable's *"value"* can be deferred as explained in the defer-evaluation attribute.

defer-*evaluation* =*"yes-no"*

This attribute specifies if the evaluation of the variable's value should be deferred (indicated by value "yes") or not (indicated by value "no"). The *yes-no* must be an expression that yields value "yes" or "no." The XVCL processor reports an error otherwise. If omitted, the default value is "no."

The value of that variable is evaluated at the reference point rather than at the point where the variable is <set>. The processor stores the expression in the symbol table, and the evaluation takes place each time the variable is referenced.

For example, as the result of the following <set> command:

```
<set var="x" value="?@y?" defer-evaluation= "yes"/>
```

the expression ?@y? is entered into the symbol table as is, without evaluating its value. At each point of reference to variable x, the processor evaluates expression ?@y? to come up with the value for variable x at a given reference point.

If **defer-evaluation** is "no," the current value of variable y is assigned to x.

We refer the reader to Section C.8.3 and Section C.8.4 for more examples of deferred evaluation.

C.11 <set-multi Command>

C.11.1 Syntax

set-multi	:=	**<set-muti var="**$multi\text{-}var\text{-}name$**" value="**$value$ (, $value$)*$"$
		[**defer-evaluation**="$yes\text{-}no$"]/>
$multi\text{-}var\text{-}name$	:=	Expression
$value$	:=	Expression

C.11.2 Command Description

The <set-multi> command defines the multivalue variable. The multivalue variables are mainly used in <while> commands for iteration (see Section C.14).

The <set-multi> command assigns a list of values specified in the **value** attribute to *multi-var-name*. Values must be separated by commas. The values are expressions.

If a specific *value* is a reference to a multivalue variable, e.g., ?@MULTI?, then the whole list of values of variable MULTI is included into the list of values of the *multi-var-name* (unless variable MULTI happens to be a control variable in the <while> loop enclosing a given <set-multi> command; see Section C.14).

The *value*s are processed from the left to the right, creating a list of values. This list of values is assigned to the "*multi-var-name*" described in the **var** attribute.

This is illustrated in the following example:

```
<set-multi var="A" value="1,2"/>
<set var="B" value="3"/>
<set-multi var="C" value="?@A?, ?@B?"/>
<set-multi var="D" value="A, B"/>
```

For <set-multi> variable C, the multivalue variable A is first evaluated, which yields a partial list of values: 1, 2. Next, the value of the single-value variable B is evaluated and appended to the preceding partial list of values, yielding the final list of values 1, 2, and 3. Multivalue variable C will receive values 1, 2, and 3.

Multivalue variable D will receive values A, B.

If there is only one variable *value* specified in the **value** attribute, the value(s) of that variable will be assigned to the variable *multi-var-name*. In the following example, variable C will receive values 1, 2.

```
<set-multi var="C" value="?@A?"/>
```

If the same variable appears more than once in the **value** attribute, each occurrence of that variable will contribute the resulting list of values. For example:

```
<set-multi var="C" value="?@A?, ?@A?, ?@A?"/>
```

Variable "C" will receive values 1, 2, 1, 2, 1, and 2.

The scope and overriding rules of multivalue variables is the same as for single-value variables.

The <set-multi> command is an empty tag and cannot contain any content between its start tag and end tag.

Escape character

In the **value** attribute, the comma plays the role of a separator. To avoid interpreting a comma as a separator, an escape character "\" should be used before the comma: "\,". For example, after command:

```
<set-multi var="A" value="1\,2"/>
```

the value of A is one element "1,2".

C.11.3 Attribute Definition

var *="multi-var-name"*

This attribute specifies the name of a multivalue variable. The *multi-var-name* must be an expression that yields a legal variable name. A legal name of a variable is a mixture of any characters except "?", "@", and ",".

defer-*evaluation ="yes-no"*

Deferred evaluation for multivalue variables works in the same way as deferred evaluation of single-valued variables (see Section C.10.3).

In the following example, expressions ?@a?, ?@b?, (?@c?+2) will be entered into the symbol table without evaluating them, and evaluation will takes place each time variable A is referenced. (The details of evaluation of ?@ variable? are explained in Section C.8.)

```
<set-multi var="A" value="?@b?,?@b?, (?@c? + 2)" defer-
evaluation= "yes"/>
```

Note: The "defer-evaluation" affects only the **value** attribute. If variables appear in any other attributes of a <set-multi> command, the evaluation will take place immediately.

C.12 Additional Rules for <set> and <set-multi> Commands

The single-value variable defined by <set> and the multivalue variable defined by the <set-multi> command must not be the same. The processor will report an error otherwise.

When an x-frame is <adapt>ed with **samelevel** = "yes," all the <set> and <set-multi> commands defined in that x-frame behave as if they were originally written in their parent x-frame in place of the <adapt> command. This is illustrated in the following example. This example uses the <set> command for illustration, but the same rule applies for the <set-multi> command as well.

X-Frame A

```
<set var="x" value="XA1"/>
 value of variable x is <value-of expr="?@x?"/> //
variable x value is XA1
 <adapt x-frame="B.xvcl" samelevel="yes"/> // variables x
and y in x-frame B is
                // raised here and behave as if they
                // are written here. So the value of
                //x is reset to XB1.
 value of variable x is reset to <value-of expr="?@x?"/>
                // x's value is reset to XB1
 value of variable y is <value-of expr="?@y?"/> //
variable y's value comes from  //x-frame B
 <adapt x-frame="C.xvcl"/>
```

X-Frame B

```
<set var="y" value="YB1"/>
<set var="x" value="XB1"/>
```

X-Frame C

```
Because of same level, Now x-frame C has:
value of variable x is <value-of expr="?@x?"/>
value of variable y is <value-of expr="?@y?"/>
```

Result

value of variable x is XA1

value of variable x is reset to XB1

value of variable y is YB1

Because of same level, now x-frame C has:

value of variable x is XB1

value of variable y YB1

variable x and y are got from the **samelevel** effects from
  B.xvcl

Comments

Note that x-frame B is adapted with **samelevel** defined yes in x-frame A. This causes the variables x and y in x-frame B to be raised to the adapting x-frame A. These variables behave as if they are originally written in x-frame A. Thus, the original x value defined in A is reset to XB1. Note that before adapting x-frame B, the value of variable x is XA1. After adapting x-frame B, the value of x becomes XB1. When adapting x-frame C from x-frame A, variable x with the new value XB1, together with variable y with value XY1, will be passed down to x-frame C.

C.13 <select> Command
C.13.1 Syntax

select   := <**select option**= *"control-variable"*>
                   (<**option value**= *"value (| value)*"* [**comp-operator**=*"comp-operator (, comp-operator)*"*]>
                   option-body
                   </**option**>)*
                   [<**otherwise**>
                   option-body
                   </**otherwise**>]

</**select**>
control-variable   := *single-var-name*
option-body   := (textual-content | break | adapt | set | set-multi | select |

$$\text{ifdef} \mid \text{ifndef} \mid \text{value-of} \mid \text{message} \mid \text{while} \mid \text{remove})^*$$

value	:=	Expression
comp-operator	:=	Expression

C.13.2 Command Description

The <select> command selects zero or more from the listed option clauses. The XVCL processor processes each of the selected option clauses immediately upon selection.

Options are selected based on the value of control-variable specified in the **option** attribute. If control-variable is undefined (that is, it does not exist in the symbol table), the processor issues an error message and terminates processing.

As indicated in the syntax section, the <select> command can contain zero or more <option> commands followed by an optional <otherwise> command. We use the term option clause to denote either <option> or <otherwise> commands.

The order of the appearance of the <option> and <otherwise> commands is strictly controlled. The XVCL processor will report an error if the order is not obeyed. The option clauses can only be written inside a <select> command.

The XVCL processor checks <option>s in sequential order and selects for processing <option>s as follows: The value of control-variable of <select> is compared against the *value*s specified in the **value** attribute of each <option> using the *comp-operator*s specified in the **comp-operator** attribute. If the **comp-operator** attribute is omitted, the processor uses the equality operator (=) by default for matching all the *value*s specified in the value attribute of <option> against the value of control-variable.

If none of the <option>s are selected, then the <otherwise> command is selected, if present.

C.13.3 Attribute Definition for <select> Command

<option= *"control-variable"*>

This attribute specifies a single-value variable name. The *control-variable* must be an expression that yields a valid single-value variable name whose value will be used by <option>s in selecting <option>s for processing.

C.13.4 The Attributes of the <option> Command

<option value= *"value (| value)*" [comp-*
operator=*"comp-operator (, comp-operator)*"]*>

Each *value* and *comp-operator* must be an expression. The *comp-operator* expression must yield one of the following comparison operators: <, >, !=, =, <=, and >=.

The *values* in **value** attribute are separated by the OR symbol "|" and their corresponding *comp-operators* in attribute **comp-operator** are separated by commas. If the **comp-operator** is omitted, the processor uses the equality operator (=) by default for all the *values*. If the **comp-operator** is specified, the number of *values* in the value attribute and the number of *comp-operators* in the **comp-operator** attribute must be the same.

The following is the general format of the <option> command:

```
<option value="value1|value2|...|valuen" comp-operator="comp-
operator1,comp-operator2,... ,comp-operatorn">
```

To determine whether a given <option> should be selected or not, the value of control-variable is compared against the i-th *value* using the i-th *comp-operator*. If any of these comparisons is TRUE, the <option> is selected. If all the comparisons are FALSE, the <option> is not selected.

The following example illustrates selection of options:

```
<set var ="x" value="a"/>
<select option="x">
<option value="a | b" comp-operator="=,="> // this option
is selected if variable x has the
 // value "a" OR "b"
</option>
....
</select>
```

The comparison is made based on the type of the *value*. A string comparison is made for alphanumeric and alphabetic values, and a numeric comparison is made for numeric values. To make a numeric comparison, the value of both the control-variable and *value* must be numeric. Otherwise, string comparison will be made.

For example, if the option value is "1" and control-variable value is "2," then numeric comparison is made. If the option value is "A1" and control-variable value is "2," then a string comparison is made.

C.14 <while> Command

C.14.1 Syntax

```
<while using-items-in = "multi-var-name (, multi-var-name)* ">
while-body
</while>
while-body := ( textual-content | break | adapt | set |
set-multi | select |
```

```
ifdef | ifndef | value-of | message | while | remove )*
```

C.14.2 Command Description

The <while> command iterates over its body. All the multivalue variables listed in the **using-items-in** attribute must have the same number of values. Each iteration uses the i-th value of each of the multivalue variables listed in the **using-items-in** attribute. Starting with 1, <while> implicitly increments the value of the index i by 1 in each iteration and terminates after processing the last values of variables. It follows that the number of iterations is equal to the number of values in each of the multivalue variables listed in the attribute **using-items-in**.

Values of the multivalue variables listed in the attribute **using-items-in** can be referenced in the body of a <while> command. If used inside a <while> command, these multivalue variables behave like a single-value variable and can be referenced just like a single-value variable.

This is illustrated in the following example:

x-Frame A

```
<set-multi var="xxx" value="1,2,3"/>
<adapt x-frame="B.xvcl"/>
```

x-Frame B

```
<while using-items-in="xxx">
value of xxx is <value-of expr="?@xxx?"/>
</while>
```

Results

```
value of xxx is 1
value of xxx is 2
value of xxx is 3
```

Comments

The multivalue variable xxx has the values 1, 2, and 3. The <while> command in x-frame B uses the multivalue variable xxx. The <while> command iterates over its body for each value in the multivalue variable xxx. In the first iteration the value of xxx is 1. The value of xxx becomes 2 and 3 in the subsequent iterations. It follows that the number of iterations is equal to the number of values in a multivalue variable.

The following example illustrates the use of one or more multivalue variables in a <while> loop.

```
<set-multi var="x" value="1,3"/>
<set-multi var="y" value="2,3"/>
<while using-items-in="x, y">
 <select option="x">
 <option value="?@y?">
 The value of x is <value-of var="?@x?"/>
 and the value of y is "<value-of var="?@y?"/>
 </option>...
 </select>...
</while>
```

In the preceding example, during the first iteration the value of x is 1 and the value of y is 2. In the first iteration, the <option> command checks if the value of variable x equals the value of variable y; therefore, this condition is not satisfied. In the second iteration, both variables have the same value of 3 and the condition is met. As a result, the text:

> The value of x is 3
> and the value of y is 3
is emitted.

The <while> command is often used for code generation, for example, generating code that creates database tables, creating user interface buttons and menus, etc.

Dynamic invocation of multivalue variables is also possible with <while> commands, as illustrated in the following example:

```
<set-multi var="index" value="1,2"/>
<set-multi var="multi1" value="a,b,c"/>
<set-multi var="multi2" value="d,e"/>...
<while using-items-in="index">
 <while using-items-in="multi?@index?">

   ...
 </while>
</while>
```

The variable index is used to create the names of multivalue variables: multi1 and multi2. For each iteration of the outer <while>, the expression multi?@index? will generate the new multivalue variable name in the inner <while> loop.

This is further illustrated in the following complete example.

X-Frame A

```
<set-multi var="multi1" value="A,B"/>
<set-multi var="multi2" value="C,D"/>
<set-multi var="index" value="1,2"/>
<adapt x-frame="B.xvcl"/>
```

X-Frame B

```
<while using-items-in="index">
<while using-items-in="multi?@index?"> // in the first
iteration VA1 is used
 // in the second iteration VA2 is used
 <value-of expr="?@multi@index?"/>
 </while>
</while>
```

Result

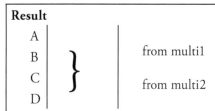

A	from multi1
B	
C	from multi2
D	

Comments

In the first iteration the value of "index" is 1 and multi1 is used in the inner loop as a result of evaluating multi?@index?. Thus A and B are emitted in the inner loop iterations.

Similarly in the second loop multi2 is used in the inner loop and as a result C and D are emitted in the inner loop iteration. In that way the name of the multivalue variable in the inner <while> loop keeps changing in each iteration of the outer loop.

If there is an <adapt> command inside <while>, these multivalue variables (currently acting as single-value variable) with corresponding i-th values are passed down to that x-frame and all its descendant x-frames. The variables that are passed down in this way have the same privileges as the single-value variables, i.e., they can be referred to in other XVCL commands. The following example illustrates this.

```
<set-multi var="x" value="1,2,3"/>
<while using-items-in="x">
  <adapt x-frame="B.xvcl"/> // for each iteration x with
                                new value is passed
                            //down to x-frame B
</while>
<!-- <value-of var="?@x?"> --> // if this is not
commented the processor will
                                //produce an error. x cannot
                                be referenced here
```

X-Frame B

```
Value of multi-value variable x in x-frame B is <value-of
  expr="?@x?"/>
```

Result

```
Value of multi-value variable x in x-frame B is 1
Value of multi-value variable x in x-frame B is 2
Value of multi-value variable x in x-frame B is 3
```

Comments

Note the <adapt> command inside <while> in x-frame A.

The <while> in x-frame A passes the single-value behavior of variable x with different values in each iteration. Referring to the example, in the first iteration the single-value variable with value 1 is passed down to x-frame B. Similarly, single-value variables with values 2 and 3 are passed down to x-frame B in the second and third iteration of the <while> loop.

It is important to note the commented <value-of> command in the x-frame A outside of the <while> loop. If the <value-of> command is not commented, the processor will produce the variable-undefined error. This is because multivalue variables cannot be referenced like single-value variables, outside of the <while> and the scope explained previously.

When <while> commands are nested, as shown in the following example, both multivalue variables x and y can be referenced as single-value variables inside the inner <while> loop.

```
<while using-items-in="x">

  <wile using-items-in="y">

    // both "x" and "y" can be referenced as single-value
      variables here

</while>

  </while>
```

C.14.3 Attribute Definition

using-items-in = "*multi-var-name* (, *multi-var-name*)*"

This attribute specifies one or more multivalue variables to be used by the <while> command. The *multi-var-name* must be an expression that yields the name of a multivalue variable existing in the symbol table. Otherwise, a warning will be produced and the <while> will be skipped.

C.15   Definition of <ifdef> Command

C.15.1 Syntax

ifdef   := **<ifdef var**="*var-name*">
                if-body

</ifdef>

var-name   := Expression

if-body := (textual-content | break | adapt | set | set-multi | select |
                ifdef | ifndef | value-of | message | while | remove)*

C.15.2 Command Description

If variable *var-name* is defined (i.e., it exists in the symbol table), the XVCL processor processes the if-body. Otherwise, the if-body is not processed.

C.15.3 Attribute Definition

var=*"var-name"*

The expression must yield a legal name of a variable (either single-value or multi-value) that may or may not exist in the symbol table.

C.16 Definition of <ifndef> Command

C.16.1 Syntax

ifndef   := **<ifndef var**=*"var-name"*>
                 if-body
</ifndef>

C.16.2 Command Description

If variable *var-name* is undefined (i.e., it does not exist in the symbol table), the XVCL processor processes the if-body. Otherwise, the if-body is not processed.

C.16.3 Attribute Definition

var=*"var-name"*

The expression must yield a legal name of a variable (either single-value or multi-value) that may or may not exist in the symbol table.

C.17 Definition of <remove> Command

C.17.1 Syntax

C.17.2 Command Description

This command undefines a variable *"var-name"* described in the **var** attribute by removing it from the symbol table. The *"var-name"* should have been previously defined by a <set> or <set-multi> command. Otherwise, the command is ignored and a warning message is produced. The variable is removed if and only if the <remove> command appears in the x-frame that originally defines that variable (i.e., the x-frame that entered that variable into the symbol table). Otherwise, the command is ignored and a warning message is produced.

The following example illustrates this.

X-Frame A

```
<set var= "x" value="XA"/>
<adapt x-frame="B.xvcl"/>
```

X-Frame B

```
<remove var="x"/> // warning! variable x cannot be
removed
```

Result

warning will be produced when processing <remove> command in x-frame B.

Comments

The warning is generated because the descendant x-frames are not allowed to <remove> any variables defined by ancestor x-frames.

C.17.3 Attribute Definition

var =*"var-name"*

This attribute specifies a variable name to be removed from the symbol table. It can be the name of a single-value or a multivalue variable. The *var-name* must be an expression that yields the name of the variable to be removed.

C.18 Definition of <message> Command

C.18.1 Syntax

<message text=" *message* " [**continue** = " *yes-no* "] />

C.18.2 Command Description

When the XVCL processor encounters the <message> command, it will display a message on the screen. This command does not affect the output emitted by the processor. The <message> command can be used for debugging purposes such as checking variable values and trapping error situations. The typical usage of this command is in the <select> command. However, it is also useful for tracking variable values by displaying them to the screen during processing.

C.18.3 Attribute Definition

message = *"text"*

This attribute specifies a message to be displayed. The *message* must be an expression.

continue = *"yes-no"*

This attribute specifies if the processing should continue (value "yes") or not (value "no"). The *yes-no* must be an expression that yields value "yes" or "no." If this attribute is omitted, the default value is "yes."

C.19 Processor Options and Configuration File

The following extra features can be activated via processor options and the configuration file:

-T option and variable optionT

When the processor is invoked with the -T option, for example:

```
java -jar xvcl.jar -T SPC
```

the processor will include the comment line with the name of an x-frame as the first line in the output emitted from that x-frame.

The user should specify comment symbols in "begin-comment" and "end-comment" variables. The default for begin-comment is //. The default for end-comment is nil (nothing).

Currently, we do not provide trace information for <insert> commands.

-B option and variable optionB

When the processor is invoked with the -B option, all the whitespaces (blank, space, etc.) in the textual content around an XVCL command (any command with the exception of <value-of>) are trimmed. XVCL whitespace characters are the same as in Java. A character is an XVCL whitespace character if and only if it satisfies one of the following criteria:

- It is a Unicode space character (SPACE_SEPARATOR, LINE_SEPARA-TOR, or PARAGRAPH_SEPARATOR) but is not also a nonbreaking space ('\u00A0', '\u2007', '\u202F').
- It is '\u0009', HORIZONTAL TABULATION.
- It is '\u000A', LINEFEED.
- It is '\u000B', VERTICAL TABULATION.
- It is '\u000C', FORM FEED.
- It is '\u000D', CARRIAGE RETURN.
- It is '\u001C', FILE SEPARATOR.
- It is '\u001D', GROUP SEPARATOR.
- It is '\u001E', RECORD SEPARATOR.
- It is '\u001F', UNIT SEPARATOR.

Option –B does not remove whitespaces (and any textual contents) inside CDATA tags. Therefore, if you want to keep blank lines after or before a command, you can put them into CDATA tags.

-N option and variable optionN (version 2.07 only)

Option –N was used to instruct the processor to recognize a namespace "xvcl". The processor 2.10 recognizes regular XVCL commands (e.g., <adapt>, as well as in namespace notation (e.g., <xvcl:adapt>), without specifying –N. Therefore, option –N has been removed.

-V option

Option –V runs the processor in validation mode, i.e., to process an x-framework without emitting the output.

-L option

Option –L instructs the processor to log the names of the files generated during processing into a file named [SPC].log placed in the same directory as SPC.

Index

A

AHEAD technique, 113, 312, 313, 316
AOP. *See* Aspect-oriented programming (AOP)
Aspect-oriented programming (AOP), 113, 126, 311
Assembly pass, 289

B

Block reservation, 268
Buffer library, 189–201
    extending, 231–234
    quantitative comparison of solutions, 228–230
    summary chart, 230
Byte ordering scheme, 190

C

C++, 180, 202
    template metaprogramming, 203, 308
    XVCL and, 296
CDT. *See* Customization decision tree (CDT)
Change-design, design for change *vs.,* 127–128
Changeability, 3, 113, 122, 128, 230, 295, 319
Clone(s)
    automated detection, 210–212
    detection, 181, 183, 191, 210–212, 315
    elimination, 183
    multiple classes, 211
    scatter plot, 211
    simple, 192

size, 181
token-based, 211
Clone Miner, 203, 211–212, 321
COBOL, 9, 210, 308
    PQL for, 44
    SPA for, 20
COBOL85, 333–338
    abstract syntax structure for, 334
    assignment statements, 337
    classification of statements, 335, 338
    design models, 333–338
    global program design abstractions in, 333
Code fragment, 192
CompareTo, 233
Complex/Buffer, 233
Component-based design, xxiv, 48, 114, 184
Concurrent versions systems (CVS), 14
    branch and merge facilities, 101
    development of new system release, 243
    FRS evolution with, 99–100
    problems working with, 108
    release history, 101
    repository, 95, 103
    update operations, 107
Context-sensitive composition, 152
Customization decision tree (CDT), 266, 271, 272, 282

D

Decision tree, customization of, 266, 271, 272, 282
Design decision(s), 42, 50, 238, 314
    tree, 282

Printed and bound by CPI Group (UK) Ltd, Croydon, CR0 4YY

17/10/2024

01775692-0004